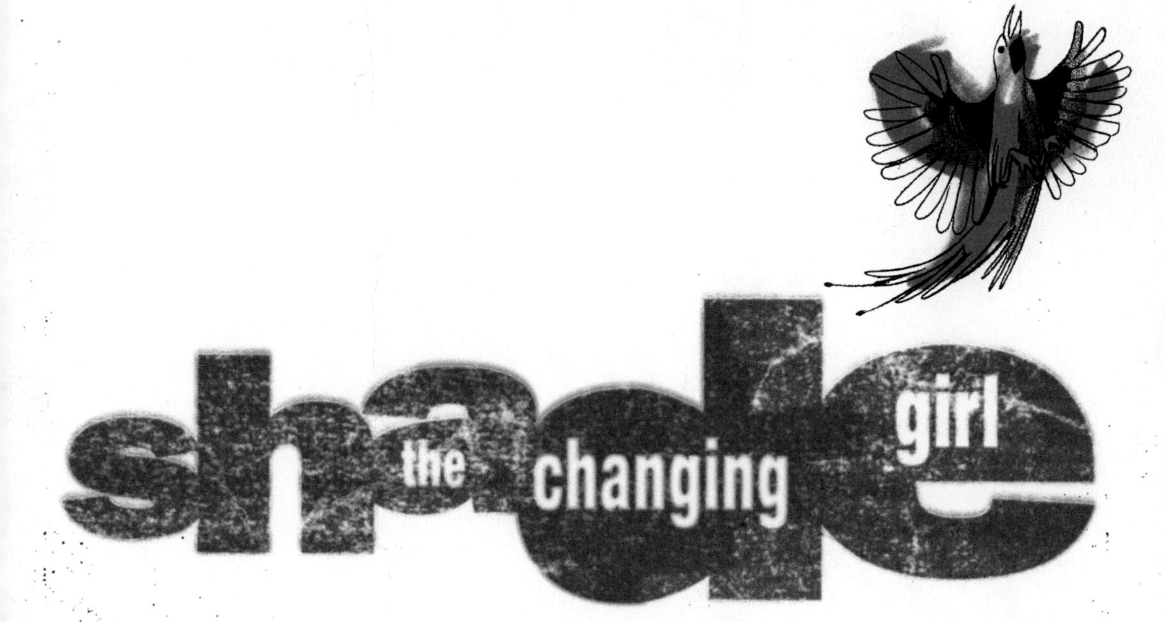

shade the changing girl

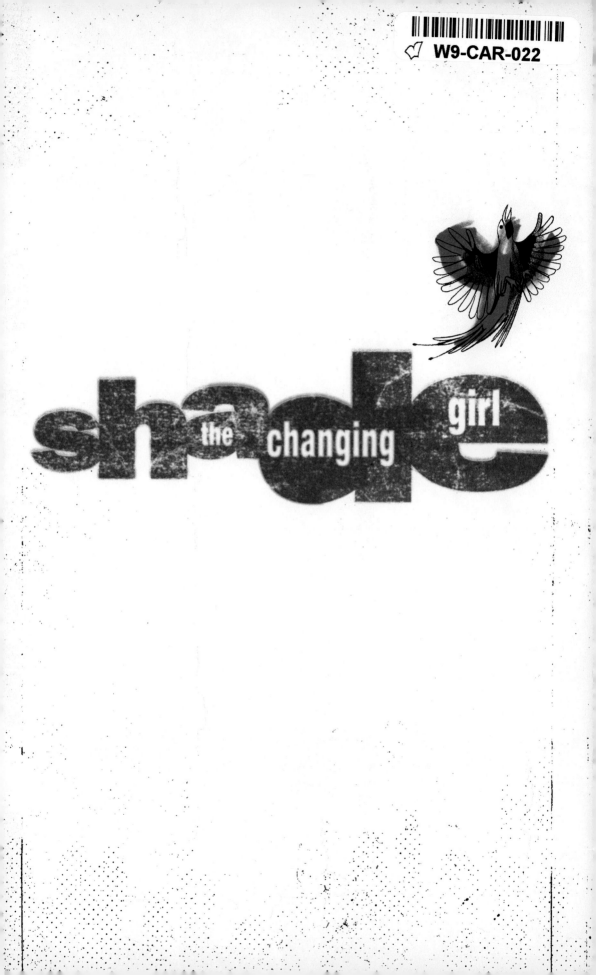

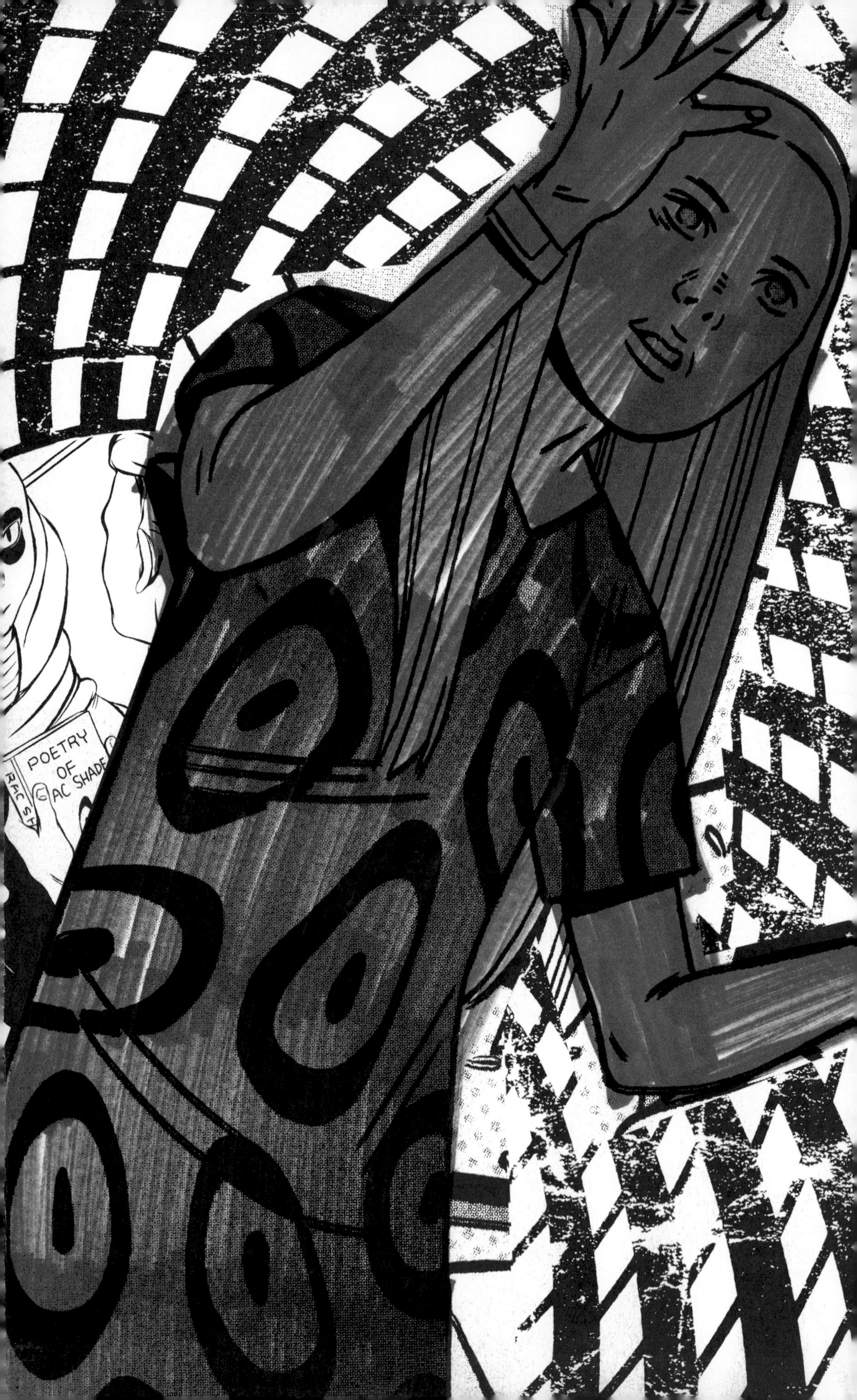
POETRY
OF
AC SHADE

shade the changing girl

VOL. 1: EARTH GIRL MADE EASY

CECIL CASTELLUCCI Writer

MARLEY ZARCONE Artist

ANDE PARKS RYAN KELLY Inkers

KELLY FITZPATRICK Colorist

SAIDA TEMOFONTE Letterer

BECKY CLOONAN Cover Art and Original Series Covers

GERARD WAY DC's Young Animal Curator

SHADE, THE CHANGING MAN CREATED BY STEVE DITKO

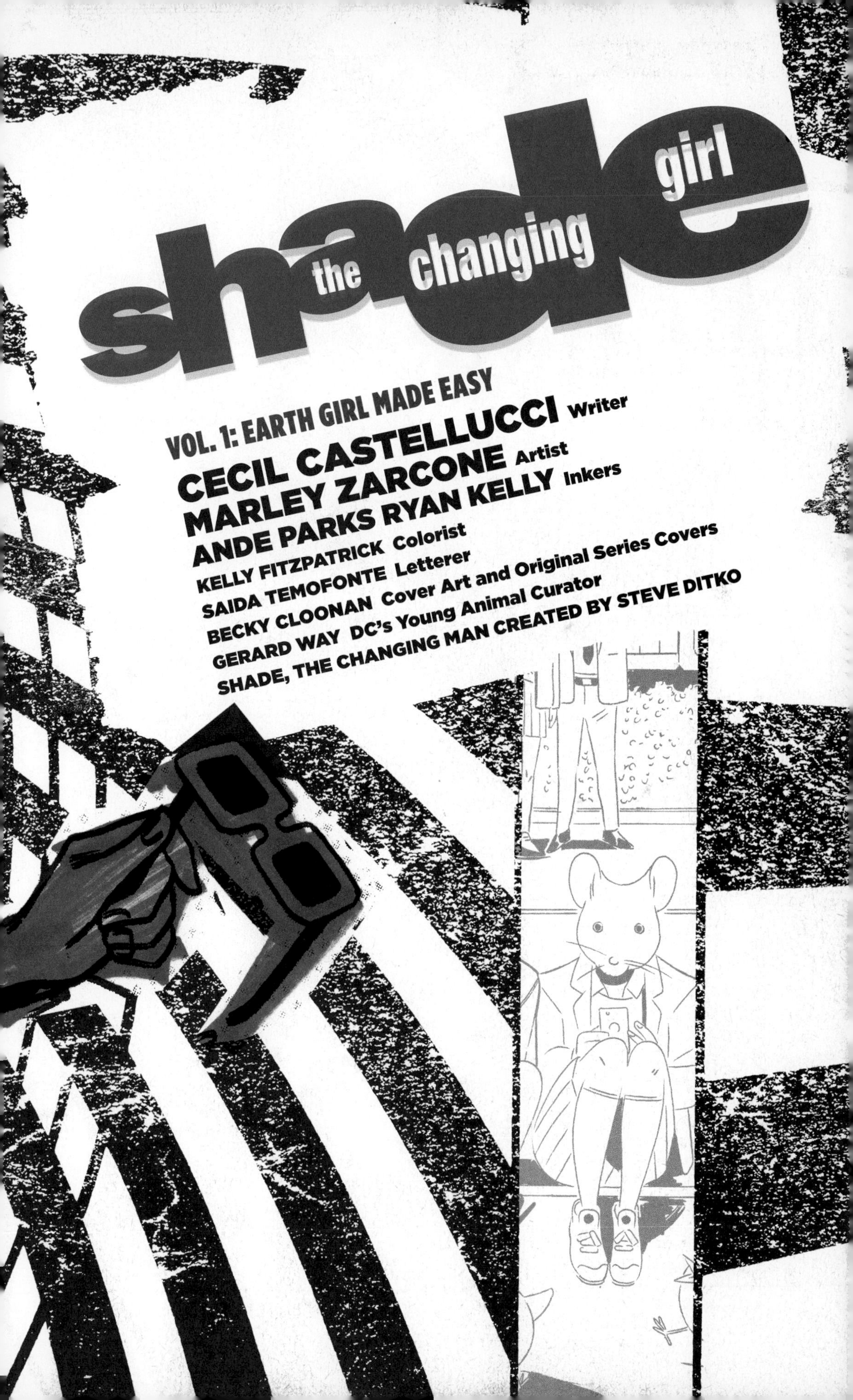

Shelly Bond
Molly Mahan
Jamie S. Rich Editors – Original Series
Jeb Woodard Group Editor – Collected Editions
Scott Nybakken Editor – Collected Edition
Steve Cook Design Director – Books
Louis Prandi Publication Design

Bob Harras Senior VP – Editor-in-Chief, DC Comics

Diane Nelson President
Dan DiDio Publisher
Jim Lee Publisher
Geoff Johns President & Chief Creative Officer
Amit Desai Executive VP – Business & Marketing Strategy,
Direct to Consumer & Global Franchise Management
Sam Ades Senior VP – Direct to Consumer
Bobbie Chase VP – Talent Development
Mark Chiarello Senior VP – Art, Design & Collected Editions
John Cunningham Senior VP – Sales & Trade Marketing
Anne DePies Senior VP – Business Strategy, Finance & Administration
Don Falletti VP – Manufacturing Operations
Lawrence Ganem VP – Editorial Administration & Talent Relations
Alison Gill Senior VP – Manufacturing & Operations
Hank Kanalz Senior VP – Editorial Strategy & Administration
Jay Kogan VP – Legal Affairs
Thomas Loftus VP – Business Affairs
Jack Mahan VP – Business Affairs
Nick J. Napolitano VP – Manufacturing Administration
Eddie Scannell VP – Consumer Marketing
Courtney Simmons Senior VP – Publicity & Communications
Jim (Ski) Sokolowski VP – Comic Book Specialty Sales & Trade Marketing
Nancy Spears VP – Mass, Book, Digital Sales & Trade Marketing

SHADE, THE CHANGING GIRL VOL. 1: EARTH GIRL MADE EASY

DC Comics
2900 West Alameda Avenue
Burbank, CA 91505
Printed by LSC Communications, Salem, VA, USA. 6/9/17. First Printing.
ISBN: 978-1-4012-7099-5

Library of Congress Cataloging-in-Publication Data is available.

MIX
Paper from
responsible sources
FSC® C132124

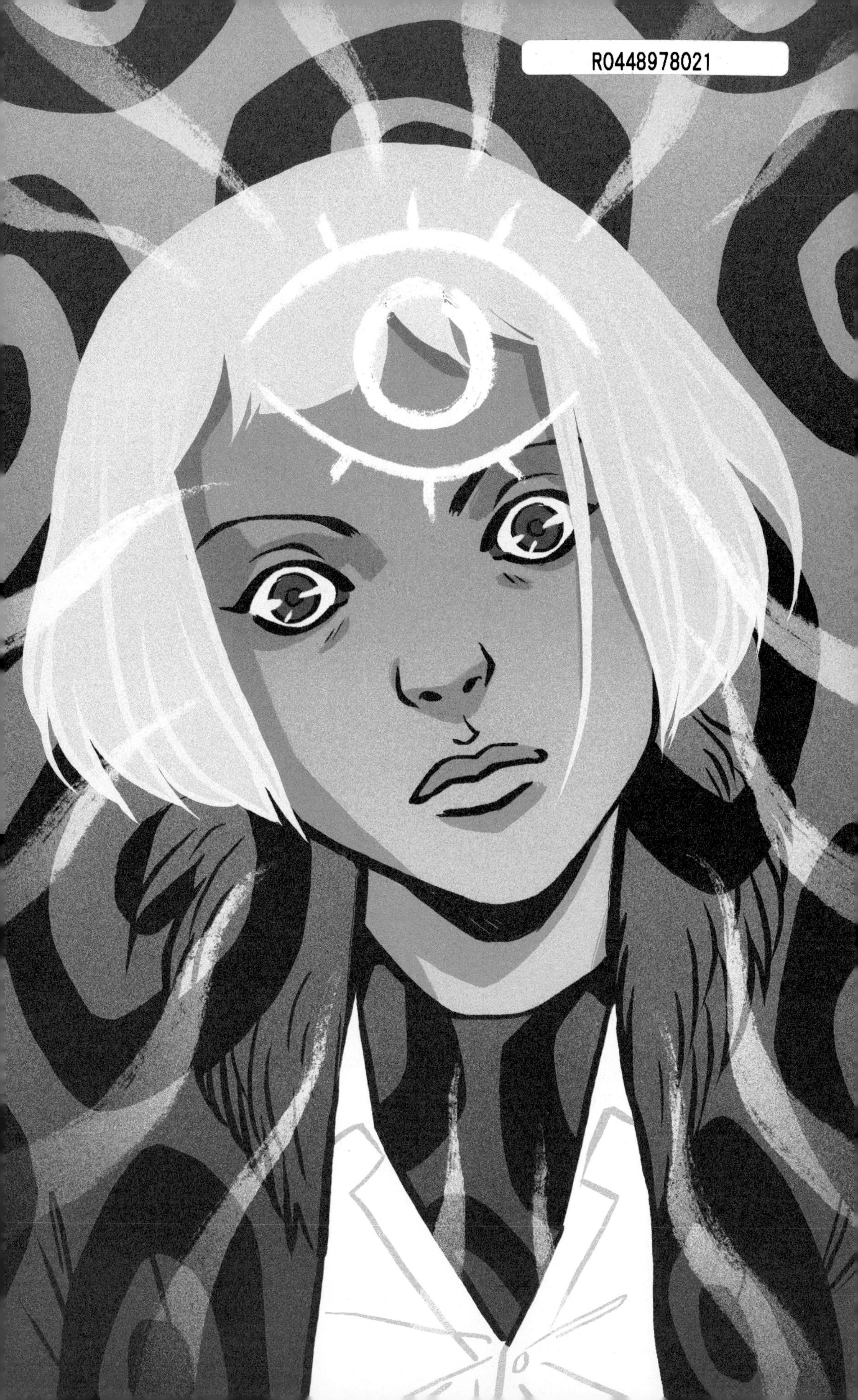

Variant cover art by Tula Lotay

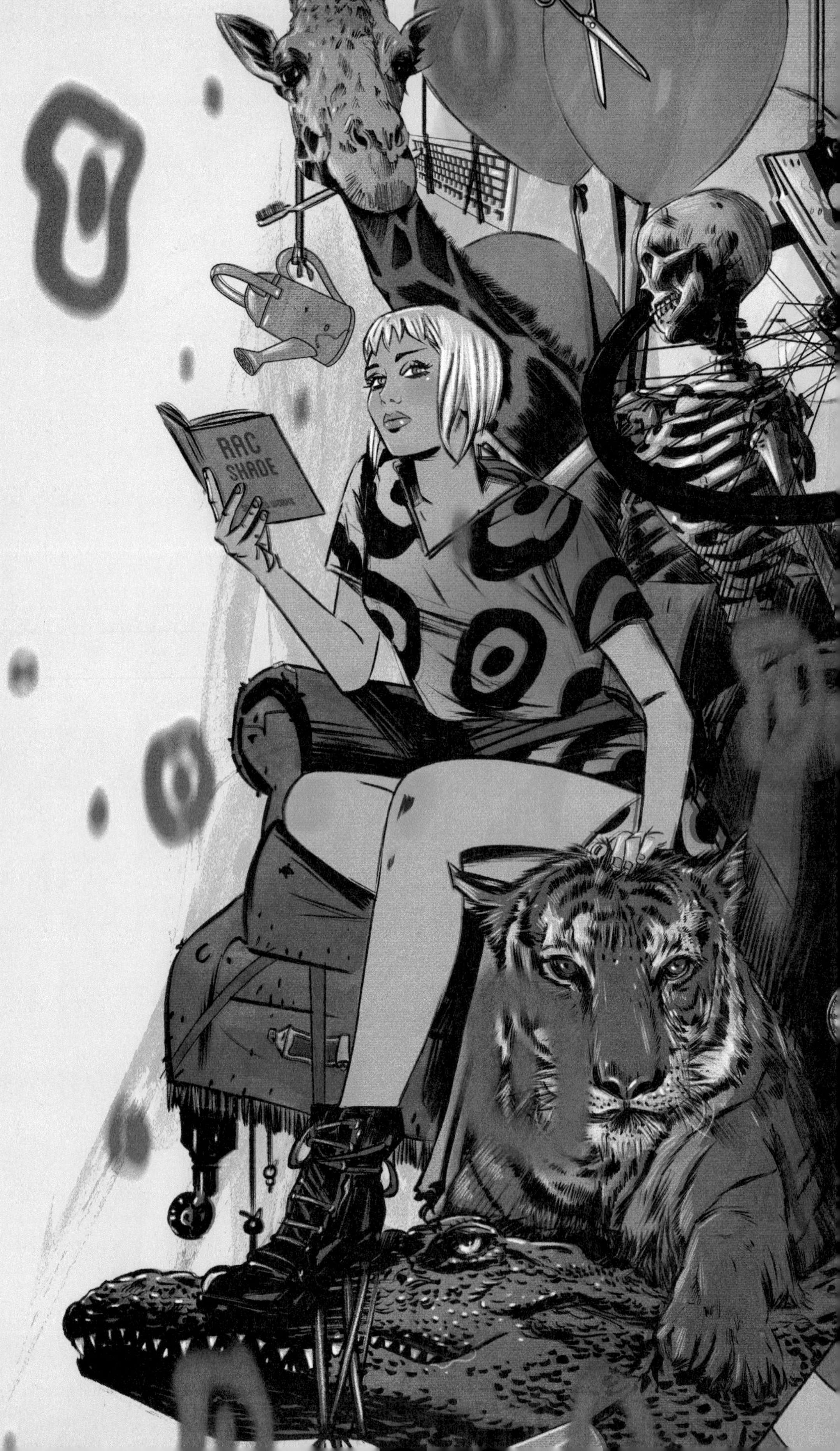
RAC
SHADE

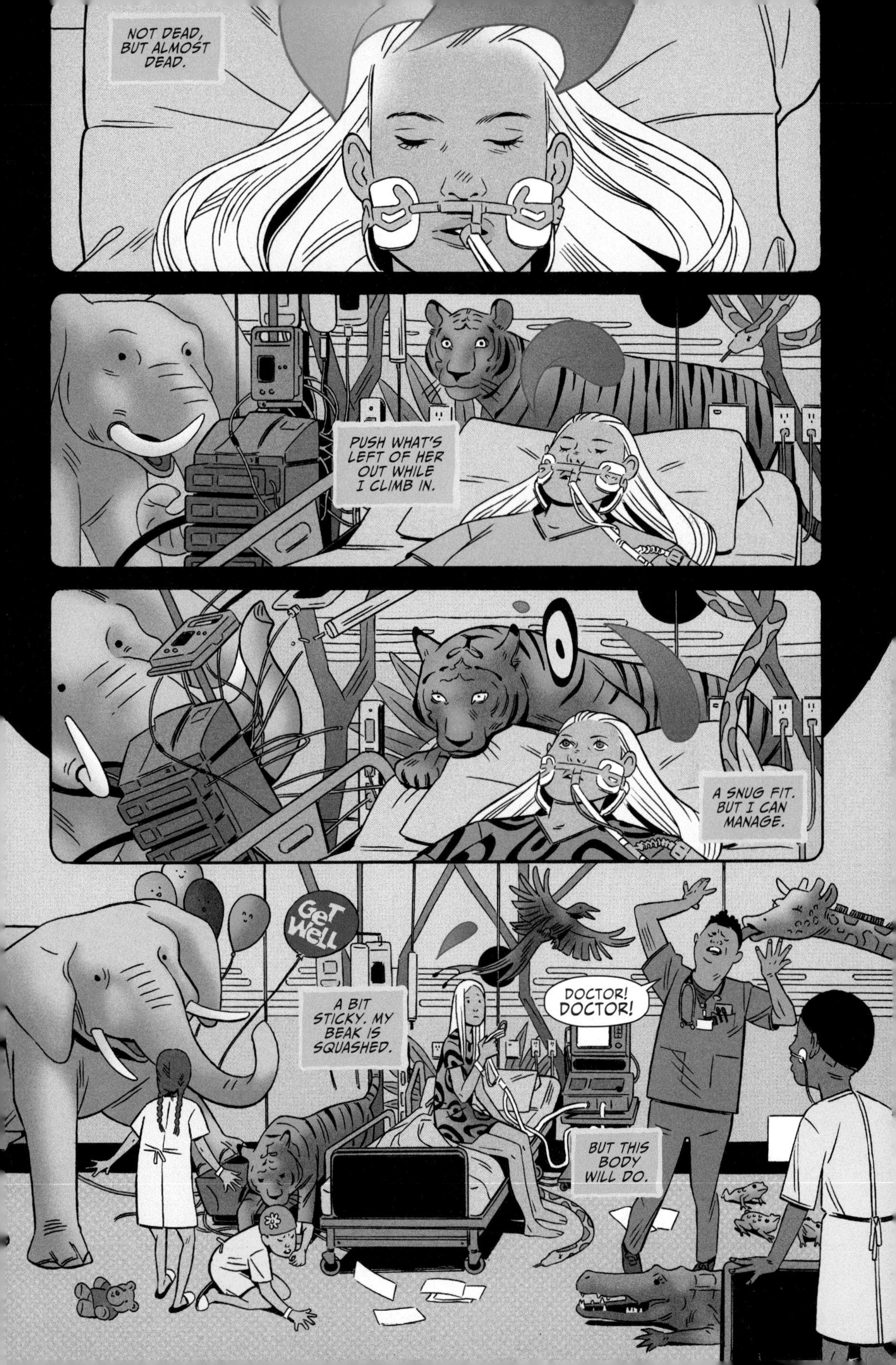
NOT DEAD, BUT ALMOST DEAD.
PUSH WHAT'S LEFT OF HER OUT WHILE I CLIMB IN.
A SNUG FIT. BUT I CAN MANAGE.
GET WELL
A BIT STICKY. MY BEAK IS SQUASHED.
DOCTOR! DOCTOR!
BUT THIS BODY WILL DO.

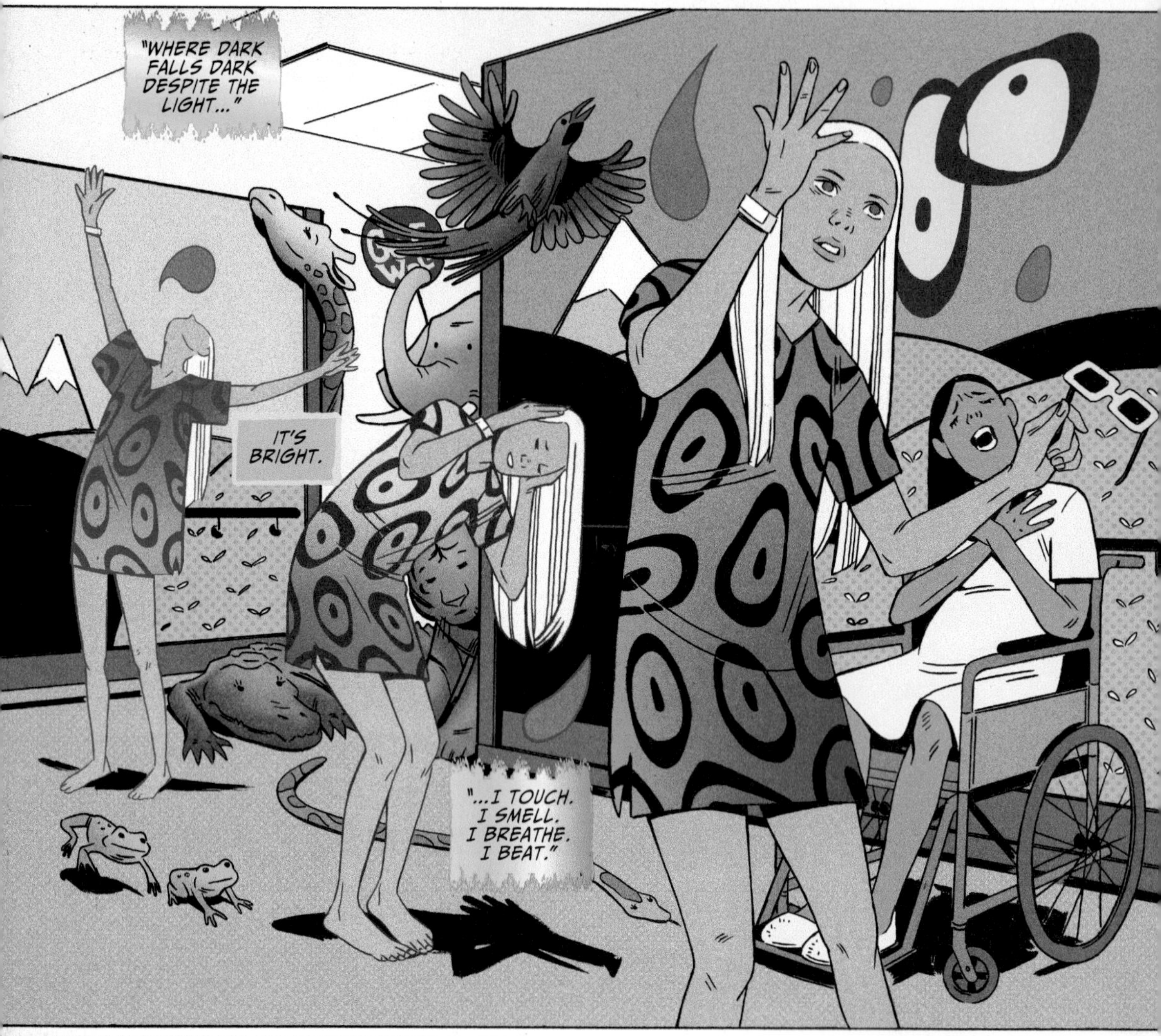
"WHERE DARK FALLS DARK DESPITE THE LIGHT..."
IT'S BRIGHT.
"...I TOUCH. I SMELL. I BREATHE. I BEAT."

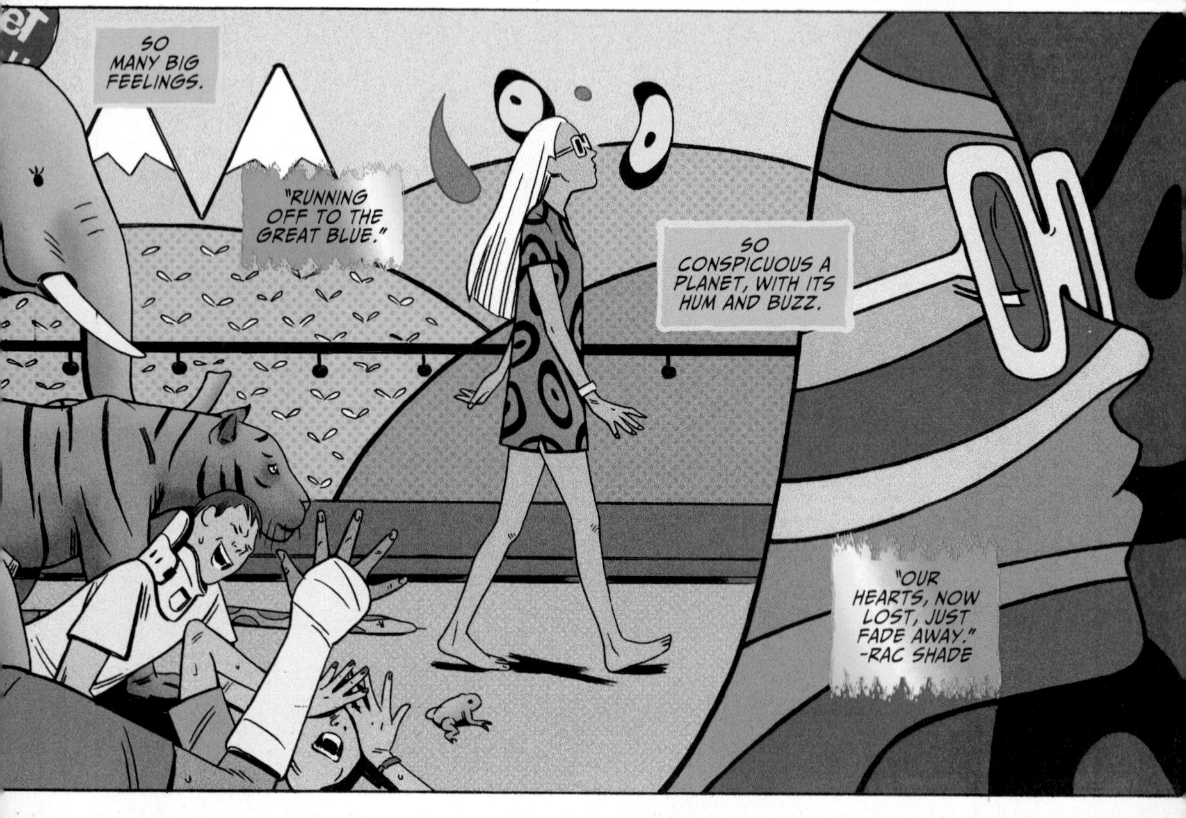
SO MANY BIG FEELINGS.
"RUNNING OFF TO THE GREAT BLUE."
SO CONSPICUOUS A PLANET, WITH ITS HUM AND BUZZ.
"OUR HEARTS, NOW LOST, JUST FADE AWAY." -RAC SHADE

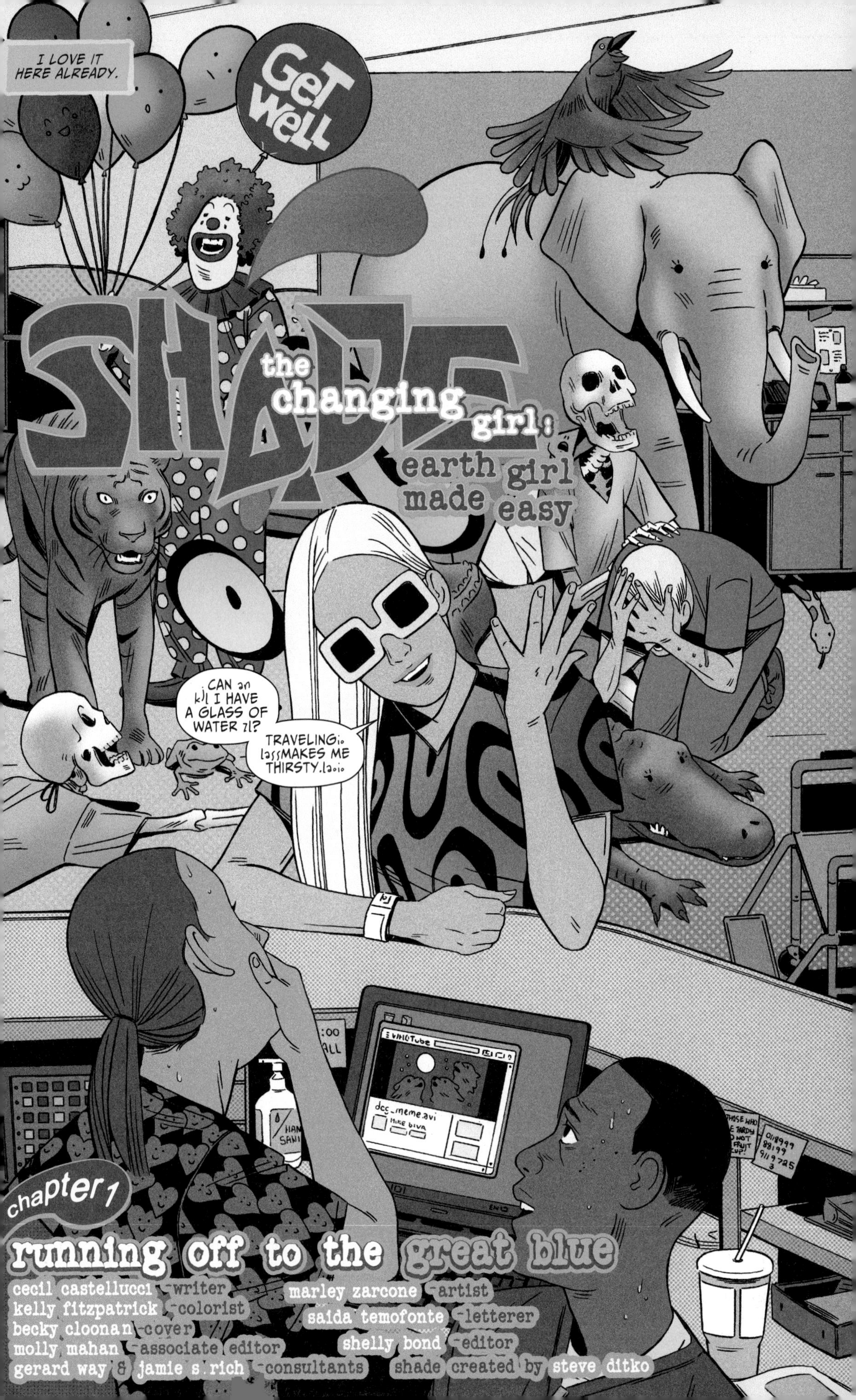

I LOVE IT HERE ALREADY.
GET WELL
SHADE the changing girl: earth girl made easy
CAN an kjl I HAVE A GLASS OF WATER zl?
TRAVELING:o lassMAKES ME THIRSTY.la:o:o
WHOTube
dog_meme.avi
chapter 1
running off to the great blue
cecil castellucci - writer
marley zarcone - artist
kelly fitzpatrick - colorist
saida temofonte - letterer
becky cloonan - cover
molly mahan - associate editor
shelly bond - editor
gerard way & jamie s. rich - consultants
shade created by steve ditko

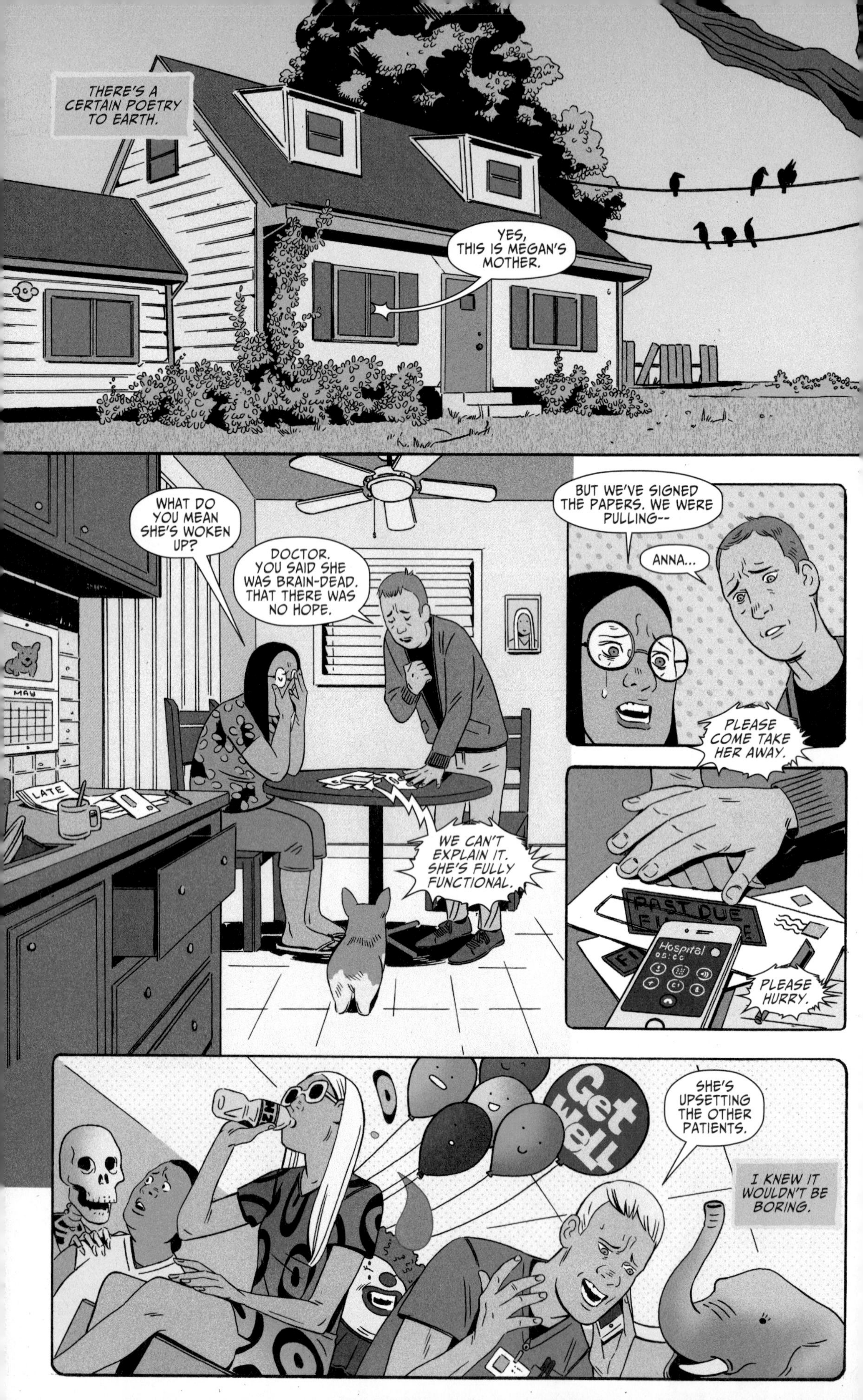
THERE'S A CERTAIN POETRY TO EARTH.
YES, THIS IS MEGAN'S MOTHER.
WHAT DO YOU MEAN SHE'S WOKEN UP?
DOCTOR. YOU SAID SHE WAS BRAIN-DEAD. THAT THERE WAS NO HOPE.
MAY
LATE
WE CAN'T EXPLAIN IT. SHE'S FULLY FUNCTIONAL.
BUT WE'VE SIGNED THE PAPERS. WE WERE PULLING--
ANNA...
PLEASE COME TAKE HER AWAY.
PAST DUE
Hospital
PLEASE HURRY.
Get well
SHE'S UPSETTING THE OTHER PATIENTS.
I KNEW IT WOULDN'T BE BORING.

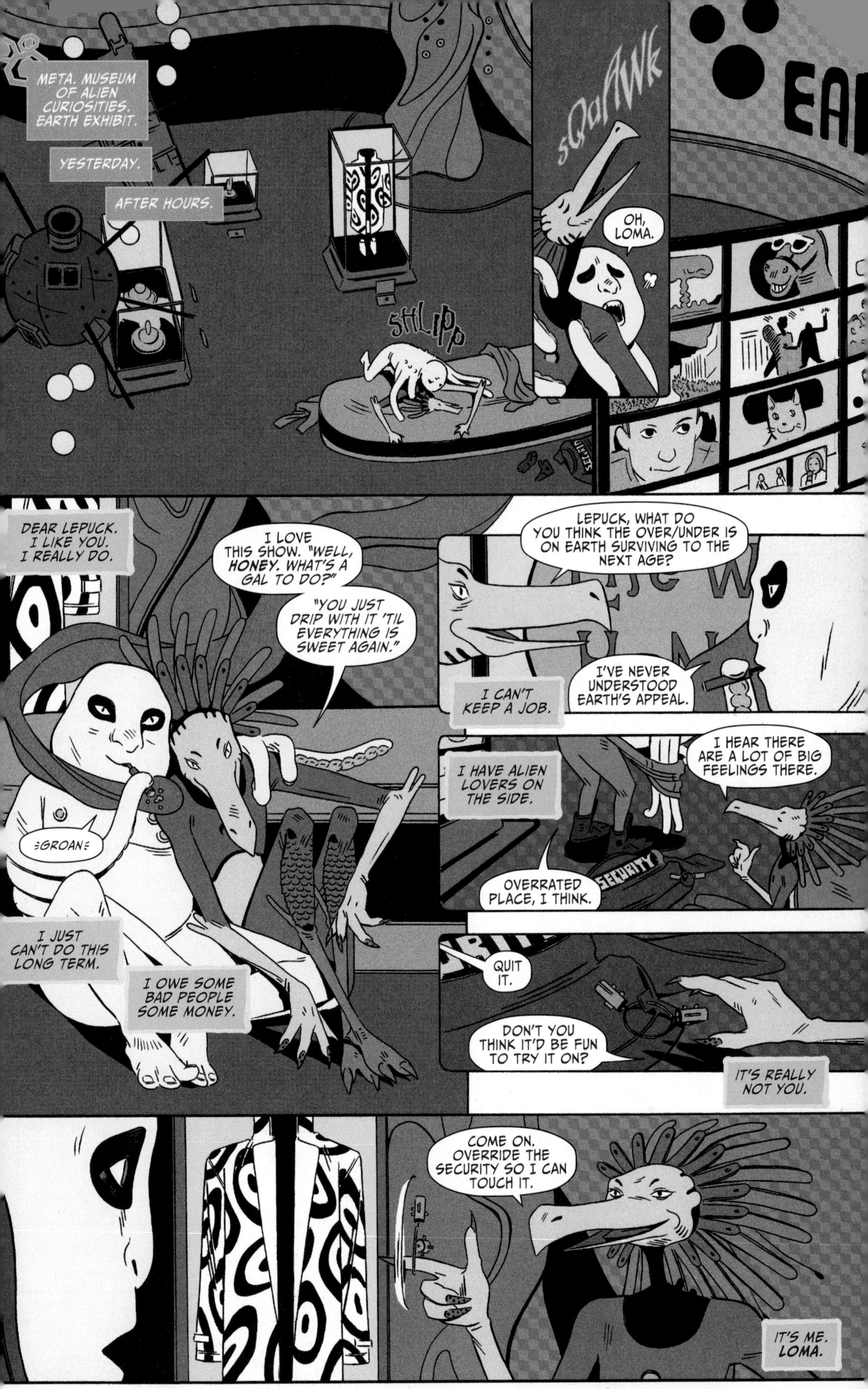
META. MUSEUM OF ALIEN CURIOSITIES. EARTH EXHIBIT.
YESTERDAY.
AFTER HOURS.
SHLIPP
SQUAWK
OH, LOMA.
EAR
DEAR LEPUCK. I LIKE YOU. I REALLY DO.
I LOVE THIS SHOW. "WELL, HONEY. WHAT'S A GAL TO DO?"
"YOU JUST DRIP WITH IT 'TIL EVERYTHING IS SWEET AGAIN."
GROAN
LEPUCK, WHAT DO YOU THINK THE OVER/UNDER IS ON EARTH SURVIVING TO THE NEXT AGE?
I CAN'T KEEP A JOB.
I'VE NEVER UNDERSTOOD EARTH'S APPEAL.
I HAVE ALIEN LOVERS ON THE SIDE.
I HEAR THERE ARE A LOT OF BIG FEELINGS THERE.
OVERRATED PLACE, I THINK.
SECURITY
I JUST CAN'T DO THIS LONG TERM.
I OWE SOME BAD PEOPLE SOME MONEY.
QUIT IT.
DON'T YOU THINK IT'D BE FUN TO TRY IT ON?
IT'S REALLY NOT YOU.
COME ON. OVERRIDE THE SECURITY SO I CAN TOUCH IT.
IT'S ME. LOMA.

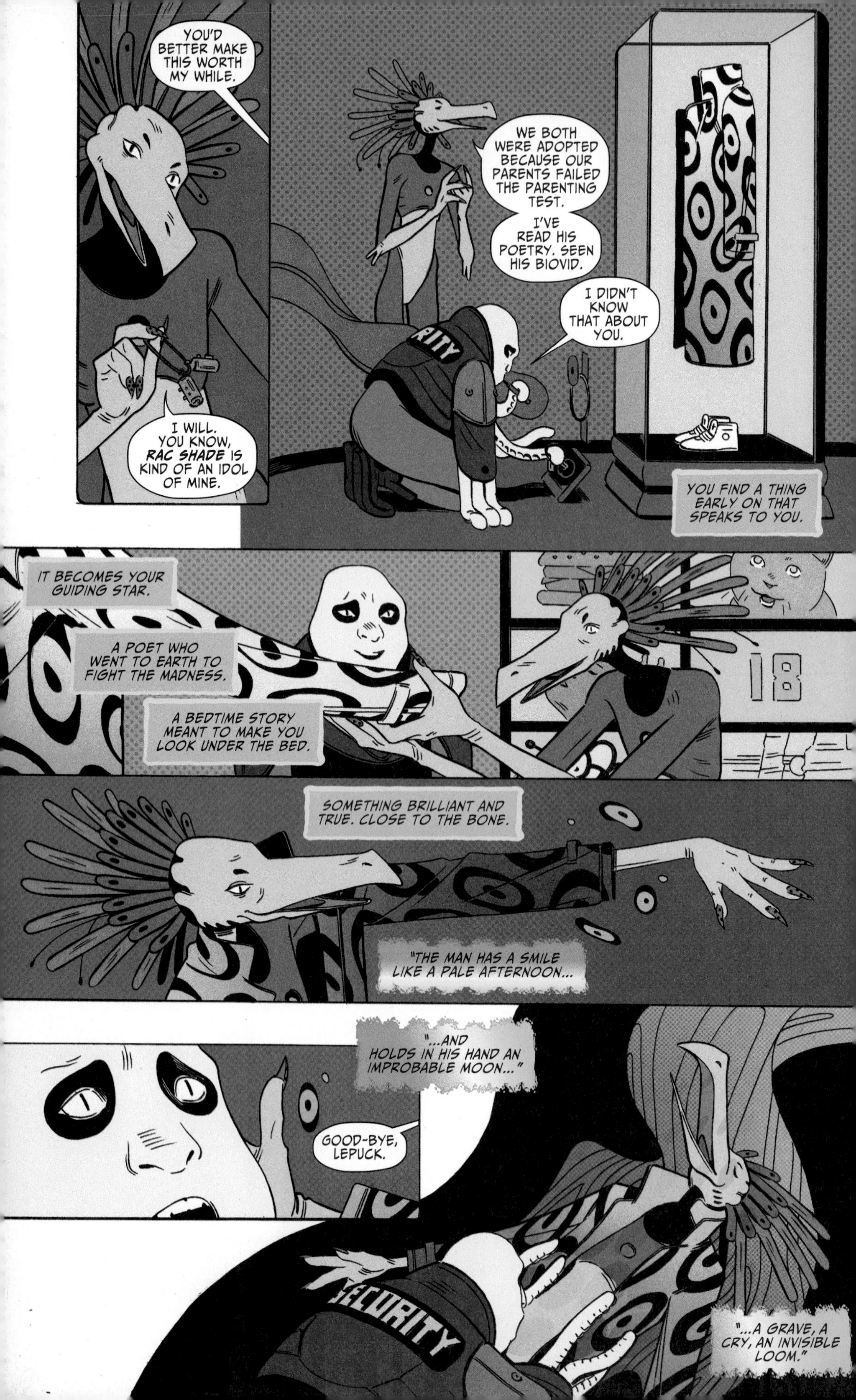
YOU'D BETTER MAKE THIS WORTH MY WHILE.
I WILL. YOU KNOW, RAC SHADE IS KIND OF AN IDOL OF MINE.
WE BOTH WERE ADOPTED BECAUSE OUR PARENTS FAILED THE PARENTING TEST.
I'VE READ HIS POETRY. SEEN HIS BIOVID.
I DIDN'T KNOW THAT ABOUT YOU.
RITY
YOU FIND A THING EARLY ON THAT SPEAKS TO YOU.
IT BECOMES YOUR GUIDING STAR.
A POET WHO WENT TO EARTH TO FIGHT THE MADNESS.
A BEDTIME STORY MEANT TO MAKE YOU LOOK UNDER THE BED.
18
SOMETHING BRILLIANT AND TRUE. CLOSE TO THE BONE.
"THE MAN HAS A SMILE LIKE A PALE AFTERNOON...
"...AND HOLDS IN HIS HAND AN IMPROBABLE MOON..."
GOOD-BYE, LEPUCK.
SECURITY
"...A GRAVE, A CRY, AN INVISIBLE LOOM."

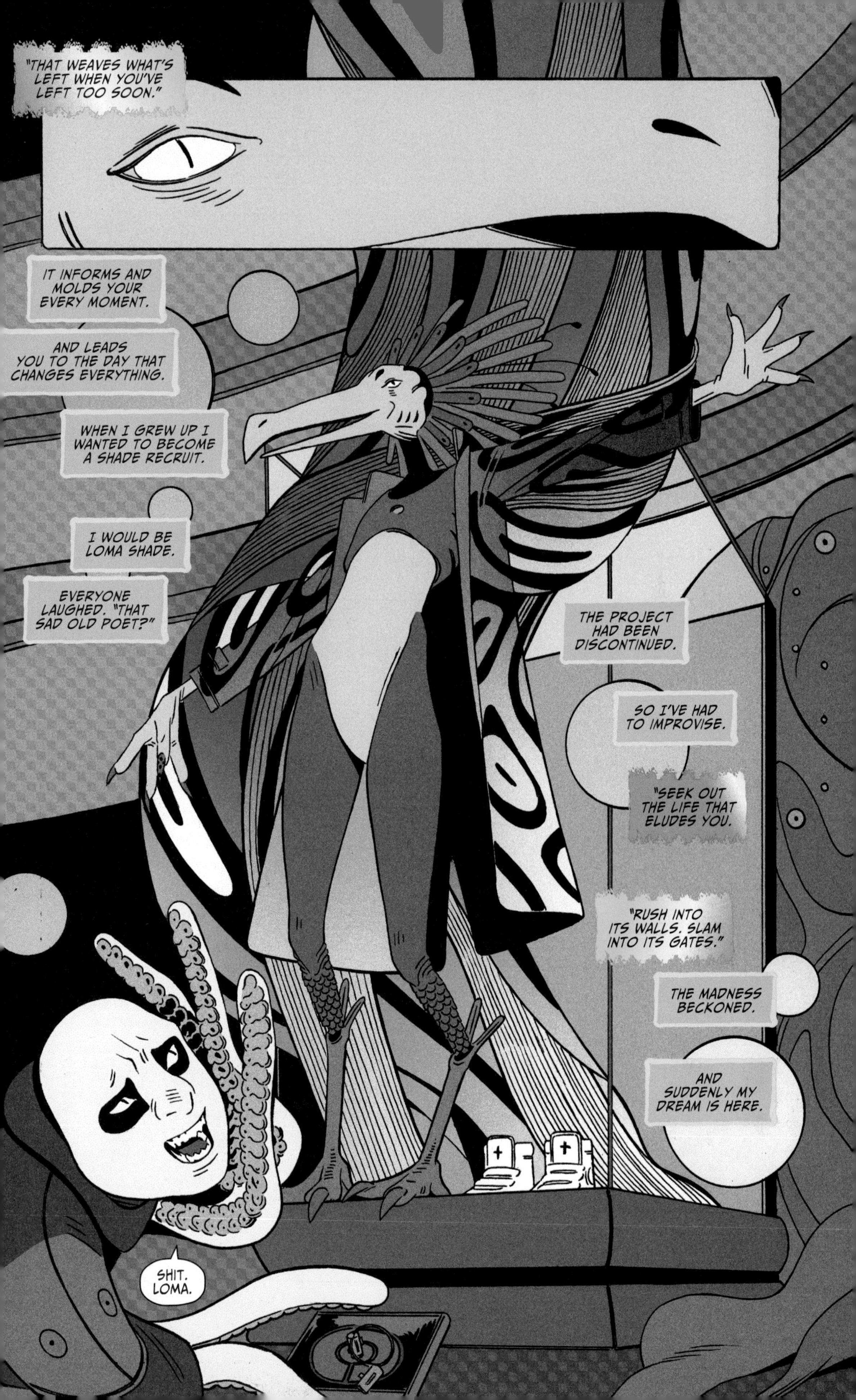
"THAT WEAVES WHAT'S LEFT WHEN YOU'VE LEFT TOO SOON."
IT INFORMS AND MOLDS YOUR EVERY MOMENT.
AND LEADS YOU TO THE DAY THAT CHANGES EVERYTHING.
WHEN I GREW UP I WANTED TO BECOME A SHADE RECRUIT.
I WOULD BE LOMA SHADE.
EVERYONE LAUGHED. "THAT SAD OLD POET?"
THE PROJECT HAD BEEN DISCONTINUED.
SO I'VE HAD TO IMPROVISE.
"SEEK OUT THE LIFE THAT ELUDES YOU.
"RUSH INTO ITS WALLS. SLAM INTO ITS GATES."
THE MADNESS BECKONED.
AND SUDDENLY MY DREAM IS HERE.
SHIT. LOMA.

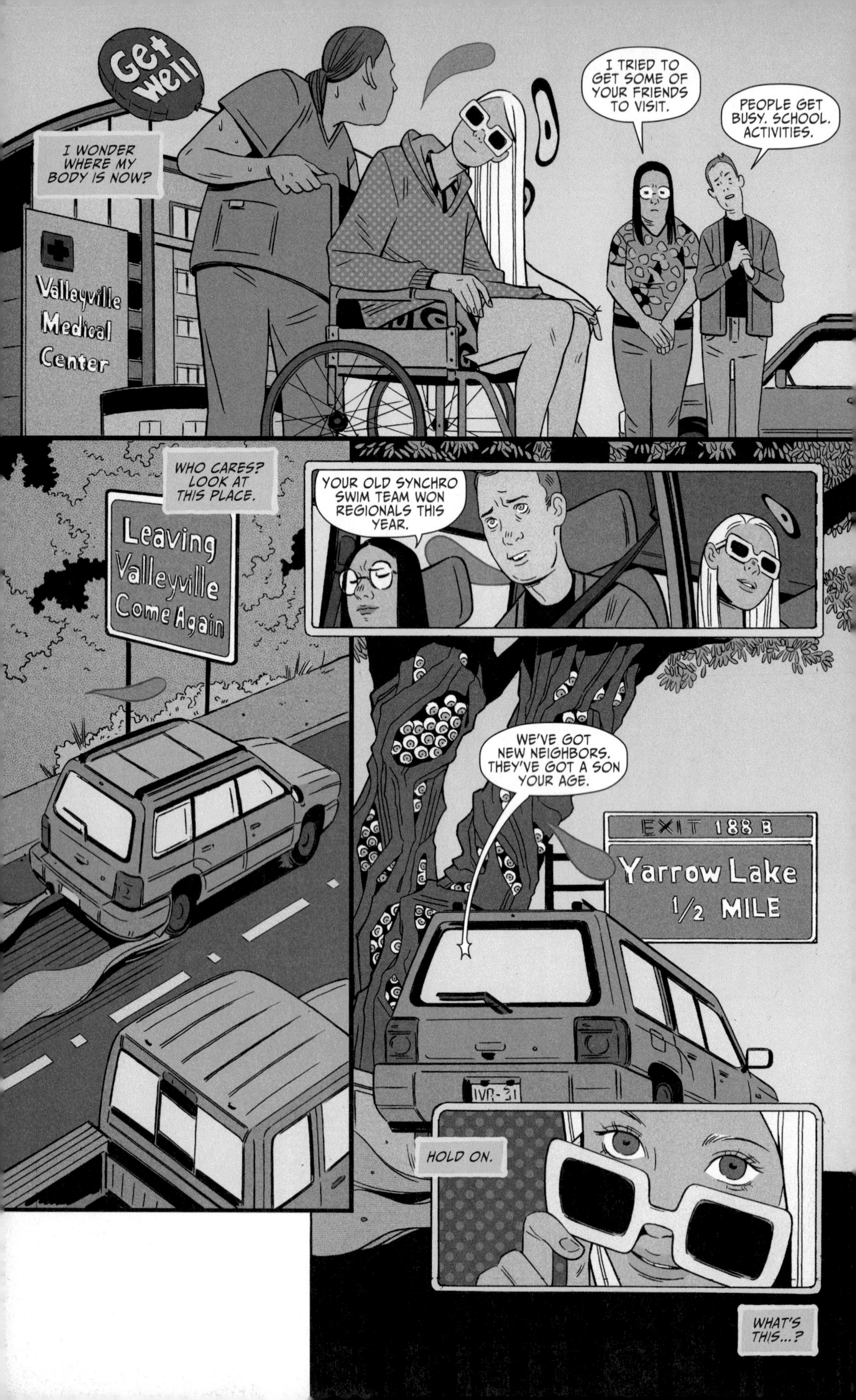
Get Well
I WONDER WHERE MY BODY IS NOW?
Valleyville Medical Center
I TRIED TO GET SOME OF YOUR FRIENDS TO VISIT.
PEOPLE GET BUSY. SCHOOL. ACTIVITIES.
WHO CARES? LOOK AT THIS PLACE.
Leaving Valleyville Come Again
YOUR OLD SYNCHRO SWIM TEAM WON REGIONALS THIS YEAR.
WE'VE GOT NEW NEIGHBORS. THEY'VE GOT A SON YOUR AGE.
EXIT 188 B
Yarrow Lake 1/2 MILE
HOLD ON.
WHAT'S THIS...?

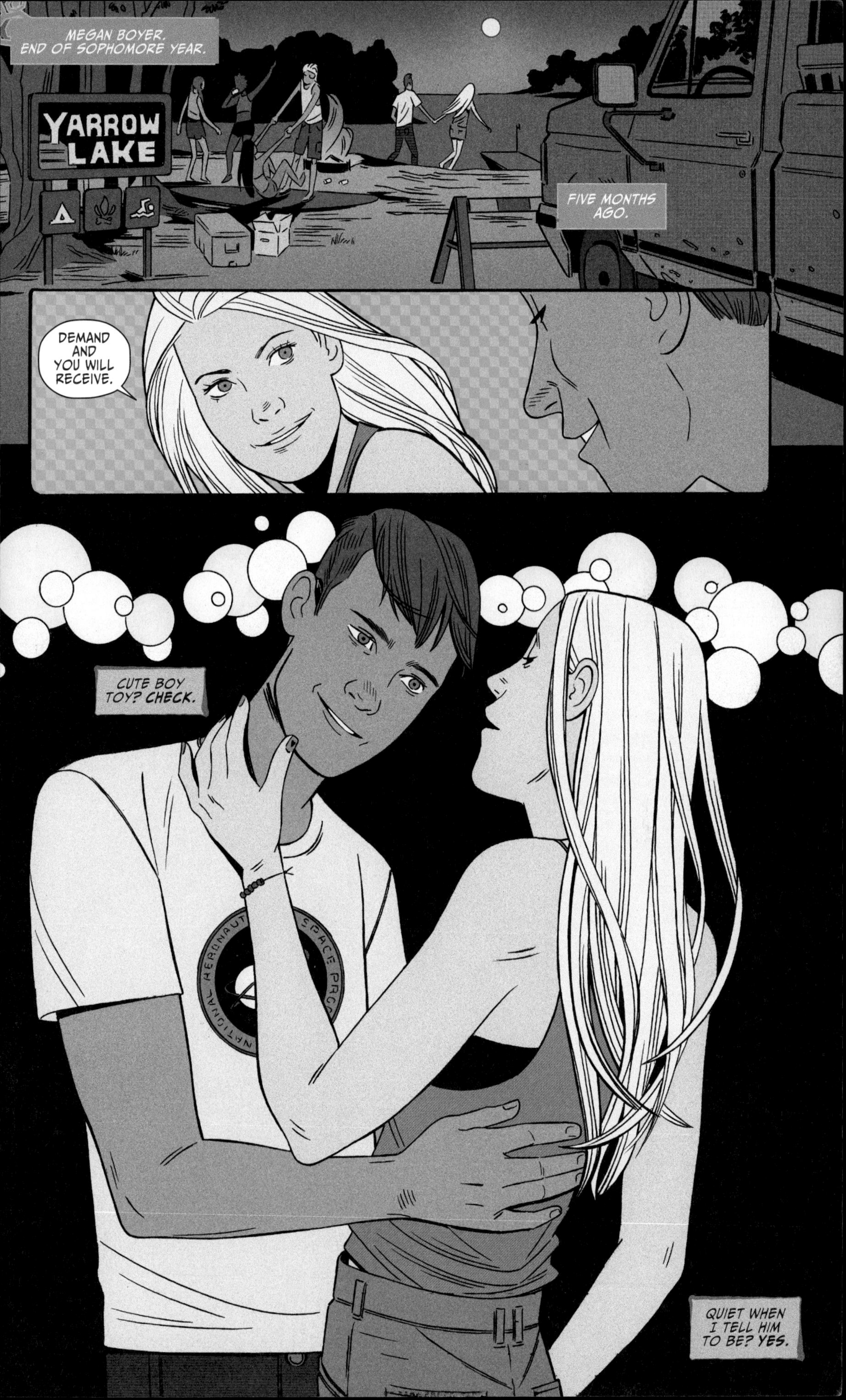
MEGAN BOYER.
END OF SOPHOMORE YEAR.
YARROW LAKE
FIVE MONTHS AGO.
DEMAND AND YOU WILL RECEIVE.
CUTE BOY TOY? CHECK.
QUIET WHEN I TELL HIM TO BE? YES.

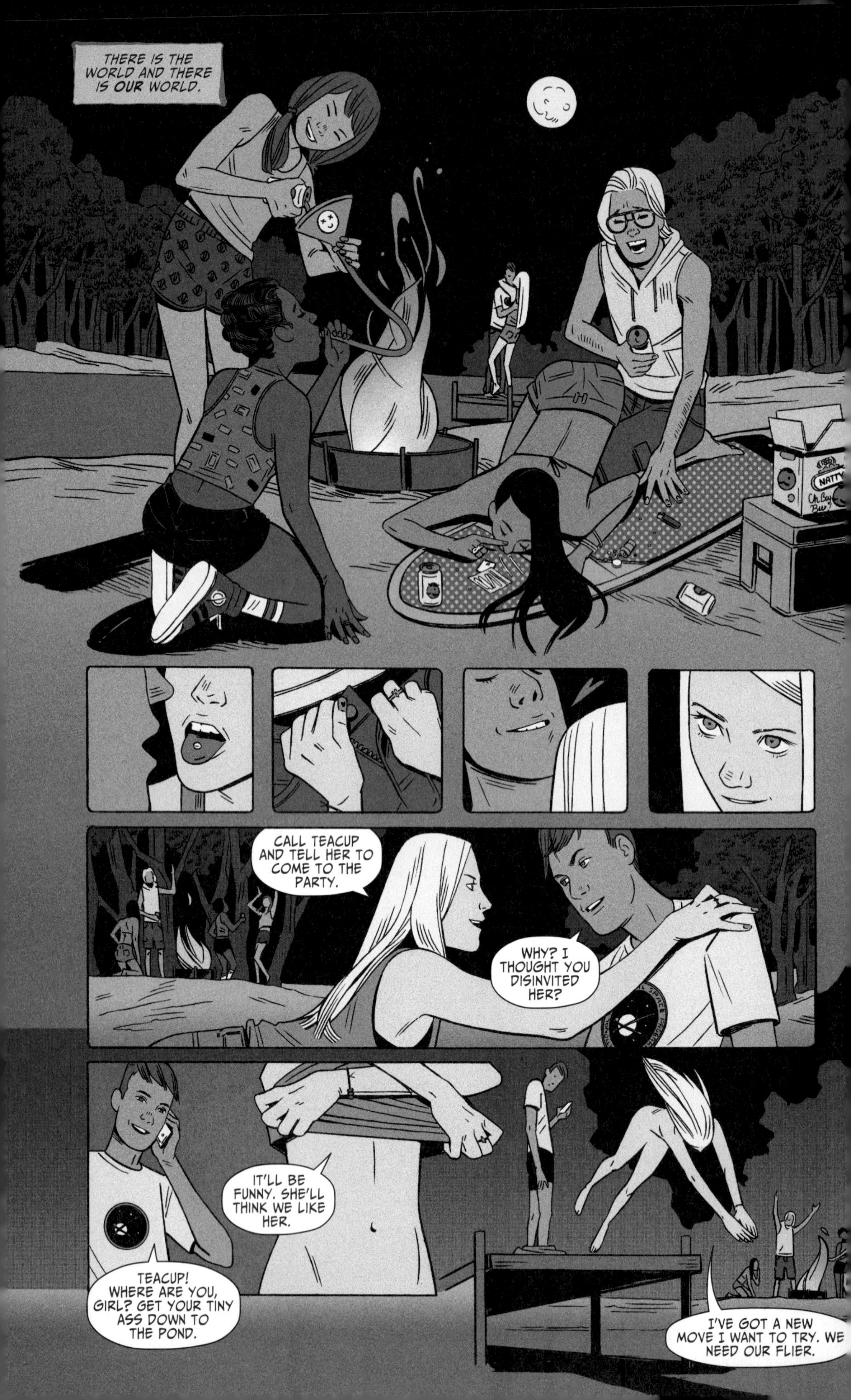
THERE IS THE WORLD AND THERE IS OUR WORLD.
NATTY
CALL TEACUP AND TELL HER TO COME TO THE PARTY.
WHY? I THOUGHT YOU DISINVITED HER?
IT'LL BE FUNNY. SHE'LL THINK WE LIKE HER.
TEACUP! WHERE ARE YOU, GIRL? GET YOUR TINY ASS DOWN TO THE POND.
I'VE GOT A NEW MOVE I WANT TO TRY. WE NEED OUR FLIER.

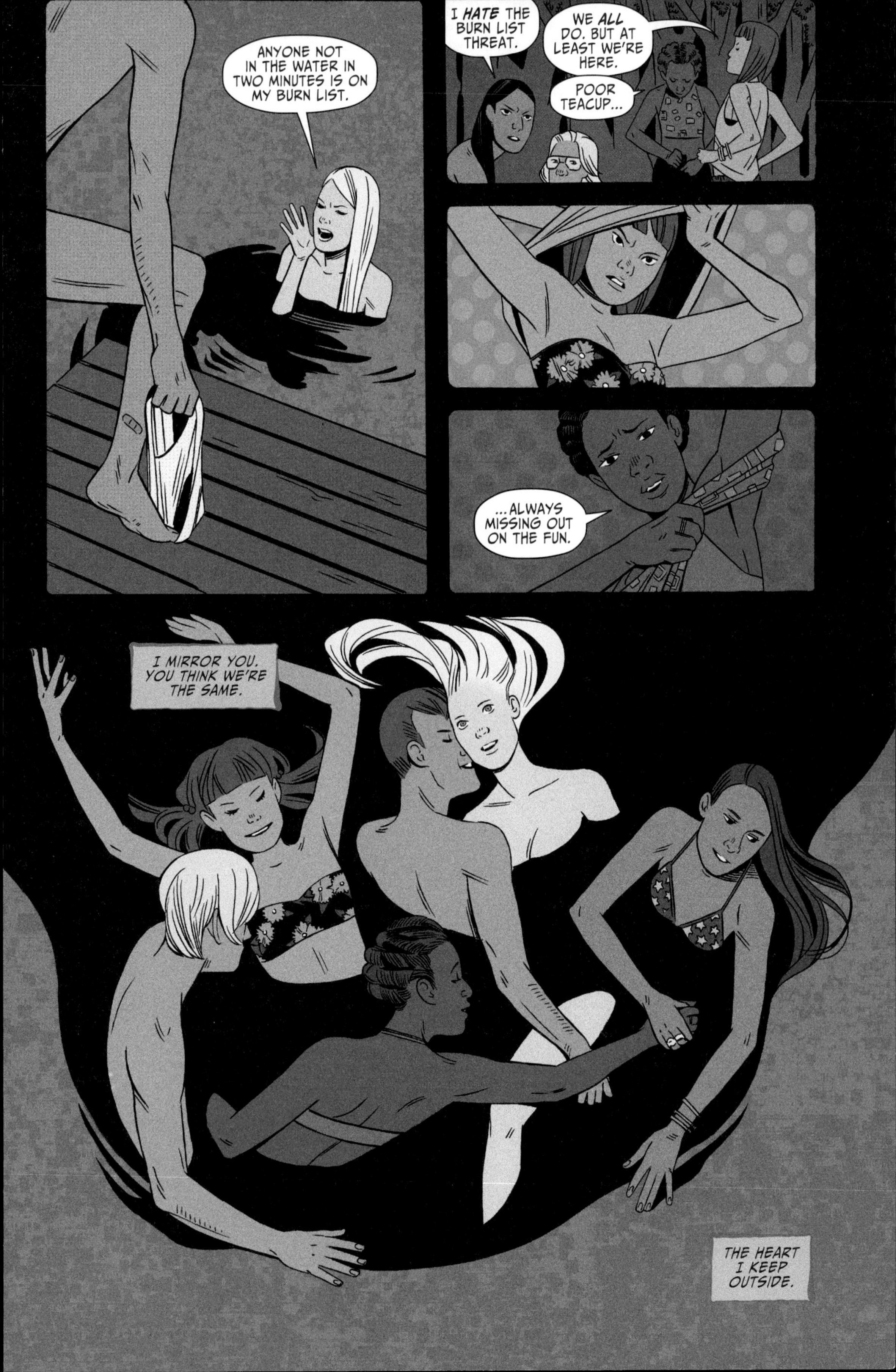
ANYONE NOT IN THE WATER IN TWO MINUTES IS ON MY BURN LIST.
I *HATE* THE BURN LIST THREAT.
WE *ALL* DO. BUT AT LEAST WE'RE HERE.
POOR TEACUP...
...ALWAYS MISSING OUT ON THE FUN.
I MIRROR YOU. YOU THINK WE'RE THE SAME.
THE HEART I KEEP OUTSIDE.

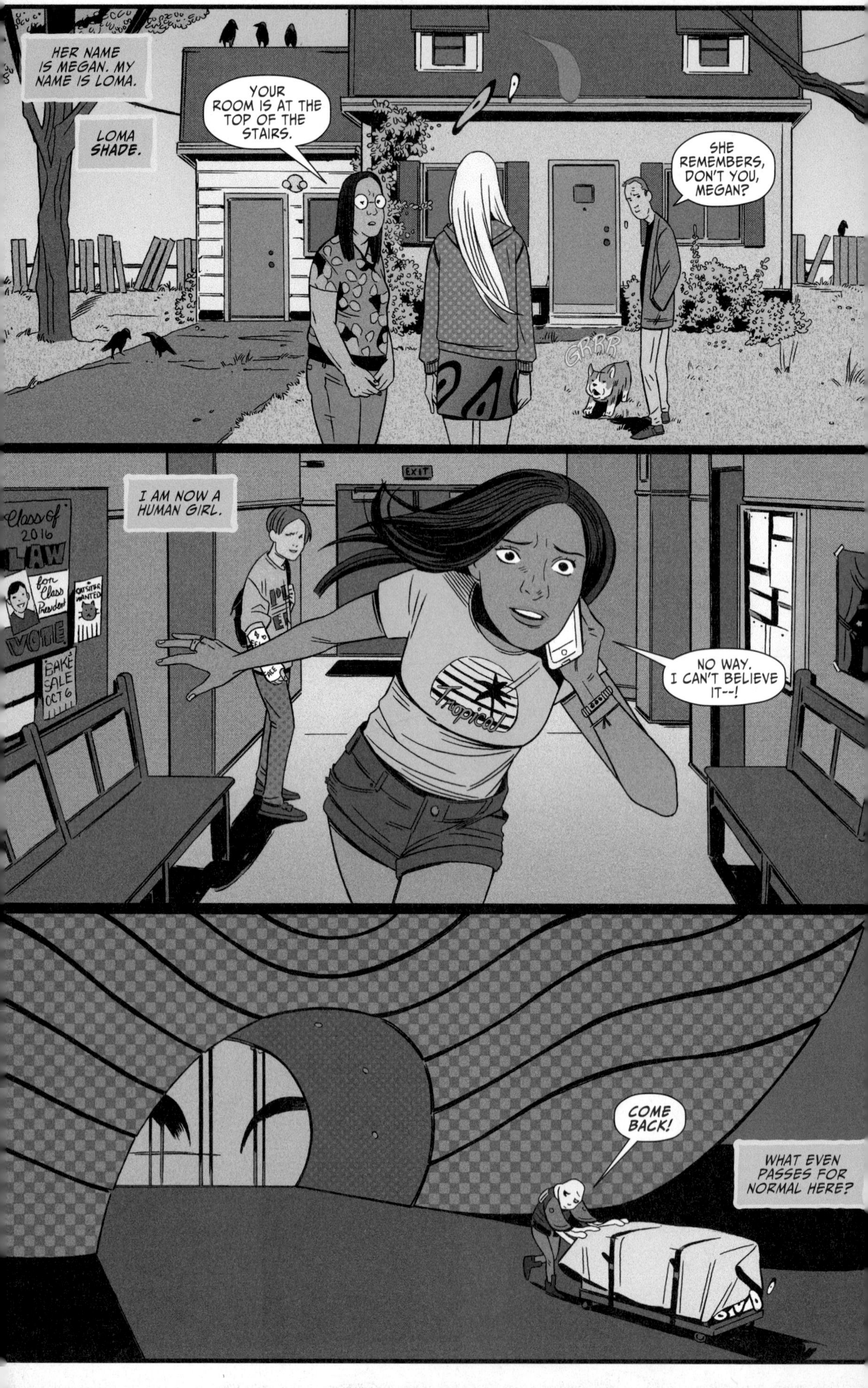
HER NAME IS MEGAN. MY NAME IS LOMA.
LOMA SHADE.
YOUR ROOM IS AT THE TOP OF THE STAIRS.
SHE REMEMBERS, DON'T YOU, MEGAN?
GRRR
EXIT
I AM NOW A HUMAN GIRL.
Class of 2016
LAW for Class President
VOTE
BAKE SALE OCT 6
Tropical
NO WAY. I CAN'T BELIEVE IT--!
COME BACK!
WHAT EVEN PASSES FOR NORMAL HERE?

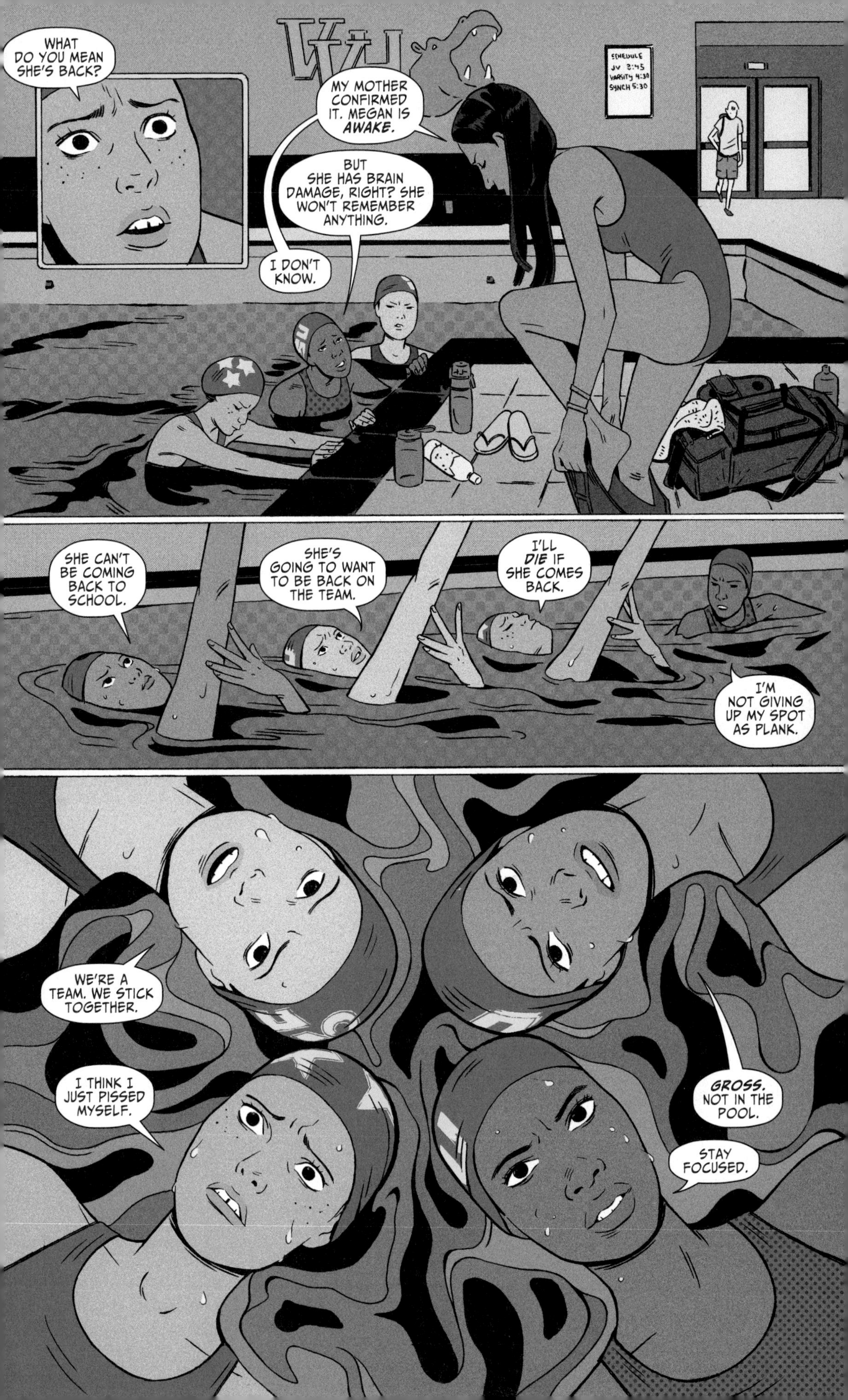
WHAT DO YOU MEAN SHE'S BACK?
MY MOTHER CONFIRMED IT. MEGAN IS AWAKE.
BUT SHE HAS BRAIN DAMAGE, RIGHT? SHE WON'T REMEMBER ANYTHING.
I DON'T KNOW.
SCHEDULE JV 3:45 VARSITY 4:30 SYNCH 5:30
SHE CAN'T BE COMING BACK TO SCHOOL.
SHE'S GOING TO WANT TO BE BACK ON THE TEAM.
I'LL DIE IF SHE COMES BACK.
I'M NOT GIVING UP MY SPOT AS PLANK.
WE'RE A TEAM. WE STICK TOGETHER.
I THINK I JUST PISSED MYSELF.
GROSS. NOT IN THE POOL.
STAY FOCUSED.

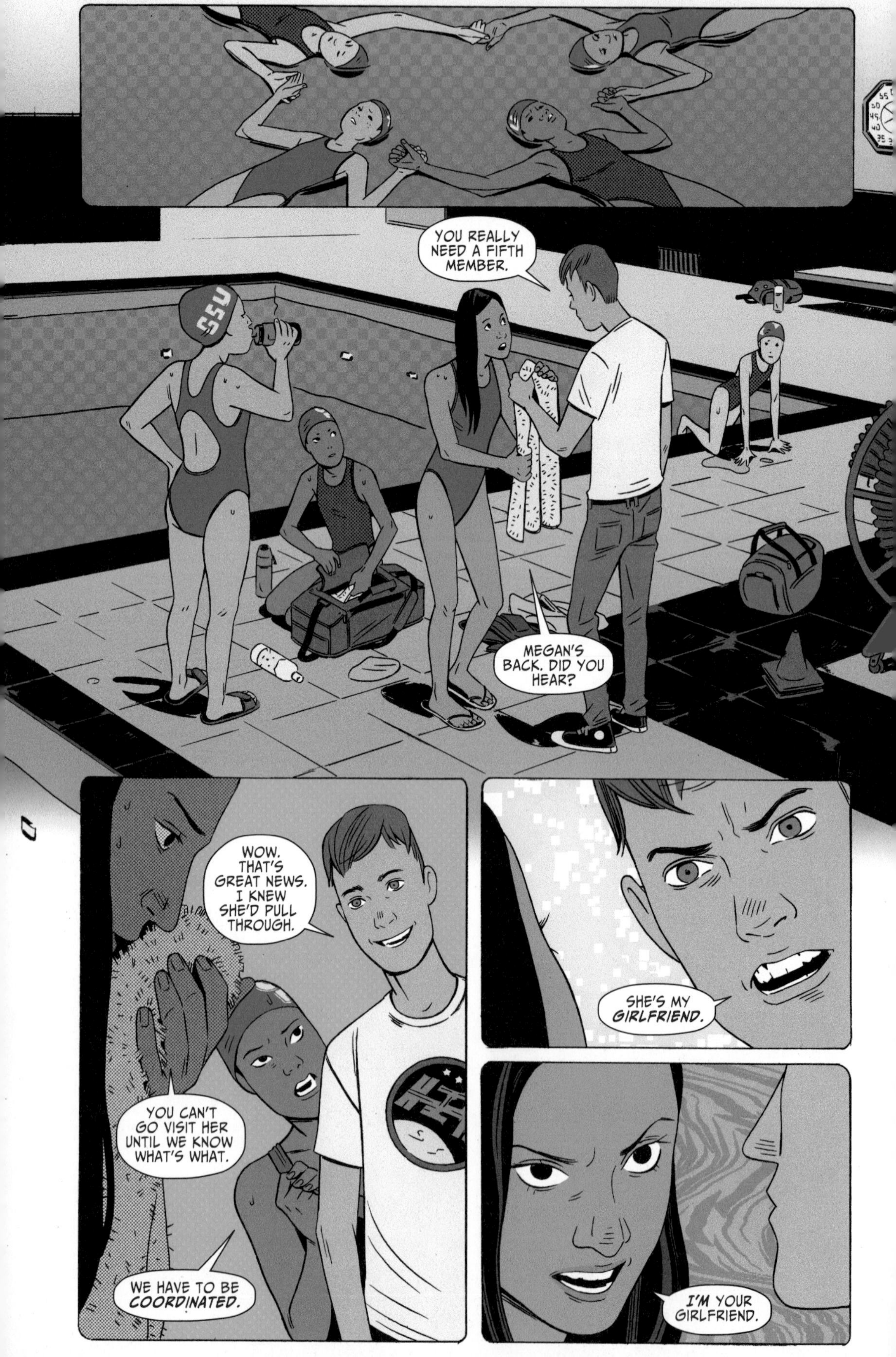
YOU REALLY NEED A FIFTH MEMBER.
MEGAN'S BACK. DID YOU HEAR?
WOW. THAT'S GREAT NEWS. I KNEW SHE'D PULL THROUGH.
YOU CAN'T GO VISIT HER UNTIL WE KNOW WHAT'S WHAT.
WE HAVE TO BE COORDINATED.
SHE'S MY GIRLFRIEND.
I'M YOUR GIRLFRIEND.

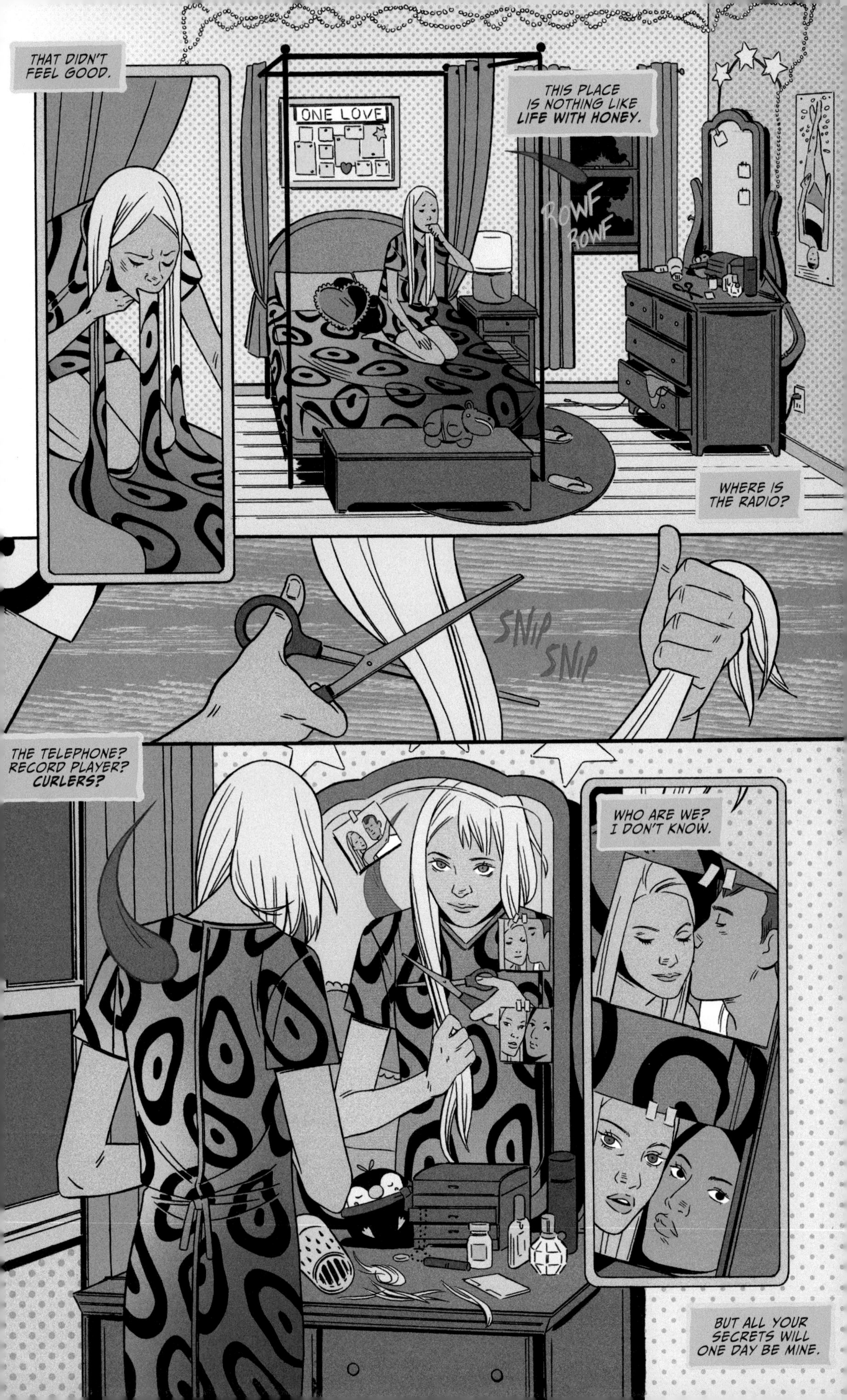
THAT DIDN'T FEEL GOOD.
THIS PLACE IS NOTHING LIKE LIFE WITH HONEY.
ONE LOVE
ROWF ROWF
WHERE IS THE RADIO?
SNIP SNIP
THE TELEPHONE? RECORD PLAYER? CURLERS?
WHO ARE WE? I DON'T KNOW.
BUT ALL YOUR SECRETS WILL ONE DAY BE MINE.

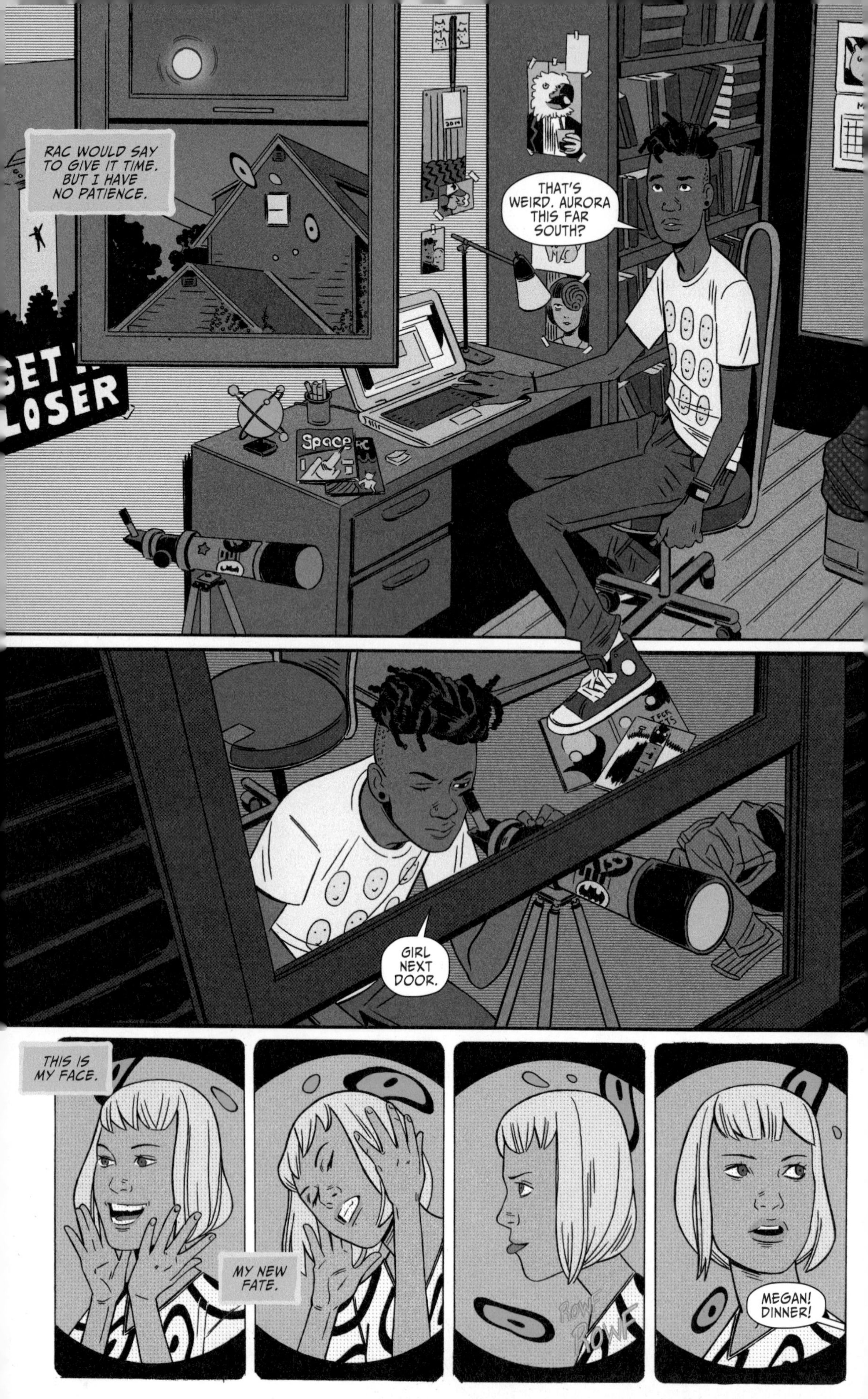
RAC WOULD SAY TO GIVE IT TIME. BUT I HAVE NO PATIENCE.
THAT'S WEIRD. AURORA THIS FAR SOUTH?
GIRL NEXT DOOR.
THIS IS MY FACE.
MY NEW FATE.
ROWF ROWF
MEGAN! DINNER!

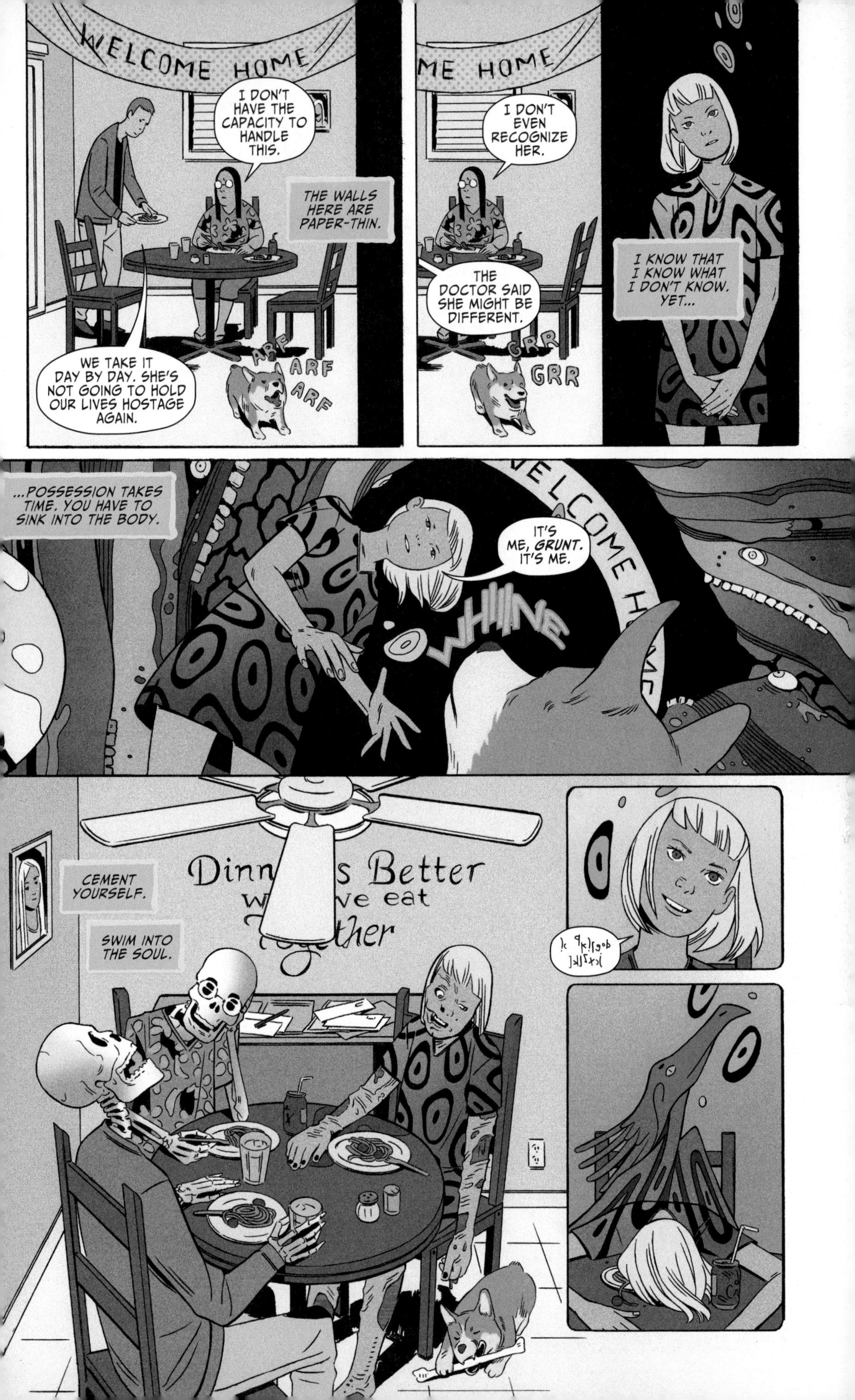
WELCOME HOME
I DON'T HAVE THE CAPACITY TO HANDLE THIS.
THE WALLS HERE ARE PAPER-THIN.
WE TAKE IT DAY BY DAY. SHE'S NOT GOING TO HOLD OUR LIVES HOSTAGE AGAIN.
ARF ARF ARF
ME HOME
I DON'T EVEN RECOGNIZE HER.
THE DOCTOR SAID SHE MIGHT BE DIFFERENT.
GRR GRR
I KNOW THAT I KNOW WHAT I DON'T KNOW. YET...
...POSSESSION TAKES TIME. YOU HAVE TO SINK INTO THE BODY.
IT'S ME, GRUNT. IT'S ME.
WHIIINE
CEMENT YOURSELF.
SWIM INTO THE SOUL.

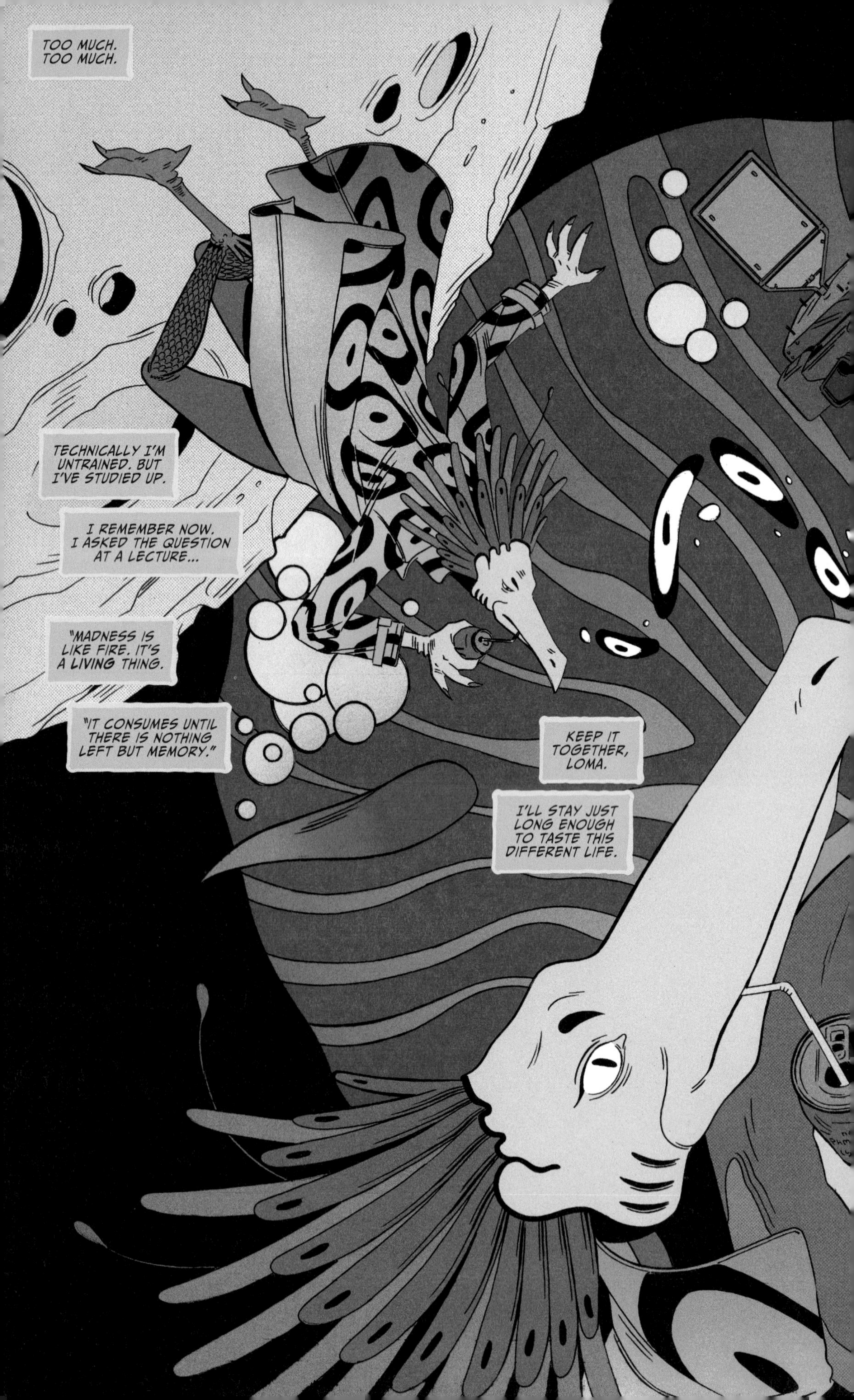
TOO MUCH. TOO MUCH.
TECHNICALLY I'M UNTRAINED. BUT I'VE STUDIED UP.
I REMEMBER NOW. I ASKED THE QUESTION AT A LECTURE...
"MADNESS IS LIKE FIRE. IT'S A LIVING THING.
"IT CONSUMES UNTIL THERE IS NOTHING LEFT BUT MEMORY."
KEEP IT TOGETHER, LOMA.
I'LL STAY JUST LONG ENOUGH TO TASTE THIS DIFFERENT LIFE.

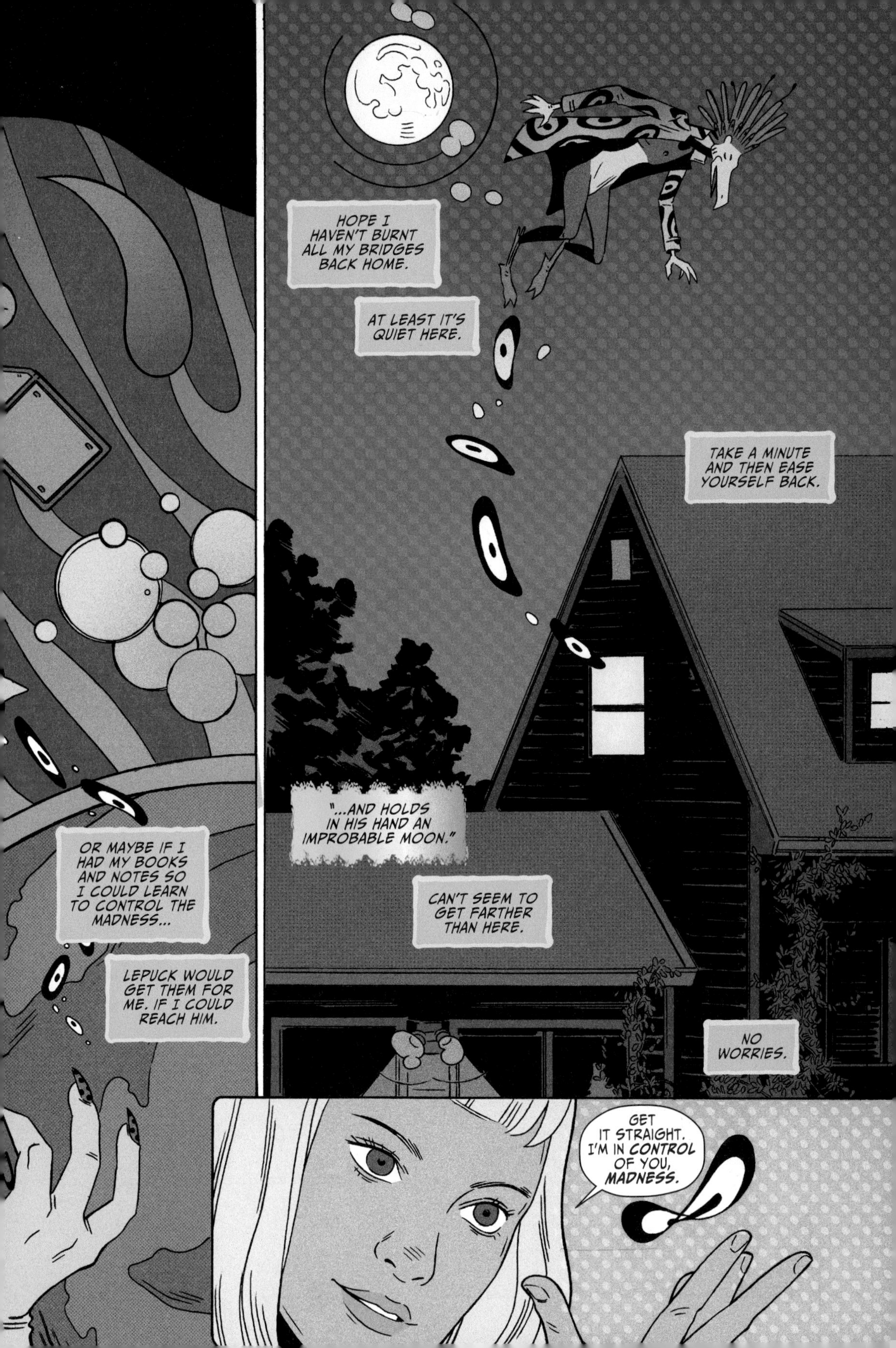
OR MAYBE IF I HAD MY BOOKS AND NOTES SO I COULD LEARN TO CONTROL THE MADNESS...
LEPUCK WOULD GET THEM FOR ME. IF I COULD REACH HIM.
HOPE I HAVEN'T BURNT ALL MY BRIDGES BACK HOME.
AT LEAST IT'S QUIET HERE.
TAKE A MINUTE AND THEN EASE YOURSELF BACK.
"...AND HOLDS IN HIS HAND AN IMPROBABLE MOON."
CAN'T SEEM TO GET FARTHER THAN HERE.
NO WORRIES.
GET IT STRAIGHT. I'M IN CONTROL OF YOU, MADNESS.

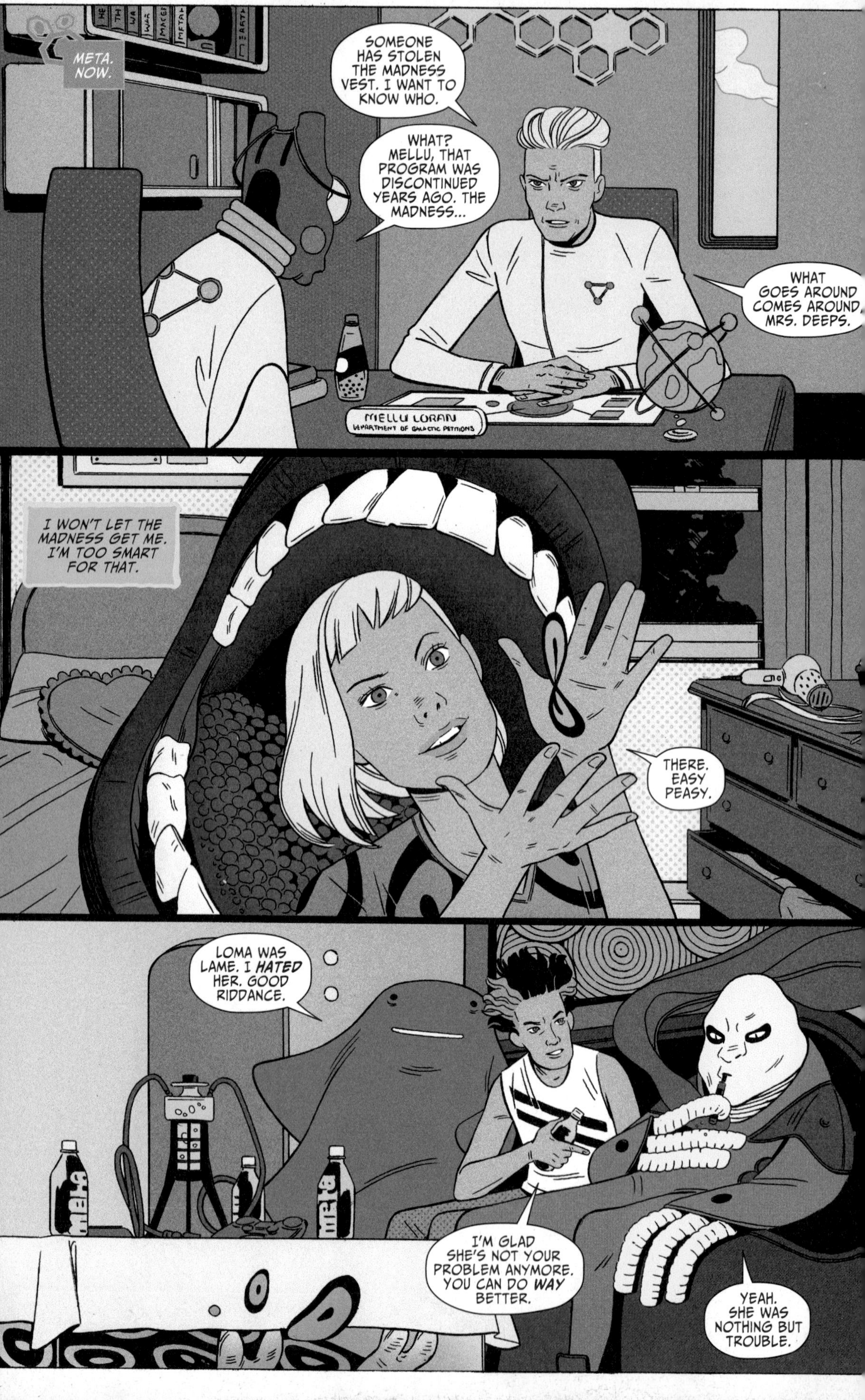
META. NOW.
SOMEONE HAS STOLEN THE MADNESS VEST. I WANT TO KNOW WHO.
WHAT? MELLU, THAT PROGRAM WAS DISCONTINUED YEARS AGO. THE MADNESS...
WHAT GOES AROUND COMES AROUND, MRS. DEEPS.
MELLU LORAN
DEPARTMENT OF GALACTIC PETITIONS
I WON'T LET THE MADNESS GET ME. I'M TOO SMART FOR THAT.
THERE. EASY PEASY.
LOMA WAS LAME. I *HATED* HER. GOOD RIDDANCE.
meta
I'M GLAD SHE'S NOT YOUR PROBLEM ANYMORE. YOU CAN DO *WAY* BETTER.
YEAH. SHE WAS NOTHING BUT TROUBLE.

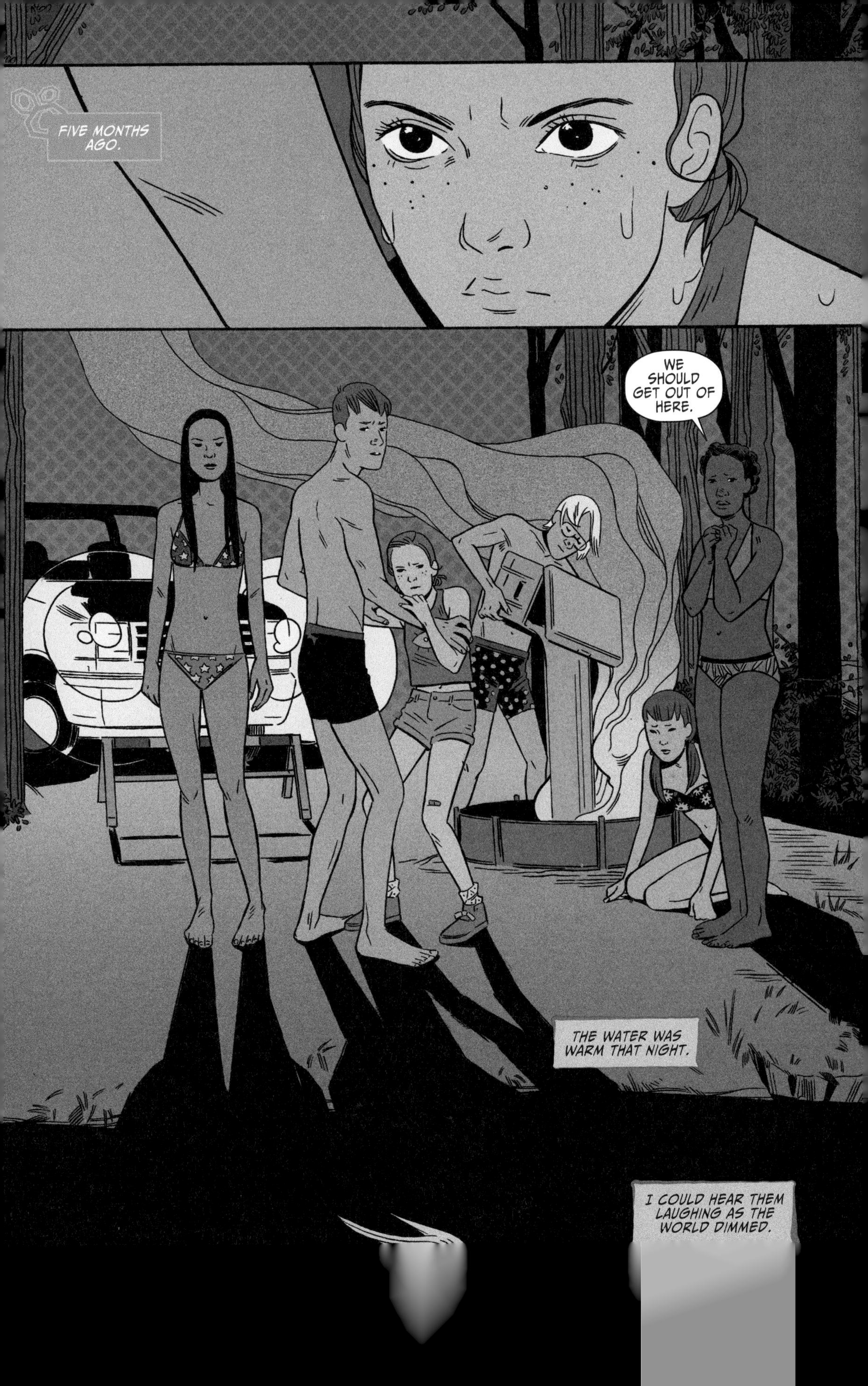
FIVE MONTHS AGO.
WE SHOULD GET OUT OF HERE.
THE WATER WAS WARM THAT NIGHT.
I COULD HEAR THEM LAUGHING AS THE WORLD DIMMED.

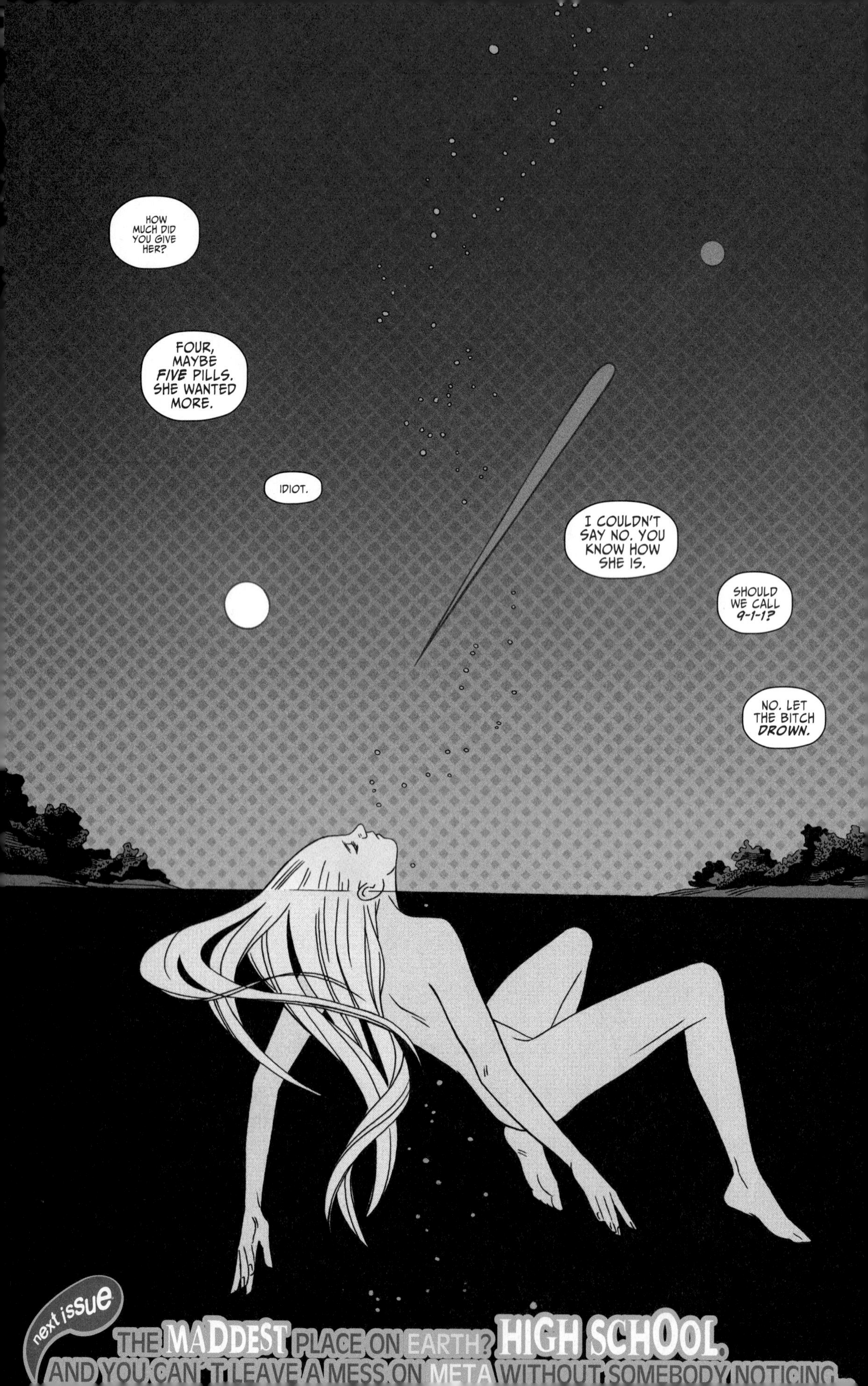
HOW MUCH DID YOU GIVE HER?
FOUR, MAYBE FIVE PILLS. SHE WANTED MORE.
IDIOT.
I COULDN'T SAY NO. YOU KNOW HOW SHE IS.
SHOULD WE CALL 9-1-1?
NO. LET THE BITCH DROWN.
next issue
THE MADDEST PLACE ON EARTH? HIGH SCHOOL.
AND YOU CAN'T LEAVE A MESS ON META WITHOUT SOMEBODY NOTICING...

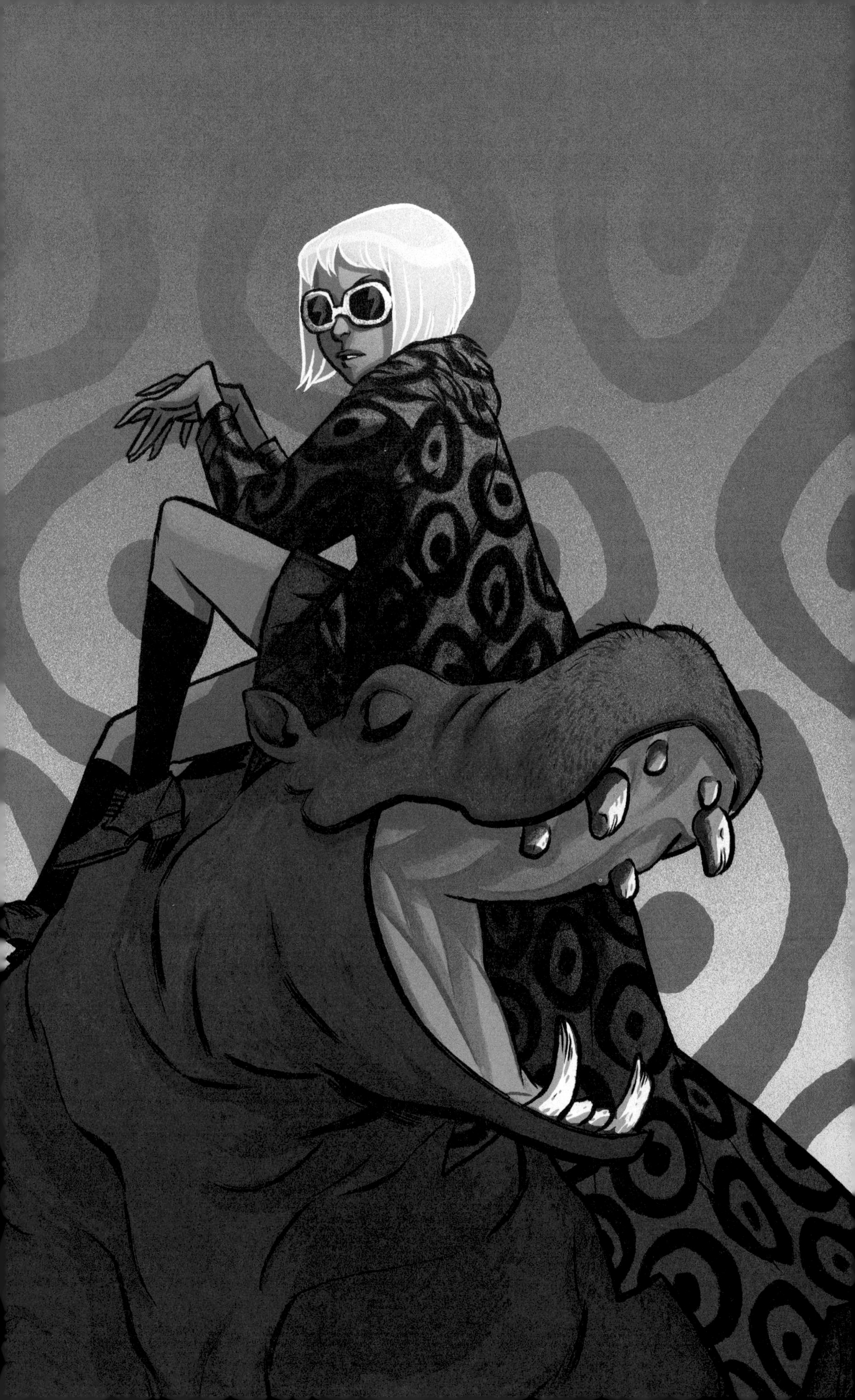

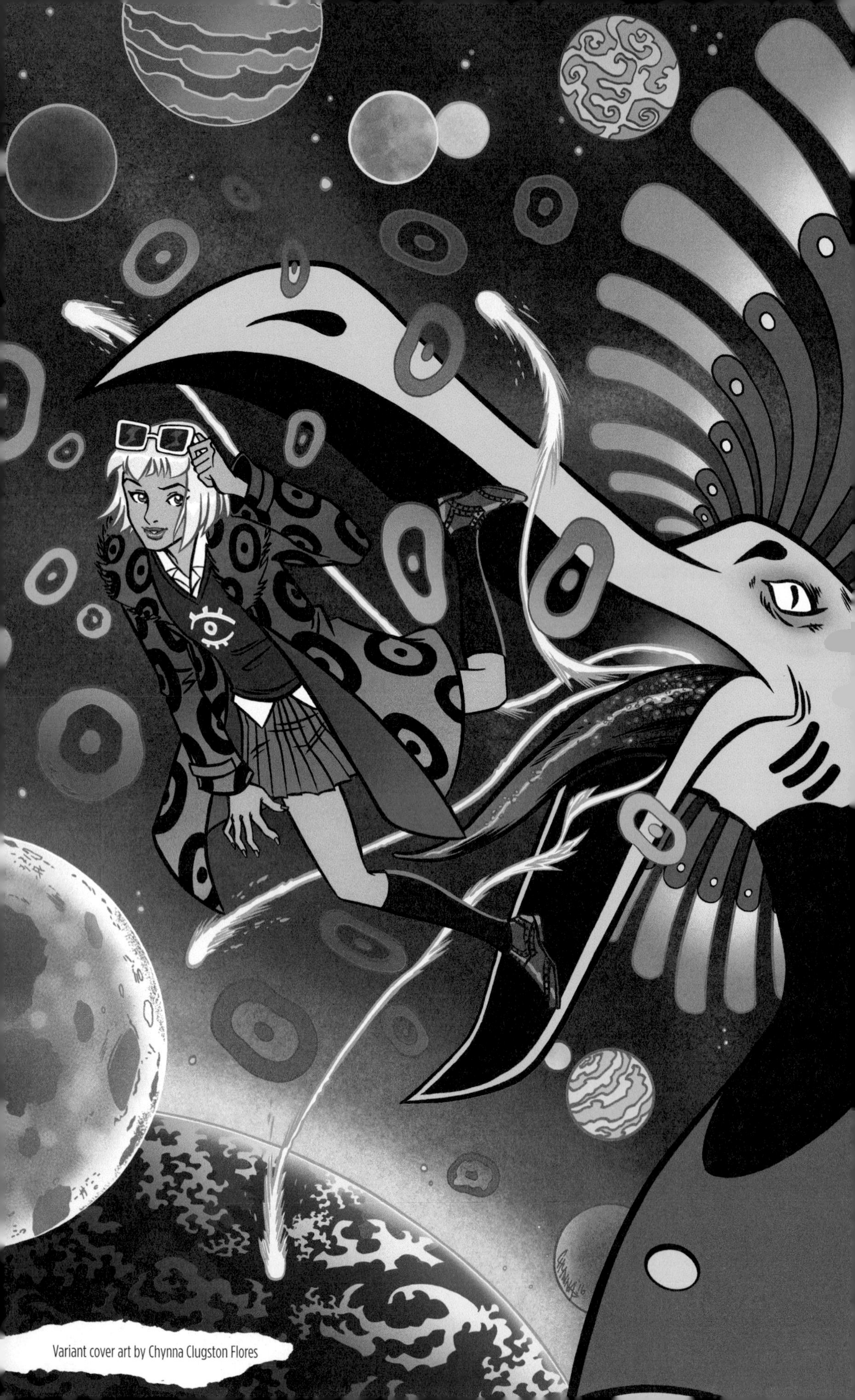

Variant cover art by Chynna Clugston Flores

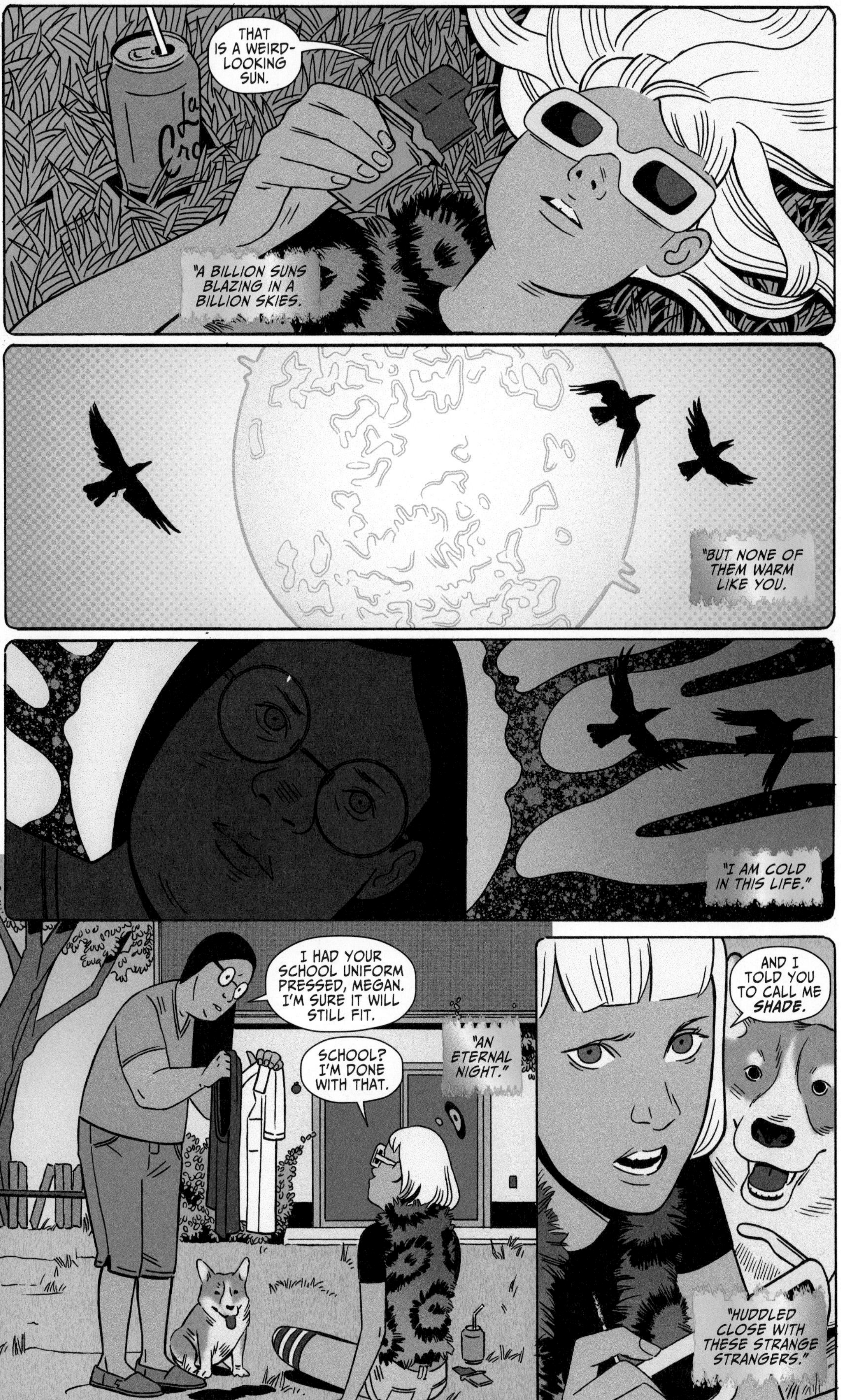
THAT IS A WEIRD-LOOKING SUN.
"A BILLION SUNS BLAZING IN A BILLION SKIES.
"BUT NONE OF THEM WARM LIKE YOU.
"I AM COLD IN THIS LIFE."
I HAD YOUR SCHOOL UNIFORM PRESSED, MEGAN. I'M SURE IT WILL STILL FIT.
SCHOOL? I'M DONE WITH THAT.
"AN ETERNAL NIGHT."
AND I TOLD YOU TO CALL ME SHADE.
"HUDDLED CLOSE WITH THESE STRANGE STRANGERS."

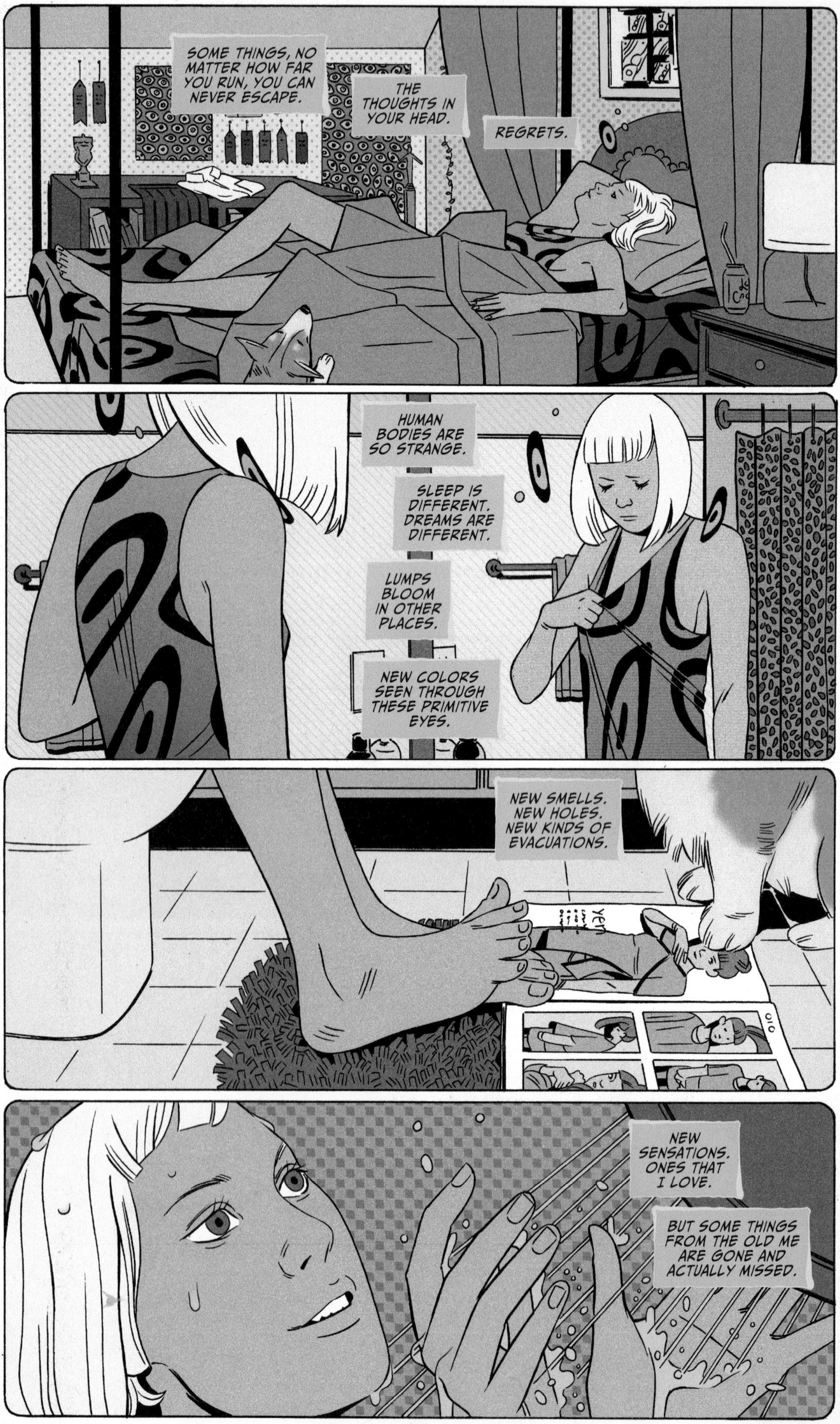
SOME THINGS, NO MATTER HOW FAR YOU RUN, YOU CAN NEVER ESCAPE.
THE THOUGHTS IN YOUR HEAD.
REGRETS.
HUMAN BODIES ARE SO STRANGE.
SLEEP IS DIFFERENT. DREAMS ARE DIFFERENT.
LUMPS BLOOM IN OTHER PLACES.
NEW COLORS SEEN THROUGH THESE PRIMITIVE EYES.
NEW SMELLS. NEW HOLES. NEW KINDS OF EVACUATIONS.
NEW SENSATIONS. ONES THAT I LOVE.
BUT SOME THINGS FROM THE OLD ME ARE GONE AND ACTUALLY MISSED.

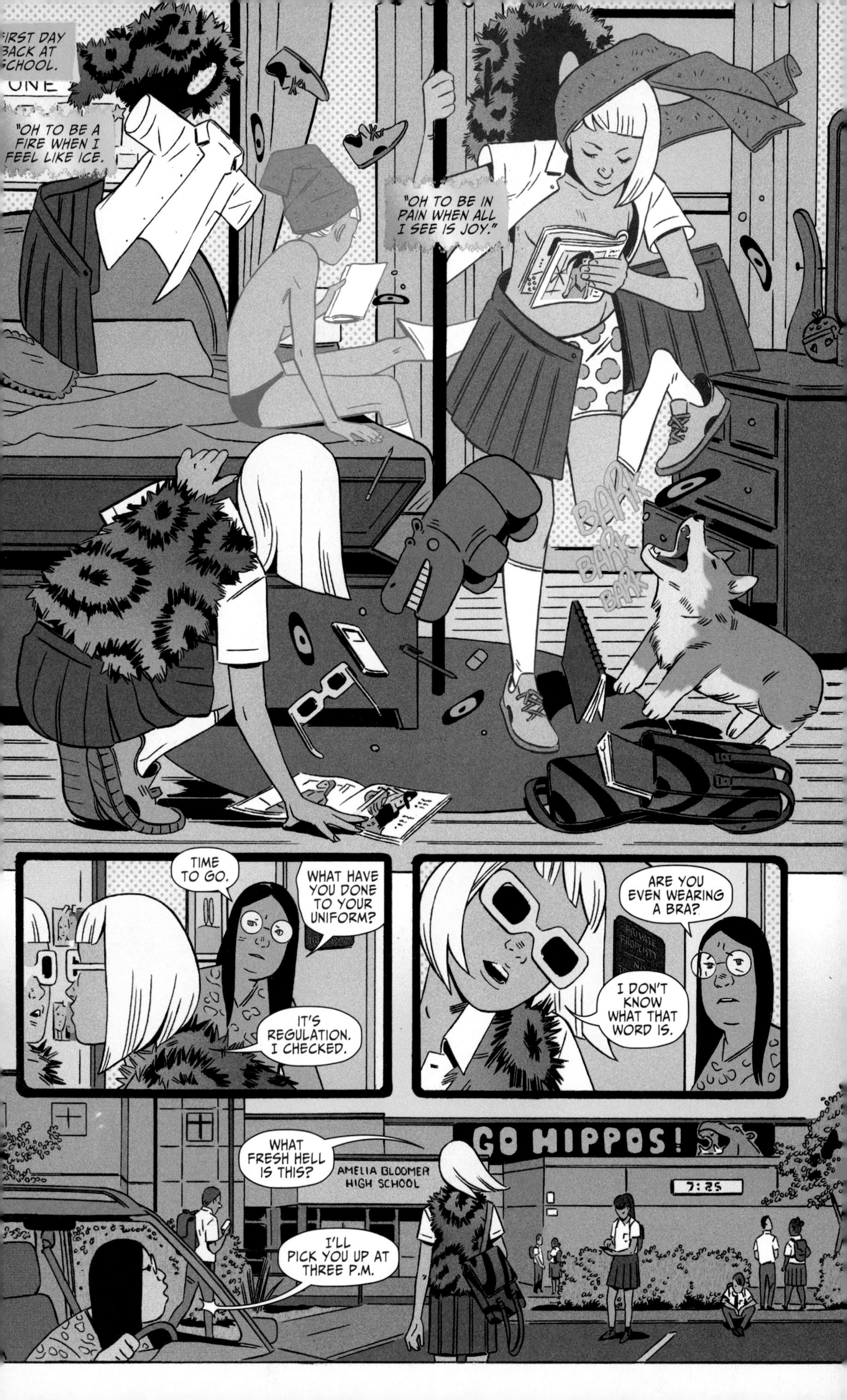
FIRST DAY BACK AT SCHOOL.
"OH TO BE A FIRE WHEN I FEEL LIKE ICE.
"OH TO BE IN PAIN WHEN ALL I SEE IS JOY."
BARK
BARK
BARK
TIME TO GO.
WHAT HAVE YOU DONE TO YOUR UNIFORM?
IT'S REGULATION. I CHECKED.
ARE YOU EVEN WEARING A BRA?
I DON'T KNOW WHAT THAT WORD IS.
PRIVATE PROPERTY
GO HIPPOS!
AMELIA BLOOMER HIGH SCHOOL
7:25
WHAT FRESH HELL IS THIS?
I'LL PICK YOU UP AT THREE P.M.

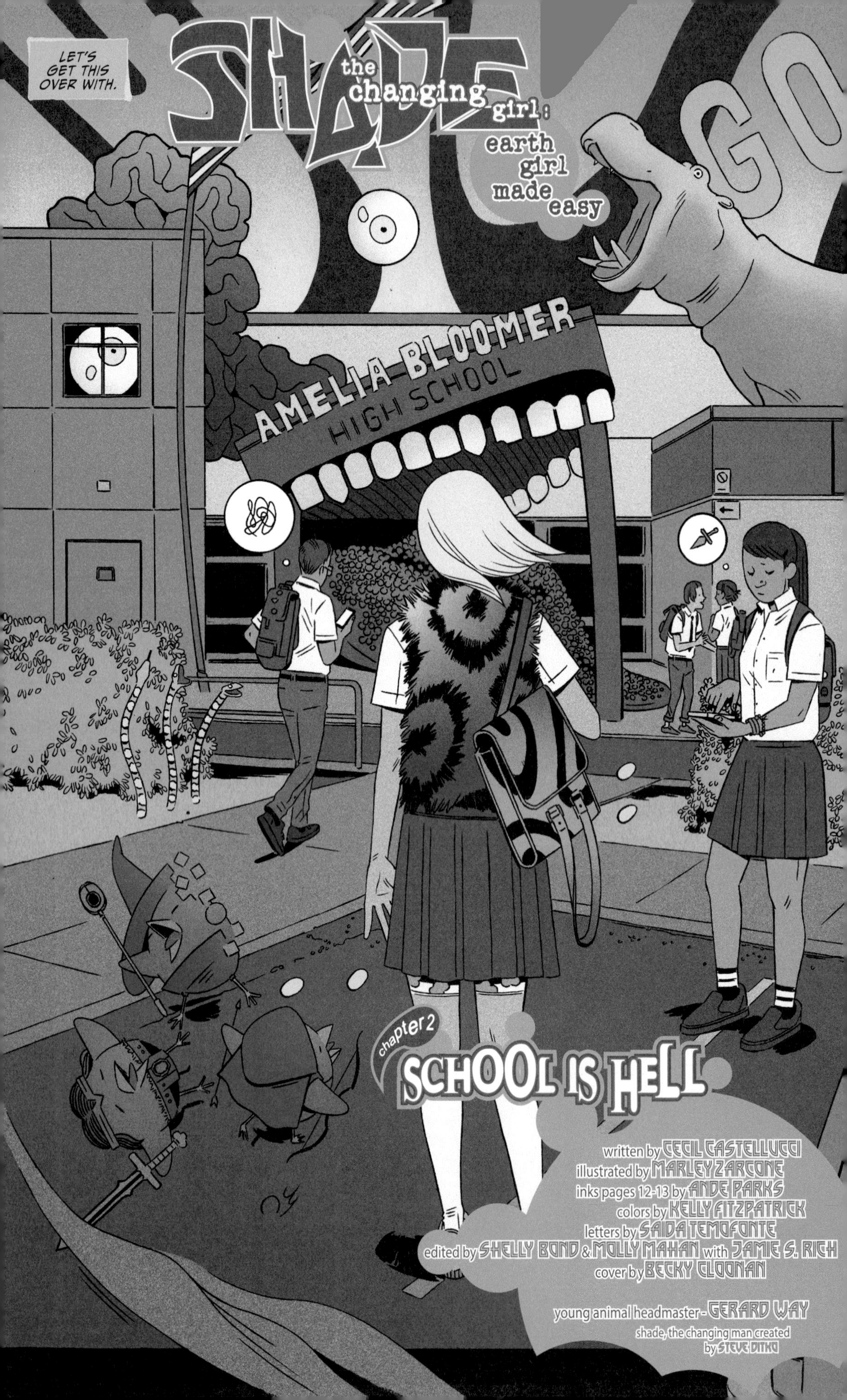
LET'S GET THIS OVER WITH.
SHADE the changing girl: earth girl made easy
GO
AMELIA BLOOMER HIGH SCHOOL
chapter 2
SCHOOL IS HELL
written by CECIL CASTELLUCCI
illustrated by MARLEY ZARCONE
inks pages 12-13 by ANDE PARKS
colors by KELLY FITZPATRICK
letters by SAIDA TEMOFONTE
edited by SHELLY BOND & MOLLY MAHAN with JAMIE S. RICH
cover by BECKY CLOONAN
young animal headmaster - GERARD WAY
shade, the changing man created by STEVE DITKO

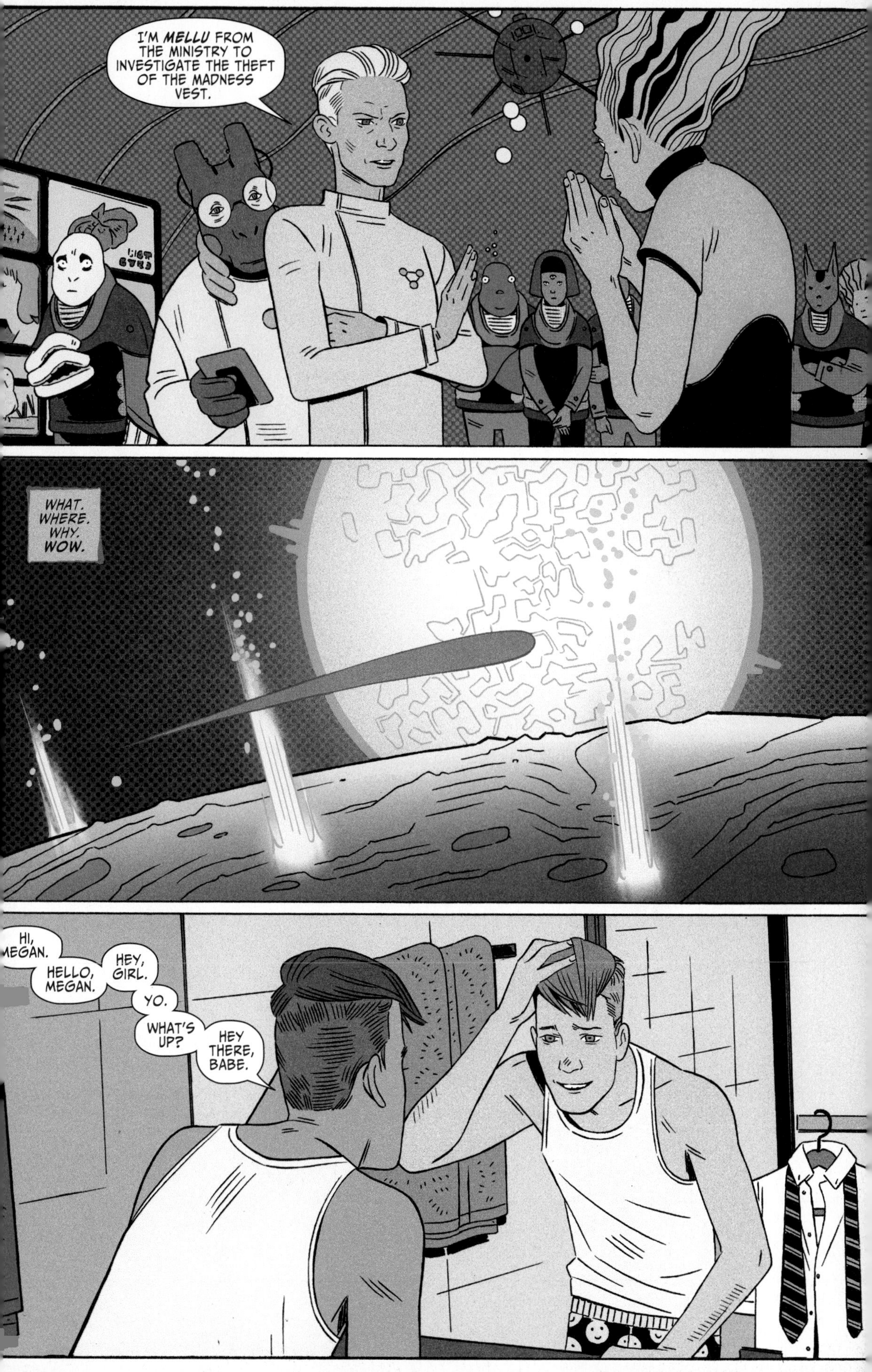
I'M MELLU FROM THE MINISTRY TO INVESTIGATE THE THEFT OF THE MADNESS VEST.
WHAT. WHERE. WHY. WOW.
HI, MEGAN.
HELLO, MEGAN.
HEY, GIRL.
YO.
WHAT'S UP?
HEY THERE, BABE.

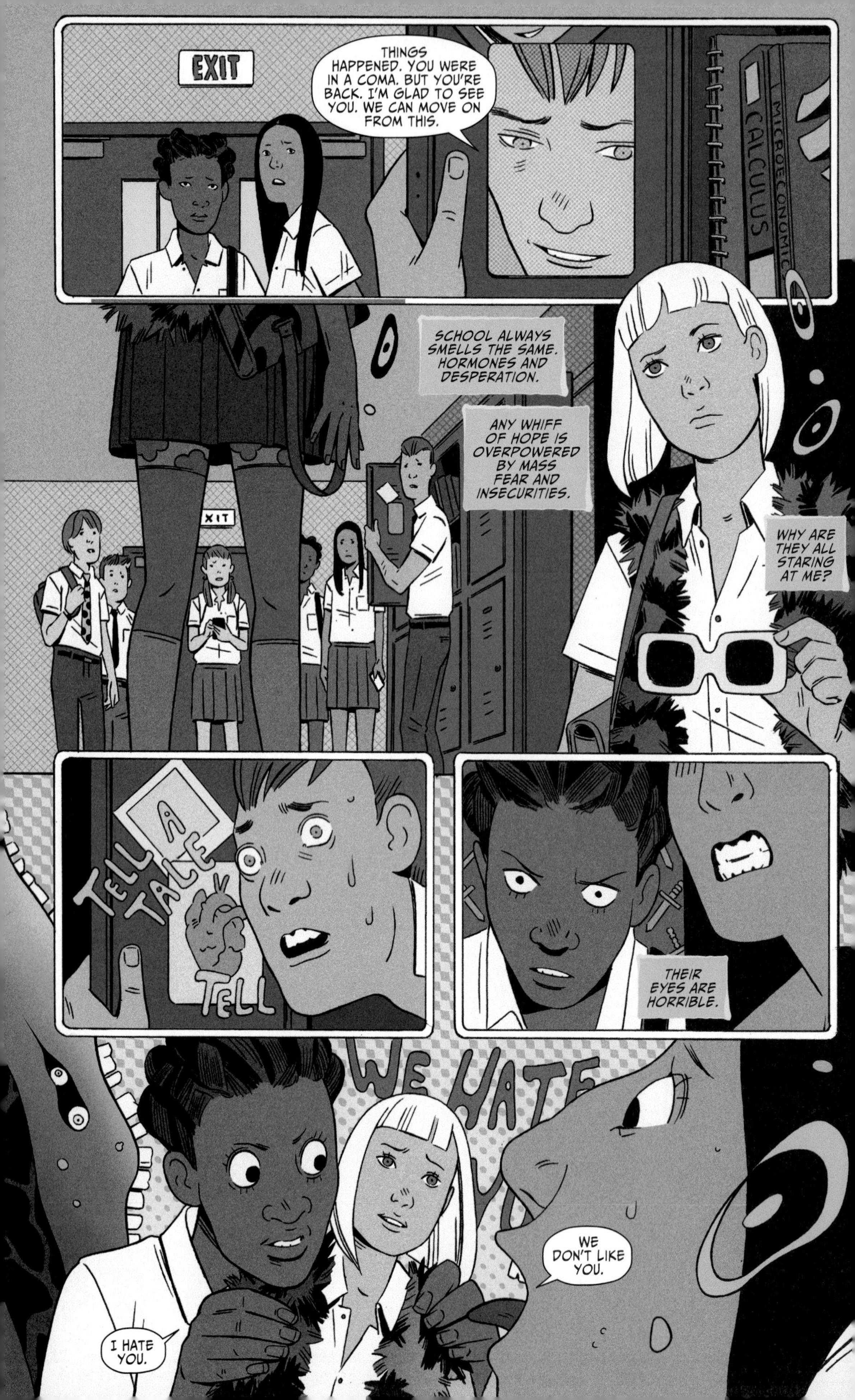
EXIT
THINGS HAPPENED. YOU WERE IN A COMA. BUT YOU'RE BACK. I'M GLAD TO SEE YOU. WE CAN MOVE ON FROM THIS.
MICROECONOMICS
CALCULUS
SCHOOL ALWAYS SMELLS THE SAME. HORMONES AND DESPERATION.
ANY WHIFF OF HOPE IS OVERPOWERED BY MASS FEAR AND INSECURITIES.
EXIT
WHY ARE THEY ALL STARING AT ME?
TELL A TALE
TELL
THEIR EYES ARE HORRIBLE.
WE HATE
WE DON'T LIKE YOU.
I HATE YOU.

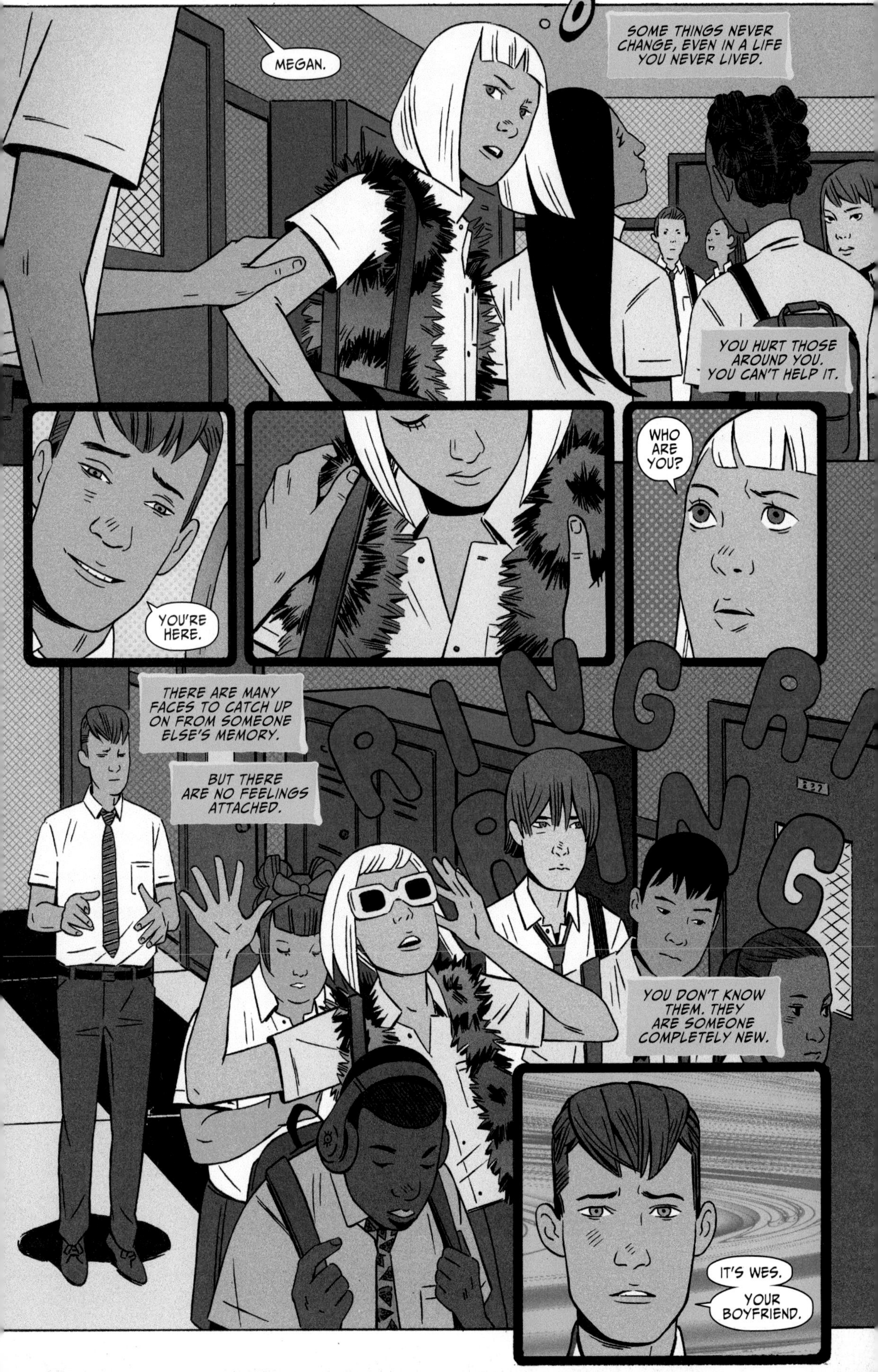
MEGAN.
SOME THINGS NEVER CHANGE, EVEN IN A LIFE YOU NEVER LIVED.
YOU HURT THOSE AROUND YOU. YOU CAN'T HELP IT.
YOU'RE HERE.
WHO ARE YOU?
THERE ARE MANY FACES TO CATCH UP ON FROM SOMEONE ELSE'S MEMORY.
BUT THERE ARE NO FEELINGS ATTACHED.
RING RING
YOU DON'T KNOW THEM. THEY ARE SOMEONE COMPLETELY NEW.
IT'S WES.
YOUR BOYFRIEND.

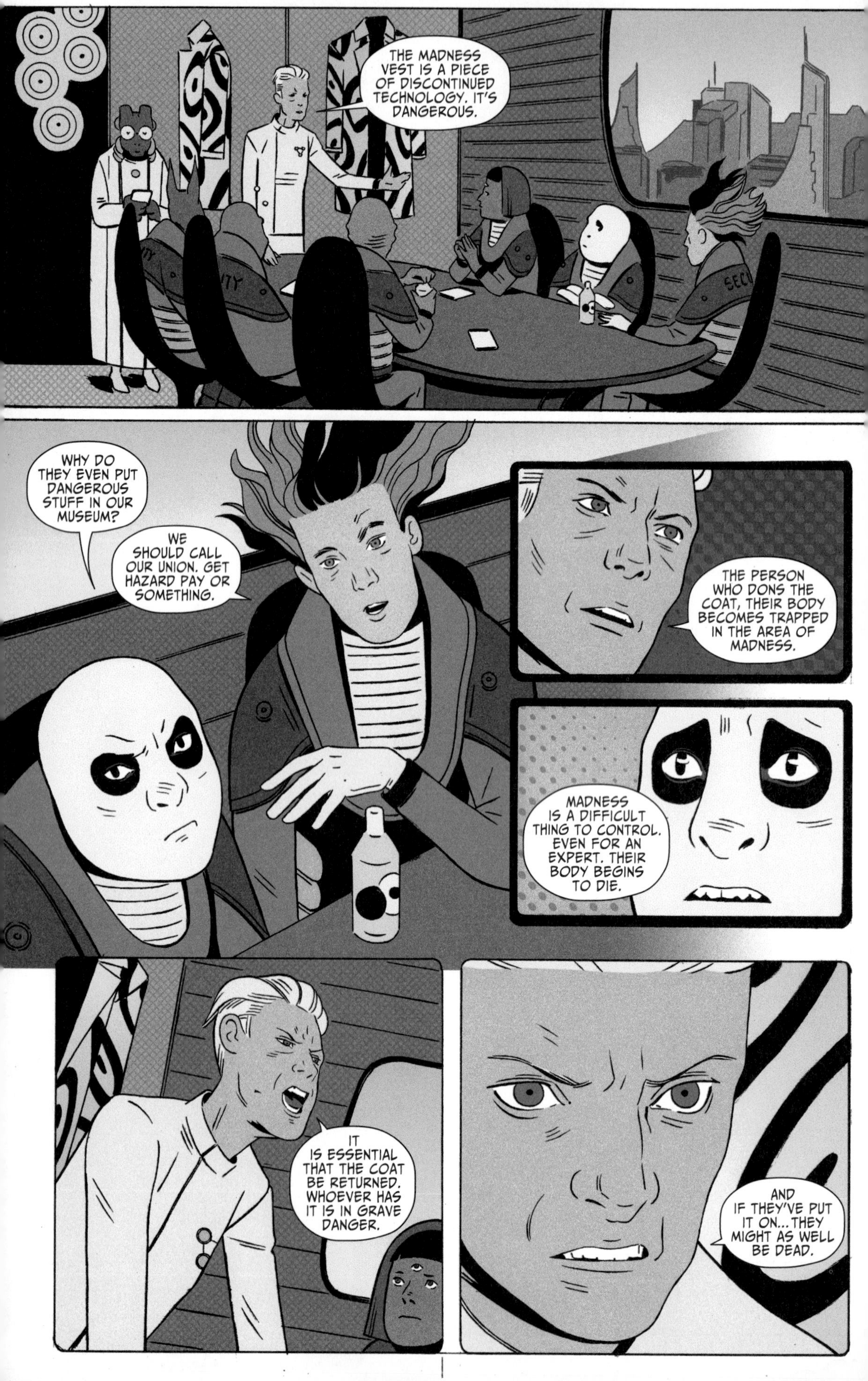
THE MADNESS VEST IS A PIECE OF DISCONTINUED TECHNOLOGY. IT'S DANGEROUS.
WHY DO THEY EVEN PUT DANGEROUS STUFF IN OUR MUSEUM?
WE SHOULD CALL OUR UNION. GET HAZARD PAY OR SOMETHING.
THE PERSON WHO DONS THE COAT, THEIR BODY BECOMES TRAPPED IN THE AREA OF MADNESS.
MADNESS IS A DIFFICULT THING TO CONTROL. EVEN FOR AN EXPERT. THEIR BODY BEGINS TO DIE.
IT IS ESSENTIAL THAT THE COAT BE RETURNED. WHOEVER HAS IT IS IN GRAVE DANGER.
AND IF THEY'VE PUT IT ON... THEY MIGHT AS WELL BE DEAD.

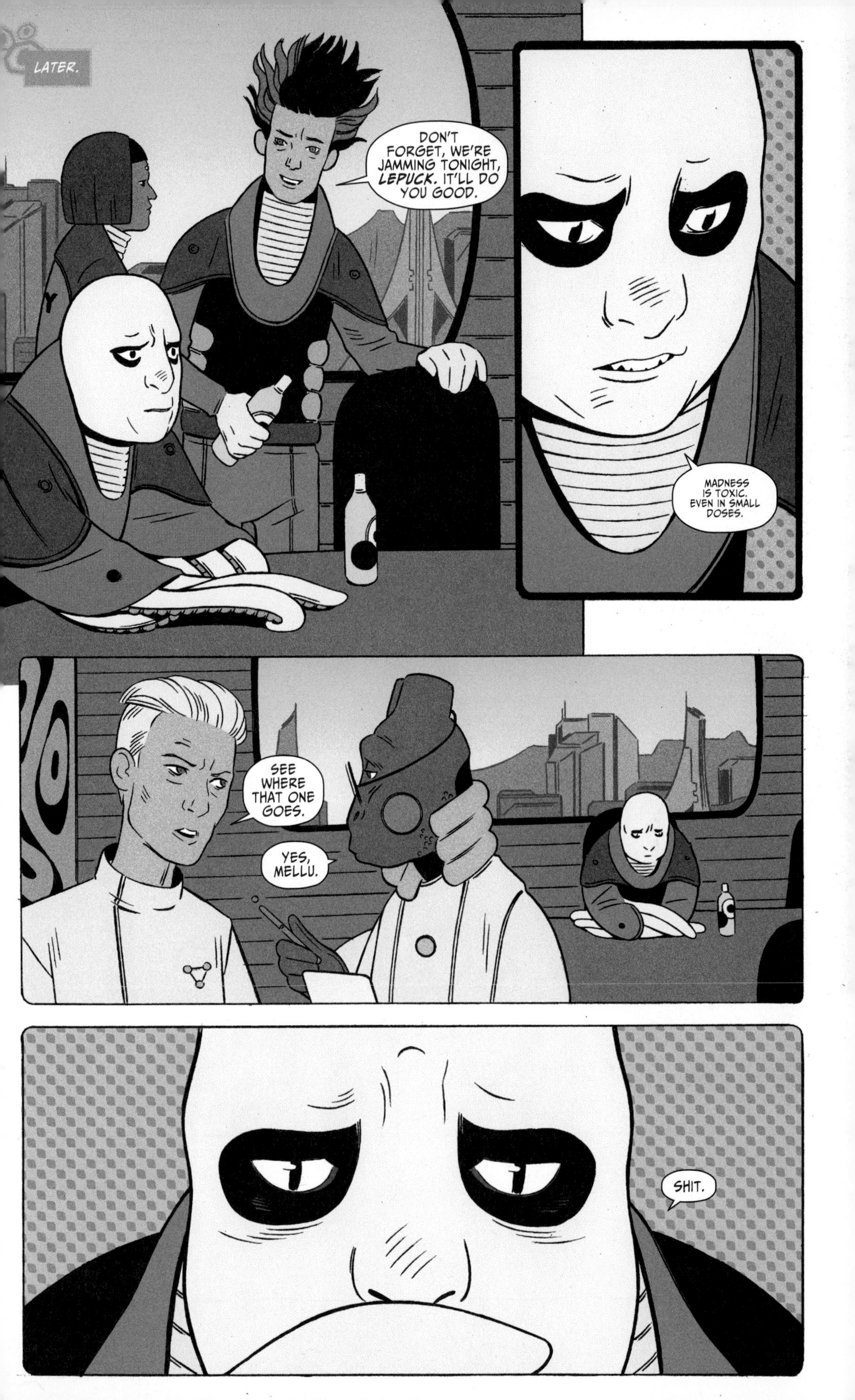
LATER.
DON'T FORGET, WE'RE JAMMING TONIGHT, LEPUCK. IT'LL DO YOU GOOD.
MADNESS IS TOXIC. EVEN IN SMALL DOSES.
SEE WHERE THAT ONE GOES.
YES, MELLU.
SHIT.

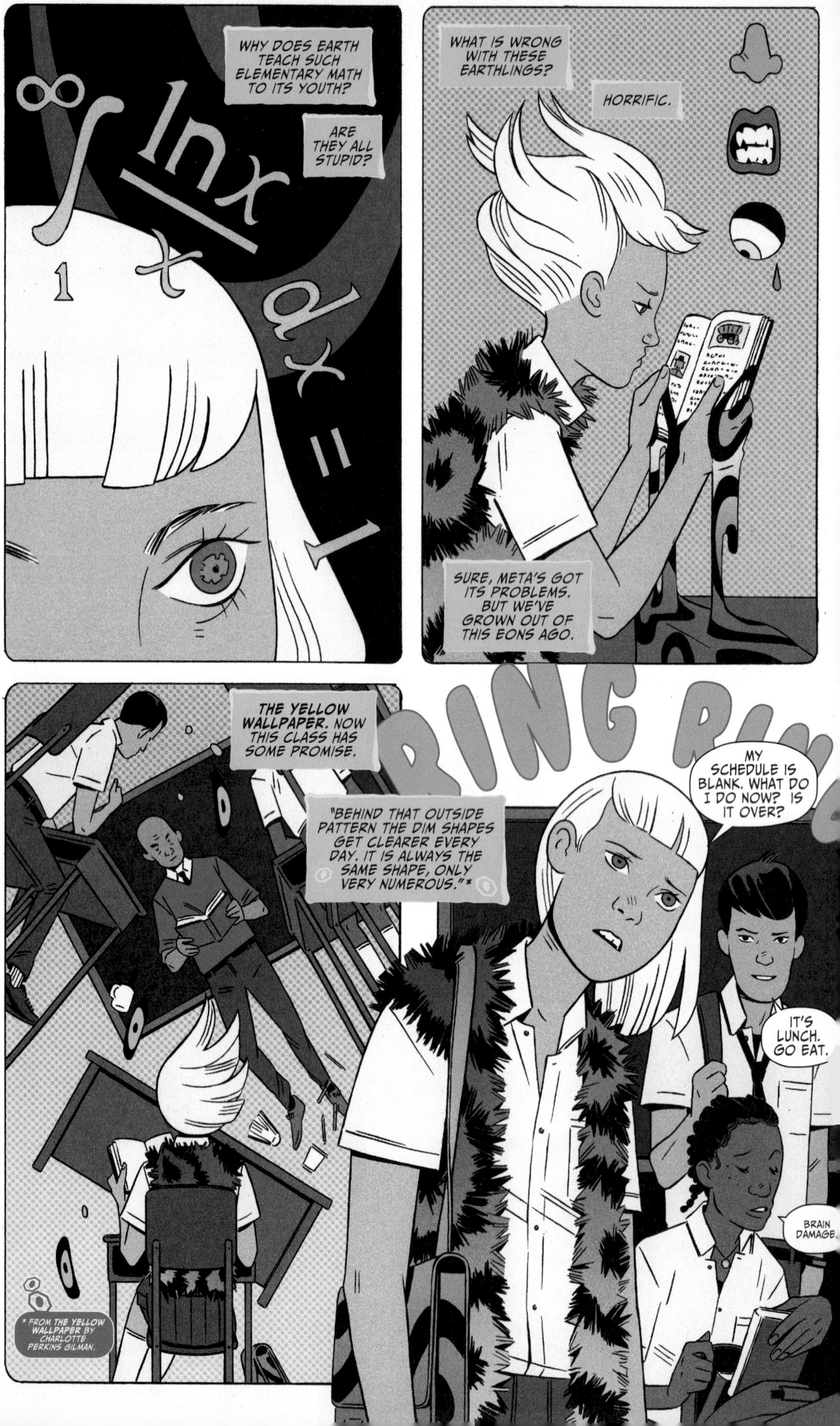
WHY DOES EARTH TEACH SUCH ELEMENTARY MATH TO ITS YOUTH?
ARE THEY ALL STUPID?
∞ ∫ 1 ln x / x dx = 1
WHAT IS WRONG WITH THESE EARTHLINGS?
HORRIFIC.
SURE, META'S GOT ITS PROBLEMS. BUT WE'VE GROWN OUT OF THIS EONS AGO.
THE YELLOW WALLPAPER. NOW THIS CLASS HAS SOME PROMISE.
"BEHIND THAT OUTSIDE PATTERN THE DIM SHAPES GET CLEARER EVERY DAY. IT IS ALWAYS THE SAME SHAPE, ONLY VERY NUMEROUS."*
* FROM THE YELLOW WALLPAPER BY CHARLOTTE PERKINS GILMAN.
RING RIN
MY SCHEDULE IS BLANK. WHAT DO I DO NOW? IS IT OVER?
IT'S LUNCH. GO EAT.
BRAIN DAMAGE.

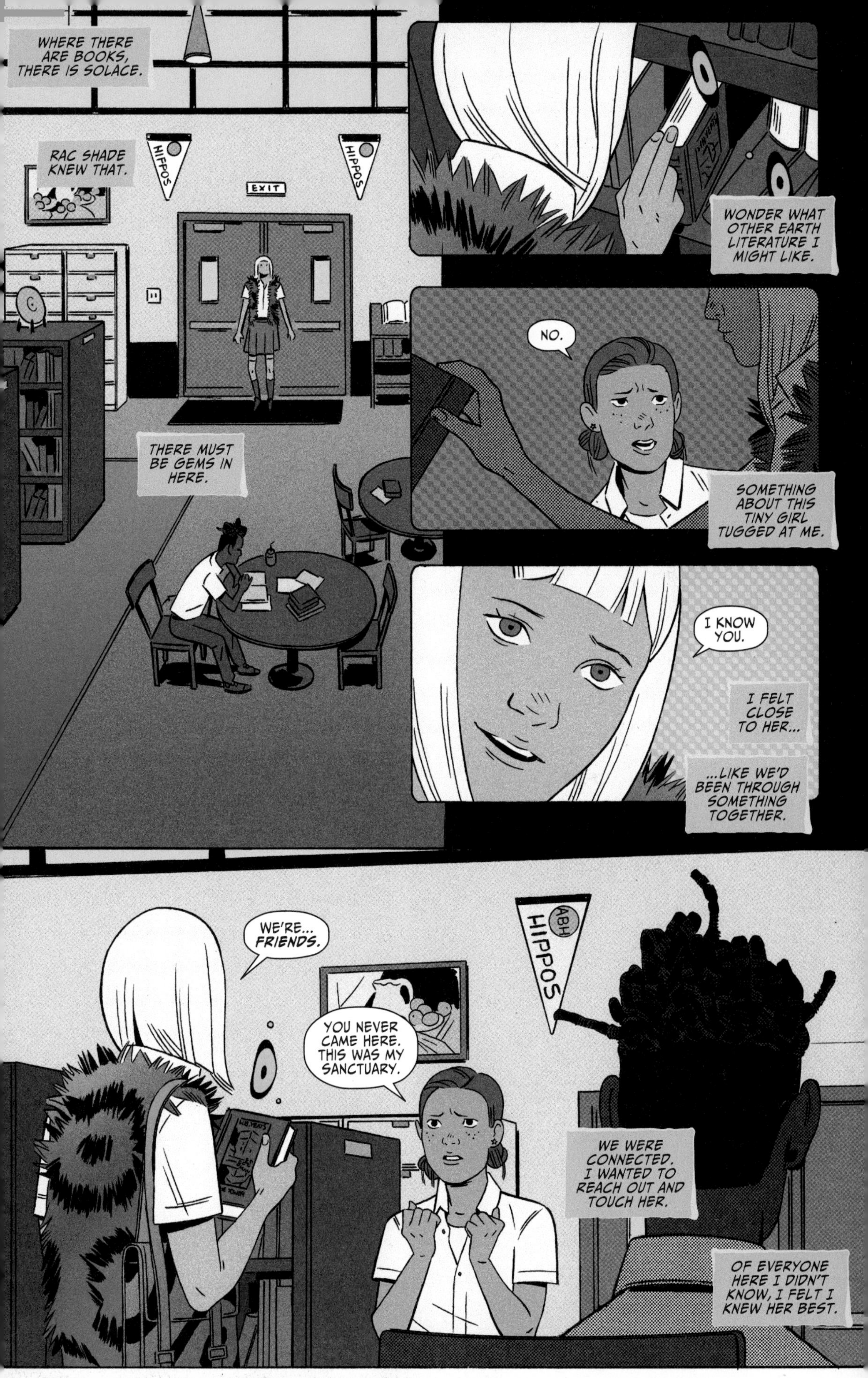
WHERE THERE ARE BOOKS, THERE IS SOLACE.
RAC SHADE KNEW THAT.
HIPPOS
HIPPOS
EXIT
THERE MUST BE GEMS IN HERE.
WONDER WHAT OTHER EARTH LITERATURE I MIGHT LIKE.
NO.
SOMETHING ABOUT THIS TINY GIRL TUGGED AT ME.
I KNOW YOU.
I FELT CLOSE TO HER...
...LIKE WE'D BEEN THROUGH SOMETHING TOGETHER.
WE'RE... FRIENDS.
ABH HIPPOS
YOU NEVER CAME HERE. THIS WAS MY SANCTUARY.
WE WERE CONNECTED. I WANTED TO REACH OUT AND TOUCH HER.
OF EVERYONE HERE I DIDN'T KNOW, I FELT I KNEW HER BEST.

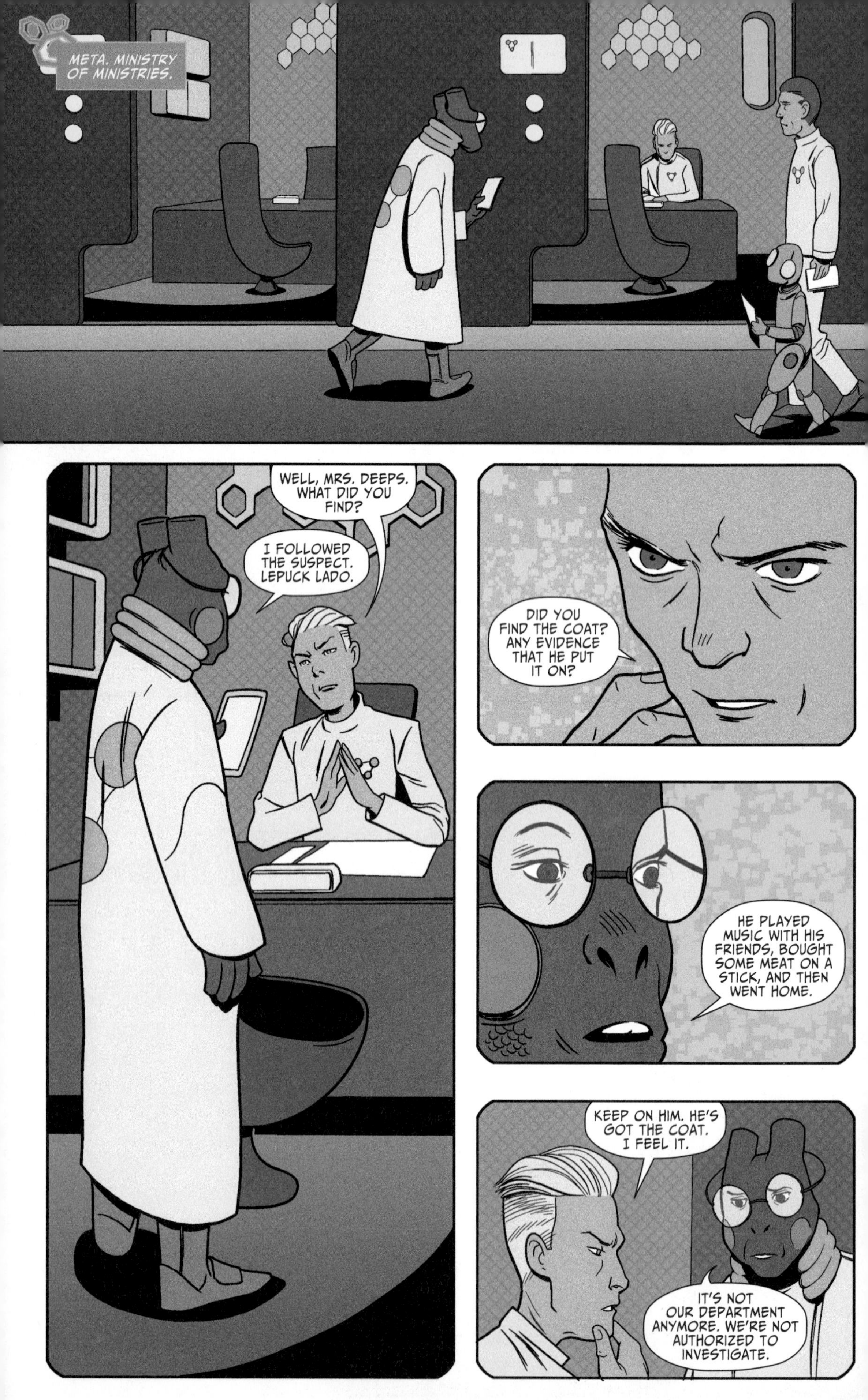

META. MINISTRY OF MINISTRIES.
WELL, MRS. DEEPS. WHAT DID YOU FIND?
I FOLLOWED THE SUSPECT. LEPUCK LADO.
DID YOU FIND THE COAT? ANY EVIDENCE THAT HE PUT IT ON?
HE PLAYED MUSIC WITH HIS FRIENDS, BOUGHT SOME MEAT ON A STICK, AND THEN WENT HOME.
KEEP ON HIM. HE'S GOT THE COAT. I FEEL IT.
IT'S NOT OUR DEPARTMENT ANYMORE. WE'RE NOT AUTHORIZED TO INVESTIGATE.

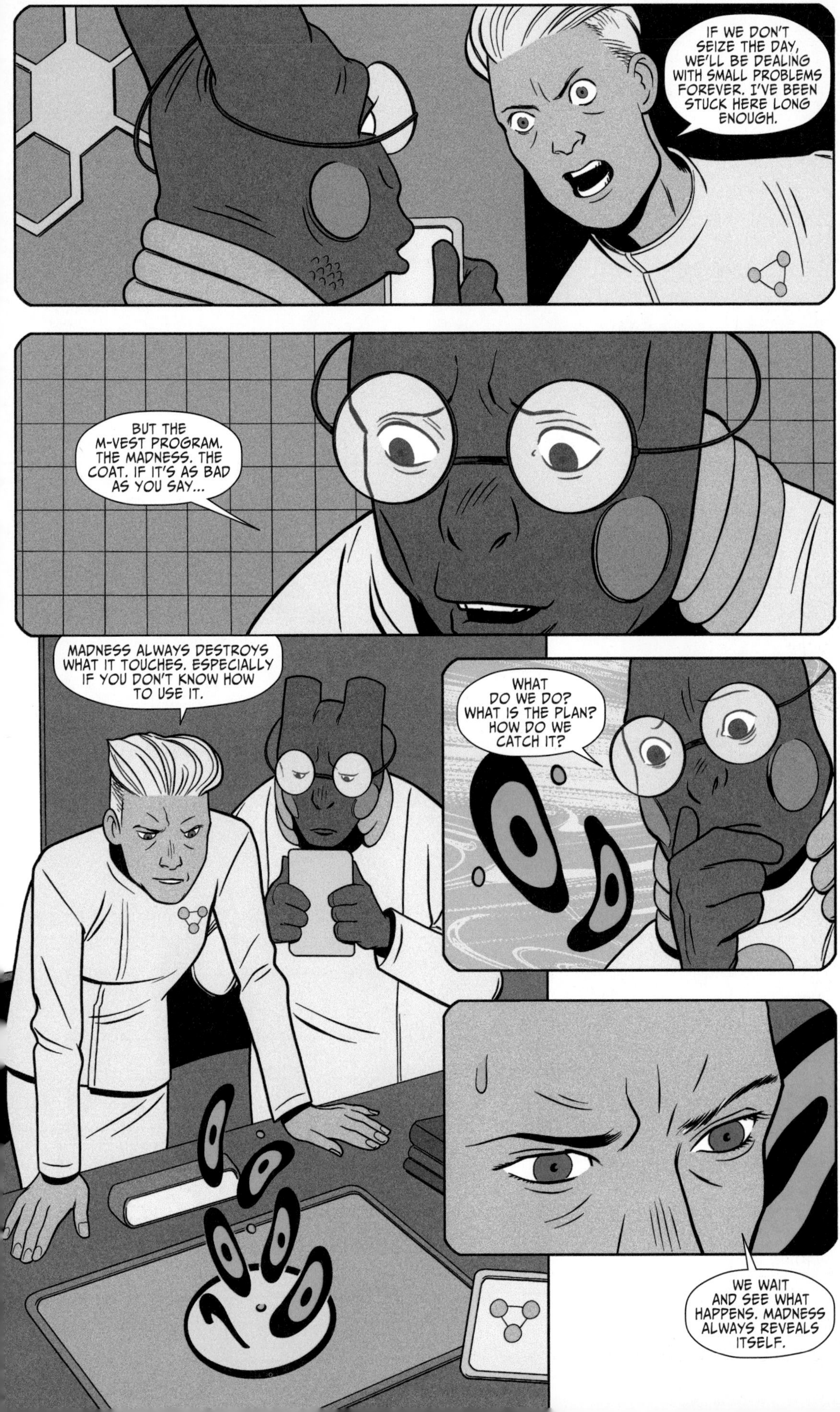
IF WE DON'T SEIZE THE DAY, WE'LL BE DEALING WITH SMALL PROBLEMS FOREVER. I'VE BEEN STUCK HERE LONG ENOUGH.
BUT THE M-VEST PROGRAM. THE MADNESS. THE COAT. IF IT'S AS BAD AS YOU SAY...
MADNESS ALWAYS DESTROYS WHAT IT TOUCHES. ESPECIALLY IF YOU DON'T KNOW HOW TO USE IT.
WHAT DO WE DO? WHAT IS THE PLAN? HOW DO WE CATCH IT?
WE WAIT AND SEE WHAT HAPPENS. MADNESS ALWAYS REVEALS ITSELF.

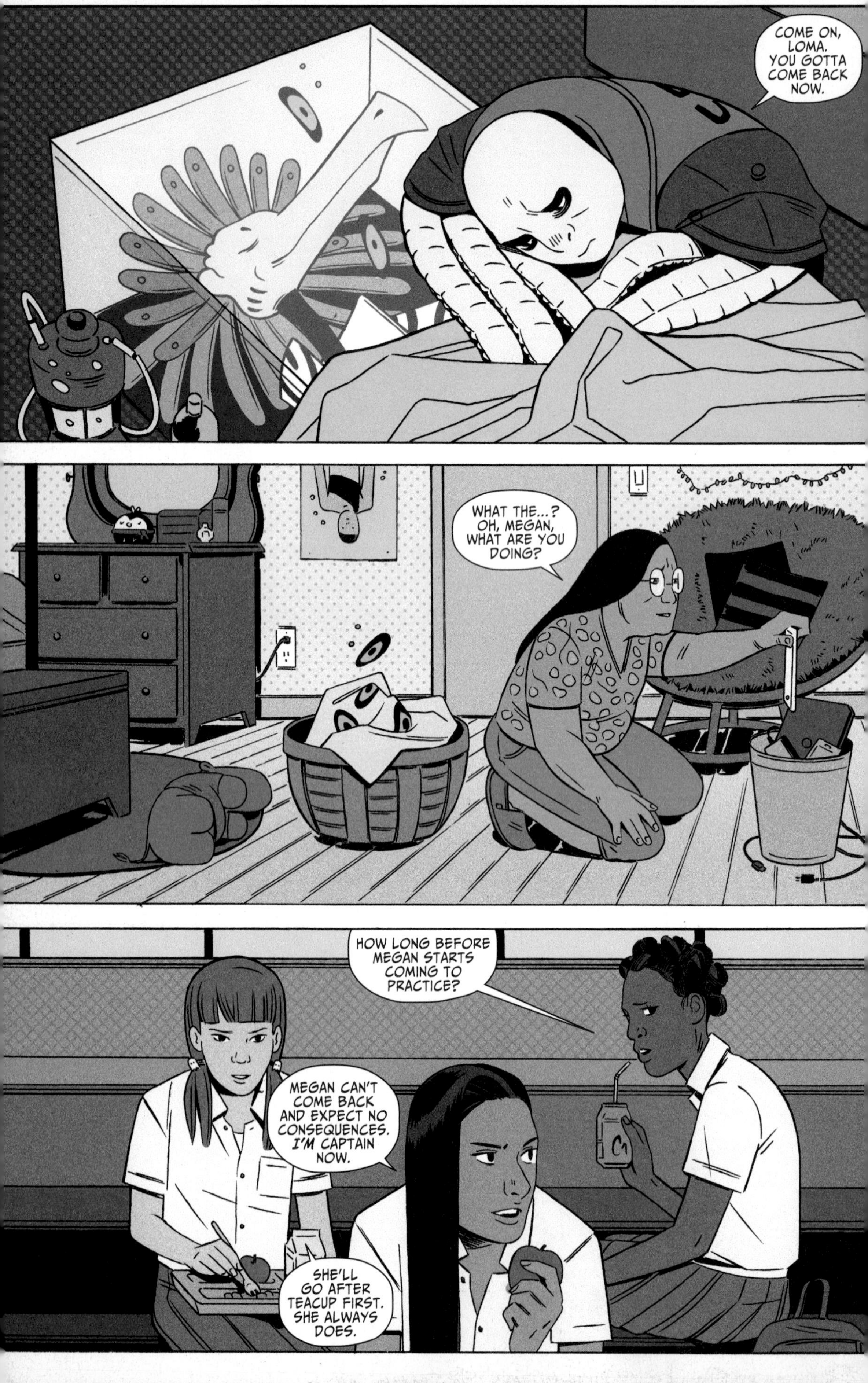
COME ON, LOMA. YOU GOTTA COME BACK NOW.
WHAT THE...? OH, MEGAN, WHAT ARE YOU DOING?
HOW LONG BEFORE MEGAN STARTS COMING TO PRACTICE?
MEGAN CAN'T COME BACK AND EXPECT NO CONSEQUENCES. *I'M* CAPTAIN NOW.
SHE'LL GO AFTER TEACUP FIRST. SHE ALWAYS DOES.

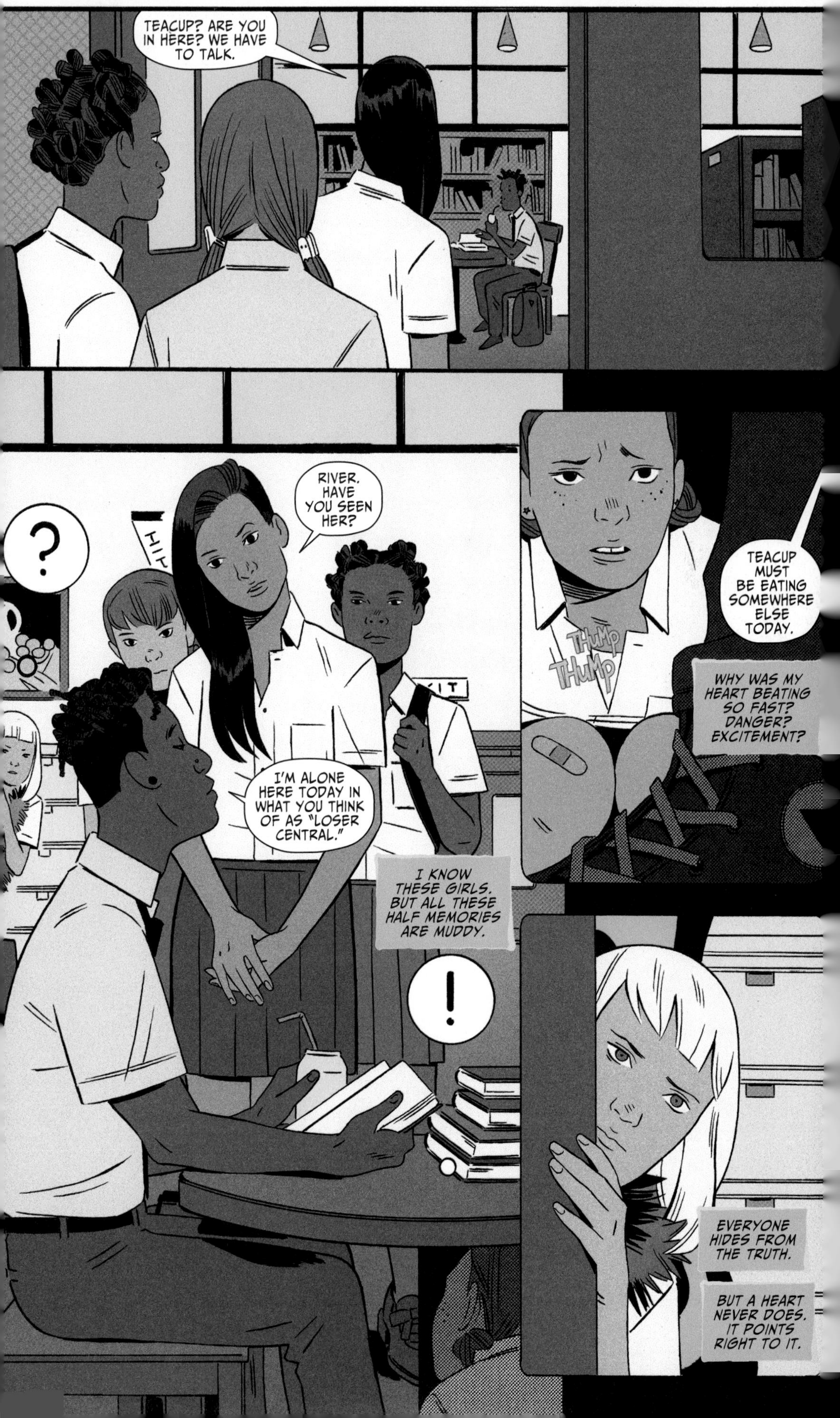

TEACUP? ARE YOU IN HERE? WE HAVE TO TALK.
?
RIVER. HAVE YOU SEEN HER?
I'M ALONE HERE TODAY IN WHAT YOU THINK OF AS "LOSER CENTRAL."
I KNOW THESE GIRLS. BUT ALL THESE HALF MEMORIES ARE MUDDY.
!
TEACUP MUST BE EATING SOMEWHERE ELSE TODAY.
THUMP THUMP
WHY WAS MY HEART BEATING SO FAST? DANGER? EXCITEMENT?
EVERYONE HIDES FROM THE TRUTH.
BUT A HEART NEVER DOES. IT POINTS RIGHT TO IT.

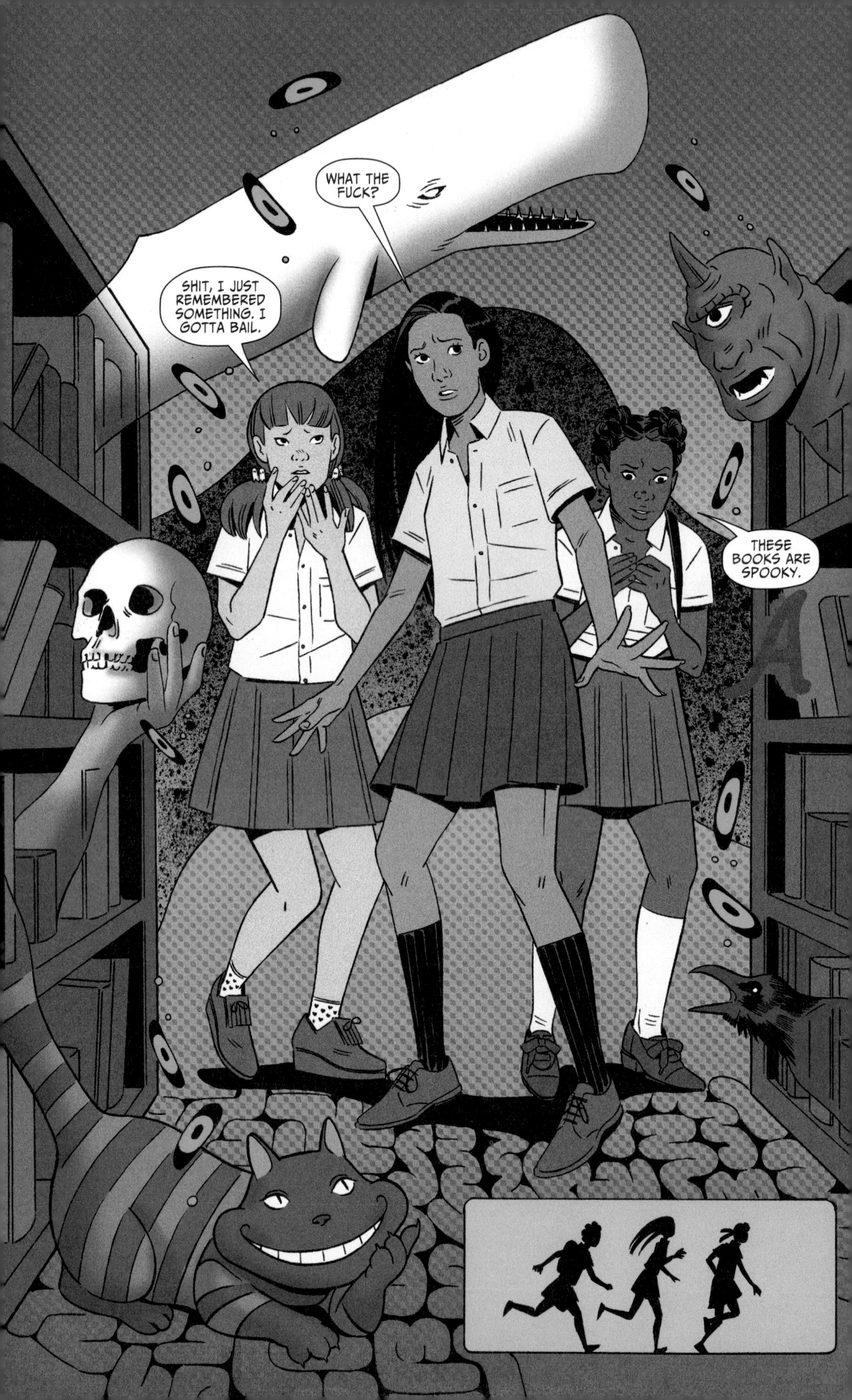
WHAT THE FUCK?
SHIT, I JUST REMEMBERED SOMETHING. I GOTTA BAIL.
THESE BOOKS ARE SPOOKY.

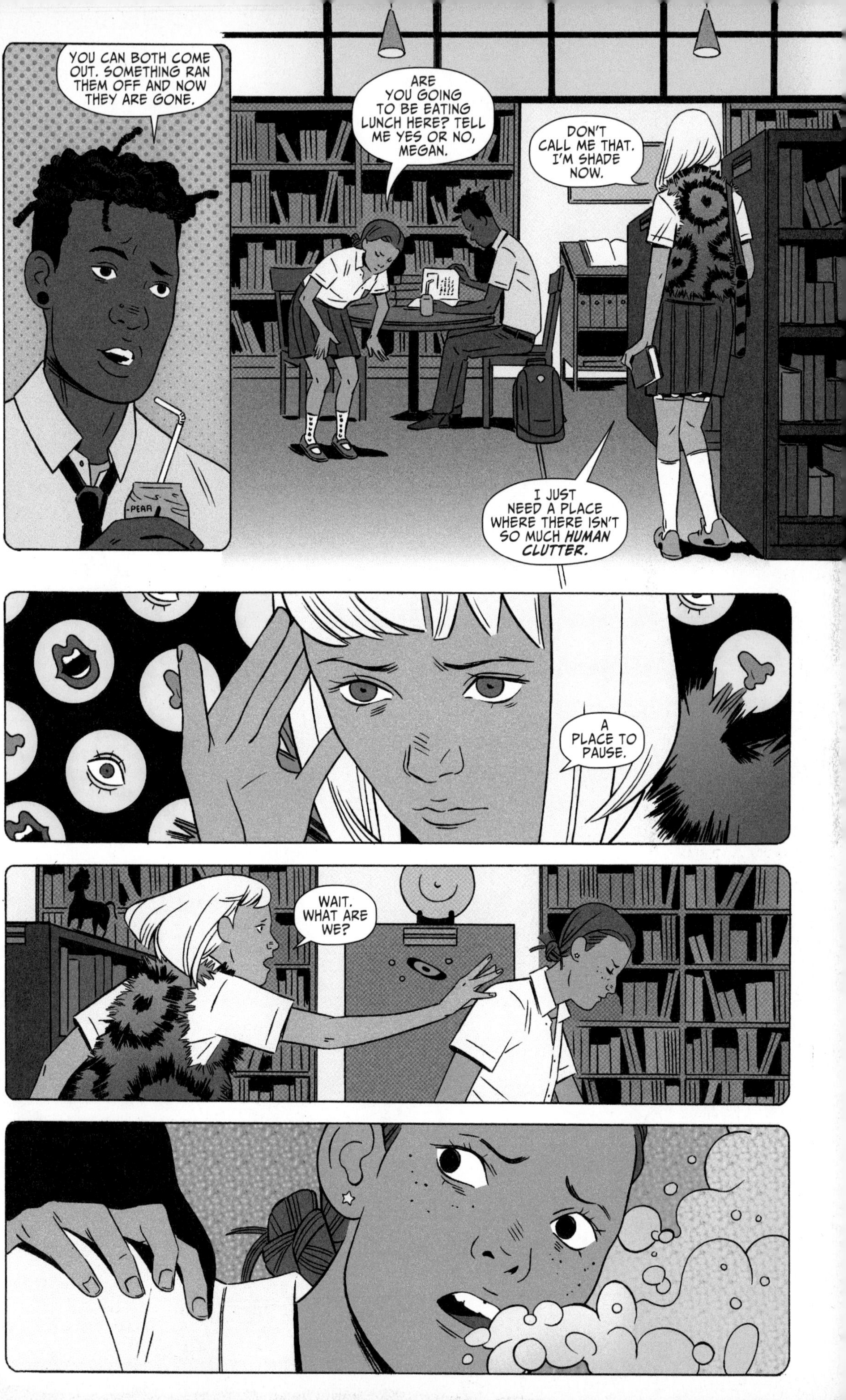
YOU CAN BOTH COME OUT. SOMETHING RAN THEM OFF AND NOW THEY ARE GONE.
PEAR
ARE YOU GOING TO BE EATING LUNCH HERE? TELL ME YES OR NO, MEGAN.
DON'T CALL ME THAT. I'M SHADE NOW.
I JUST NEED A PLACE WHERE THERE ISN'T SO MUCH *HUMAN CLUTTER.*
A PLACE TO PAUSE.
WAIT. WHAT ARE WE?

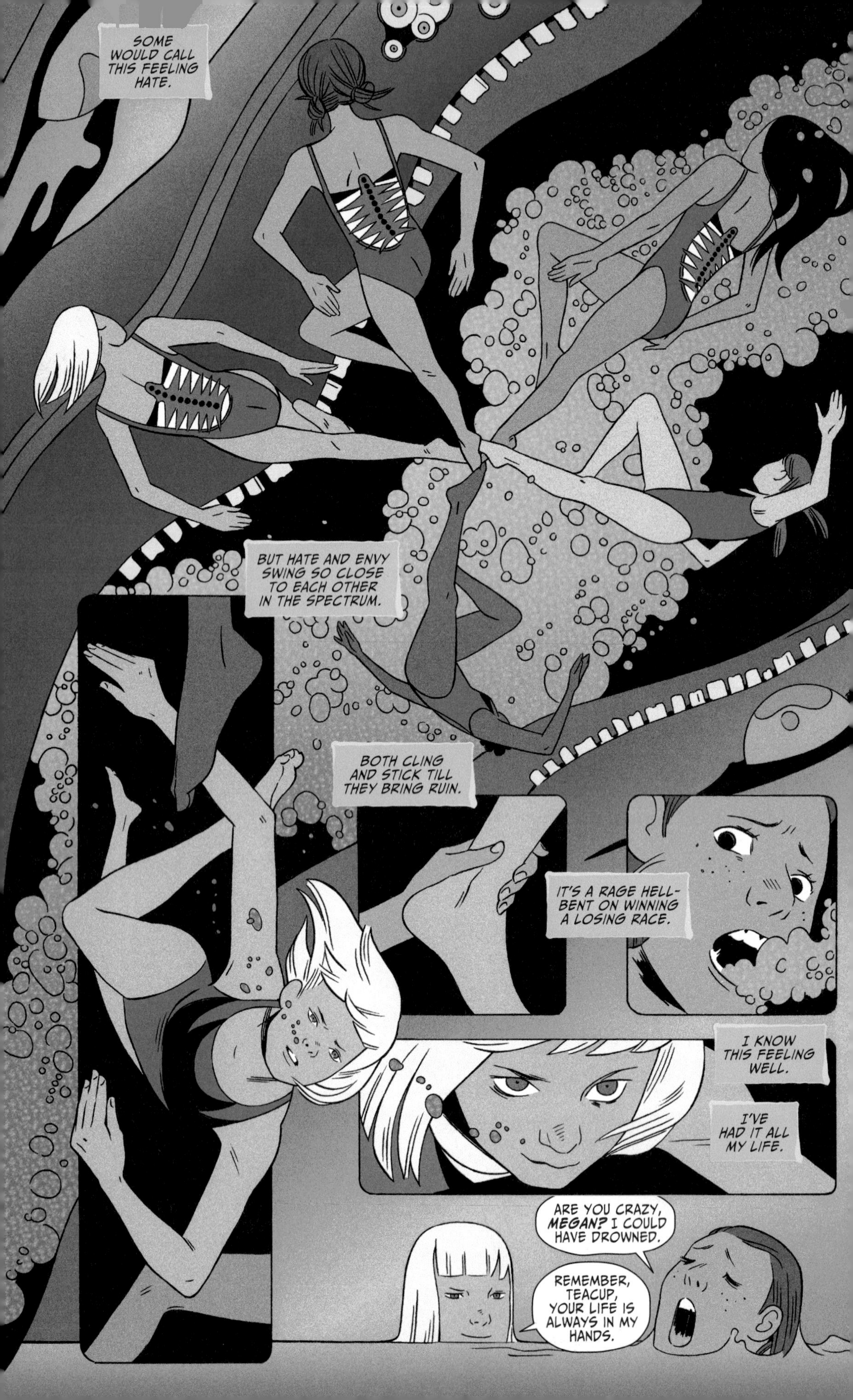
SOME WOULD CALL THIS FEELING HATE.
BUT HATE AND ENVY SWING SO CLOSE TO EACH OTHER IN THE SPECTRUM.
BOTH CLING AND STICK TILL THEY BRING RUIN.
IT'S A RAGE HELL-BENT ON WINNING A LOSING RACE.
I KNOW THIS FEELING WELL.
I'VE HAD IT ALL MY LIFE.
ARE YOU CRAZY, MEGAN? I COULD HAVE DROWNED.
REMEMBER, TEACUP, YOUR LIFE IS ALWAYS IN MY HANDS.

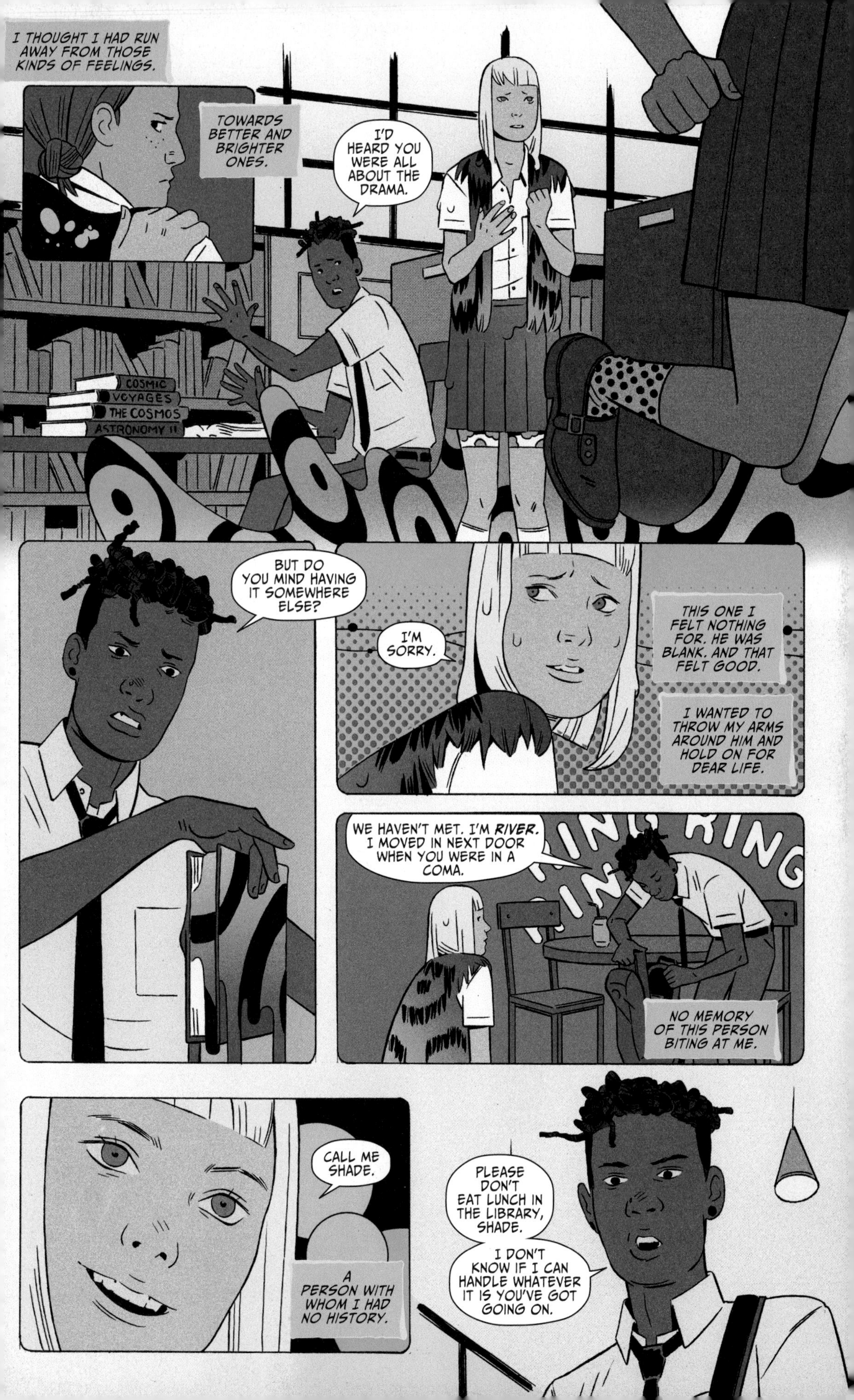

I THOUGHT I HAD RUN AWAY FROM THOSE KINDS OF FEELINGS.
TOWARDS BETTER AND BRIGHTER ONES.
I'D HEARD YOU WERE ALL ABOUT THE DRAMA.
COSMIC
VOYAGES
THE COSMOS
ASTRONOMY II
BUT DO YOU MIND HAVING IT SOMEWHERE ELSE?
I'M SORRY.
THIS ONE I FELT NOTHING FOR. HE WAS BLANK. AND THAT FELT GOOD.
I WANTED TO THROW MY ARMS AROUND HIM AND HOLD ON FOR DEAR LIFE.
WE HAVEN'T MET. I'M *RIVER.* I MOVED IN NEXT DOOR WHEN YOU WERE IN A COMA.
RING RING
NO MEMORY OF THIS PERSON BITING AT ME.
CALL ME SHADE.
A PERSON WITH WHOM I HAD NO HISTORY.
PLEASE DON'T EAT LUNCH IN THE LIBRARY, SHADE.
I DON'T KNOW IF I CAN HANDLE WHATEVER IT IS YOU'VE GOT GOING ON.

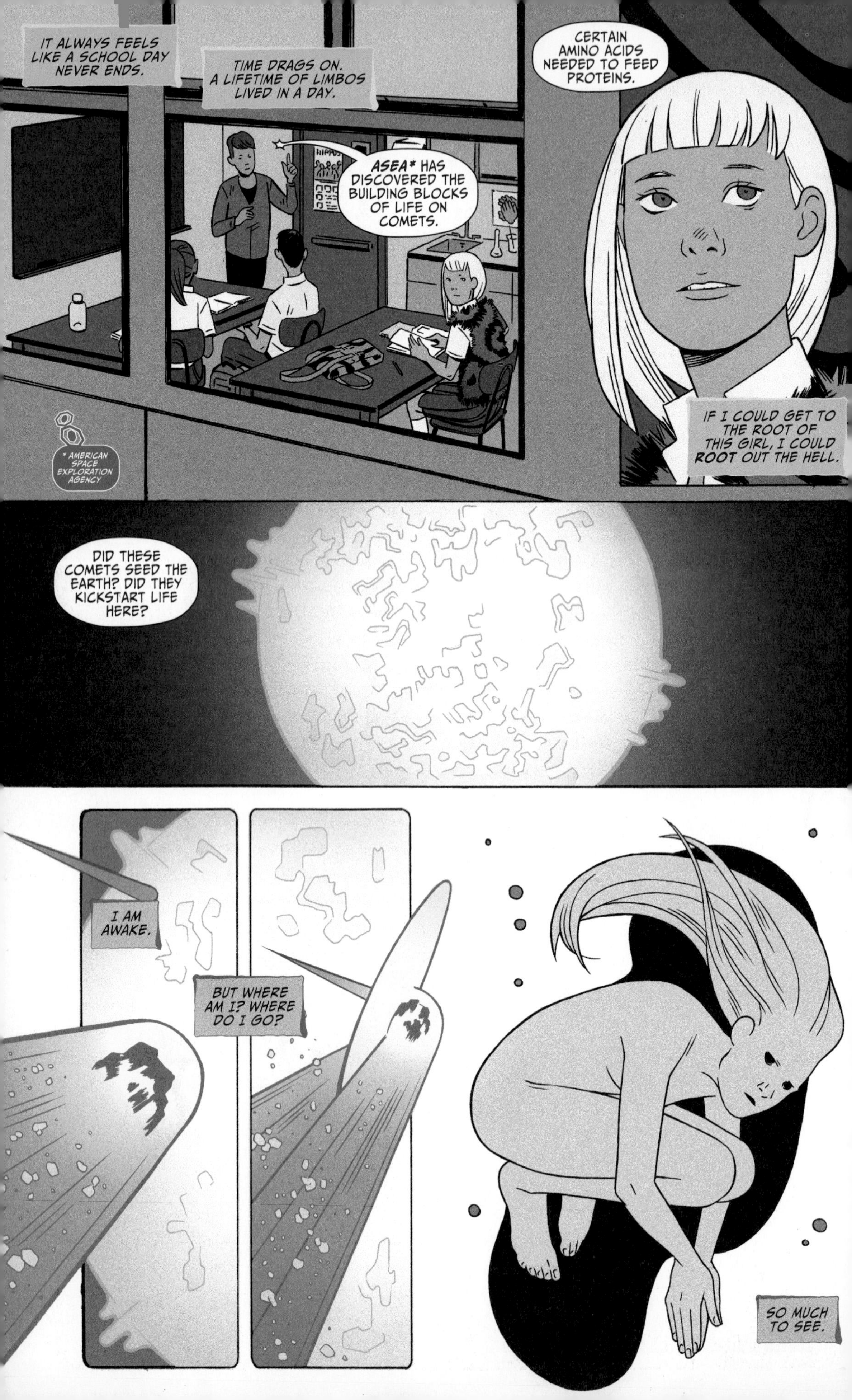
IT ALWAYS FEELS LIKE A SCHOOL DAY NEVER ENDS.
TIME DRAGS ON. A LIFETIME OF LIMBOS LIVED IN A DAY.
ASEA* HAS DISCOVERED THE BUILDING BLOCKS OF LIFE ON COMETS.
* AMERICAN SPACE EXPLORATION AGENCY
CERTAIN AMINO ACIDS NEEDED TO FEED PROTEINS.
IF I COULD GET TO THE ROOT OF THIS GIRL, I COULD ROOT OUT THE HELL.
DID THESE COMETS SEED THE EARTH? DID THEY KICKSTART LIFE HERE?
I AM AWAKE.
BUT WHERE AM I? WHERE DO I GO?
SO MUCH TO SEE.

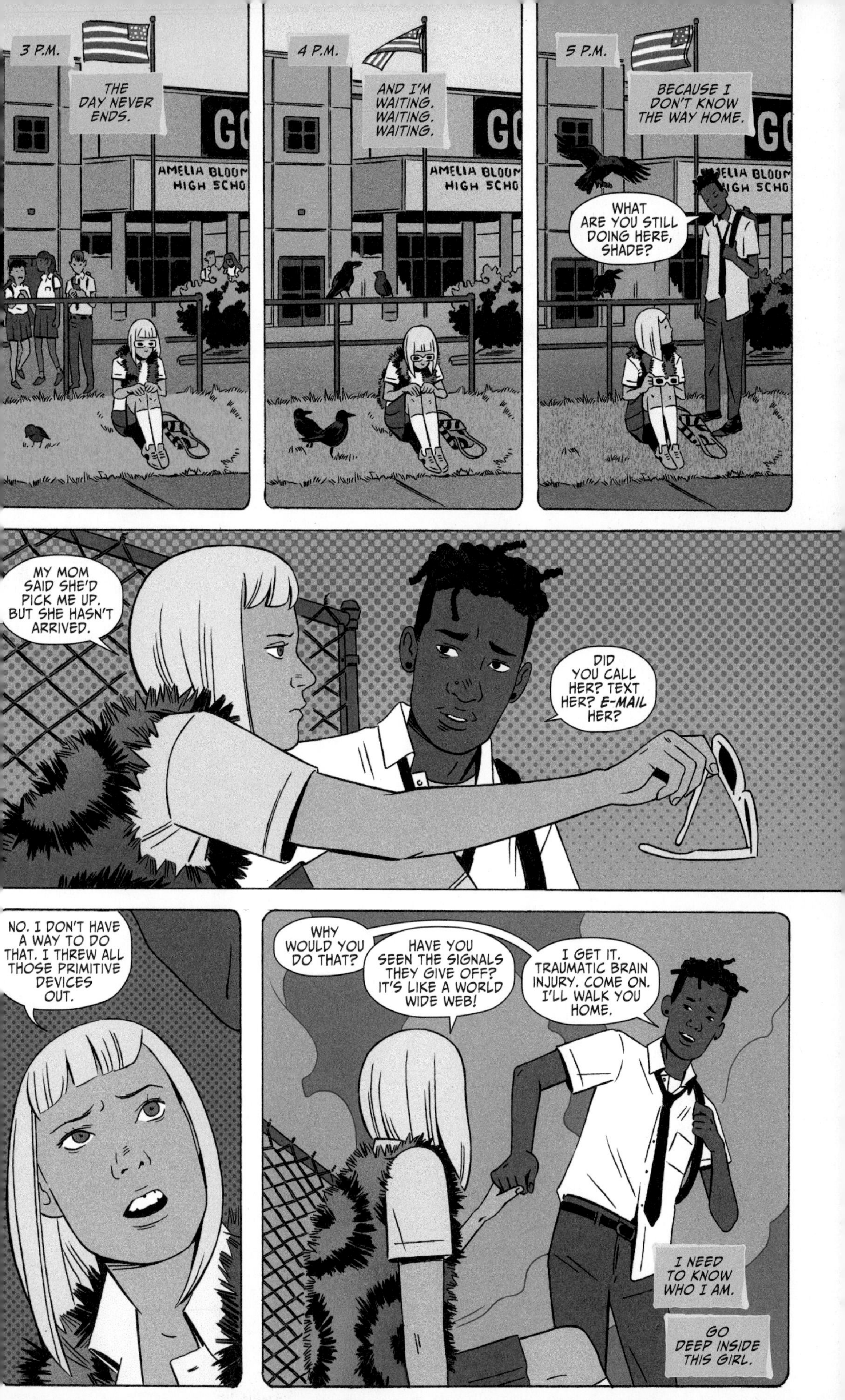

3 P.M.
THE DAY NEVER ENDS.
GO
AMELIA BLOOM HIGH SCHO
4 P.M.
AND I'M WAITING. WAITING. WAITING.
5 P.M.
BECAUSE I DON'T KNOW THE WAY HOME.
WHAT ARE YOU STILL DOING HERE, SHADE?
MY MOM SAID SHE'D PICK ME UP. BUT SHE HASN'T ARRIVED.
DID YOU CALL HER? TEXT HER? *E-MAIL* HER?
NO. I DON'T HAVE A WAY TO DO THAT. I THREW ALL THOSE PRIMITIVE DEVICES OUT.
WHY WOULD YOU DO THAT?
HAVE YOU SEEN THE SIGNALS THEY GIVE OFF? IT'S LIKE A WORLD WIDE WEB!
I GET IT. TRAUMATIC BRAIN INJURY. COME ON. I'LL WALK YOU HOME.
I NEED TO KNOW WHO I AM.
GO DEEP INSIDE THIS GIRL.

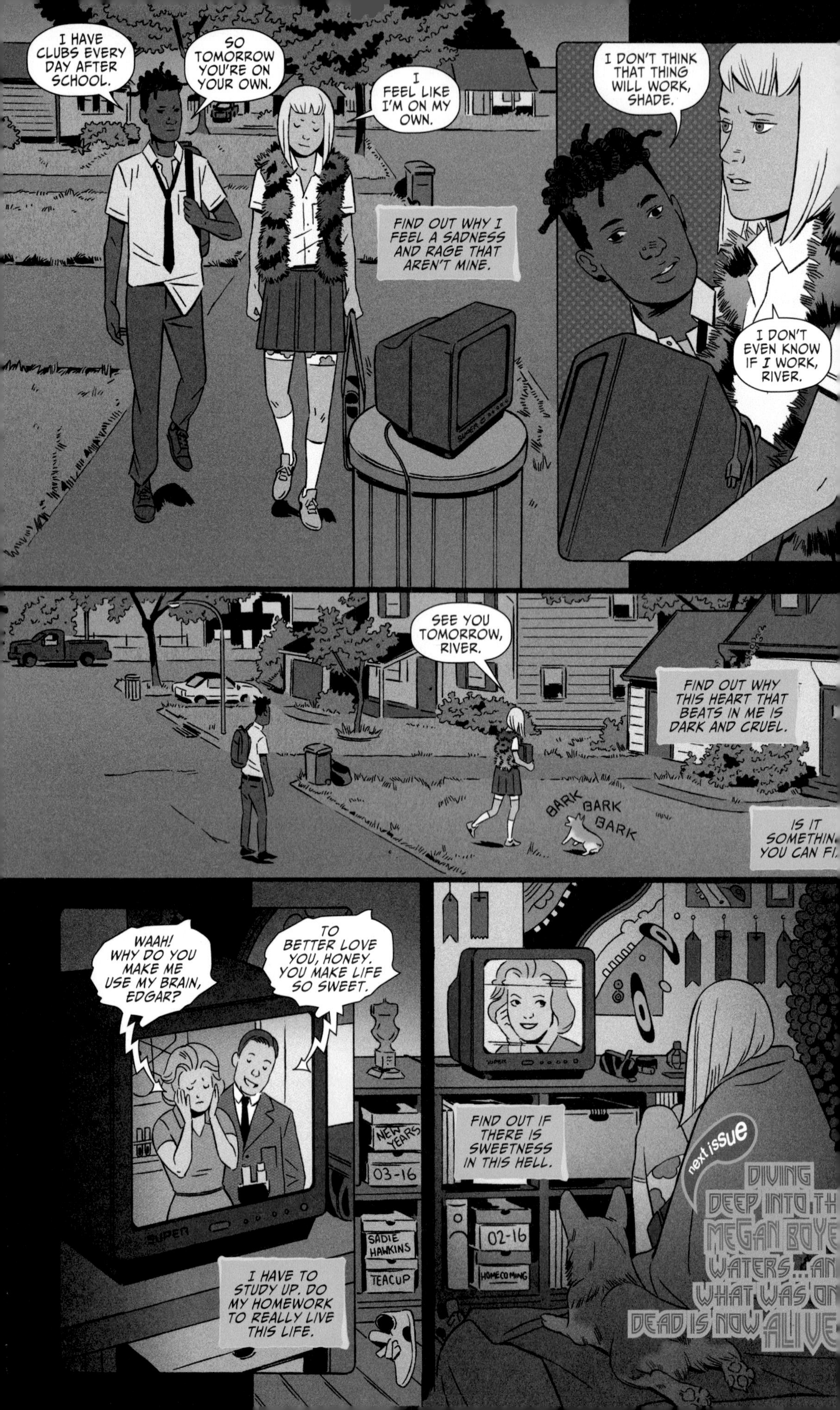
I HAVE CLUBS EVERY DAY AFTER SCHOOL.
SO TOMORROW YOU'RE ON YOUR OWN.
I FEEL LIKE I'M ON MY OWN.
FIND OUT WHY I FEEL A SADNESS AND RAGE THAT AREN'T MINE.
SUPER
I DON'T THINK THAT THING WILL WORK, SHADE.
I DON'T EVEN KNOW IF I WORK, RIVER.
SEE YOU TOMORROW, RIVER.
FIND OUT WHY THIS HEART THAT BEATS IN ME IS DARK AND CRUEL.
BARK BARK BARK
IS IT SOMETHIN YOU CAN FI
WAAH! WHY DO YOU MAKE ME USE MY BRAIN, EDGAR?
TO BETTER LOVE YOU, HONEY. YOU MAKE LIFE SO SWEET.
SUPER
I HAVE TO STUDY UP. DO MY HOMEWORK TO REALLY LIVE THIS LIFE.
NEW YEARS
03-16
SADIE HAWKINS
TEACUP
SUPER
FIND OUT IF THERE IS SWEETNESS IN THIS HELL.
02-16
HOMECOMING
next issue
DIVING DEEP INTO TH MEGAN BOYE WATERS...AN WHAT WAS ON DEAD IS NOW ALIVE

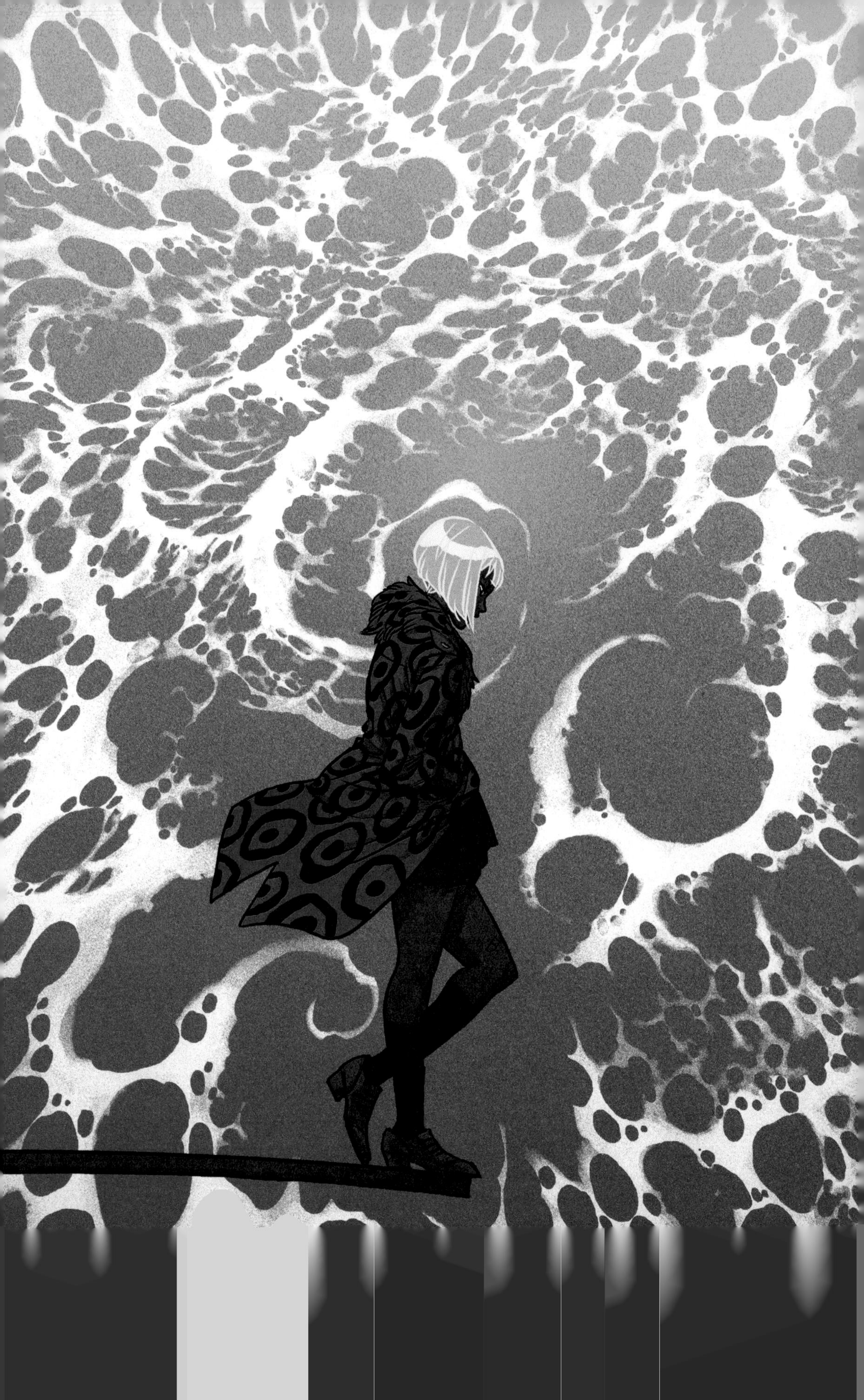

Variant cover art by Paul Rentler

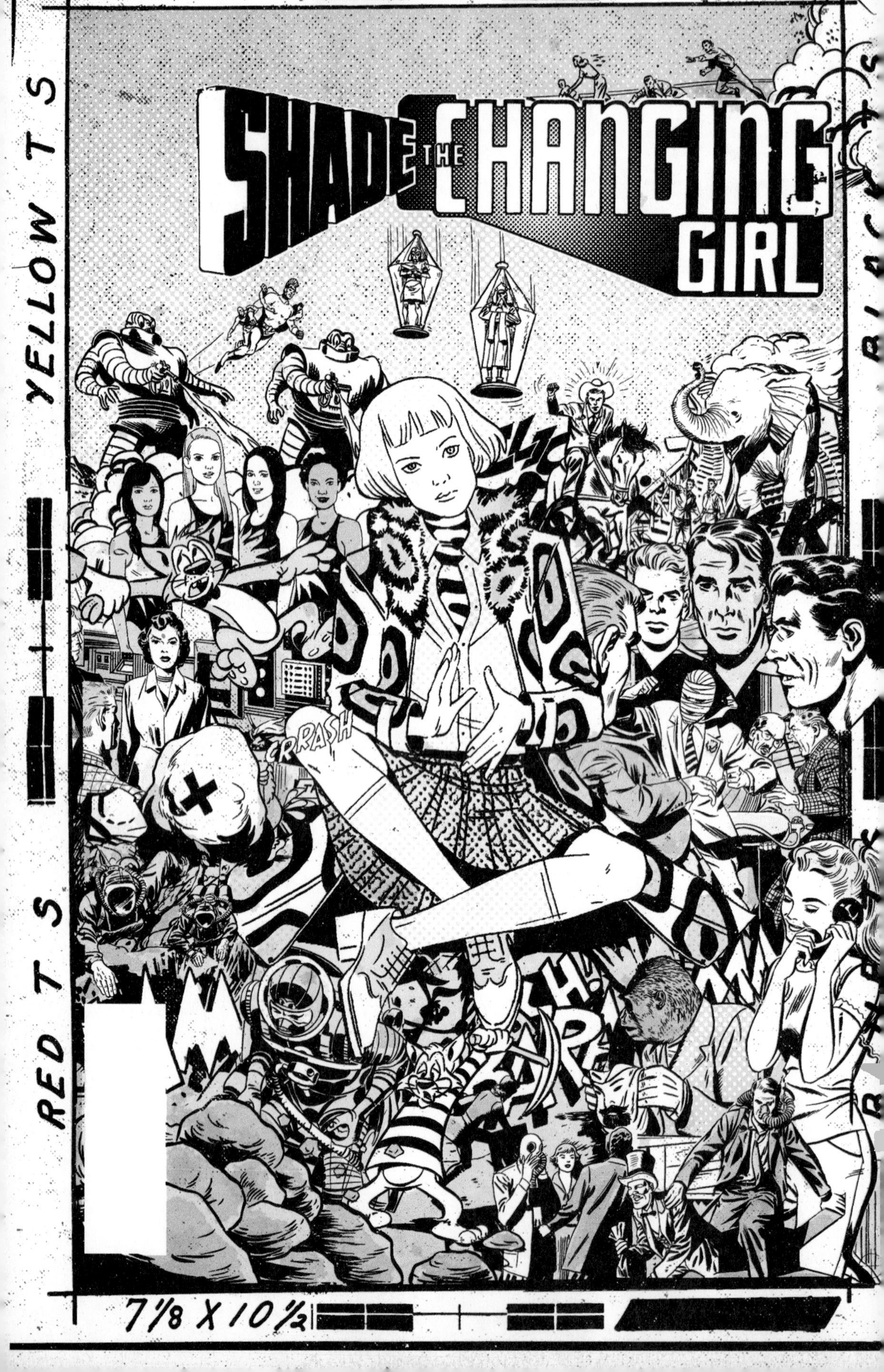

SHADE THE CHANGING GIRL
YELLOW TS
RED TS
CRRASH
7 1/8 X 10 1/2

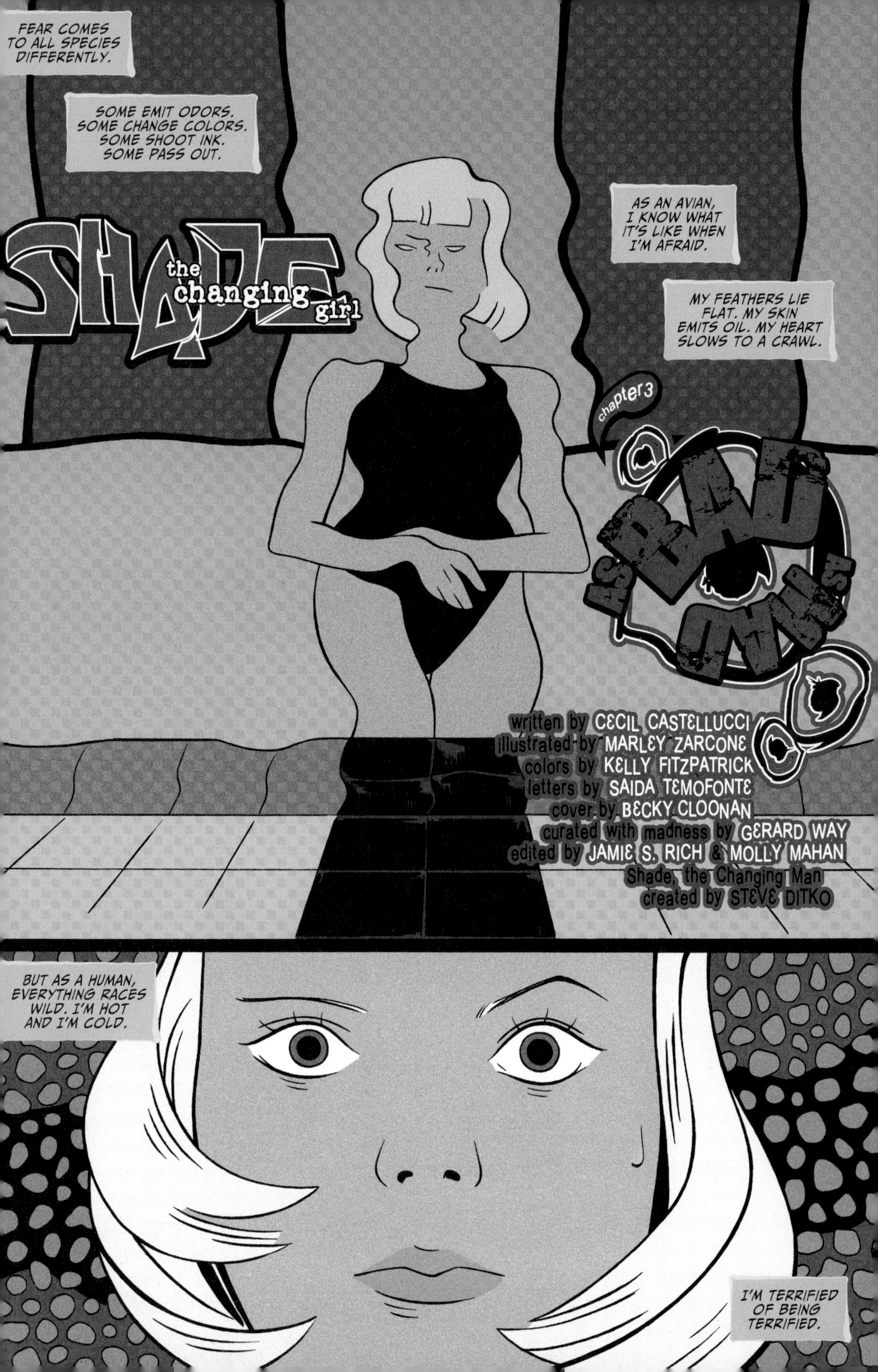
FEAR COMES TO ALL SPECIES DIFFERENTLY.
SOME EMIT ODORS. SOME CHANGE COLORS. SOME SHOOT INK. SOME PASS OUT.
SHADE the changing girl
AS AN AVIAN, I KNOW WHAT IT'S LIKE WHEN I'M AFRAID.
MY FEATHERS LIE FLAT. MY SKIN EMITS OIL. MY HEART SLOWS TO A CRAWL.
chapter 3
AS BAD AS ANYTHING
written by CECIL CASTELLUCCI
illustrated by MARLEY ZARCONE
colors by KELLY FITZPATRICK
letters by SAIDA TEMOFONTE
cover by BECKY CLOONAN
curated with madness by GERARD WAY
edited by JAMIE S. RICH & MOLLY MAHAN
Shade, the Changing Man created by STEVE DITKO
BUT AS A HUMAN, EVERYTHING RACES WILD. I'M HOT AND I'M COLD.
I'M TERRIFIED OF BEING TERRIFIED.

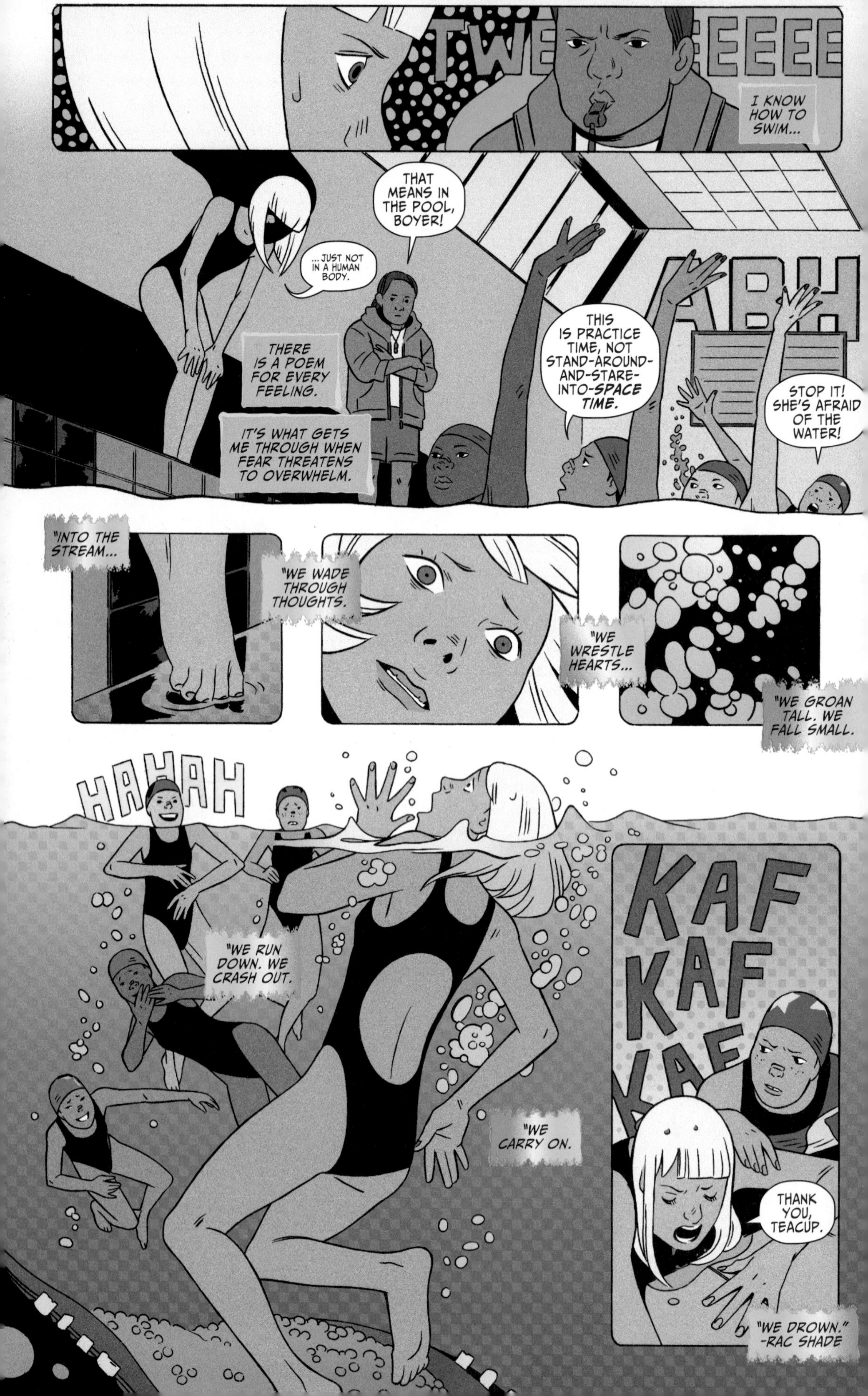
TWEEEEEE
I KNOW HOW TO SWIM...
...JUST NOT IN A HUMAN BODY.
THAT MEANS IN THE POOL, BOYER!
THERE IS A POEM FOR EVERY FEELING.
IT'S WHAT GETS ME THROUGH WHEN FEAR THREATENS TO OVERWHELM.
THIS IS PRACTICE TIME, NOT STAND-AROUND-AND-STARE-INTO-SPACE TIME.
ABH
STOP IT! SHE'S AFRAID OF THE WATER!
"INTO THE STREAM...
"WE WADE THROUGH THOUGHTS.
"WE WRESTLE HEARTS...
"WE GROAN TALL. WE FALL SMALL.
HAHAH
"WE RUN DOWN. WE CRASH OUT.
"WE CARRY ON.
KAF KAF KAF
THANK YOU, TEACUP.
"WE DROWN."
-RAC SHADE

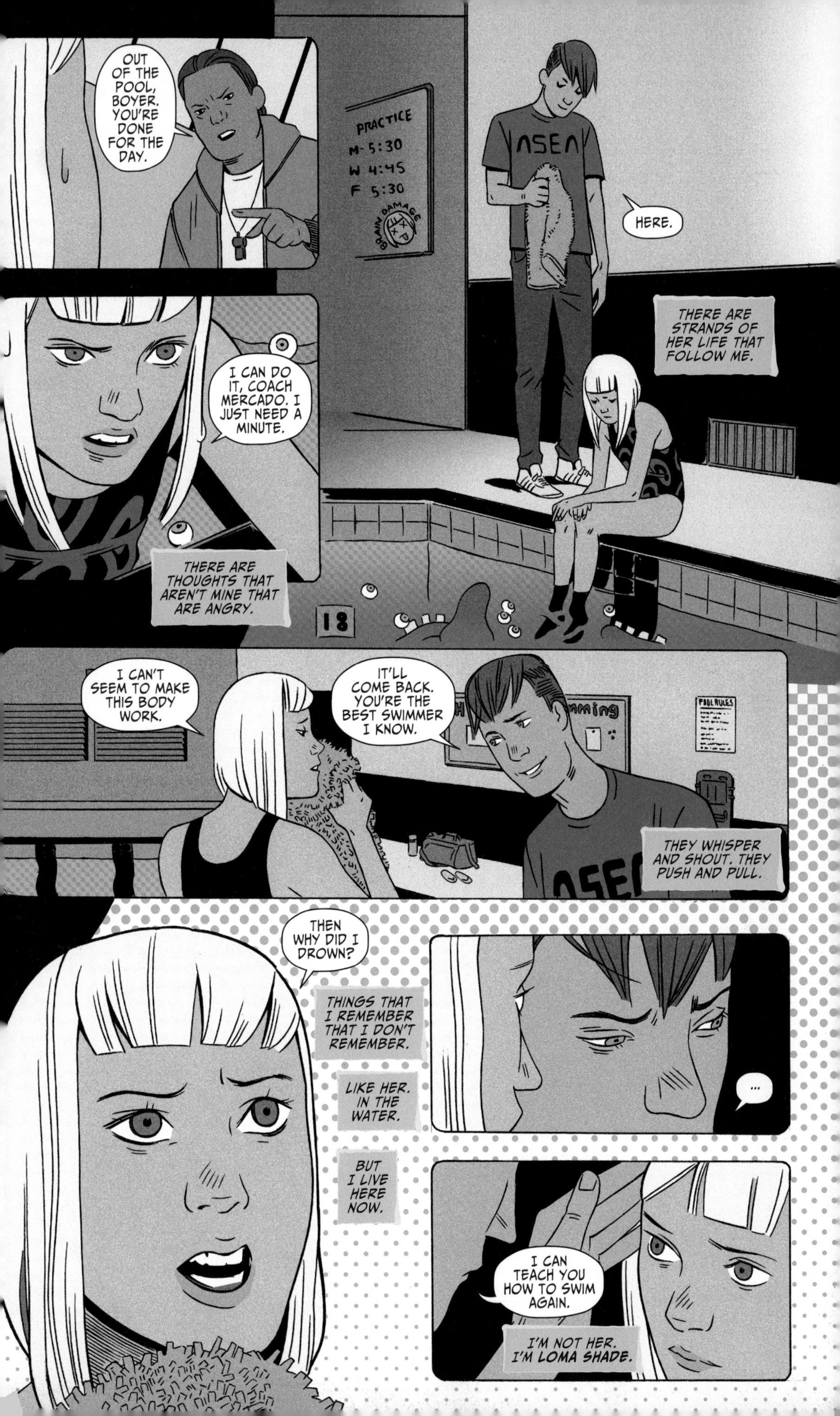
OUT OF THE POOL, BOYER. YOU'RE DONE FOR THE DAY.
PRACTICE
M-5:30
W 4:45
F 5:30
BRAIN DAMAGE
HERE.
I CAN DO IT, COACH MERCADO. I JUST NEED A MINUTE.
THERE ARE STRANDS OF HER LIFE THAT FOLLOW ME.
THERE ARE THOUGHTS THAT AREN'T MINE THAT ARE ANGRY.
18
I CAN'T SEEM TO MAKE THIS BODY WORK.
IT'LL COME BACK. YOU'RE THE BEST SWIMMER I KNOW.
POOL RULES
THEY WHISPER AND SHOUT. THEY PUSH AND PULL.
THEN WHY DID I DROWN?
THINGS THAT I REMEMBER THAT I DON'T REMEMBER.
LIKE HER. IN THE WATER.
BUT I LIVE HERE NOW.
...
I CAN TEACH YOU HOW TO SWIM AGAIN.
I'M NOT HER. I'M LOMA SHADE.

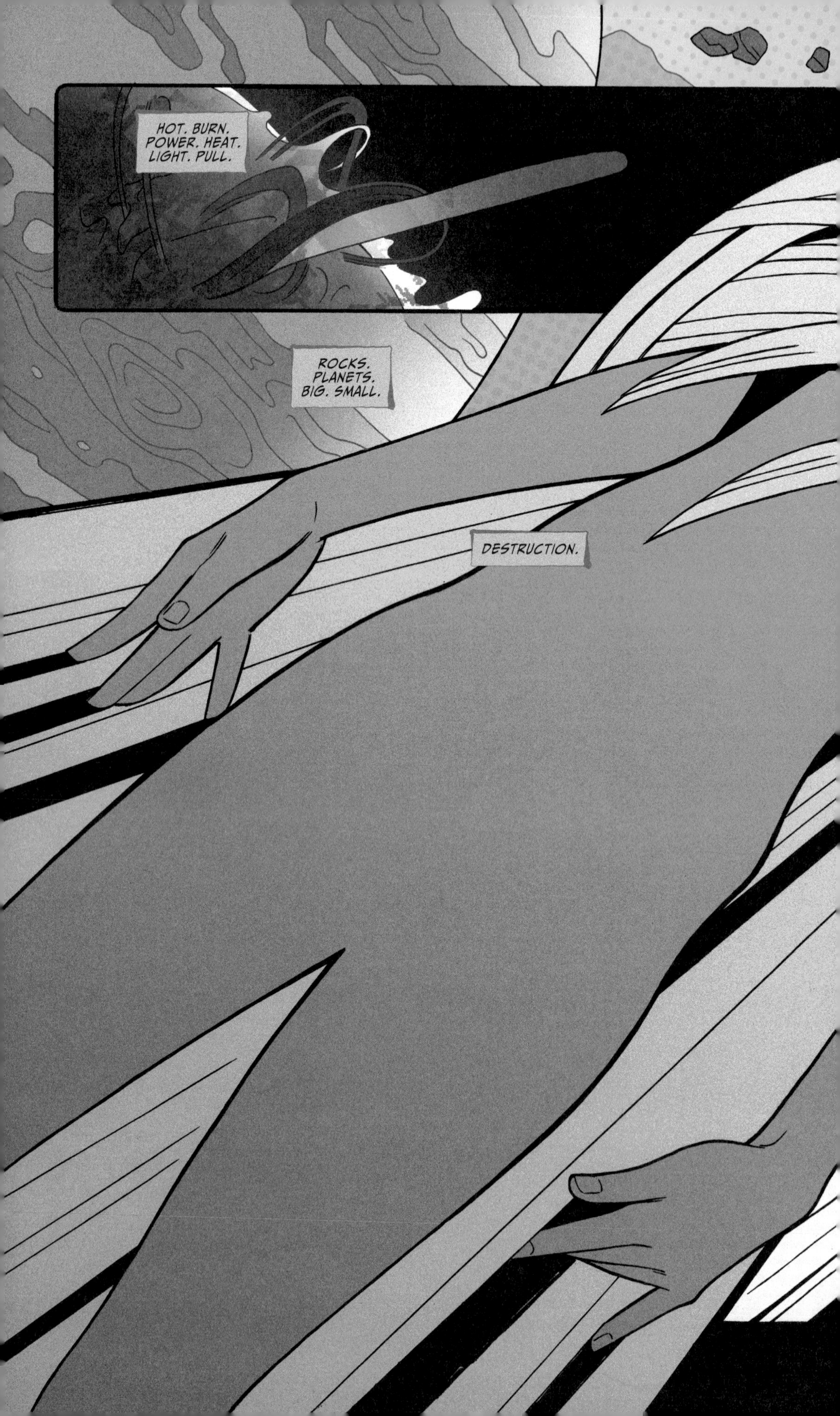
HOT. BURN. POWER. HEAT. LIGHT. PULL.
ROCKS. PLANETS. BIG. SMALL.
DESTRUCTION.

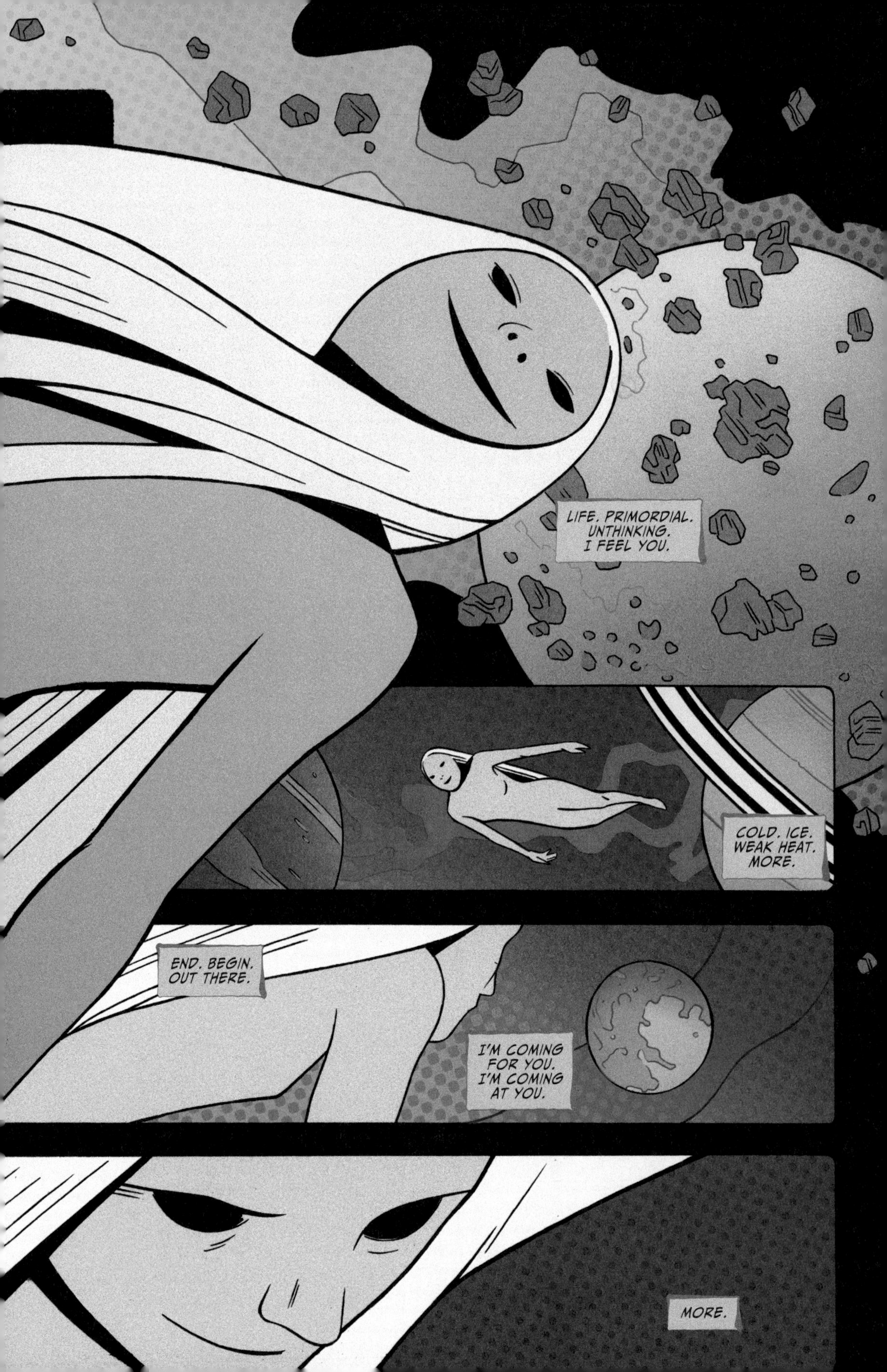
LIFE. PRIMORDIAL. UNTHINKING. I FEEL YOU.
COLD. ICE. WEAK HEAT. MORE.
END. BEGIN. OUT THERE.
I'M COMING FOR YOU. I'M COMING AT YOU.
MORE.

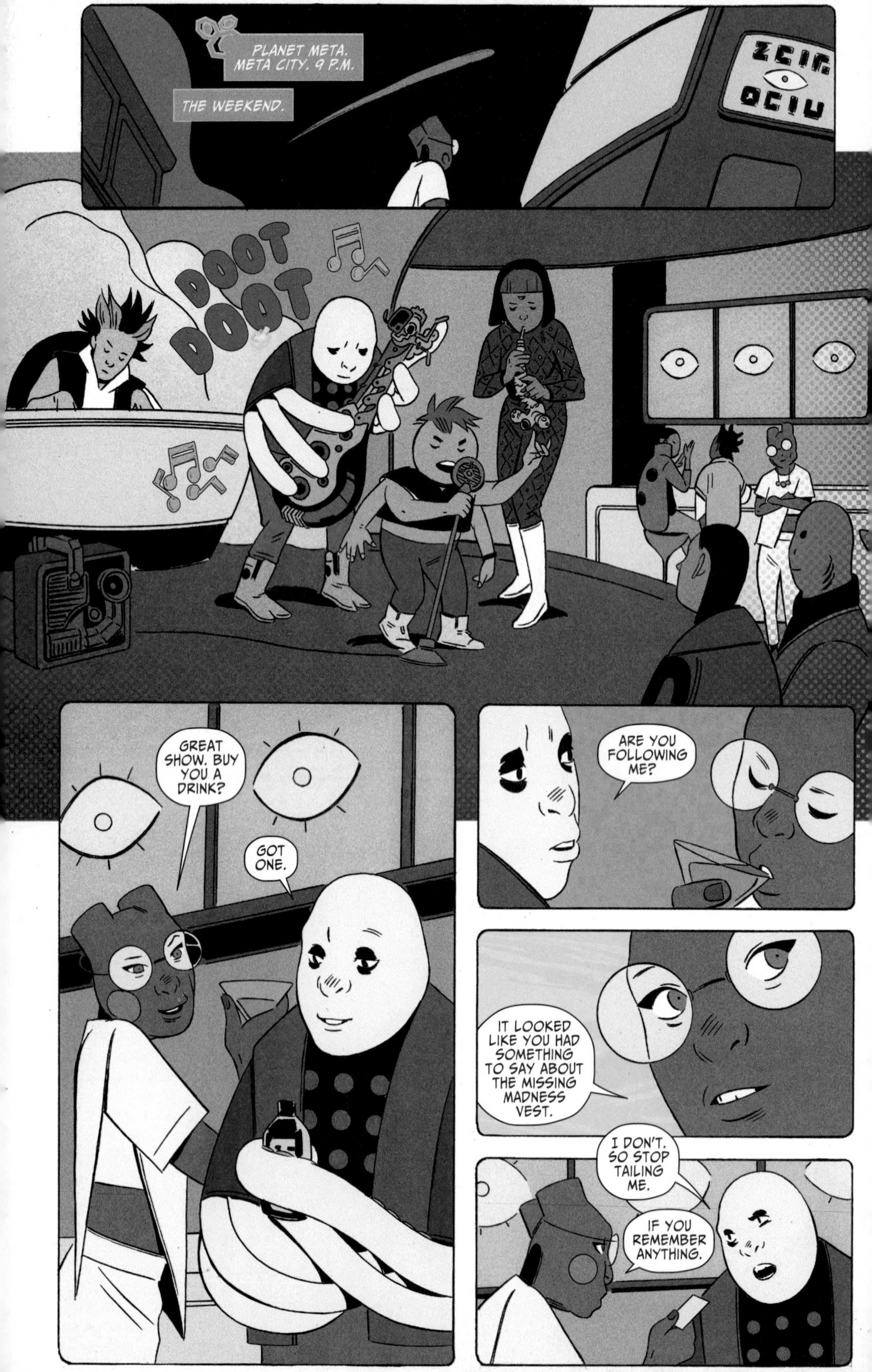
PLANET META.
META CITY. 9 P.M.
THE WEEKEND.
DOOT DOOT
GREAT SHOW. BUY YOU A DRINK?
GOT ONE.
ARE YOU FOLLOWING ME?
IT LOOKED LIKE YOU HAD SOMETHING TO SAY ABOUT THE MISSING MADNESS VEST.
I DON'T. SO STOP TAILING ME.
IF YOU REMEMBER ANYTHING.

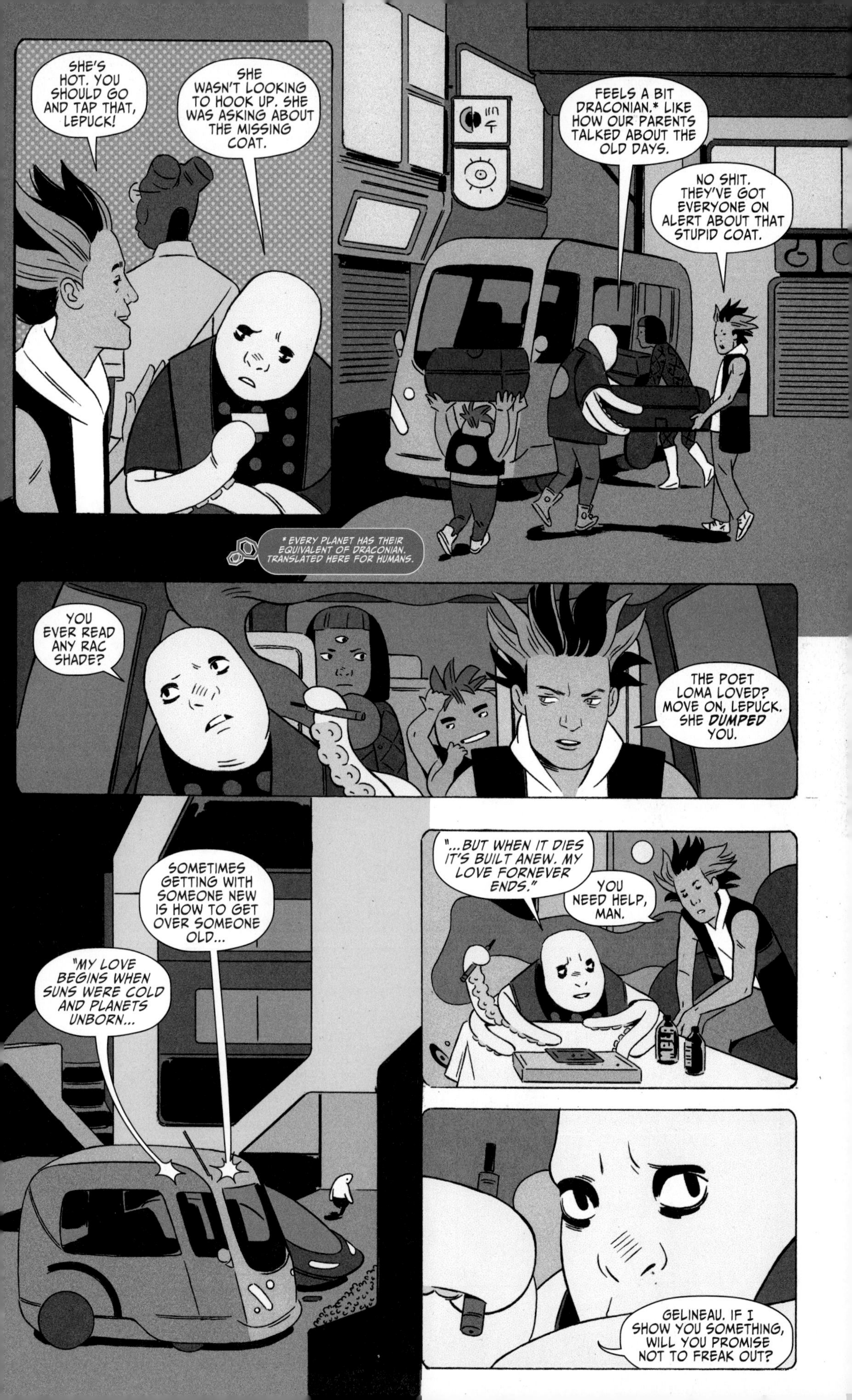
SHE'S HOT. YOU SHOULD GO AND TAP THAT, LEPUCK!
SHE WASN'T LOOKING TO HOOK UP. SHE WAS ASKING ABOUT THE MISSING COAT.
FEELS A BIT DRACONIAN.* LIKE HOW OUR PARENTS TALKED ABOUT THE OLD DAYS.
NO SHIT. THEY'VE GOT EVERYONE ON ALERT ABOUT THAT STUPID COAT.
* EVERY PLANET HAS THEIR EQUIVALENT OF DRACONIAN. TRANSLATED HERE FOR HUMANS.
YOU EVER READ ANY RAC SHADE?
THE POET LOMA LOVED? MOVE ON, LEPUCK. SHE *DUMPED* YOU.
SOMETIMES GETTING WITH SOMEONE NEW IS HOW TO GET OVER SOMEONE OLD...
"MY LOVE BEGINS WHEN SUNS WERE COLD AND PLANETS UNBORN...
"...BUT WHEN IT DIES IT'S BUILT ANEW. MY LOVE FORNEVER ENDS."
YOU NEED HELP, MAN.
GELINEAU. IF I SHOW YOU SOMETHING, WILL YOU PROMISE NOT TO FREAK OUT?

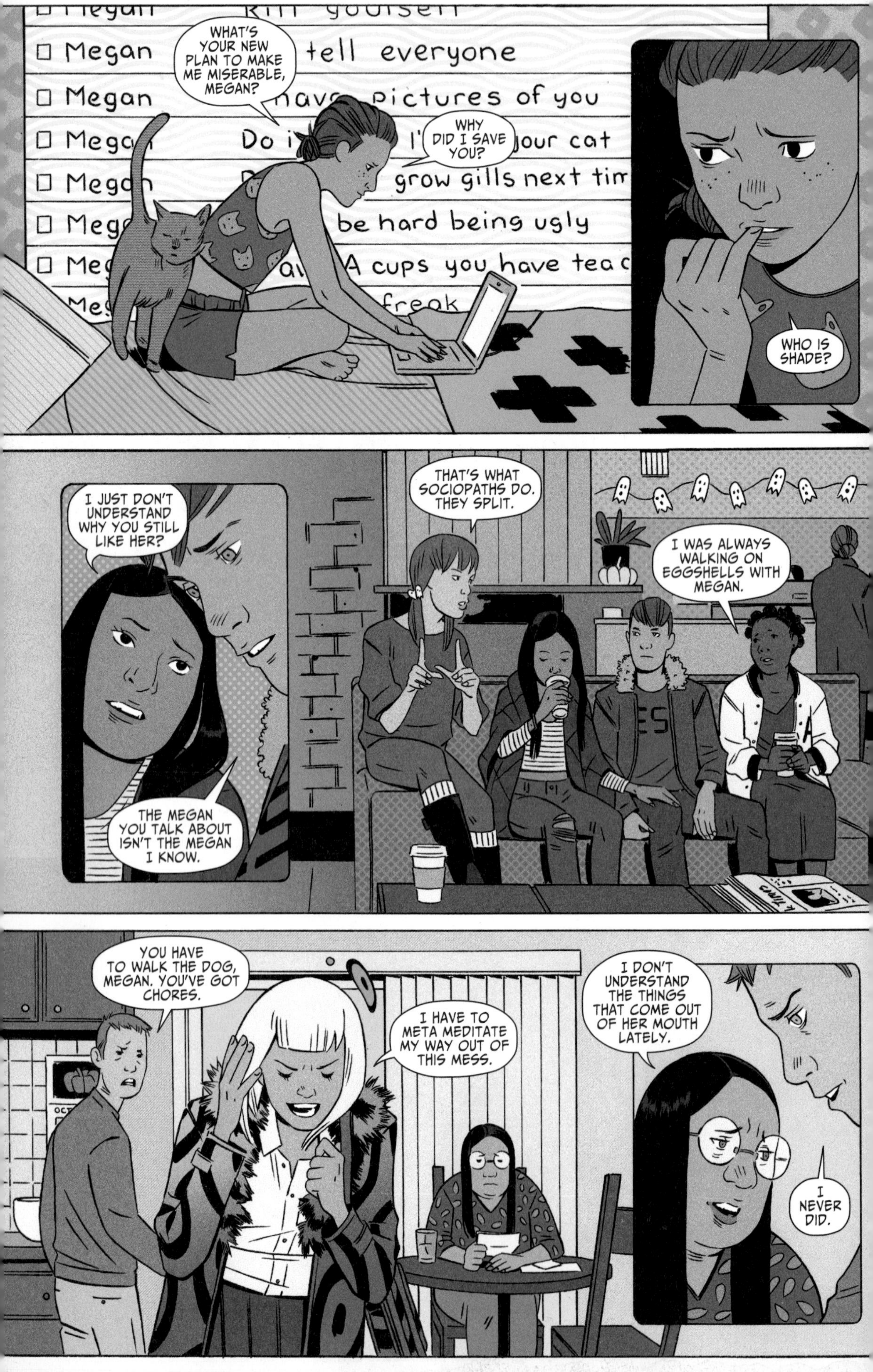

Megan tell everyone
Megan pictures of you
Megan Do i jour cat
Megan grow gills next tim
Meg be hard being ugly
Meg A cups you have teac
freak
WHAT'S YOUR NEW PLAN TO MAKE ME MISERABLE, MEGAN?
WHY DID I SAVE YOU?
WHO IS SHADE?
I JUST DON'T UNDERSTAND WHY YOU STILL LIKE HER?
THE MEGAN YOU TALK ABOUT ISN'T THE MEGAN I KNOW.
THAT'S WHAT SOCIOPATHS DO. THEY SPLIT.
I WAS ALWAYS WALKING ON EGGSHELLS WITH MEGAN.
YOU HAVE TO WALK THE DOG, MEGAN. YOU'VE GOT CHORES.
I HAVE TO META MEDITATE MY WAY OUT OF THIS MESS.
I DON'T UNDERSTAND THE THINGS THAT COME OUT OF HER MOUTH LATELY.
I NEVER DID.

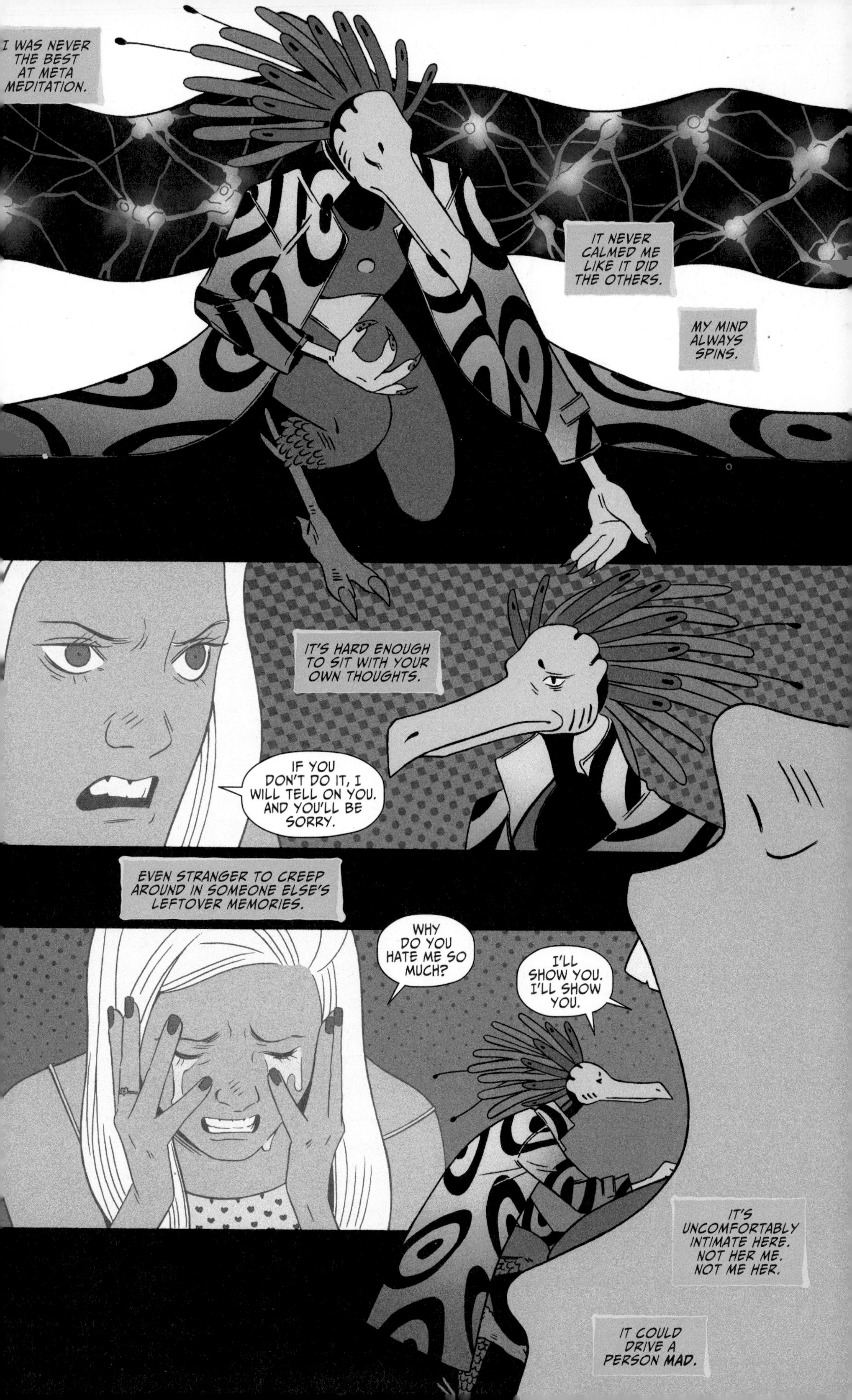

I WAS NEVER THE BEST AT META MEDITATION.
IT NEVER CALMED ME LIKE IT DID THE OTHERS.
MY MIND ALWAYS SPINS.
IT'S HARD ENOUGH TO SIT WITH YOUR OWN THOUGHTS.
IF YOU DON'T DO IT, I WILL TELL ON YOU. AND YOU'LL BE SORRY.
EVEN STRANGER TO CREEP AROUND IN SOMEONE ELSE'S LEFTOVER MEMORIES.
WHY DO YOU HATE ME SO MUCH?
I'LL SHOW YOU. I'LL SHOW YOU.
IT'S UNCOMFORTABLY INTIMATE HERE. NOT HER ME. NOT ME HER.
IT COULD DRIVE A PERSON MAD.

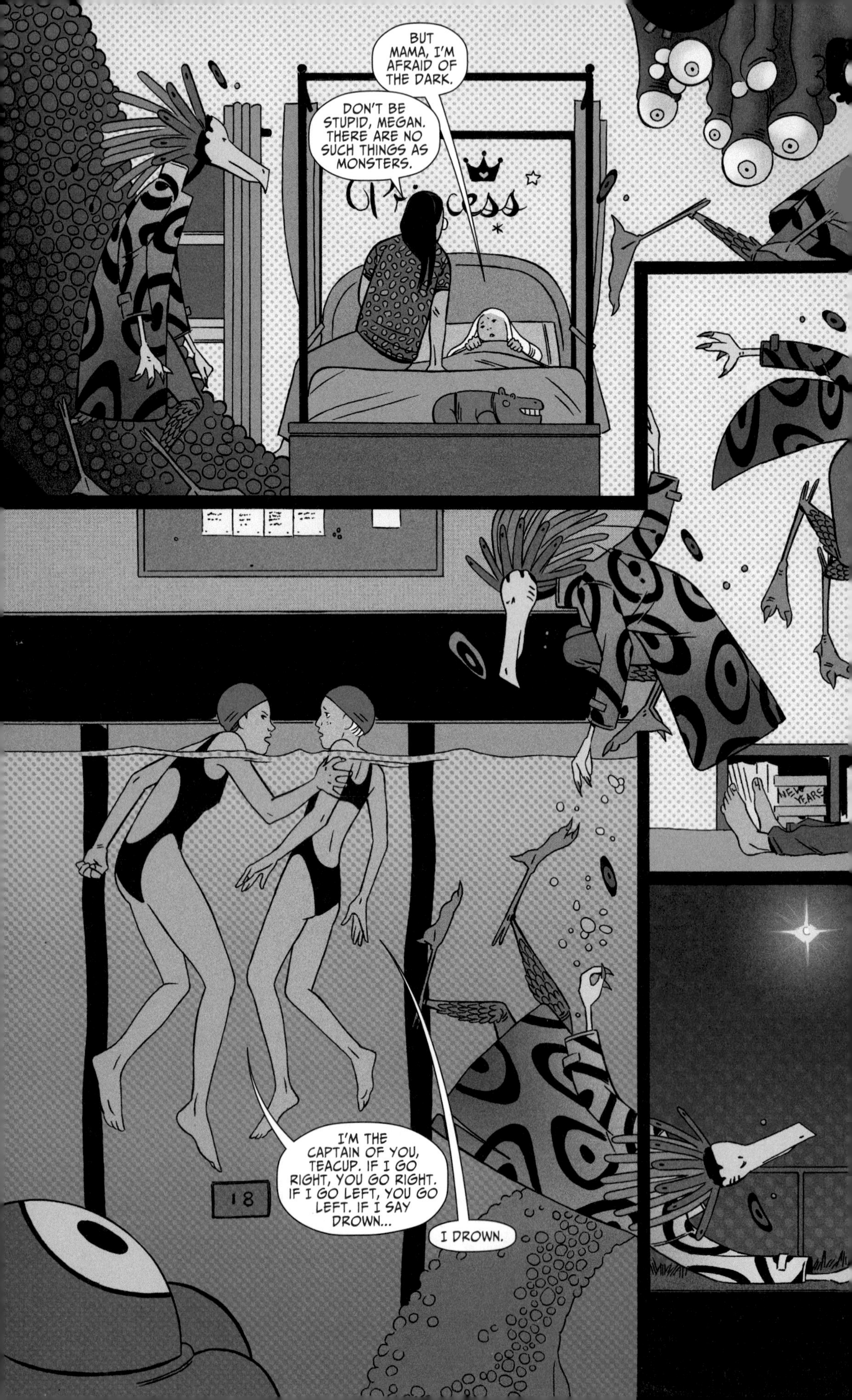
BUT MAMA, I'M AFRAID OF THE DARK.
DON'T BE STUPID, MEGAN. THERE ARE NO SUCH THINGS AS MONSTERS.
Princess
NEW YEARS
18
I'M THE CAPTAIN OF YOU, TEACUP. IF I GO RIGHT, YOU GO RIGHT. IF I GO LEFT, YOU GO LEFT. IF I SAY DROWN...
I DROWN.

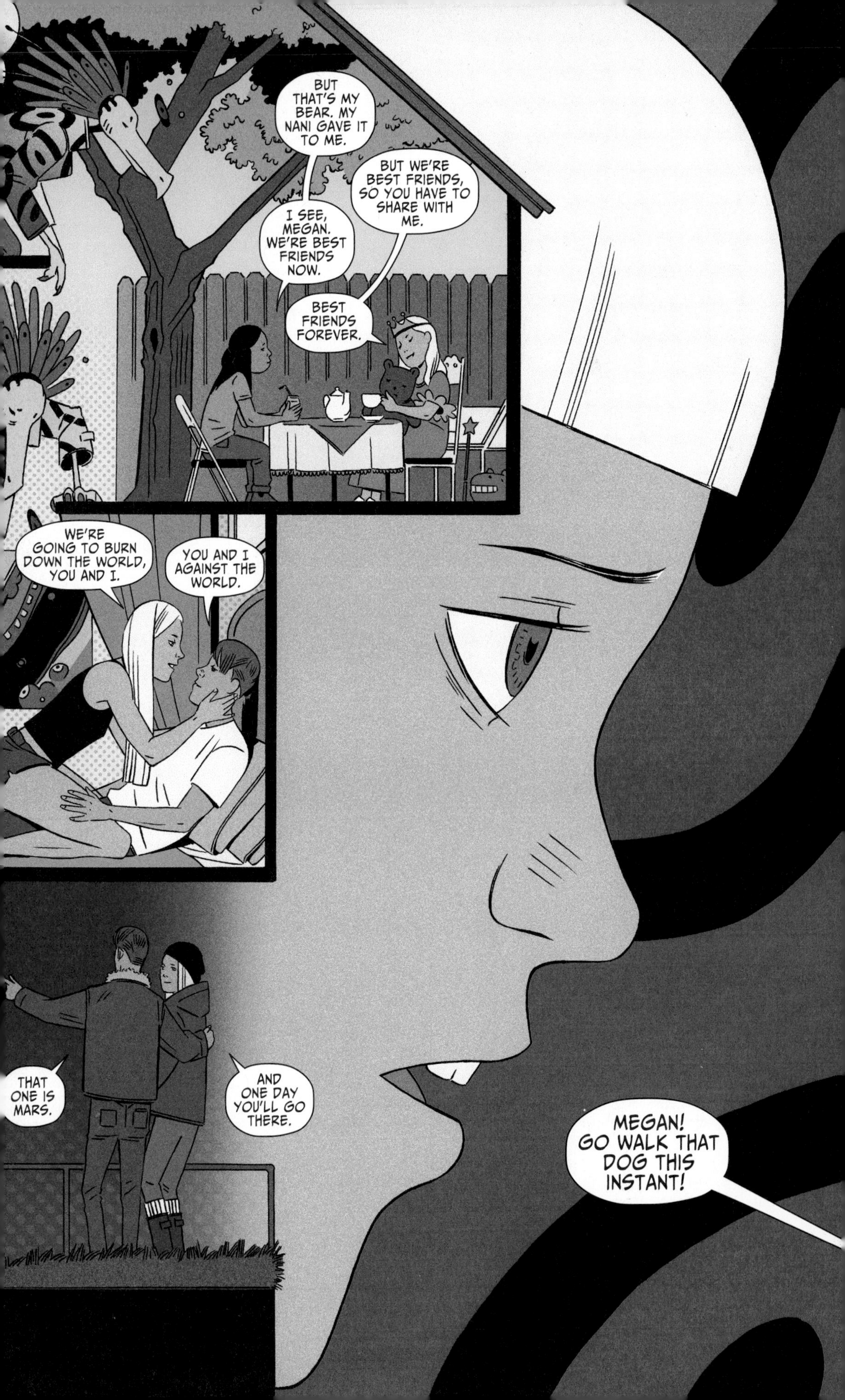
BUT THAT'S MY BEAR. MY NANI GAVE IT TO ME.
BUT WE'RE BEST FRIENDS, SO YOU HAVE TO SHARE WITH ME.
I SEE, MEGAN. WE'RE BEST FRIENDS NOW.
BEST FRIENDS FOREVER.
WE'RE GOING TO BURN DOWN THE WORLD, YOU AND I.
YOU AND I AGAINST THE WORLD.
THAT ONE IS MARS.
AND ONE DAY YOU'LL GO THERE.
MEGAN! GO WALK THAT DOG THIS INSTANT!

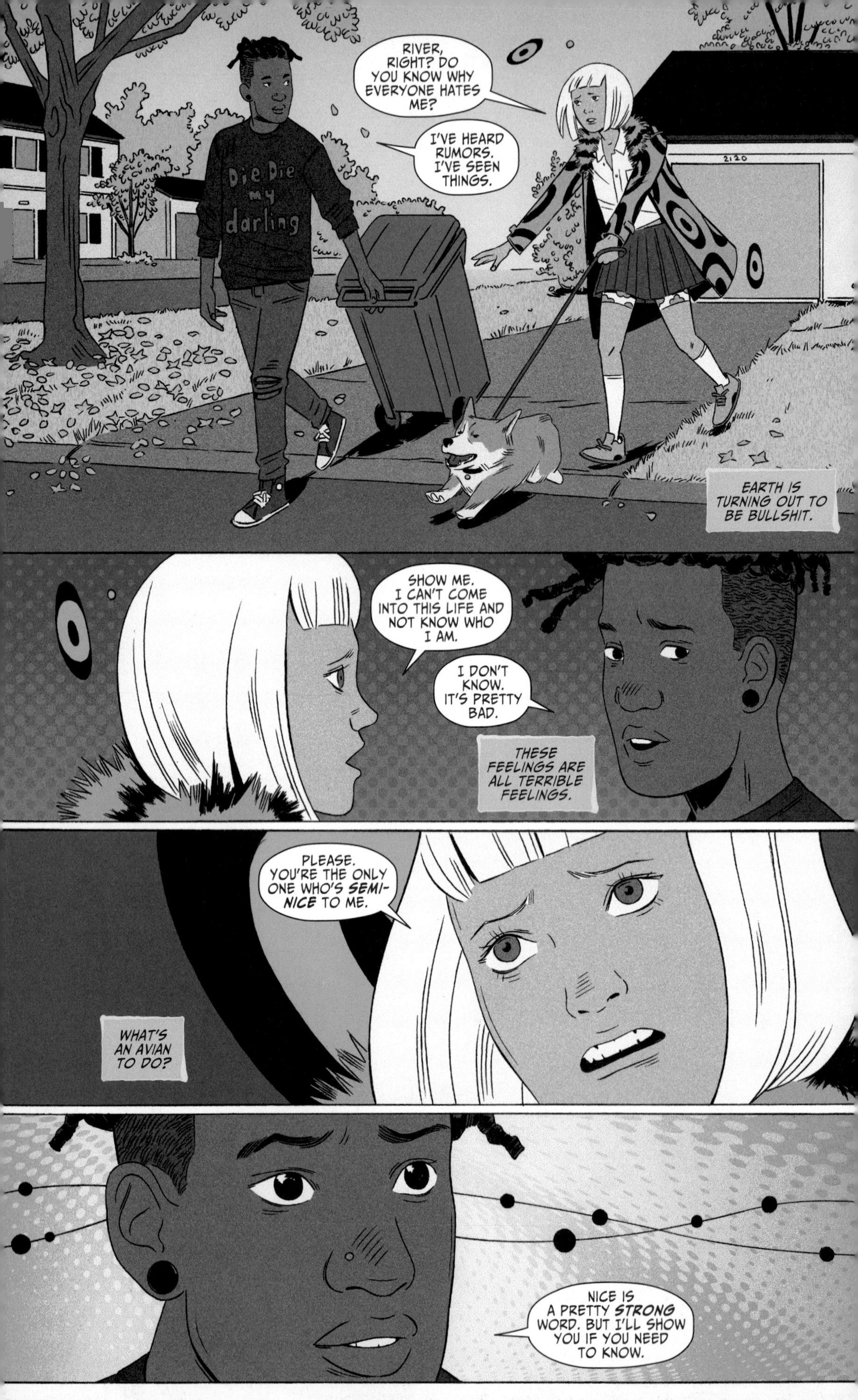
Die Die my darling
RIVER, RIGHT? DO YOU KNOW WHY EVERYONE HATES ME?
I'VE HEARD RUMORS. I'VE SEEN THINGS.
2120
EARTH IS TURNING OUT TO BE BULLSHIT.
SHOW ME. I CAN'T COME INTO THIS LIFE AND NOT KNOW WHO I AM.
I DON'T KNOW. IT'S PRETTY BAD.
THESE FEELINGS ARE ALL TERRIBLE FEELINGS.
PLEASE. YOU'RE THE ONLY ONE WHO'S *SEMI-NICE* TO ME.
WHAT'S AN AVIAN TO DO?
NICE IS A PRETTY *STRONG* WORD. BUT I'LL SHOW YOU IF YOU NEED TO KNOW.

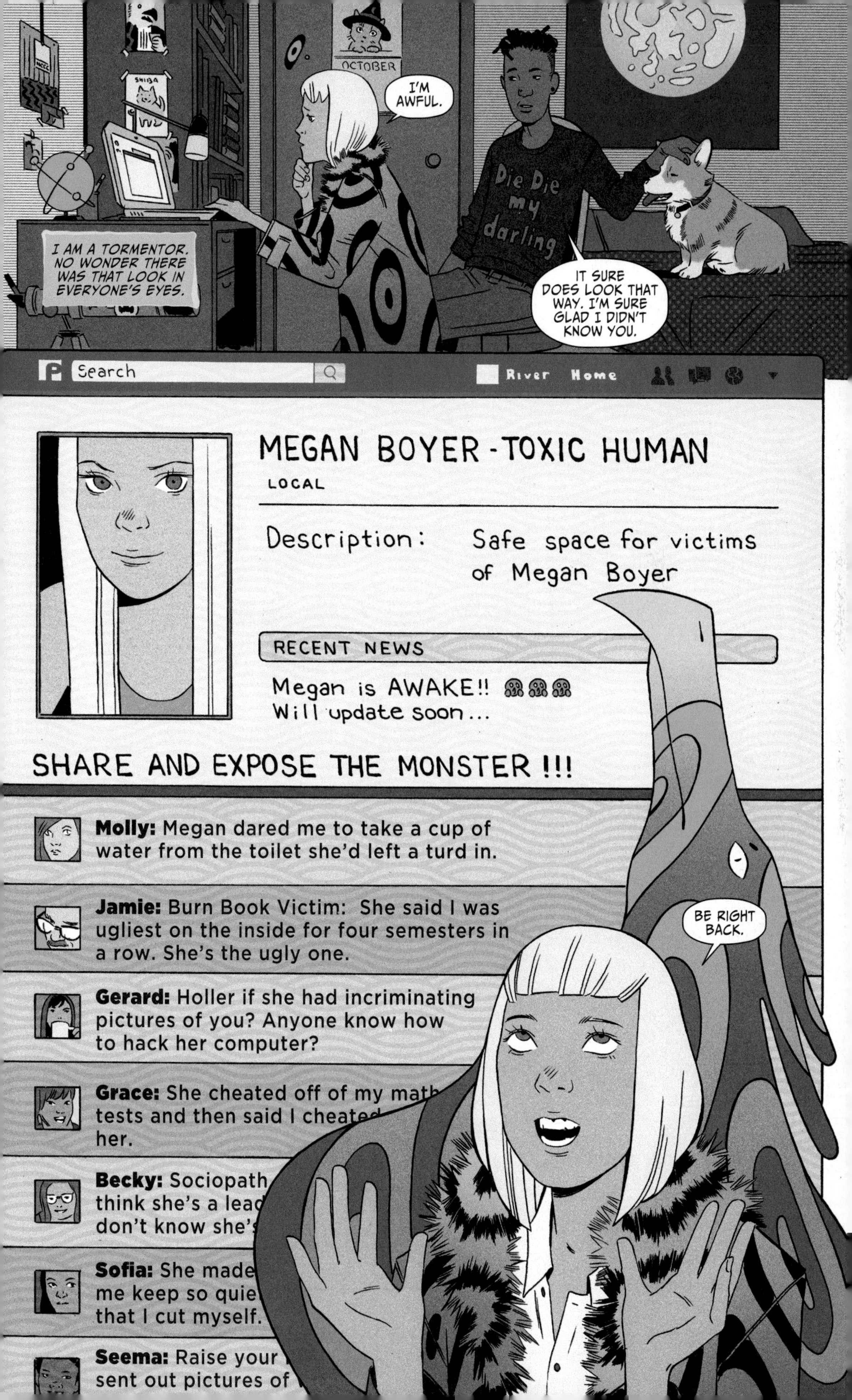
I'M AWFUL.
I AM A TORMENTOR. NO WONDER THERE WAS THAT LOOK IN EVERYONE'S EYES.
IT SURE DOES LOOK THAT WAY. I'M SURE GLAD I DIDN'T KNOW YOU.
Die Die my darling
OCTOBER
SHIBA
Search
River Home
MEGAN BOYER - TOXIC HUMAN
LOCAL
Description: Safe space for victims of Megan Boyer
RECENT NEWS
Megan is AWAKE!!
Will update soon...
SHARE AND EXPOSE THE MONSTER !!!
Molly: Megan dared me to take a cup of water from the toilet she'd left a turd in.
Jamie: Burn Book Victim: She said I was ugliest on the inside for four semesters in a row. She's the ugly one.
Gerard: Holler if she had incriminating pictures of you? Anyone know how to hack her computer?
Grace: She cheated off of my math tests and then said I cheate
her.
Becky: Sociopath
think she's a lead
don't know she's
Sofia: She made
me keep so quie
that I cut myself.
Seema: Raise your
sent out pictures of
BE RIGHT BACK.

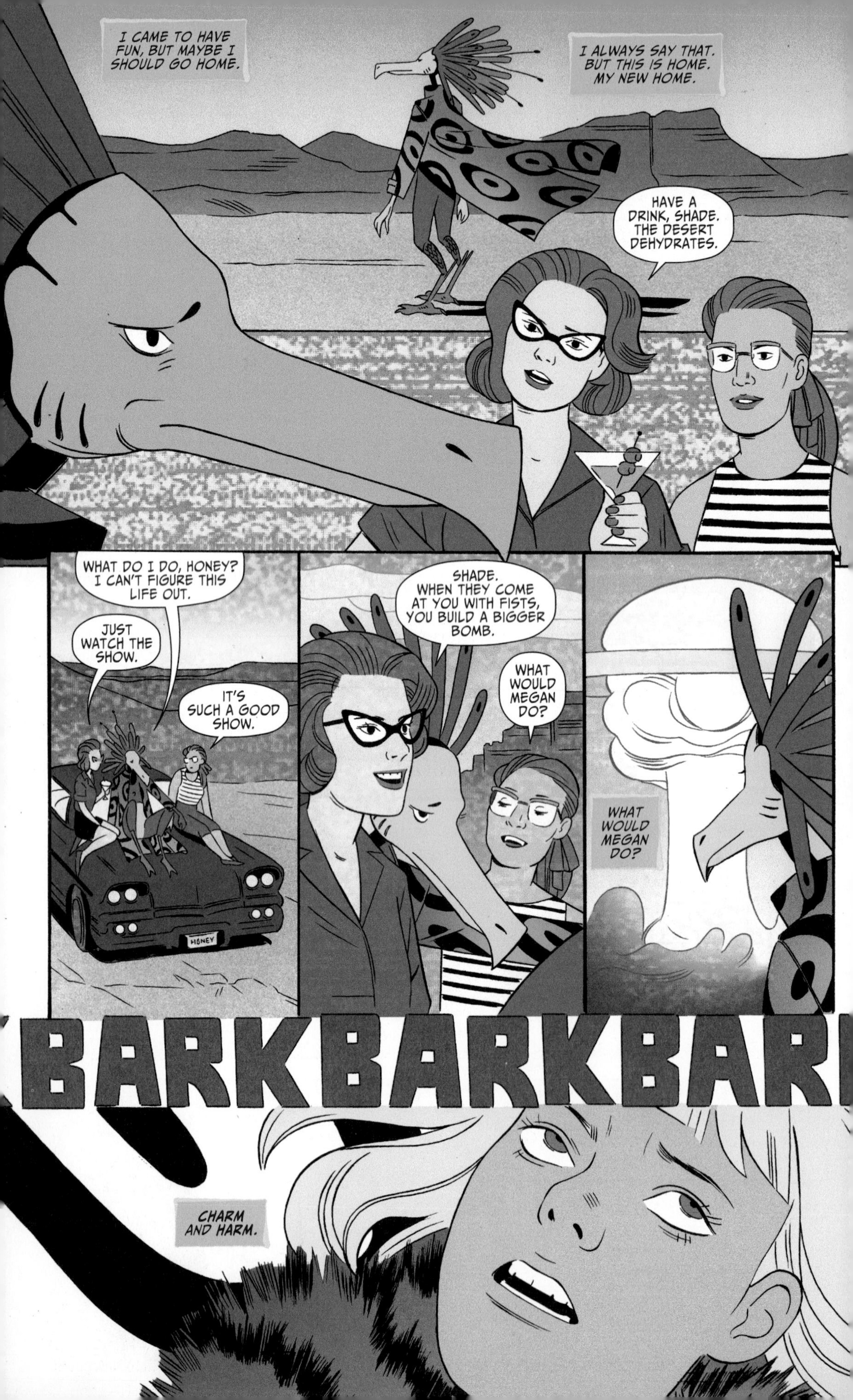
I CAME TO HAVE FUN, BUT MAYBE I SHOULD GO HOME.
I ALWAYS SAY THAT. BUT THIS IS HOME. MY NEW HOME.
HAVE A DRINK, SHADE. THE DESERT DEHYDRATES.
WHAT DO I DO, HONEY? I CAN'T FIGURE THIS LIFE OUT.
JUST WATCH THE SHOW.
IT'S SUCH A GOOD SHOW.
HONEY
SHADE. WHEN THEY COME AT YOU WITH FISTS, YOU BUILD A BIGGER BOMB.
WHAT WOULD MEGAN DO?
WHAT WOULD MEGAN DO?
BARKBARKBAR
CHARM AND HARM.

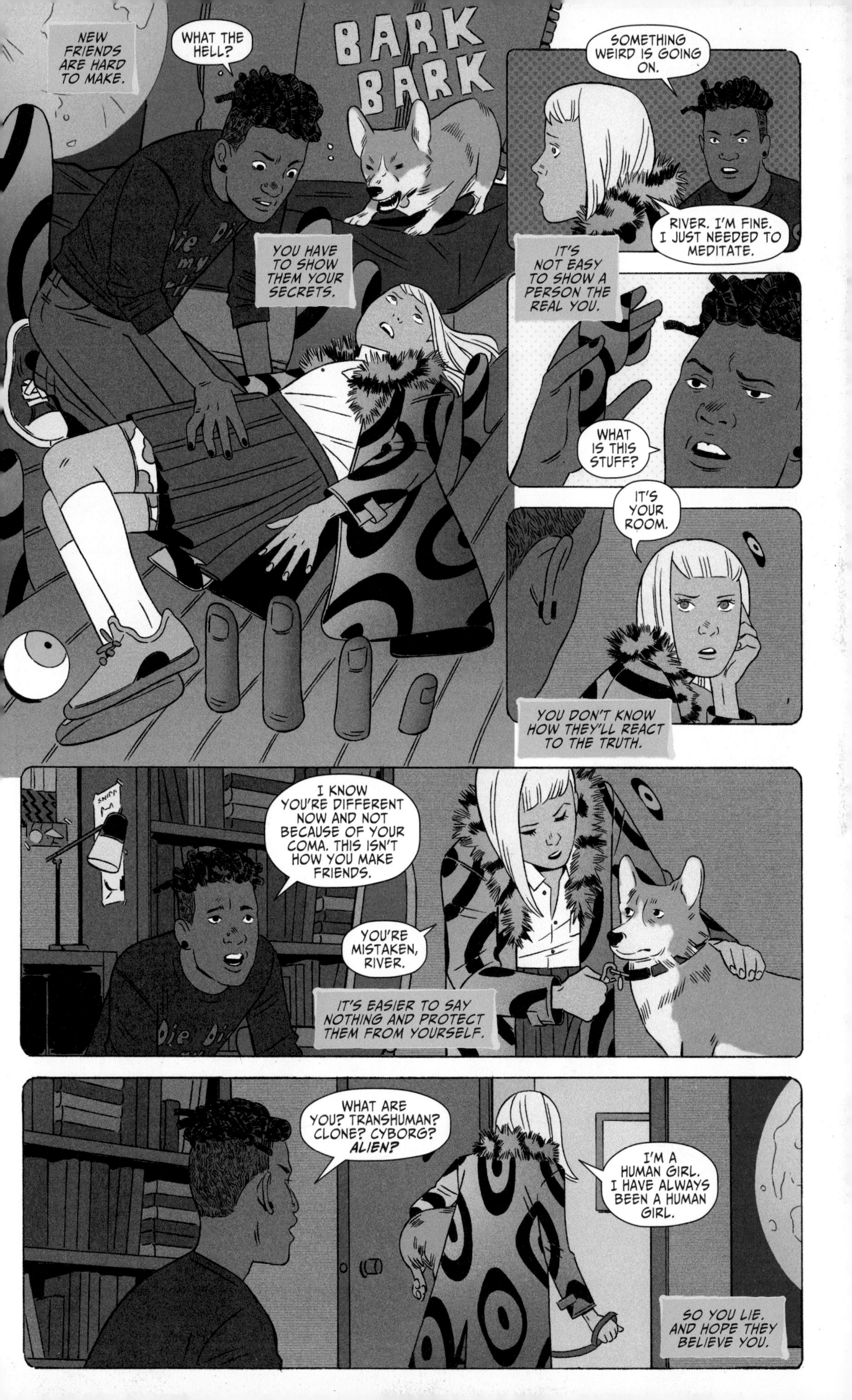
NEW FRIENDS ARE HARD TO MAKE.
WHAT THE HELL?
BARK BARK
YOU HAVE TO SHOW THEM YOUR SECRETS.
SOMETHING WEIRD IS GOING ON.
RIVER. I'M FINE. I JUST NEEDED TO MEDITATE.
IT'S NOT EASY TO SHOW A PERSON THE REAL YOU.
WHAT IS THIS STUFF?
IT'S YOUR ROOM.
YOU DON'T KNOW HOW THEY'LL REACT TO THE TRUTH.
I KNOW YOU'RE DIFFERENT NOW AND NOT BECAUSE OF YOUR COMA. THIS ISN'T HOW YOU MAKE FRIENDS.
YOU'RE MISTAKEN, RIVER.
IT'S EASIER TO SAY NOTHING AND PROTECT THEM FROM YOURSELF.
WHAT ARE YOU? TRANSHUMAN? CLONE? CYBORG? ***ALIEN?***
I'M A HUMAN GIRL. I HAVE ALWAYS BEEN A HUMAN GIRL.
SO YOU LIE. AND HOPE THEY BELIEVE YOU.

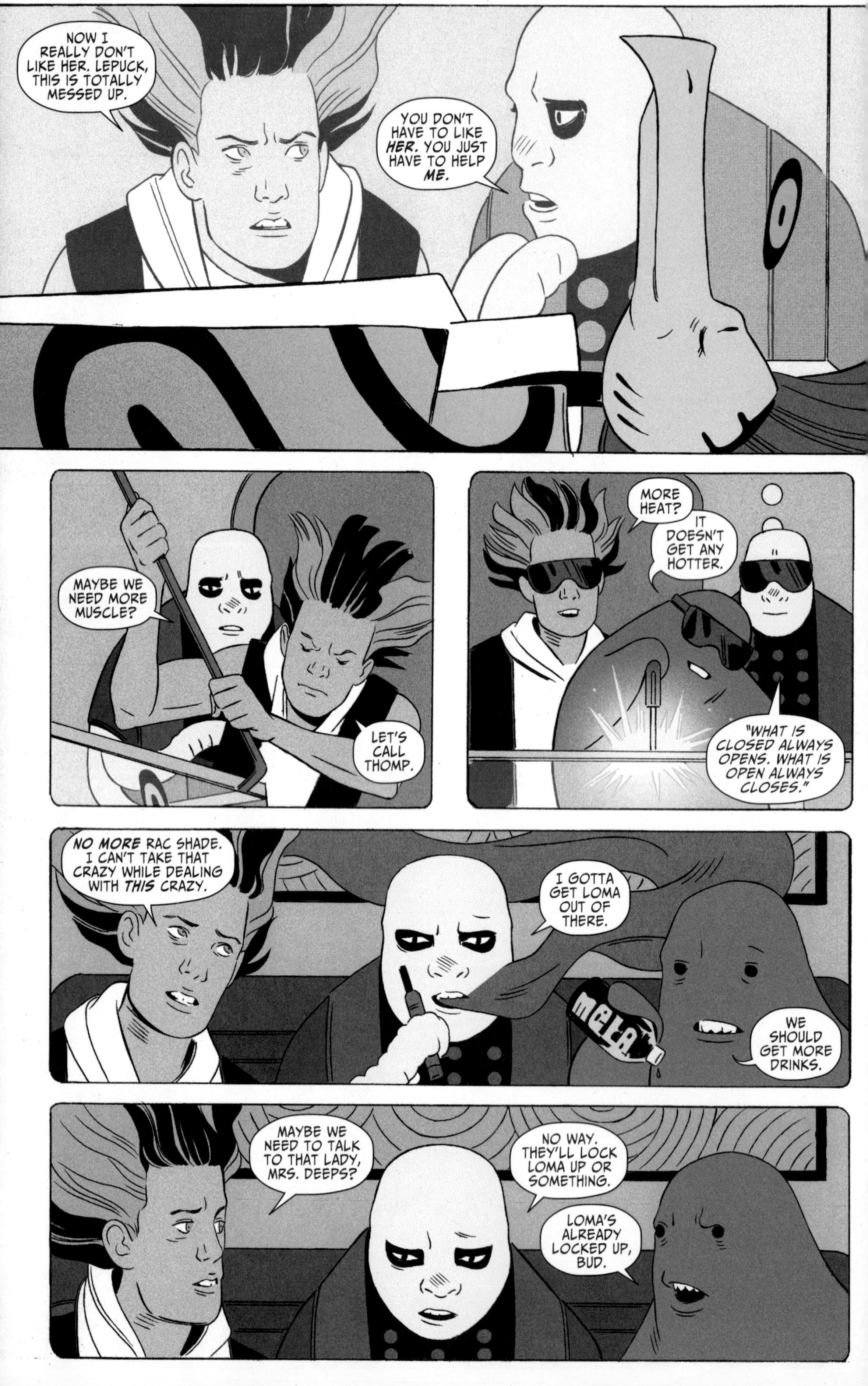

NOW I REALLY DON'T LIKE HER. LEPUCK, THIS IS TOTALLY MESSED UP.
YOU DON'T HAVE TO LIKE *HER.* YOU JUST HAVE TO HELP *ME.*
MAYBE WE NEED MORE MUSCLE?
LET'S CALL THOMP.
MORE HEAT?
IT DOESN'T GET ANY HOTTER.
"WHAT IS CLOSED ALWAYS OPENS. WHAT IS OPEN ALWAYS CLOSES."
NO MORE RAC SHADE. I CAN'T TAKE THAT CRAZY WHILE DEALING WITH *THIS* CRAZY.
I GOTTA GET LOMA OUT OF THERE.
WE SHOULD GET MORE DRINKS.
MAYBE WE NEED TO TALK TO THAT LADY, MRS. DEEPS?
NO WAY. THEY'LL LOCK LOMA UP OR SOMETHING.
LOMA'S ALREADY LOCKED UP, BUD.

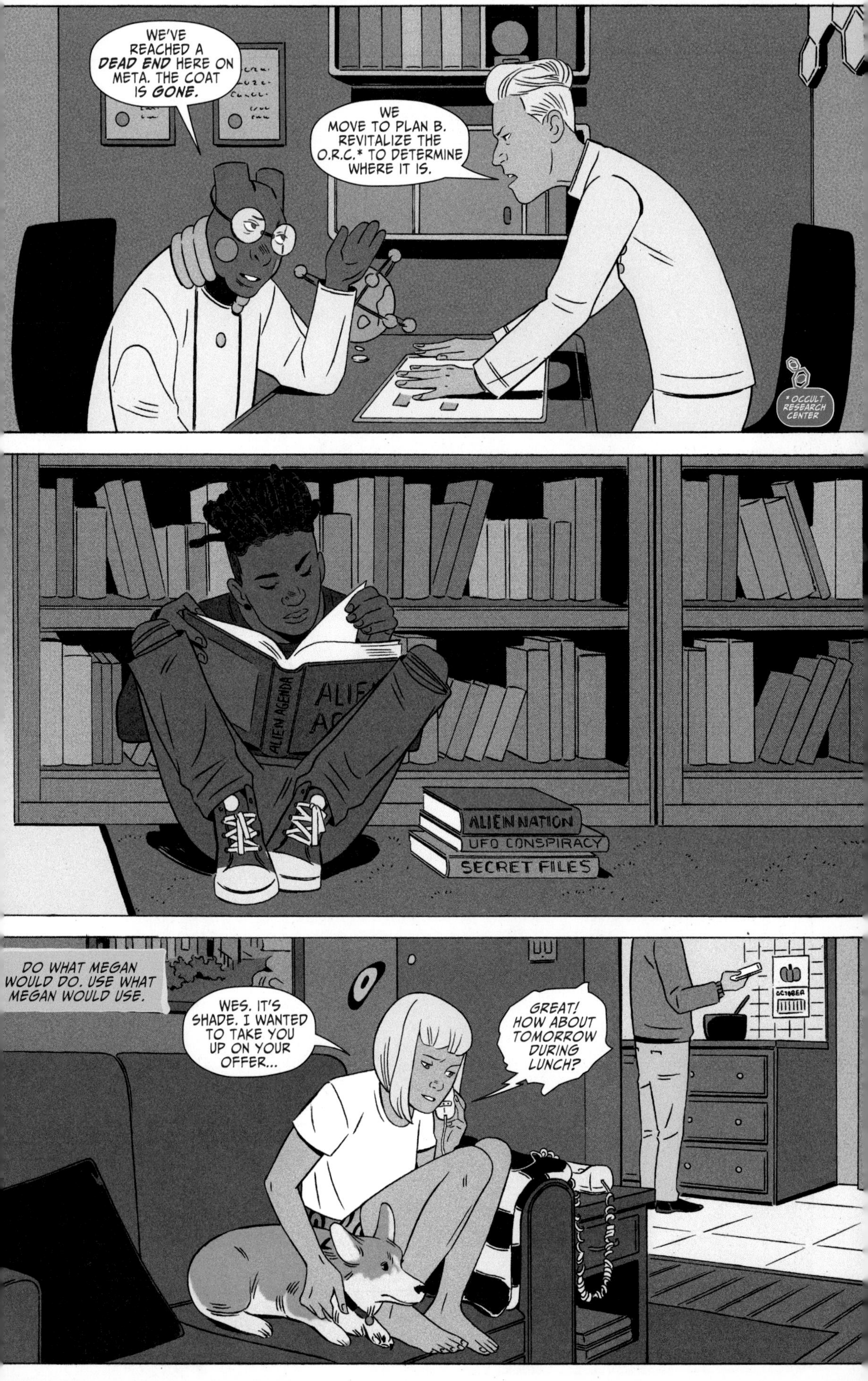
WE'VE REACHED A DEAD END HERE ON META. THE COAT IS GONE.
WE MOVE TO PLAN B. REVITALIZE THE O.R.C.* TO DETERMINE WHERE IT IS.
* OCCULT RESEARCH CENTER
ALIEN AGENDA
ALIEN NATION
UFO CONSPIRACY
SECRET FILES
DO WHAT MEGAN WOULD DO. USE WHAT MEGAN WOULD USE.
WES. IT'S SHADE. I WANTED TO TAKE YOU UP ON YOUR OFFER...
GREAT! HOW ABOUT TOMORROW DURING LUNCH?
OCTOBER

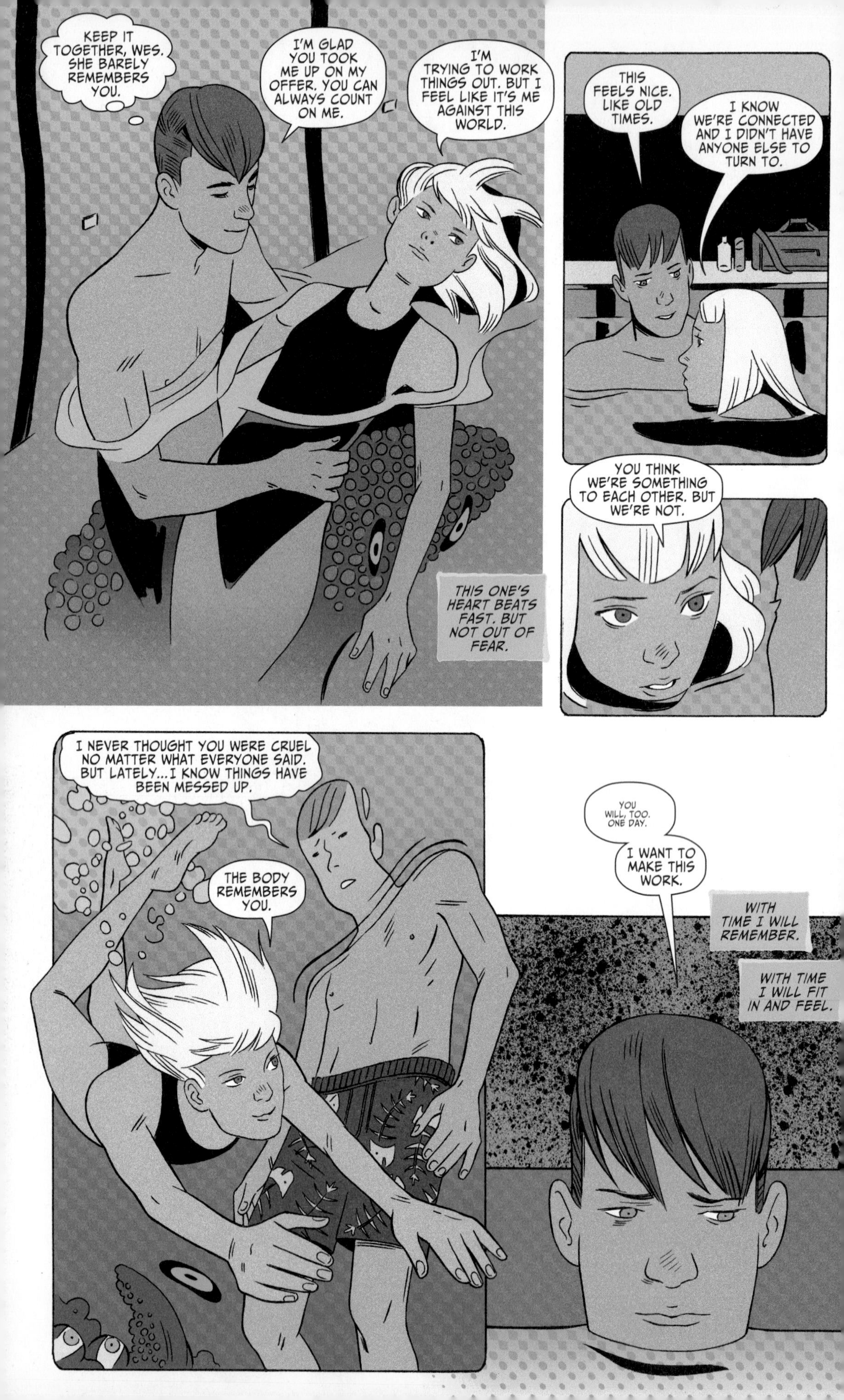
KEEP IT TOGETHER, WES. SHE BARELY REMEMBERS YOU.
I'M GLAD YOU TOOK ME UP ON MY OFFER. YOU CAN ALWAYS COUNT ON ME.
I'M TRYING TO WORK THINGS OUT. BUT I FEEL LIKE IT'S ME AGAINST THIS WORLD.
THIS ONE'S HEART BEATS FAST. BUT NOT OUT OF FEAR.
THIS FEELS NICE. LIKE OLD TIMES.
I KNOW WE'RE CONNECTED AND I DIDN'T HAVE ANYONE ELSE TO TURN TO.
YOU THINK WE'RE SOMETHING TO EACH OTHER. BUT WE'RE NOT.
I NEVER THOUGHT YOU WERE CRUEL NO MATTER WHAT EVERYONE SAID. BUT LATELY...I KNOW THINGS HAVE BEEN MESSED UP.
THE BODY REMEMBERS YOU.
YOU WILL, TOO. ONE DAY.
I WANT TO MAKE THIS WORK.
WITH TIME I WILL REMEMBER.
WITH TIME I WILL FIT IN AND FEEL.

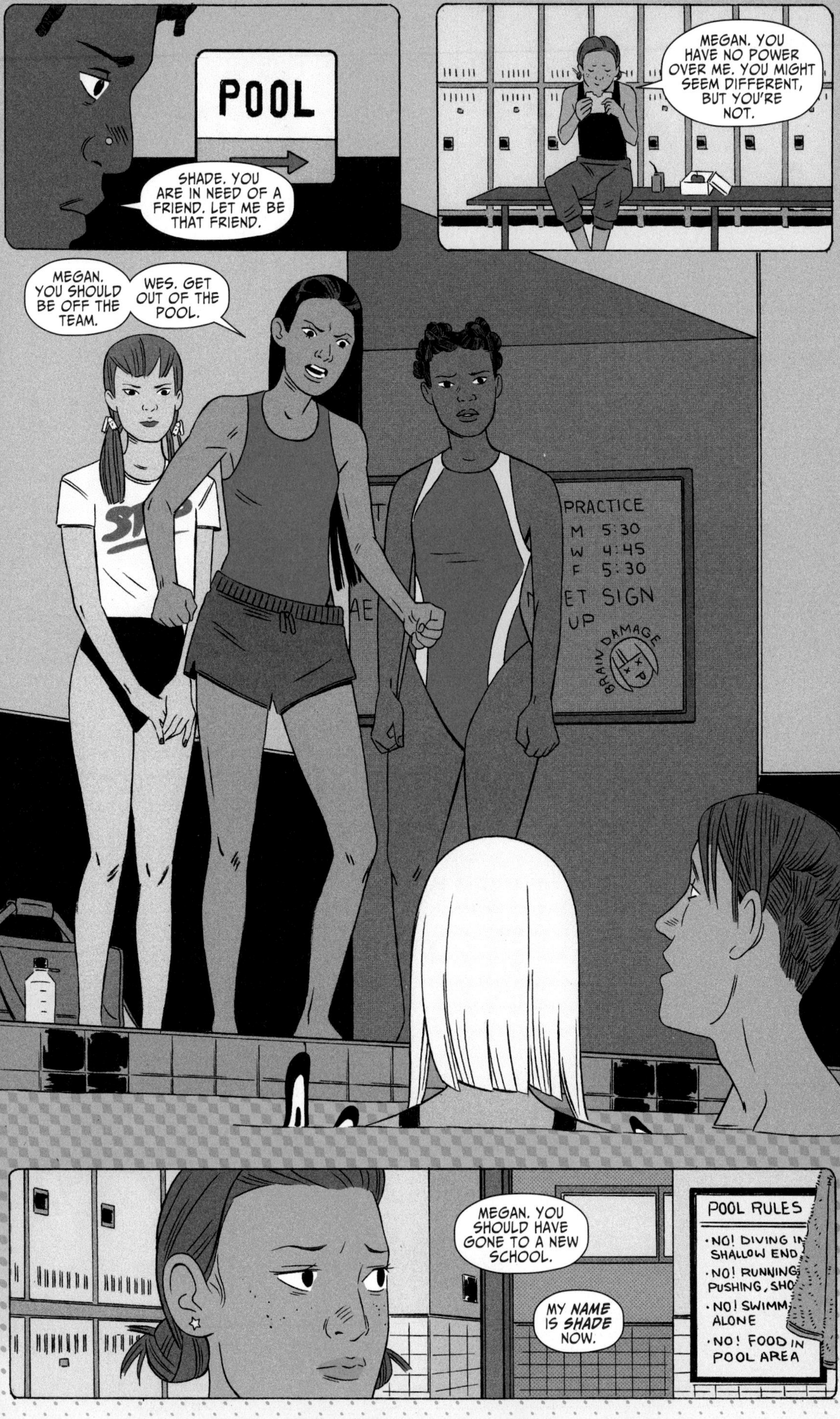
POOL
SHADE. YOU ARE IN NEED OF A FRIEND. LET ME BE THAT FRIEND.
MEGAN. YOU HAVE NO POWER OVER ME. YOU MIGHT SEEM DIFFERENT, BUT YOU'RE NOT.
MEGAN. YOU SHOULD BE OFF THE TEAM.
WES. GET OUT OF THE POOL.
PRACTICE
M 5:30
W 4:45
F 5:30
ET SIGN UP
BRAIN DAMAGE
MEGAN. YOU SHOULD HAVE GONE TO A NEW SCHOOL.
MY NAME IS SHADE NOW.
POOL RULES
·NO! DIVING IN SHALLOW END
·NO! RUNNING PUSHING, SHO
·NO! SWIMM ALONE
·NO! FOOD IN POOL AREA

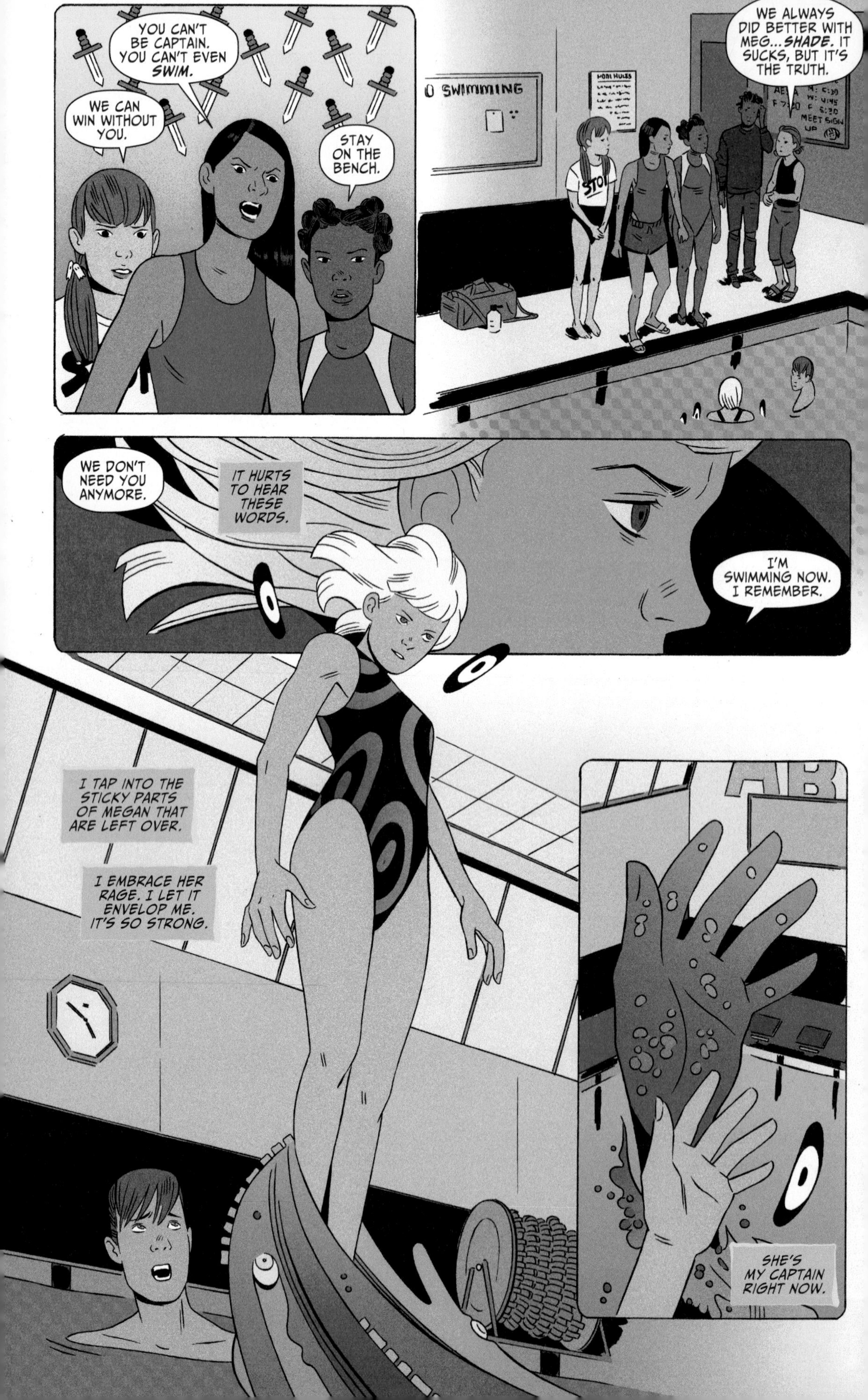
YOU CAN'T BE CAPTAIN. YOU CAN'T EVEN SWIM.
WE CAN WIN WITHOUT YOU.
STAY ON THE BENCH.
WE ALWAYS DID BETTER WITH MEG... SHADE. IT SUCKS, BUT IT'S THE TRUTH.
WE DON'T NEED YOU ANYMORE.
IT HURTS TO HEAR THESE WORDS.
I'M SWIMMING NOW. I REMEMBER.
I TAP INTO THE STICKY PARTS OF MEGAN THAT ARE LEFT OVER.
I EMBRACE HER RAGE. I LET IT ENVELOP ME. IT'S SO STRONG.
SHE'S MY CAPTAIN RIGHT NOW.

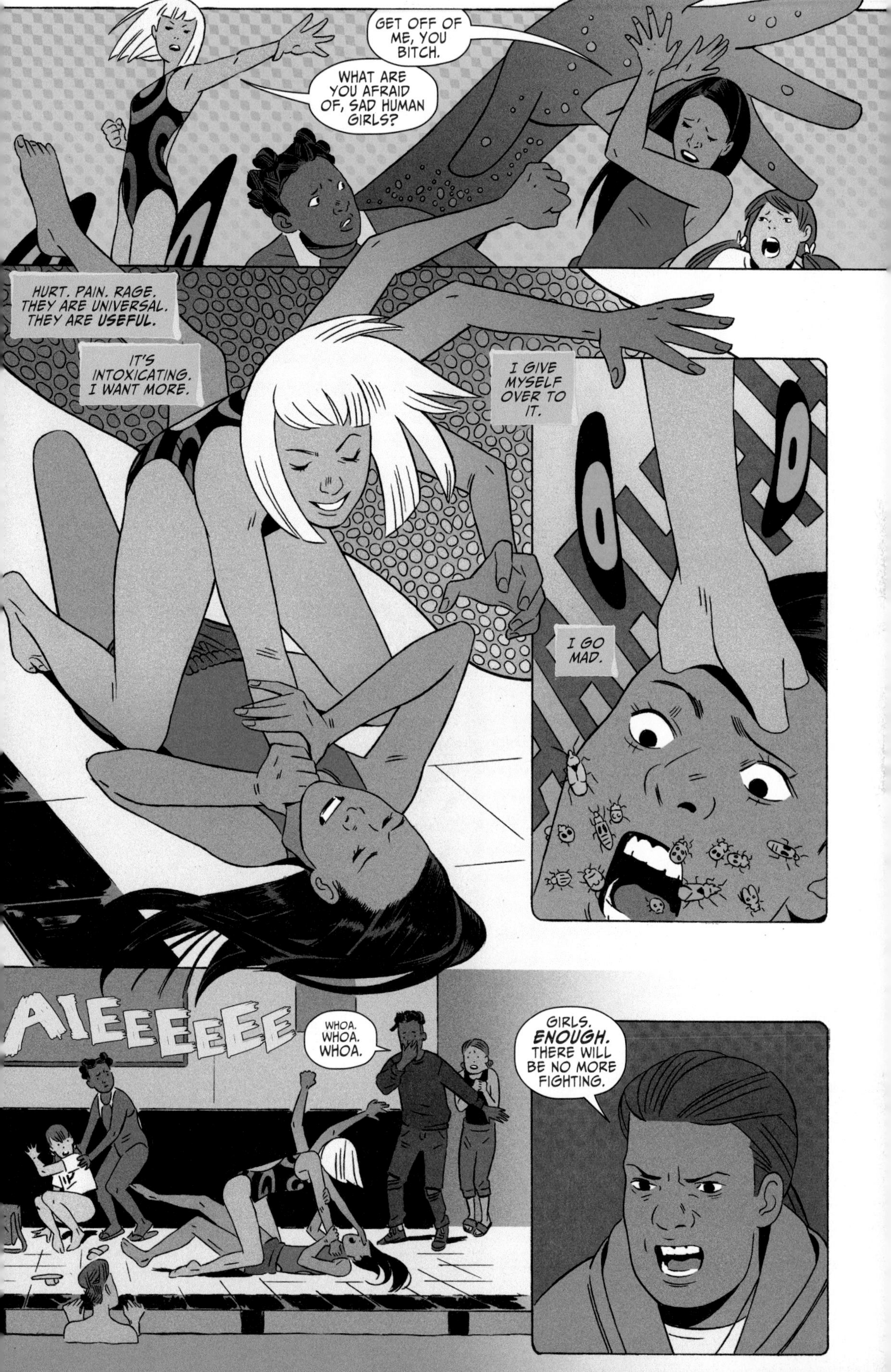
GET OFF OF ME, YOU BITCH.
WHAT ARE YOU AFRAID OF, SAD HUMAN GIRLS?
HURT. PAIN. RAGE. THEY ARE UNIVERSAL. THEY ARE USEFUL.
IT'S INTOXICATING. I WANT MORE.
I GIVE MYSELF OVER TO IT.
I GO MAD.
AIEEEEEEE
WHOA. WHOA. WHOA.
GIRLS. ENOUGH. THERE WILL BE NO MORE FIGHTING.

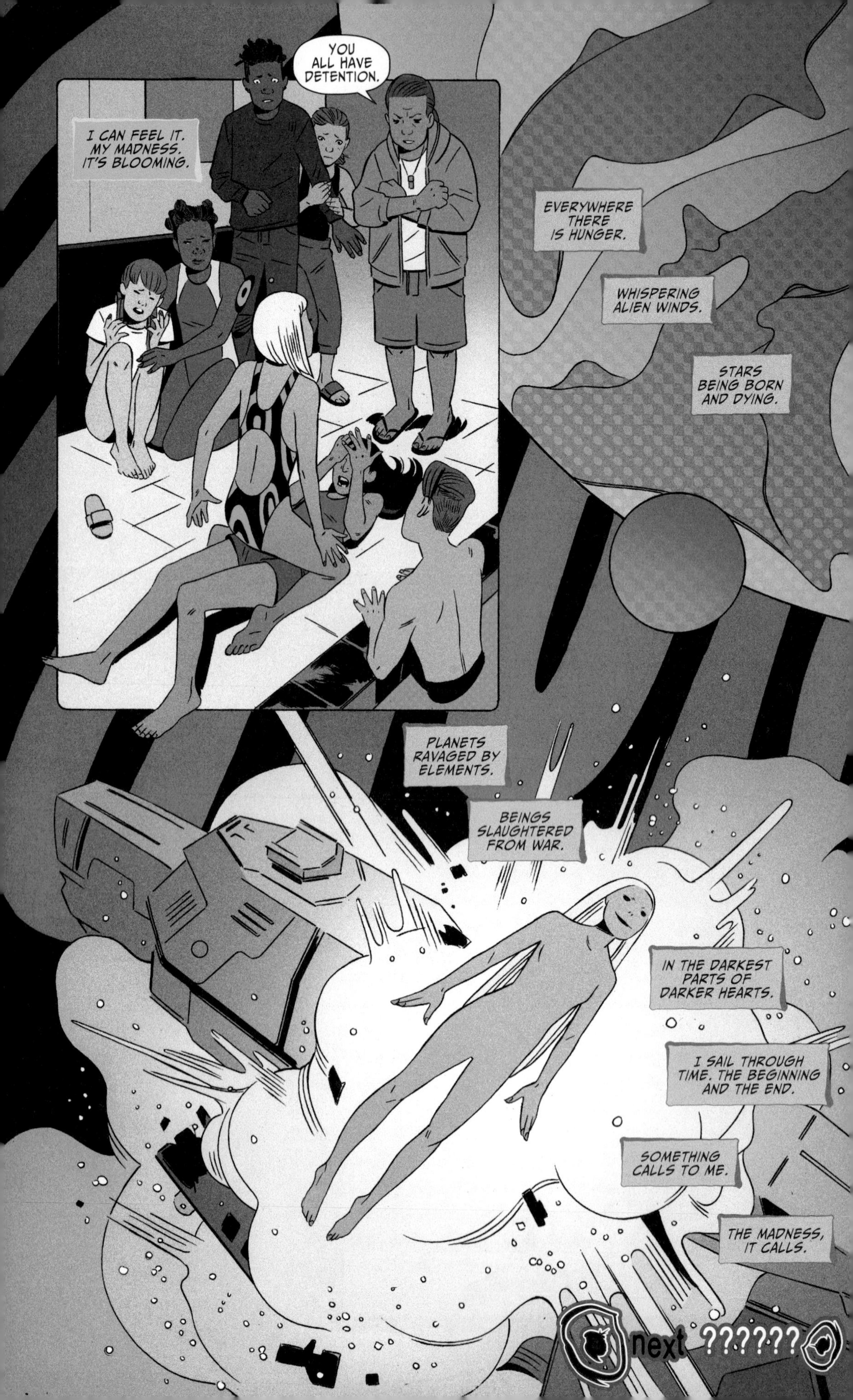
I CAN FEEL IT. MY MADNESS. IT'S BLOOMING.
YOU ALL HAVE DETENTION.
EVERYWHERE THERE IS HUNGER.
WHISPERING ALIEN WINDS.
STARS BEING BORN AND DYING.
PLANETS RAVAGED BY ELEMENTS.
BEINGS SLAUGHTERED FROM WAR.
IN THE DARKEST PARTS OF DARKER HEARTS.
I SAIL THROUGH TIME. THE BEGINNING AND THE END.
SOMETHING CALLS TO ME.
THE MADNESS, IT CALLS.
next ??????

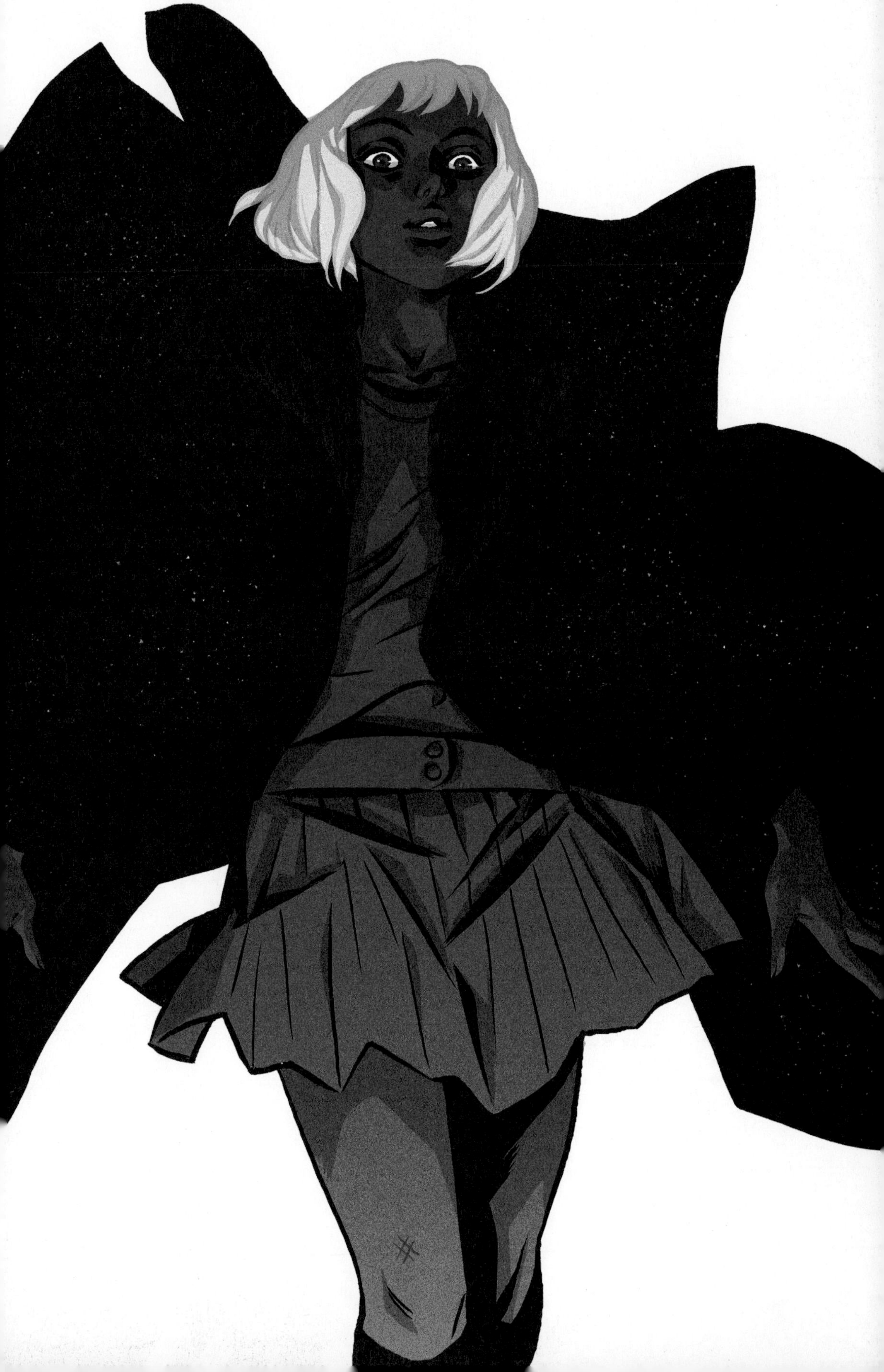

Variant cover art by Joëlle Jones and Kelly Fitzpatrick

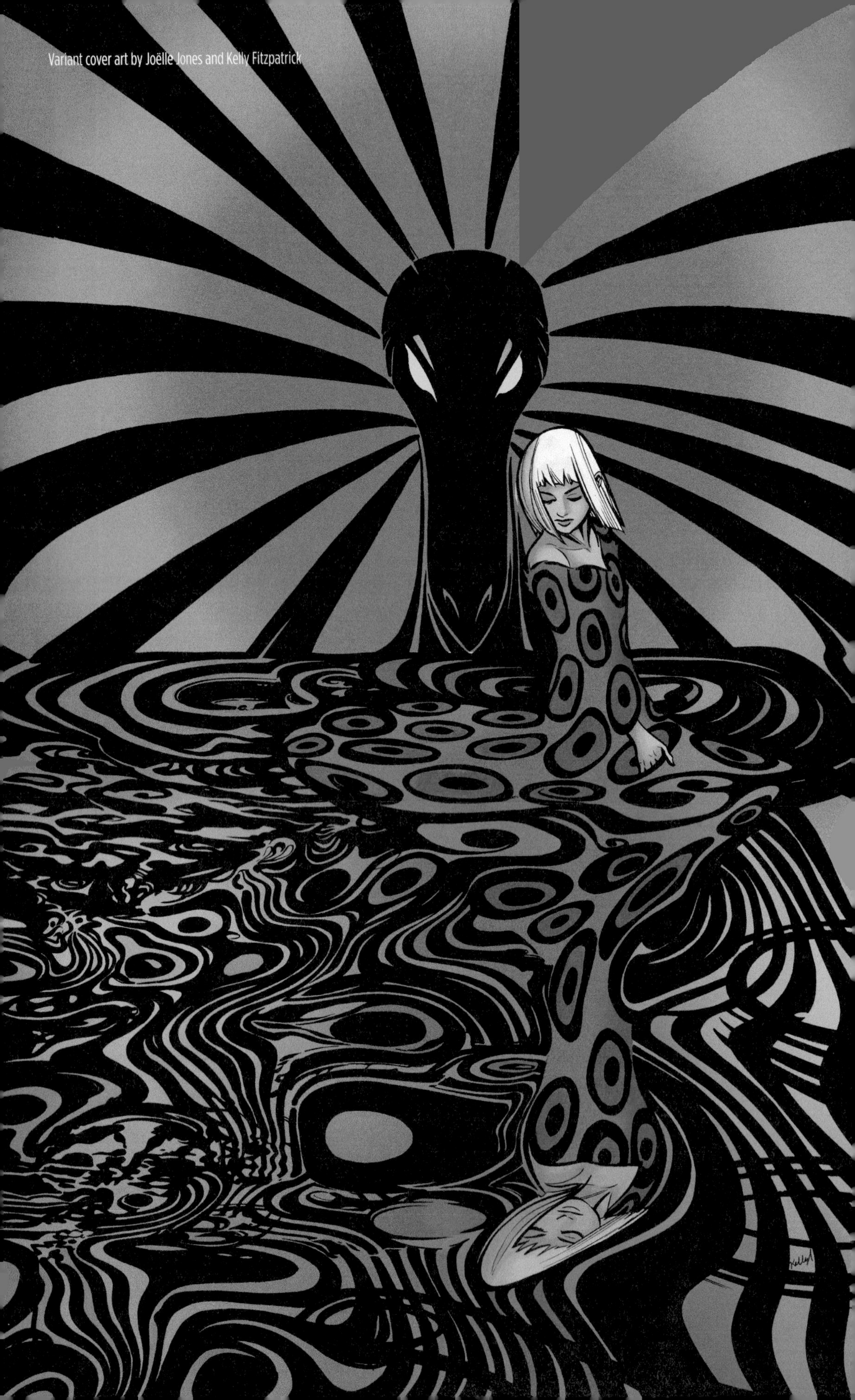

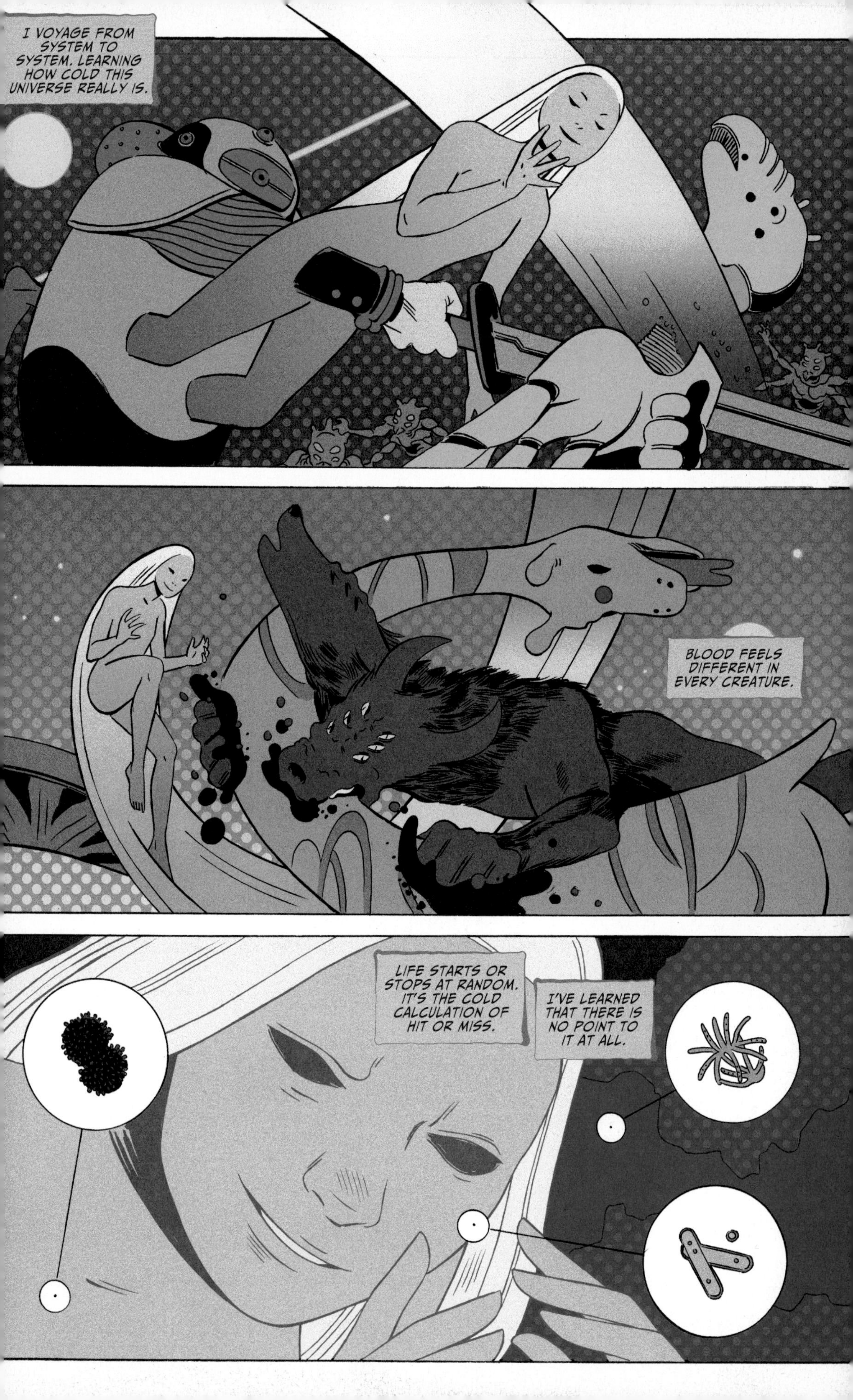
I VOYAGE FROM SYSTEM TO SYSTEM. LEARNING HOW COLD THIS UNIVERSE REALLY IS.
BLOOD FEELS DIFFERENT IN EVERY CREATURE.
LIFE STARTS OR STOPS AT RANDOM. IT'S THE COLD CALCULATION OF HIT OR MISS.
I'VE LEARNED THAT THERE IS NO POINT TO IT AT ALL.

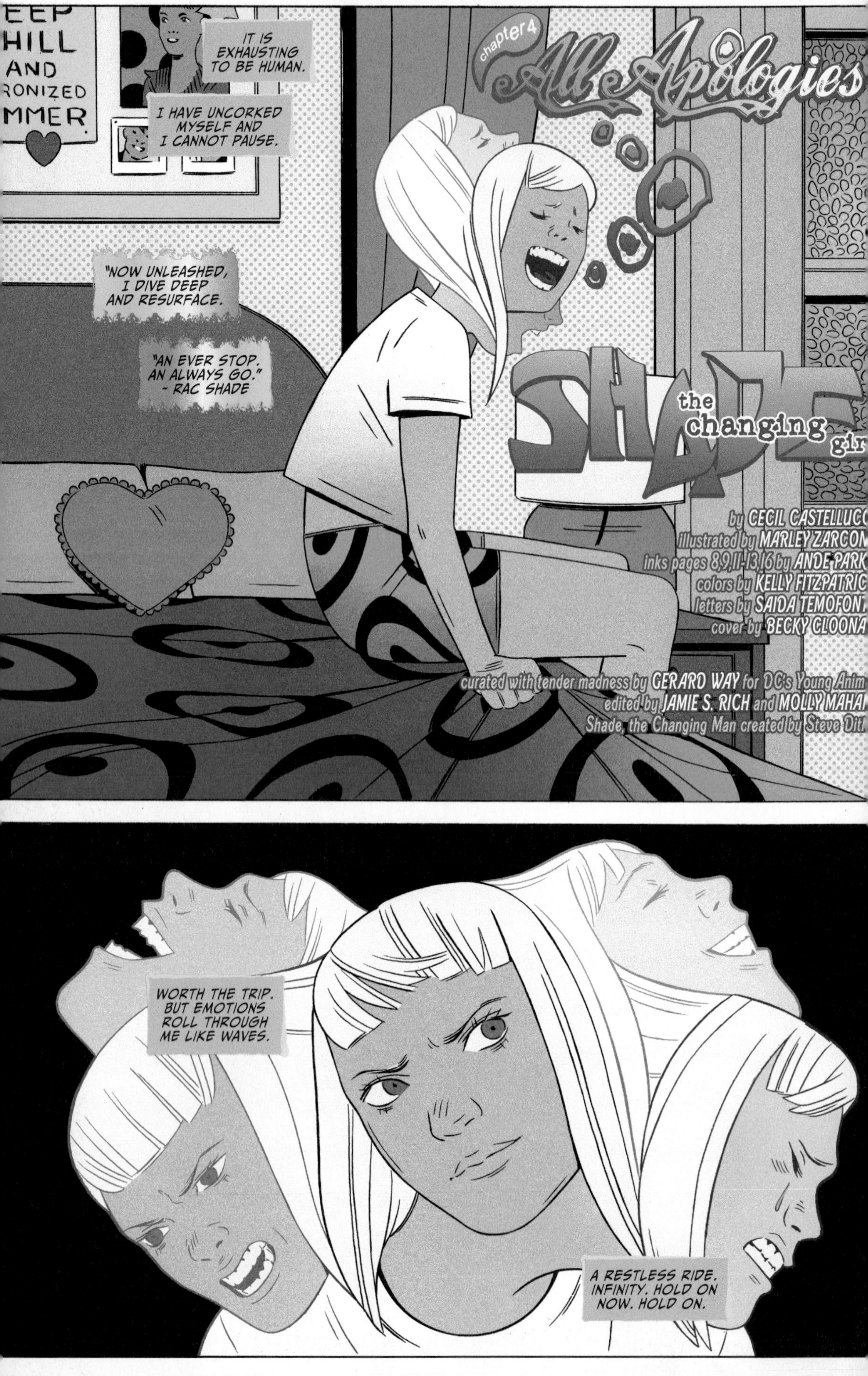
IT IS EXHAUSTING TO BE HUMAN.
I HAVE UNCORKED MYSELF AND I CANNOT PAUSE.
chapter 4
All Apologies
"NOW UNLEASHED, I DIVE DEEP AND RESURFACE.
"AN EVER STOP. AN ALWAYS GO." - RAC SHADE
SHADE the changing gir
by CECIL CASTELLUCC
illustrated by MARLEY ZARCON
inks pages 8,9,11-13,16 by ANDE PARK
colors by KELLY FITZPATRIC
letters by SAIDA TEMOFON
cover by BECKY CLOONA
curated with tender madness by GERARD WAY for DC's Young Anim
edited by JAMIE S. RICH and MOLLY MAHA
Shade, the Changing Man created by Steve Dit
WORTH THE TRIP. BUT EMOTIONS ROLL THROUGH ME LIKE WAVES.
A RESTLESS RIDE. INFINITY. HOLD ON NOW. HOLD ON.

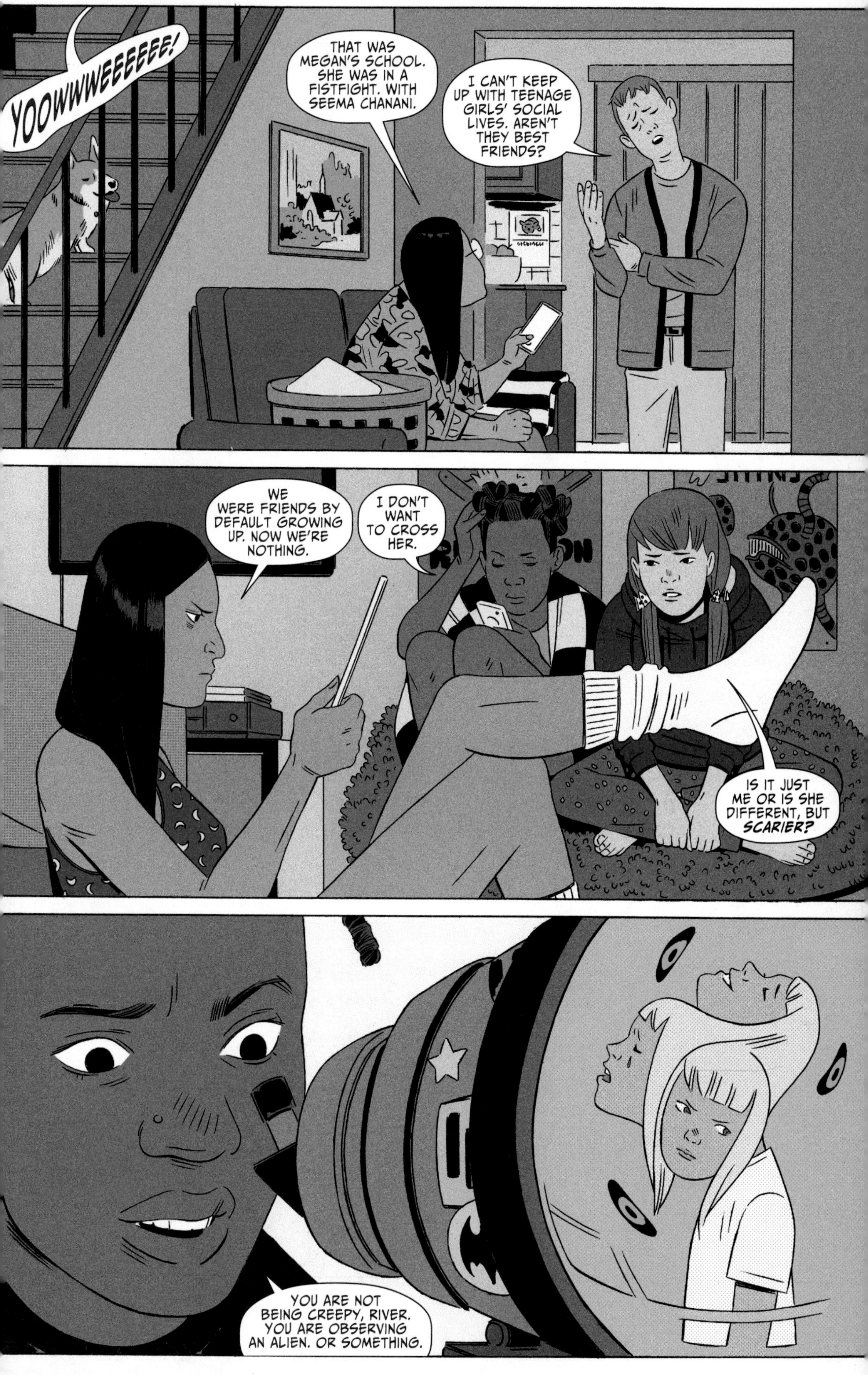
YOOWWWEEEEEEE!
THAT WAS MEGAN'S SCHOOL. SHE WAS IN A FISTFIGHT. WITH SEEMA CHANANI.
I CAN'T KEEP UP WITH TEENAGE GIRLS' SOCIAL LIVES. AREN'T THEY BEST FRIENDS?
WE WERE FRIENDS BY DEFAULT GROWING UP. NOW WE'RE NOTHING.
I DON'T WANT TO CROSS HER.
IS IT JUST ME OR IS SHE DIFFERENT, BUT SCARIER?
YOU ARE NOT BEING CREEPY, RIVER. YOU ARE OBSERVING AN ALIEN. OR SOMETHING.

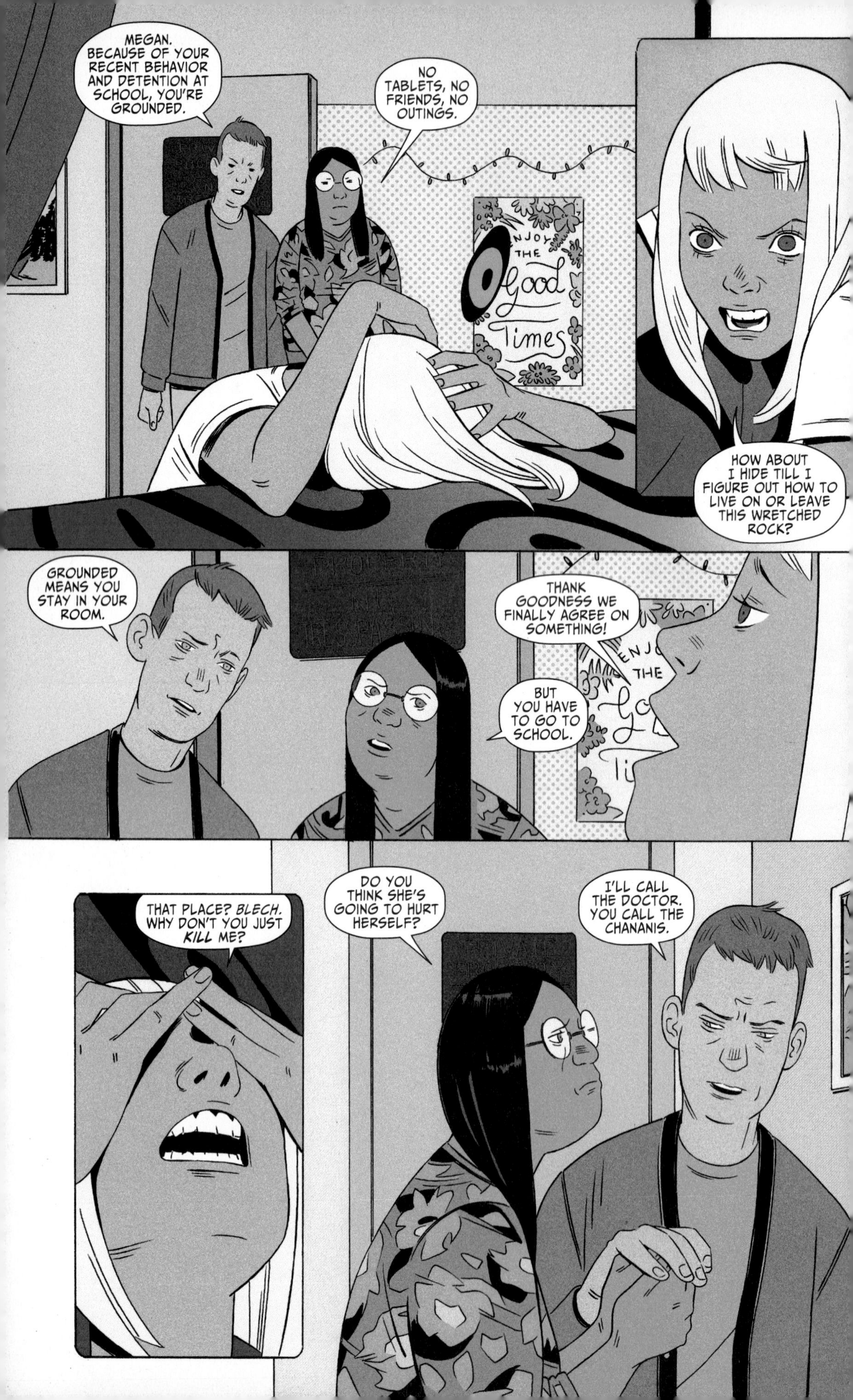
MEGAN. BECAUSE OF YOUR RECENT BEHAVIOR AND DETENTION AT SCHOOL, YOU'RE GROUNDED.
NO TABLETS, NO FRIENDS, NO OUTINGS.
ENJOY THE Good Times
HOW ABOUT I HIDE TILL I FIGURE OUT HOW TO LIVE ON OR LEAVE THIS WRETCHED ROCK?
GROUNDED MEANS YOU STAY IN YOUR ROOM.
THANK GOODNESS WE FINALLY AGREE ON SOMETHING!
BUT YOU HAVE TO GO TO SCHOOL.
THAT PLACE? *BLECH.* WHY DON'T YOU JUST *KILL* ME?
DO YOU THINK SHE'S GOING TO HURT HERSELF?
I'LL CALL THE DOCTOR. YOU CALL THE CHANANIS.

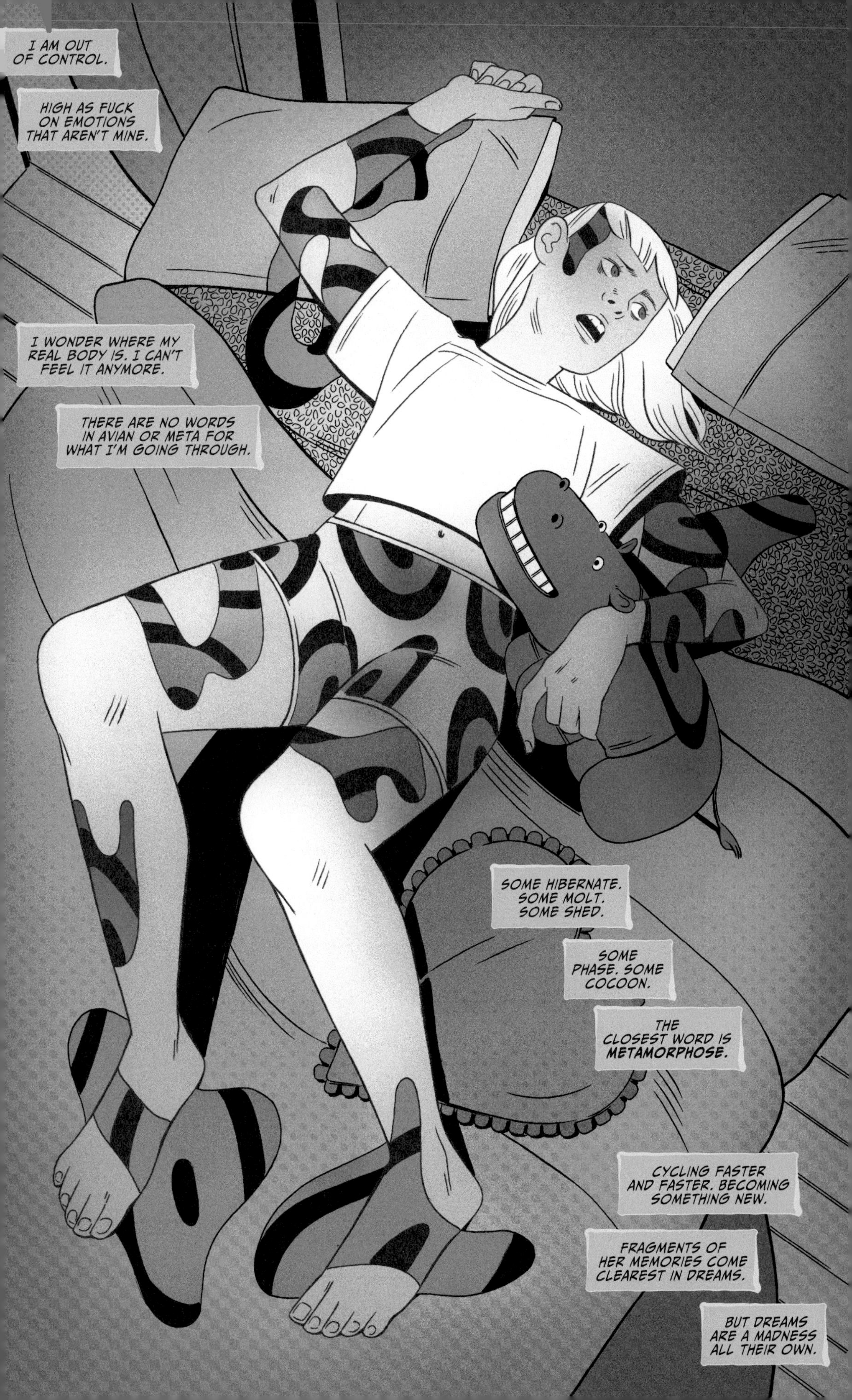
I AM OUT OF CONTROL.
HIGH AS FUCK ON EMOTIONS THAT AREN'T MINE.
I WONDER WHERE MY REAL BODY IS. I CAN'T FEEL IT ANYMORE.
THERE ARE NO WORDS IN AVIAN OR META FOR WHAT I'M GOING THROUGH.
SOME HIBERNATE. SOME MOLT. SOME SHED.
SOME PHASE. SOME COCOON.
THE CLOSEST WORD IS **METAMORPHOSE.**
CYCLING FASTER AND FASTER. BECOMING SOMETHING NEW.
FRAGMENTS OF HER MEMORIES COME CLEAREST IN DREAMS.
BUT DREAMS ARE A MADNESS ALL THEIR OWN.

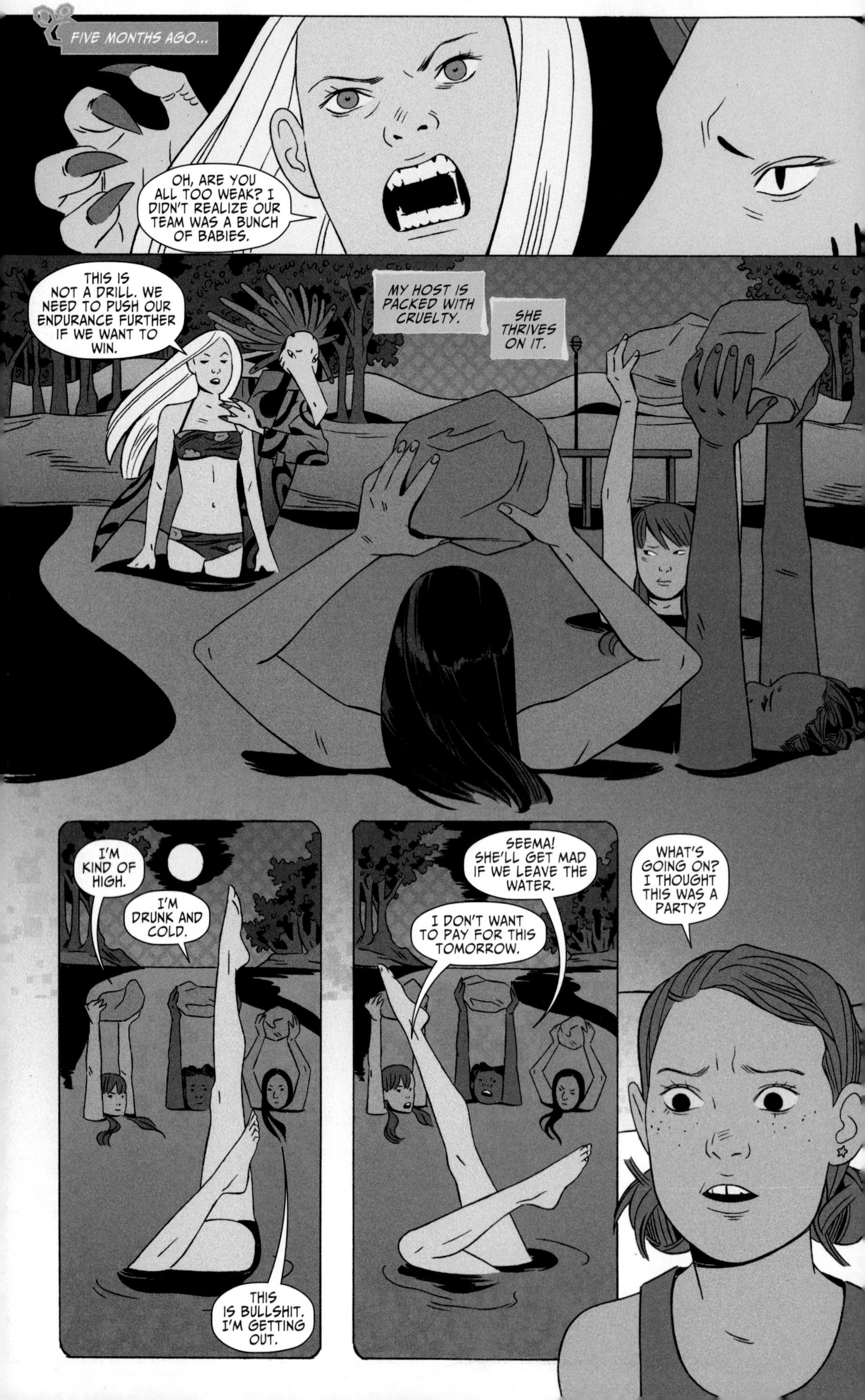
FIVE MONTHS AGO...
OH, ARE YOU ALL TOO WEAK? I DIDN'T REALIZE OUR TEAM WAS A BUNCH OF BABIES.
THIS IS NOT A DRILL. WE NEED TO PUSH OUR ENDURANCE FURTHER IF WE WANT TO WIN.
MY HOST IS PACKED WITH CRUELTY.
SHE THRIVES ON IT.
I'M KIND OF HIGH.
I'M DRUNK AND COLD.
THIS IS BULLSHIT. I'M GETTING OUT.
SEEMA! SHE'LL GET MAD IF WE LEAVE THE WATER.
I DON'T WANT TO PAY FOR THIS TOMORROW.
WHAT'S GOING ON? I THOUGHT THIS WAS A PARTY?

TRAINING NEVER STOPS, TEACUP. GET IN THE WATER.

WATCH CLOSELY AND LEARN, TEACUP. THIS IS HOW WE GET MEDALS. YOU HAVE TO *FLY*.

WITH ROCKS? THIS IS DANGEROUS. THE LAKE ISN'T DEEP ENOUGH. I DON'T HAVE MY NOSE CLIP. LET'S TRY THIS OUT ON THE LAND.

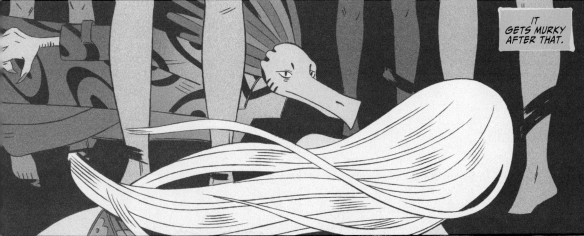

IT GETS MURKY AFTER THAT.

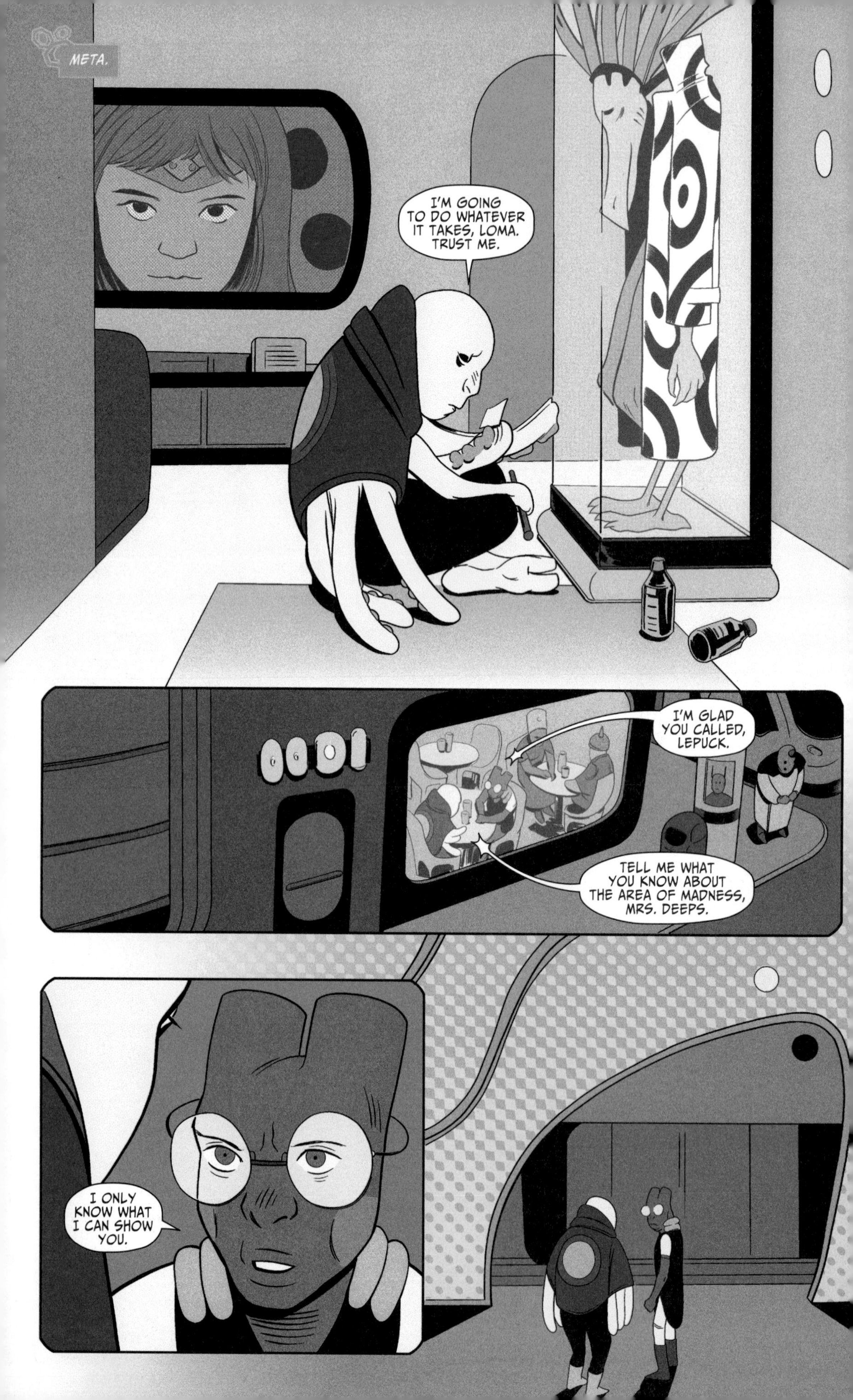
META.
I'M GOING TO DO WHATEVER IT TAKES, LOMA. TRUST ME.
I'M GLAD YOU CALLED, LEPUCK.
TELL ME WHAT YOU KNOW ABOUT THE AREA OF MADNESS, MRS. DEEPS.
I ONLY KNOW WHAT I CAN SHOW YOU.

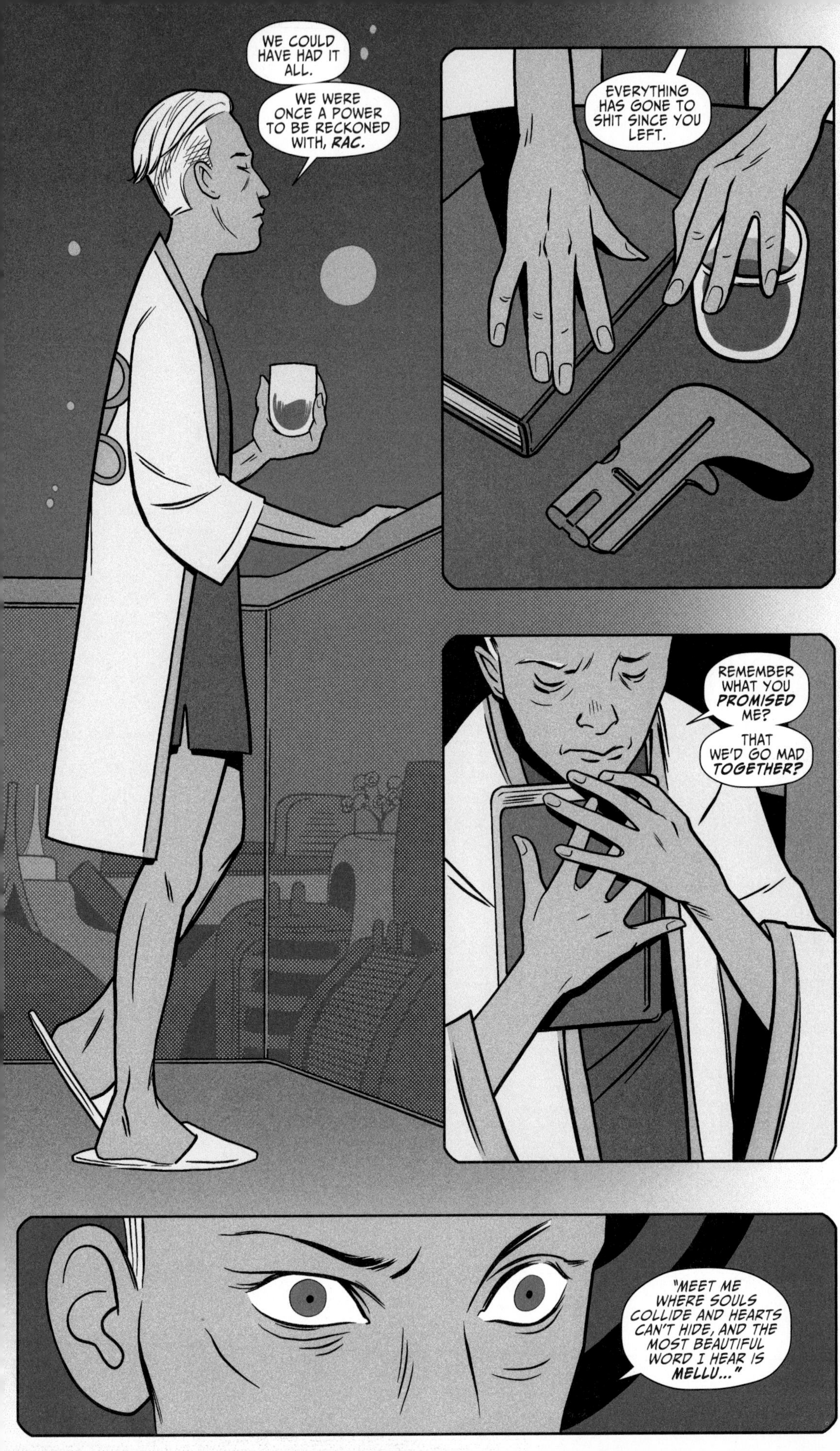
WE COULD HAVE HAD IT ALL.
WE WERE ONCE A POWER TO BE RECKONED WITH, RAC.
EVERYTHING HAS GONE TO SHIT SINCE YOU LEFT.
REMEMBER WHAT YOU PROMISED ME?
THAT WE'D GO MAD TOGETHER?
"MEET ME WHERE SOULS COLLIDE AND HEARTS CAN'T HIDE, AND THE MOST BEAUTIFUL WORD I HEAR IS MELLU..."

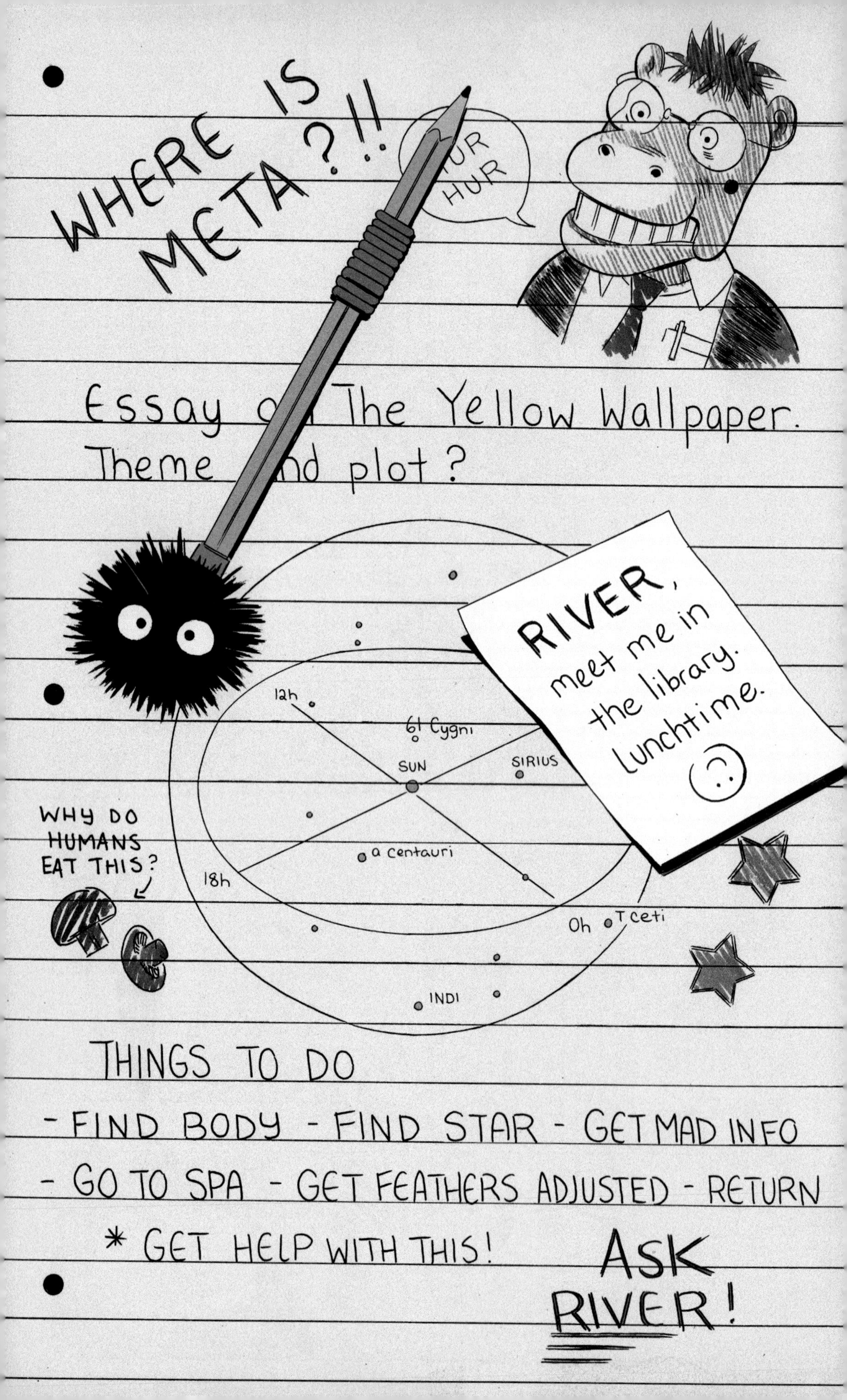
WHERE IS META?!!
HUR HUR
Essay o The Yellow Wallpaper.
Theme nd plot?
RIVER, meet me in the library. Lunchtime. :)
12h
61 Cygni
SUN
SIRIUS
a centauri
18h
0h
T ceti
INDI
WHY DO HUMANS EAT THIS?
THINGS TO DO
- FIND BODY - FIND STAR - GET MAD INFO
- GO TO SPA - GET FEATHERS ADJUSTED - RETURN
* GET HELP WITH THIS!
ASK RIVER!

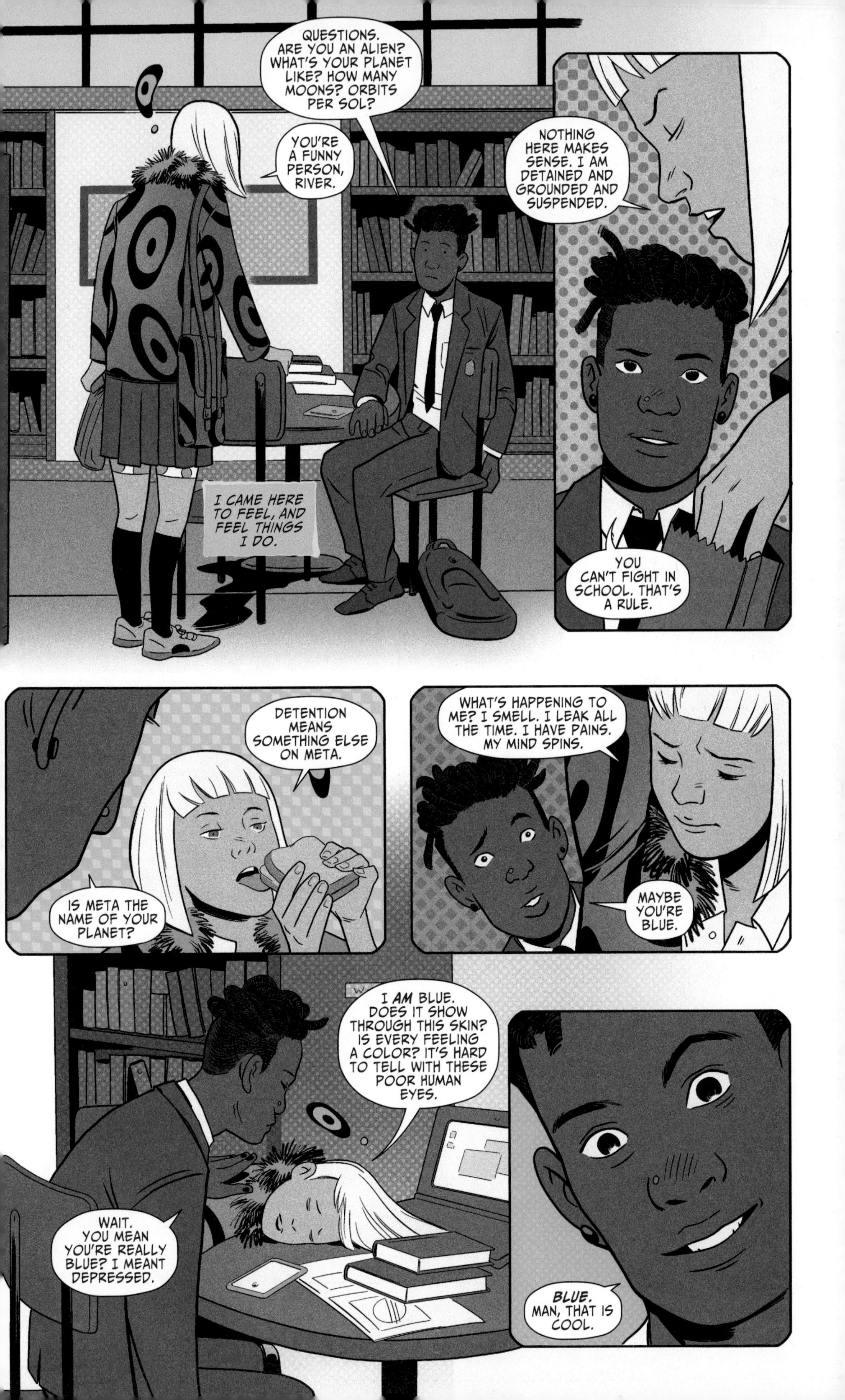
QUESTIONS. ARE YOU AN ALIEN? WHAT'S YOUR PLANET LIKE? HOW MANY MOONS? ORBITS PER SOL?
YOU'RE A FUNNY PERSON, RIVER.
I CAME HERE TO FEEL, AND FEEL THINGS I DO.
NOTHING HERE MAKES SENSE. I AM DETAINED AND GROUNDED AND SUSPENDED.
YOU CAN'T FIGHT IN SCHOOL. THAT'S A RULE.
DETENTION MEANS SOMETHING ELSE ON META.
IS META THE NAME OF YOUR PLANET?
WHAT'S HAPPENING TO ME? I SMELL. I LEAK ALL THE TIME. I HAVE PAINS. MY MIND SPINS.
MAYBE YOU'RE BLUE.
I AM BLUE. DOES IT SHOW THROUGH THIS SKIN? IS EVERY FEELING A COLOR? IT'S HARD TO TELL WITH THESE POOR HUMAN EYES.
WAIT. YOU MEAN YOU'RE REALLY BLUE? I MEANT DEPRESSED.
BLUE. MAN, THAT IS COOL.

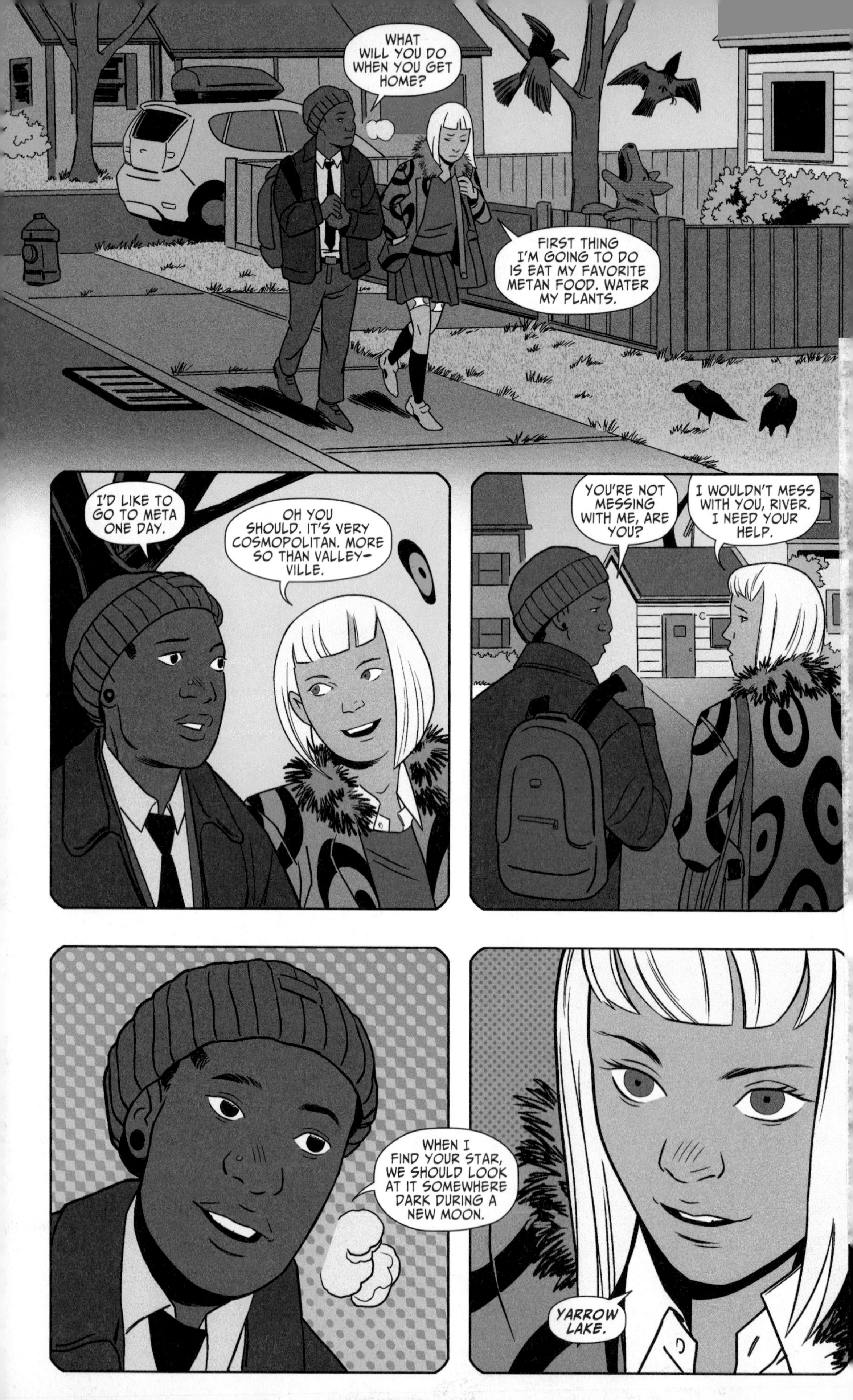
WHAT WILL YOU DO WHEN YOU GET HOME?
FIRST THING I'M GOING TO DO IS EAT MY FAVORITE METAN FOOD. WATER MY PLANTS.
I'D LIKE TO GO TO META ONE DAY.
OH YOU SHOULD. IT'S VERY COSMOPOLITAN. MORE SO THAN VALLEY-VILLE.
YOU'RE NOT MESSING WITH ME, ARE YOU?
I WOULDN'T MESS WITH YOU, RIVER. I NEED YOUR HELP.
WHEN I FIND YOUR STAR, WE SHOULD LOOK AT IT SOMEWHERE DARK DURING A NEW MOON.
YARROW LAKE.

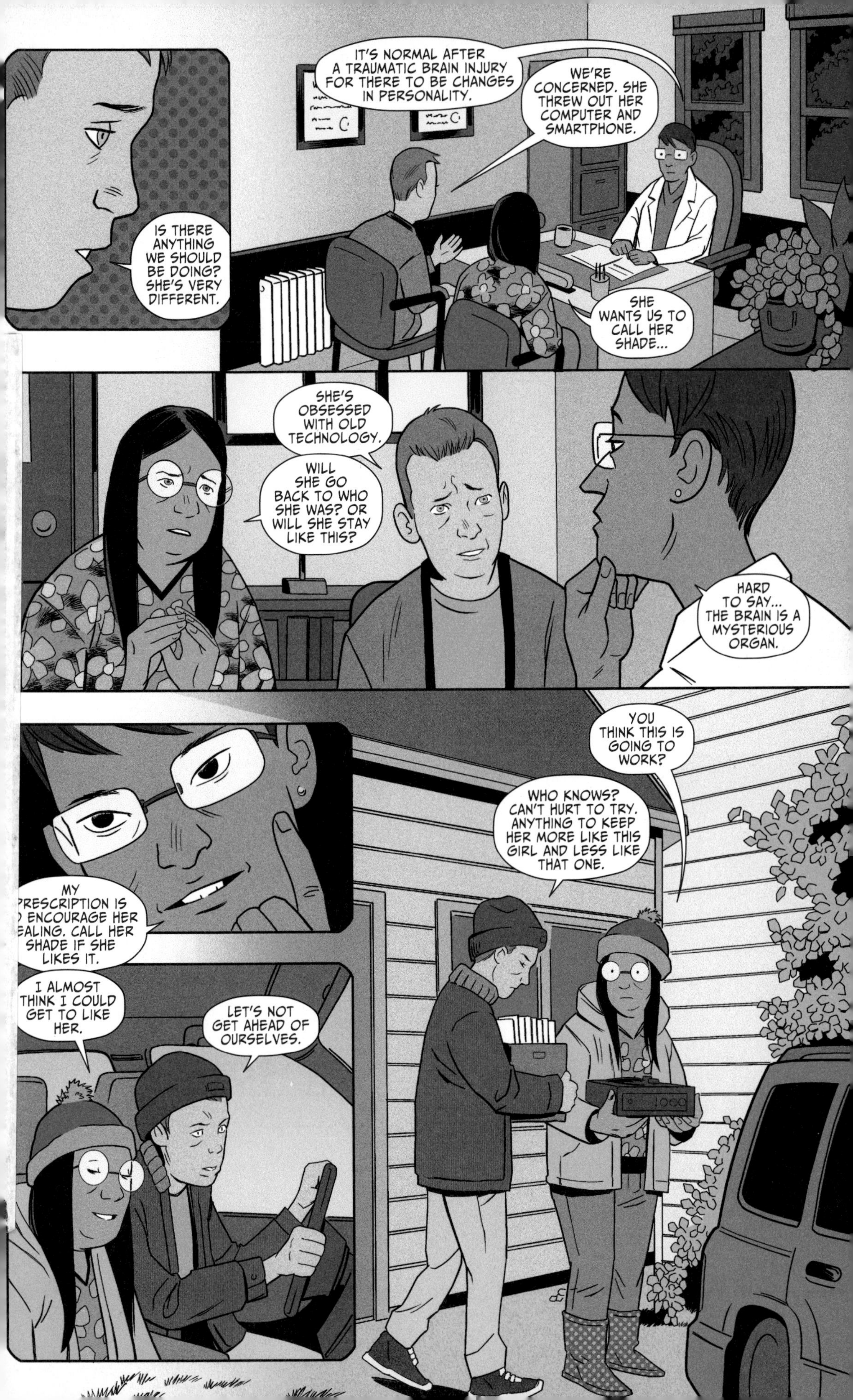
IS THERE ANYTHING WE SHOULD BE DOING? SHE'S VERY DIFFERENT.
IT'S NORMAL AFTER A TRAUMATIC BRAIN INJURY FOR THERE TO BE CHANGES IN PERSONALITY.
WE'RE CONCERNED. SHE THREW OUT HER COMPUTER AND SMARTPHONE.
SHE WANTS US TO CALL HER SHADE...
SHE'S OBSESSED WITH OLD TECHNOLOGY.
WILL SHE GO BACK TO WHO SHE WAS? OR WILL SHE STAY LIKE THIS?
HARD TO SAY... THE BRAIN IS A MYSTERIOUS ORGAN.
MY PRESCRIPTION IS ENCOURAGE HER EALING. CALL HER SHADE IF SHE LIKES IT.
I ALMOST THINK I COULD GET TO LIKE HER.
LET'S NOT GET AHEAD OF OURSELVES.
YOU THINK THIS IS GOING TO WORK?
WHO KNOWS? CAN'T HURT TO TRY. ANYTHING TO KEEP HER MORE LIKE THIS GIRL AND LESS LIKE THAT ONE.

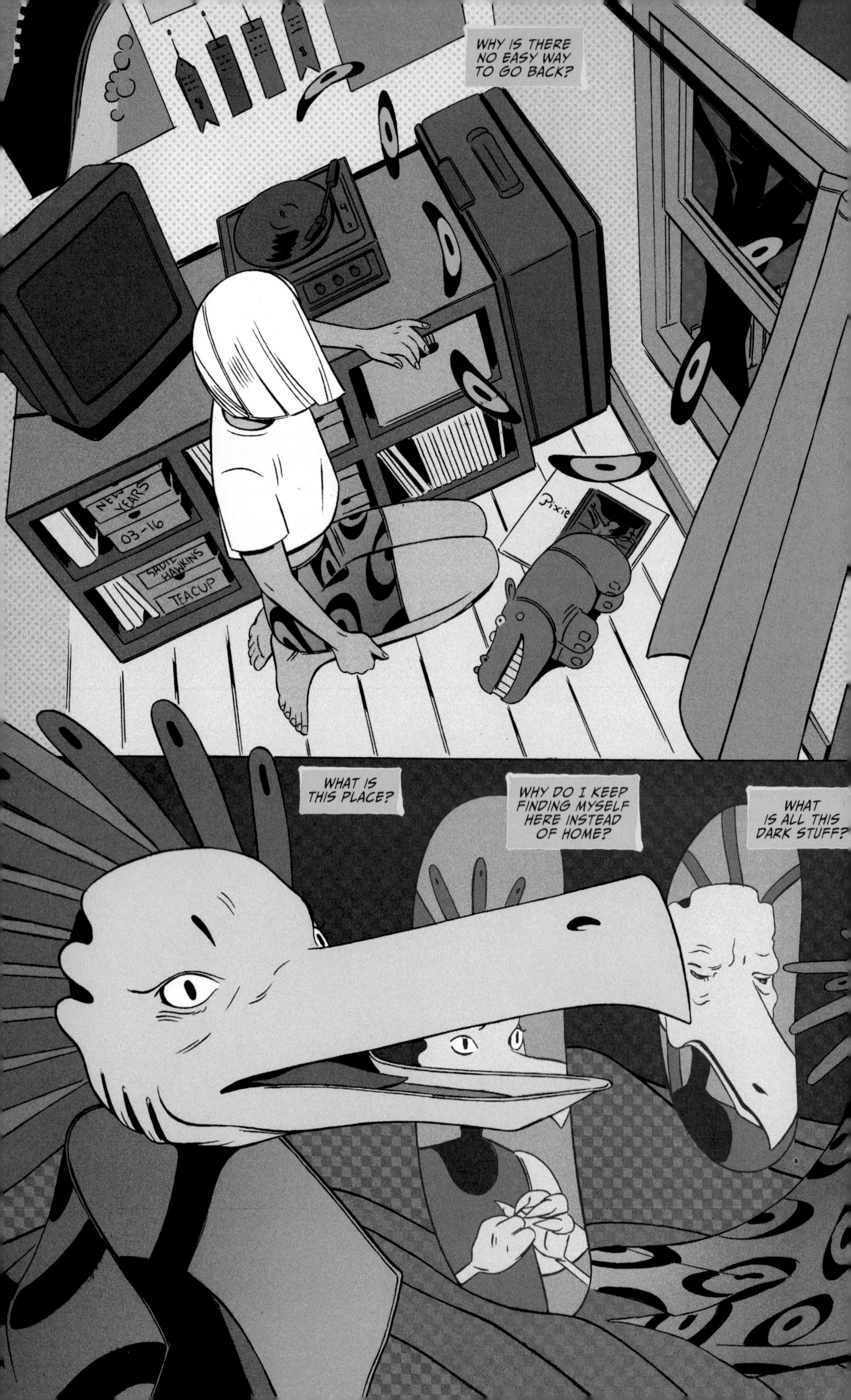
WHY IS THERE NO EASY WAY TO GO BACK?
NEW YEARS
03-16
SADIE HAWKINS
TEACUP
Pixie
WHAT IS THIS PLACE?
WHY DO I KEEP FINDING MYSELF HERE INSTEAD OF HOME?
WHAT IS ALL THIS DARK STUFF?

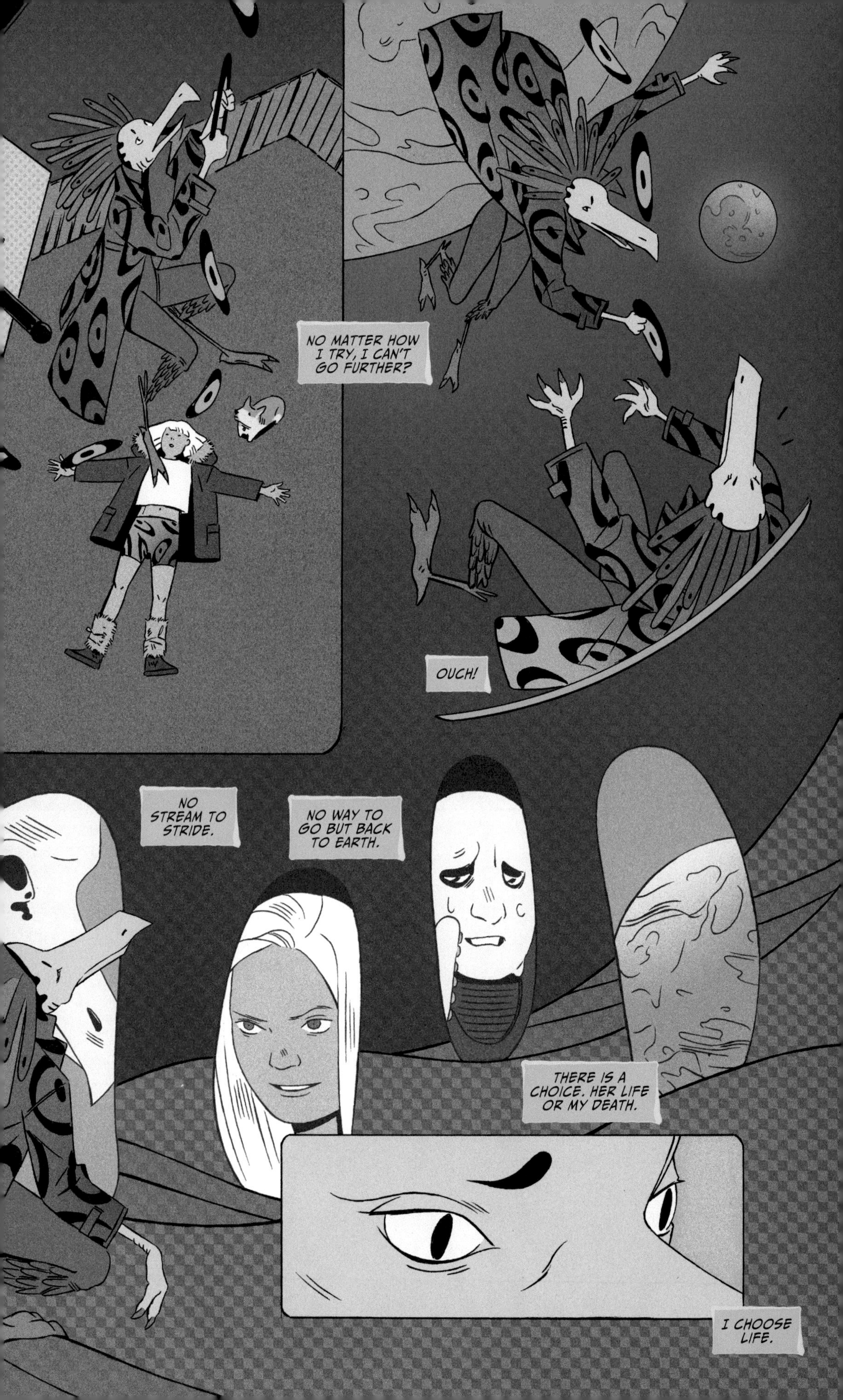
NO MATTER HOW I TRY, I CAN'T GO FURTHER?
OUCH!
NO STREAM TO STRIDE.
NO WAY TO GO BUT BACK TO EARTH.
THERE IS A CHOICE. HER LIFE OR MY DEATH.
I CHOOSE LIFE.

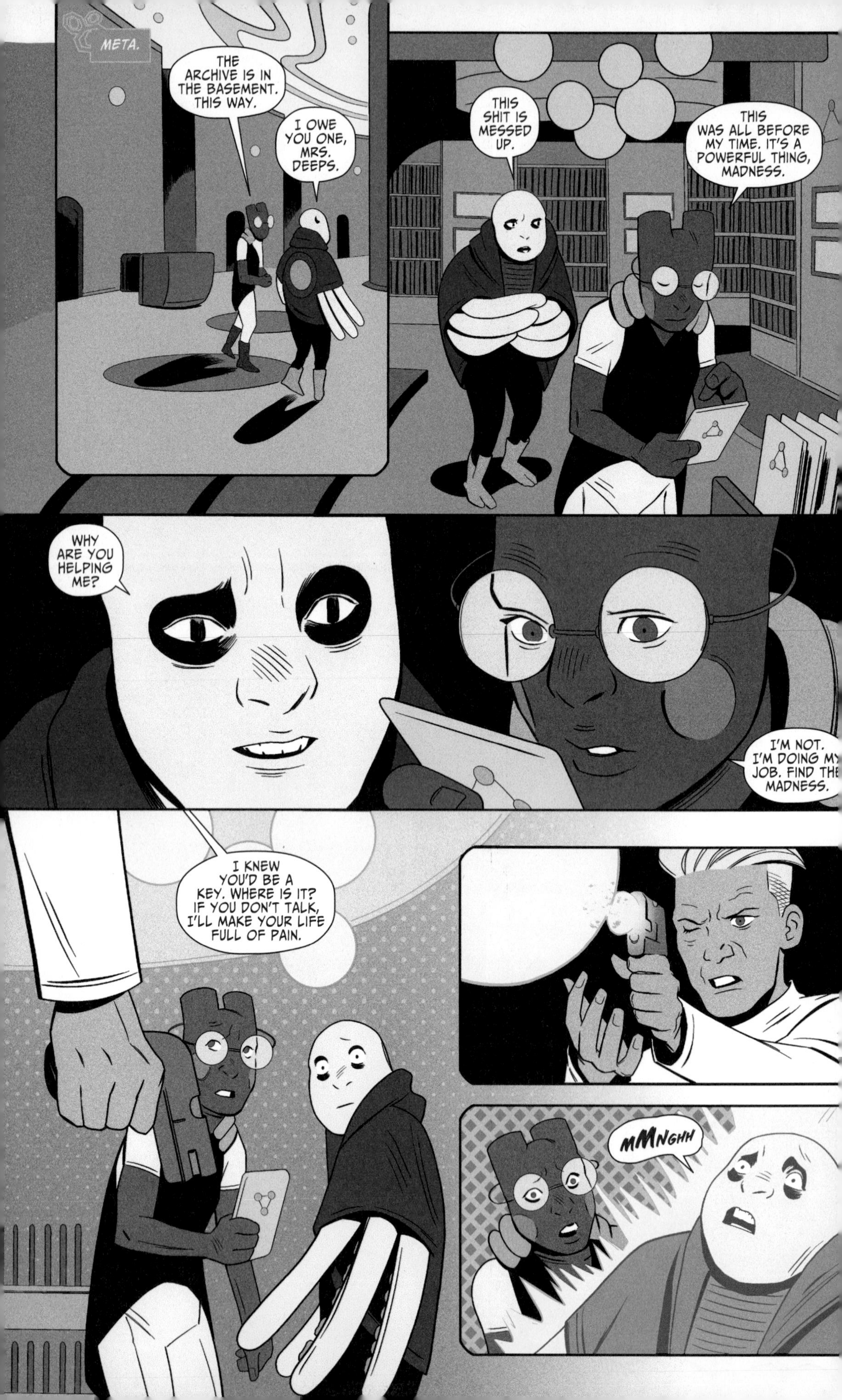
META.
THE ARCHIVE IS IN THE BASEMENT. THIS WAY.
I OWE YOU ONE, MRS. DEEPS.
THIS SHIT IS MESSED UP.
THIS WAS ALL BEFORE MY TIME. IT'S A POWERFUL THING, MADNESS.
WHY ARE YOU HELPING ME?
I'M NOT. I'M DOING MY JOB. FIND THE MADNESS.
I KNEW YOU'D BE A KEY. WHERE IS IT? IF YOU DON'T TALK, I'LL MAKE YOUR LIFE FULL OF PAIN.
MMNGHH

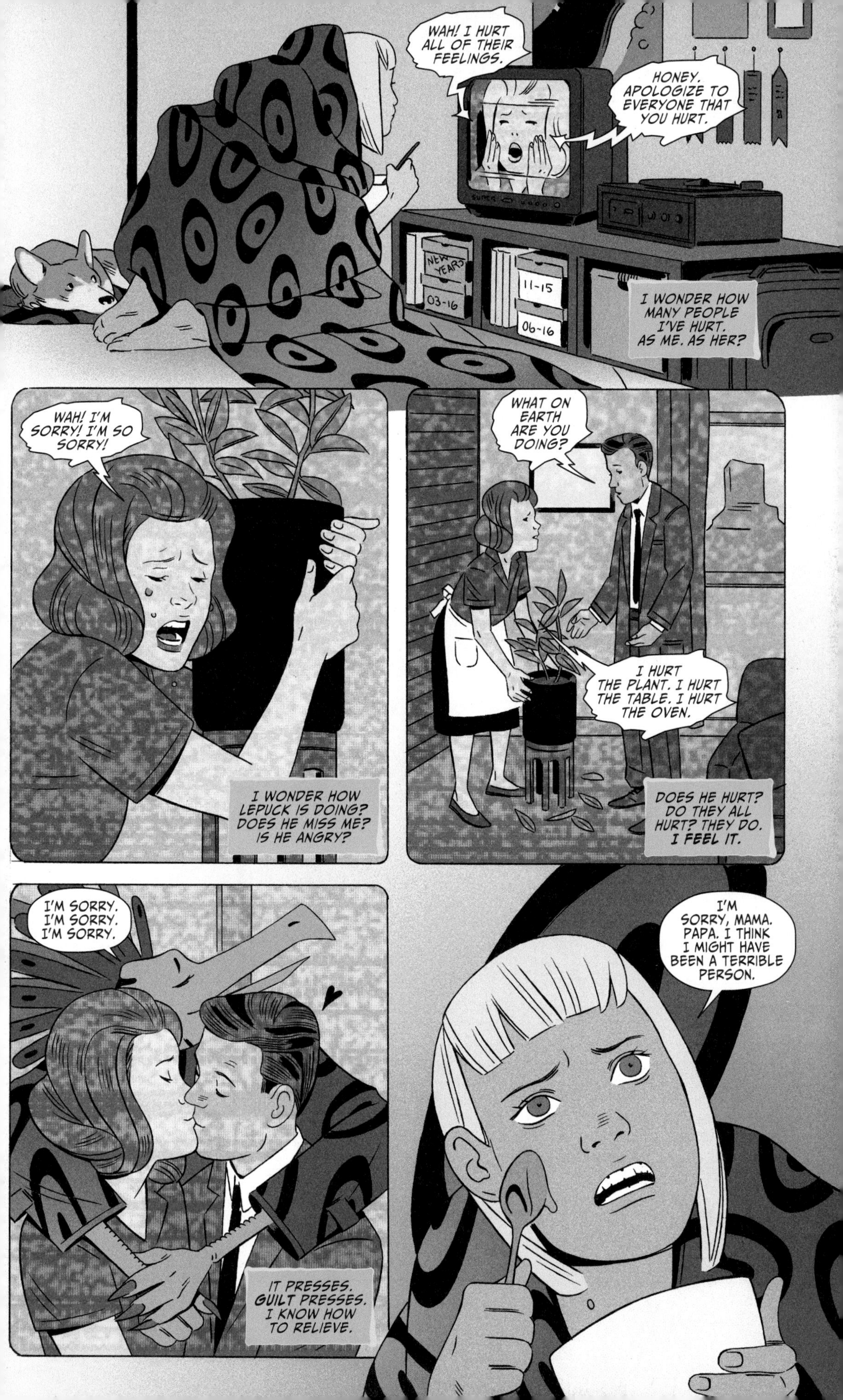
WAH! I HURT ALL OF THEIR FEELINGS.
HONEY. APOLOGIZE TO EVERYONE THAT YOU HURT.
NEW YEARS
03-16
11-15
06-16
I WONDER HOW MANY PEOPLE I'VE HURT. AS ME. AS HER?
WAH! I'M SORRY! I'M SO SORRY!
I WONDER HOW LEPUCK IS DOING? DOES HE MISS ME? IS HE ANGRY?
WHAT ON EARTH ARE YOU DOING?
I HURT THE PLANT. I HURT THE TABLE. I HURT THE OVEN.
DOES HE HURT? DO THEY ALL HURT? THEY DO. I FEEL IT.
I'M SORRY. I'M SORRY. I'M SORRY.
IT PRESSES. GUILT PRESSES. I KNOW HOW TO RELIEVE.
I'M SORRY, MAMA. PAPA. I THINK I MIGHT HAVE BEEN A TERRIBLE PERSON.

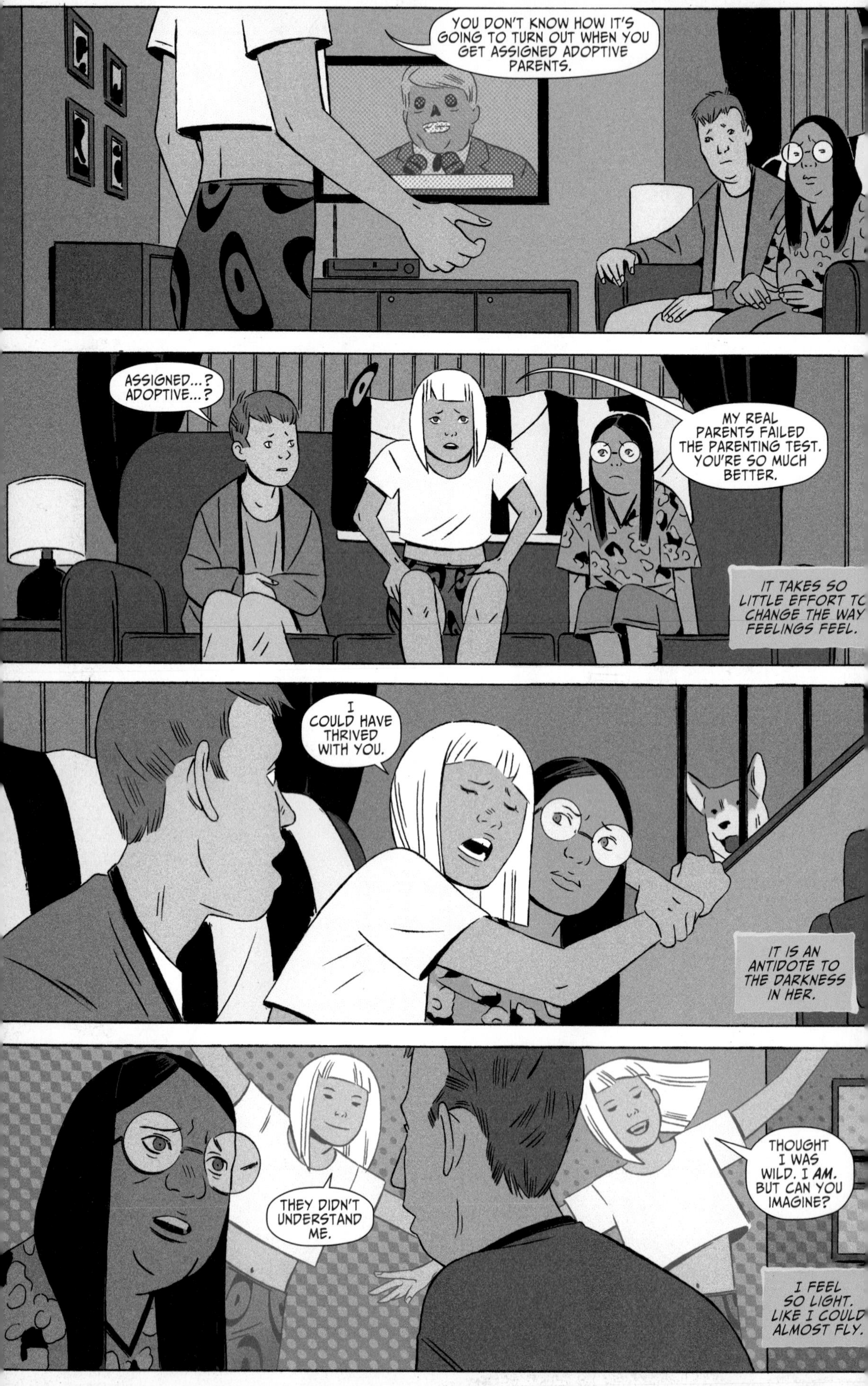
YOU DON'T KNOW HOW IT'S GOING TO TURN OUT WHEN YOU GET ASSIGNED ADOPTIVE PARENTS.
ASSIGNED...? ADOPTIVE...?
MY REAL PARENTS FAILED THE PARENTING TEST. YOU'RE SO MUCH BETTER.
IT TAKES SO LITTLE EFFORT TO CHANGE THE WAY FEELINGS FEEL.
I COULD HAVE THRIVED WITH YOU.
IT IS AN ANTIDOTE TO THE DARKNESS IN HER.
THEY DIDN'T UNDERSTAND ME.
THOUGHT I WAS WILD. I *AM.* BUT CAN YOU IMAGINE?
I FEEL SO LIGHT. LIKE I COULD ALMOST FLY.

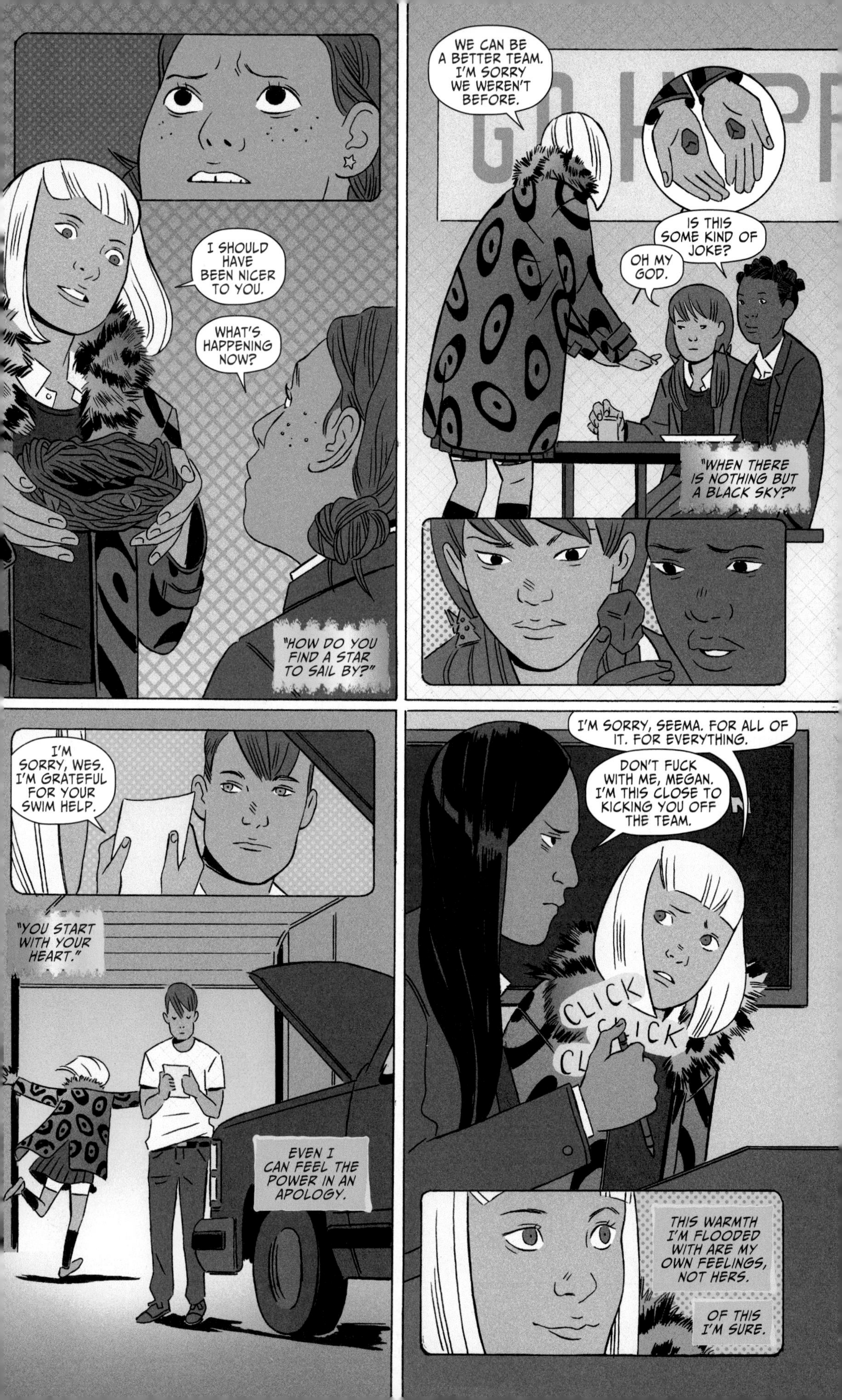
I SHOULD HAVE BEEN NICER TO YOU.
WHAT'S HAPPENING NOW?
"HOW DO YOU FIND A STAR TO SAIL BY?"
WE CAN BE A BETTER TEAM. I'M SORRY WE WEREN'T BEFORE.
IS THIS SOME KIND OF JOKE?
OH MY GOD.
"WHEN THERE IS NOTHING BUT A BLACK SKY?"
I'M SORRY, WES. I'M GRATEFUL FOR YOUR SWIM HELP.
"YOU START WITH YOUR HEART."
EVEN I CAN FEEL THE POWER IN AN APOLOGY.
I'M SORRY, SEEMA. FOR ALL OF IT. FOR EVERYTHING.
DON'T FUCK WITH ME, MEGAN. I'M THIS CLOSE TO KICKING YOU OFF THE TEAM.
CLICK
CLICK
CLICK
THIS WARMTH I'M FLOODED WITH ARE MY OWN FEELINGS, NOT HERS.
OF THIS I'M SURE.

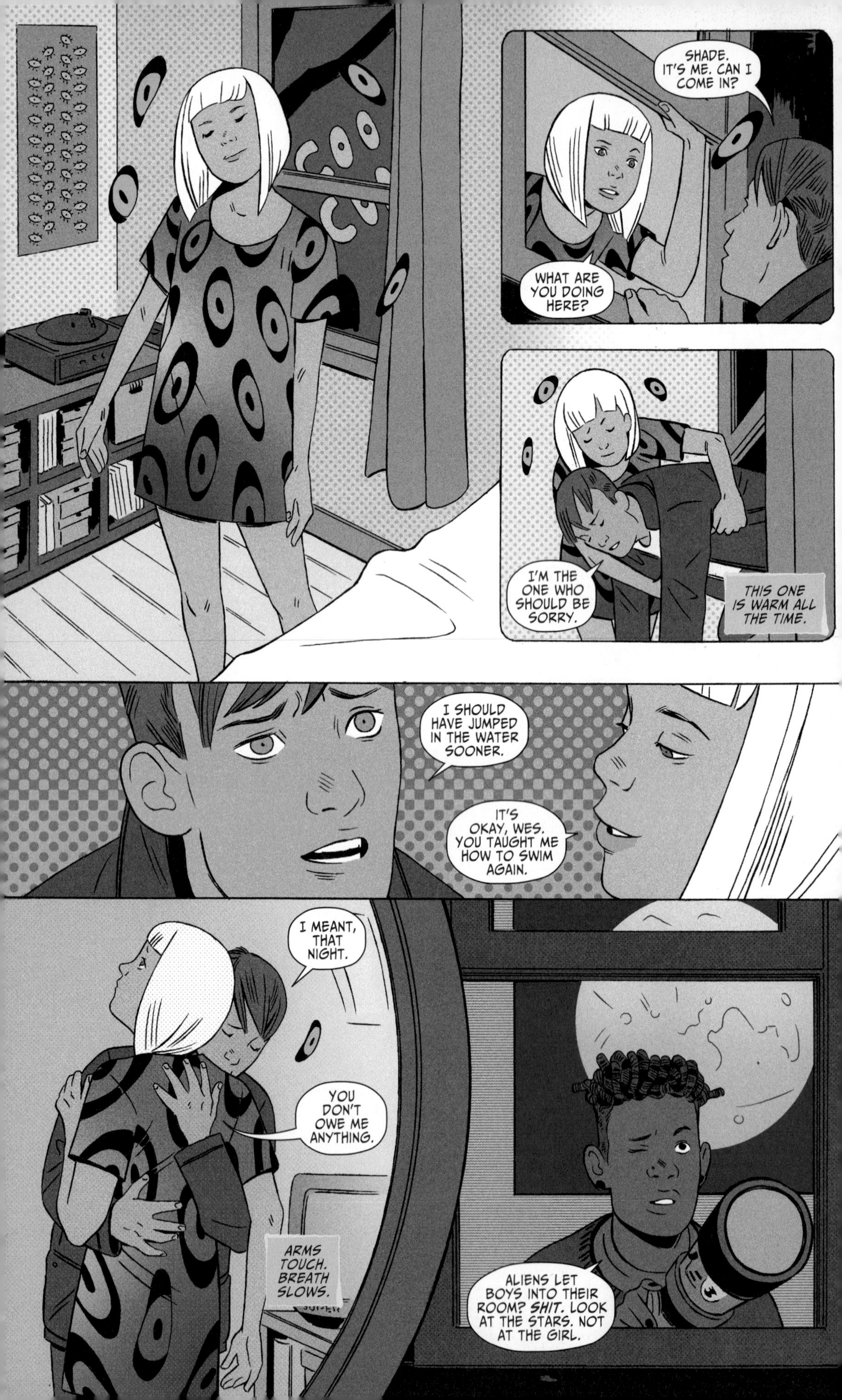

SHADE. IT'S ME. CAN I COME IN?
WHAT ARE YOU DOING HERE?
I'M THE ONE WHO SHOULD BE SORRY.
THIS ONE IS WARM ALL THE TIME.
I SHOULD HAVE JUMPED IN THE WATER SOONER.
IT'S OKAY, WES. YOU TAUGHT ME HOW TO SWIM AGAIN.
I MEANT, THAT NIGHT.
YOU DON'T OWE ME ANYTHING.
ARMS TOUCH. BREATH SLOWS.
ALIENS LET BOYS INTO THEIR ROOM? *SHIT*. LOOK AT THE STARS. NOT AT THE GIRL.

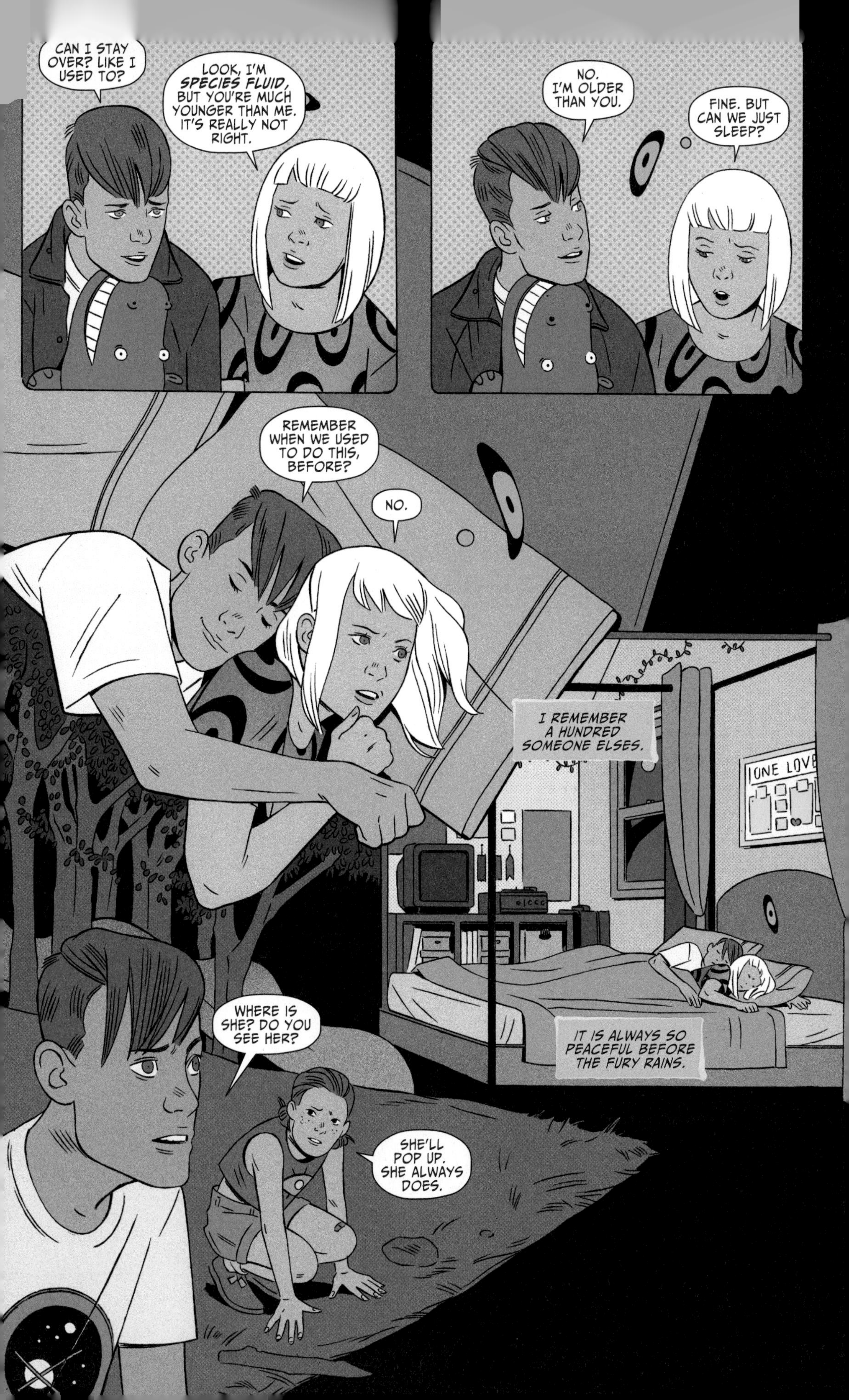
CAN I STAY OVER? LIKE I USED TO?
LOOK, I'M SPECIES FLUID, BUT YOU'RE MUCH YOUNGER THAN ME. IT'S REALLY NOT RIGHT.
NO. I'M OLDER THAN YOU.
FINE. BUT CAN WE JUST SLEEP?
REMEMBER WHEN WE USED TO DO THIS, BEFORE?
NO.
I REMEMBER A HUNDRED SOMEONE ELSES.
ONE LOVE
IT IS ALWAYS SO PEACEFUL BEFORE THE FURY RAINS.
WHERE IS SHE? DO YOU SEE HER?
SHE'LL POP UP. SHE ALWAYS DOES.

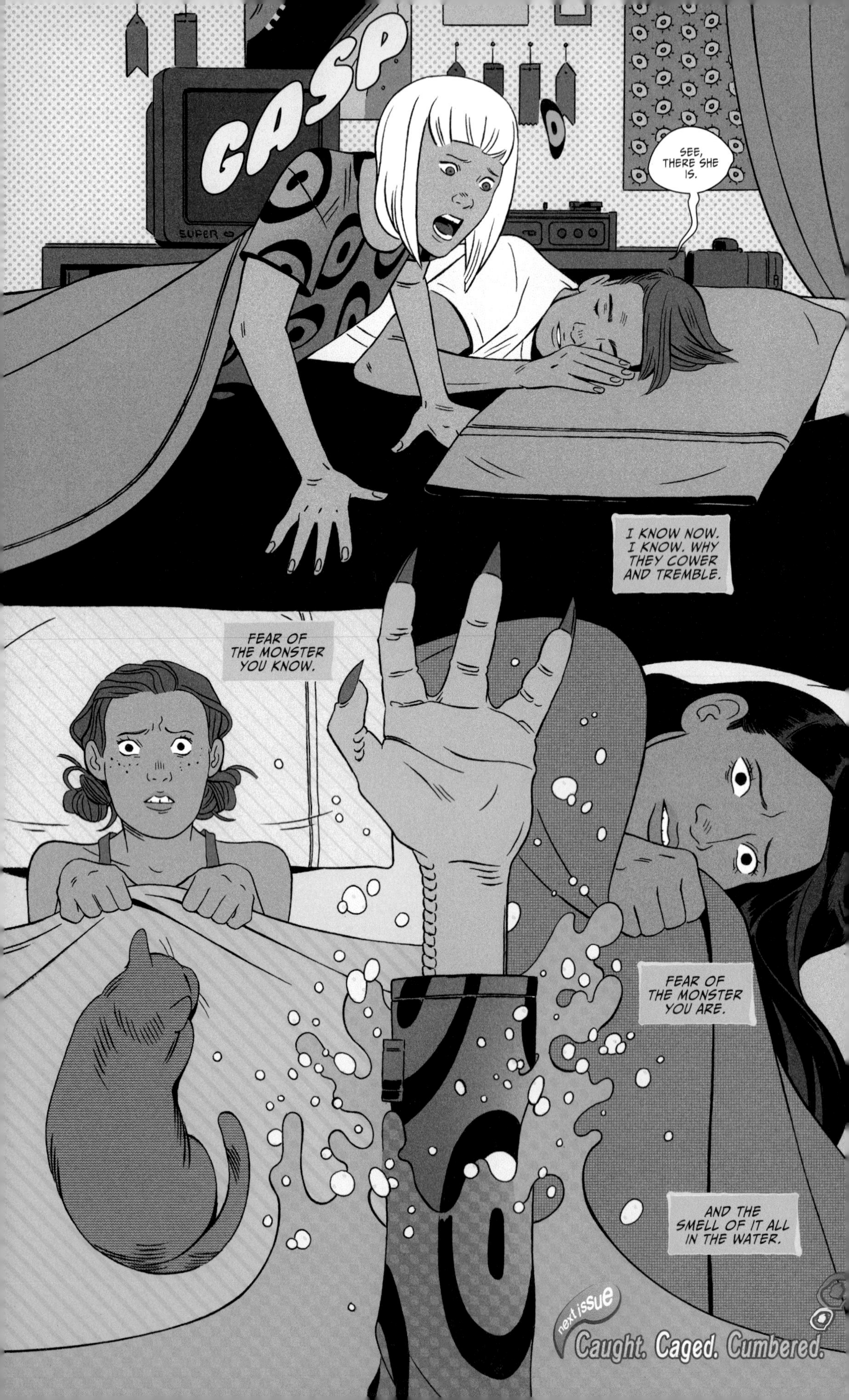
GASP
SUPER
SEE, THERE SHE IS.
I KNOW NOW. I KNOW. WHY THEY COWER AND TREMBLE.
FEAR OF THE MONSTER YOU KNOW.
FEAR OF THE MONSTER YOU ARE.
AND THE SMELL OF IT ALL IN THE WATER.
next issue
Caught. Caged. Cumbered.

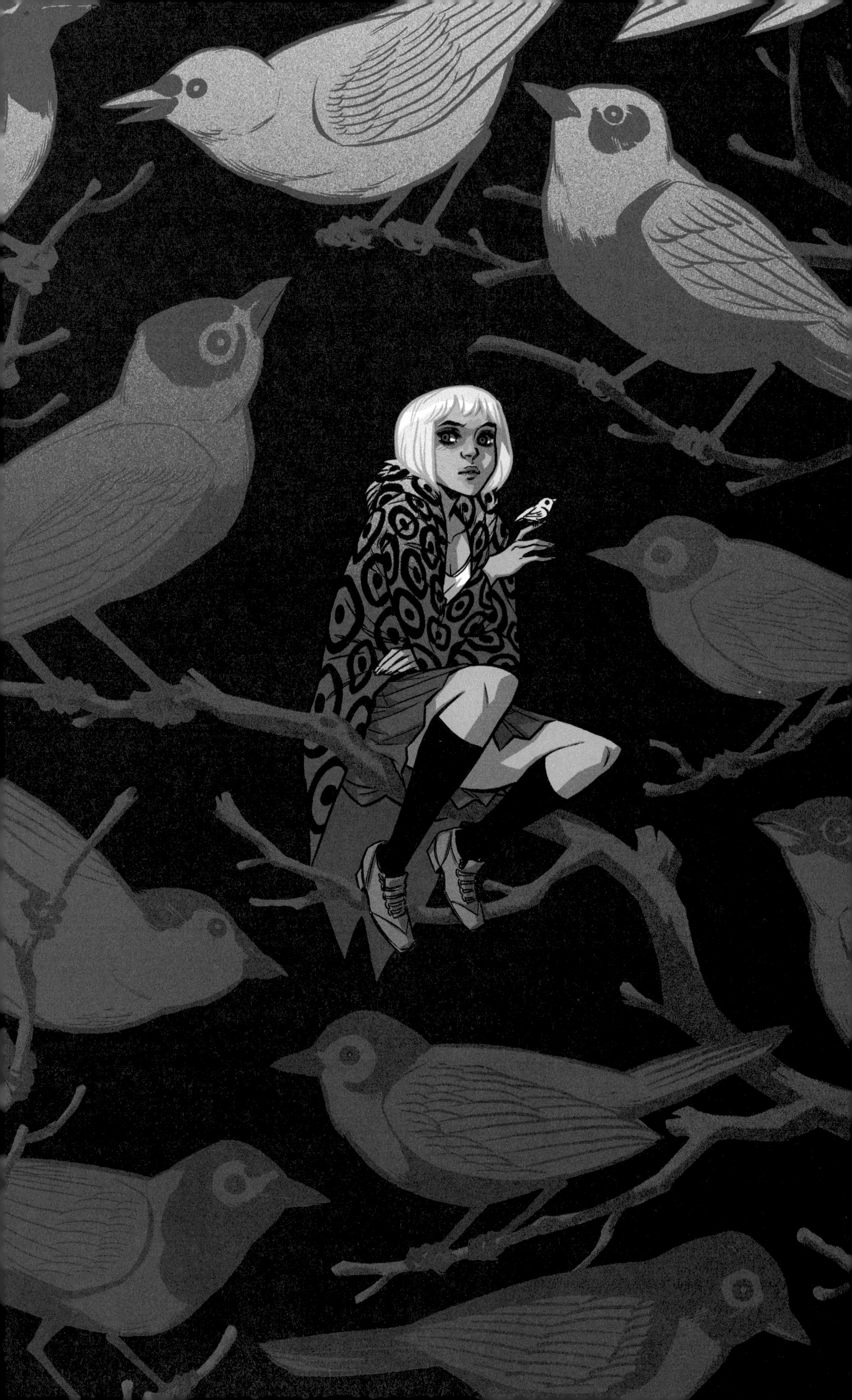

Variant cover art by Jenny Frison

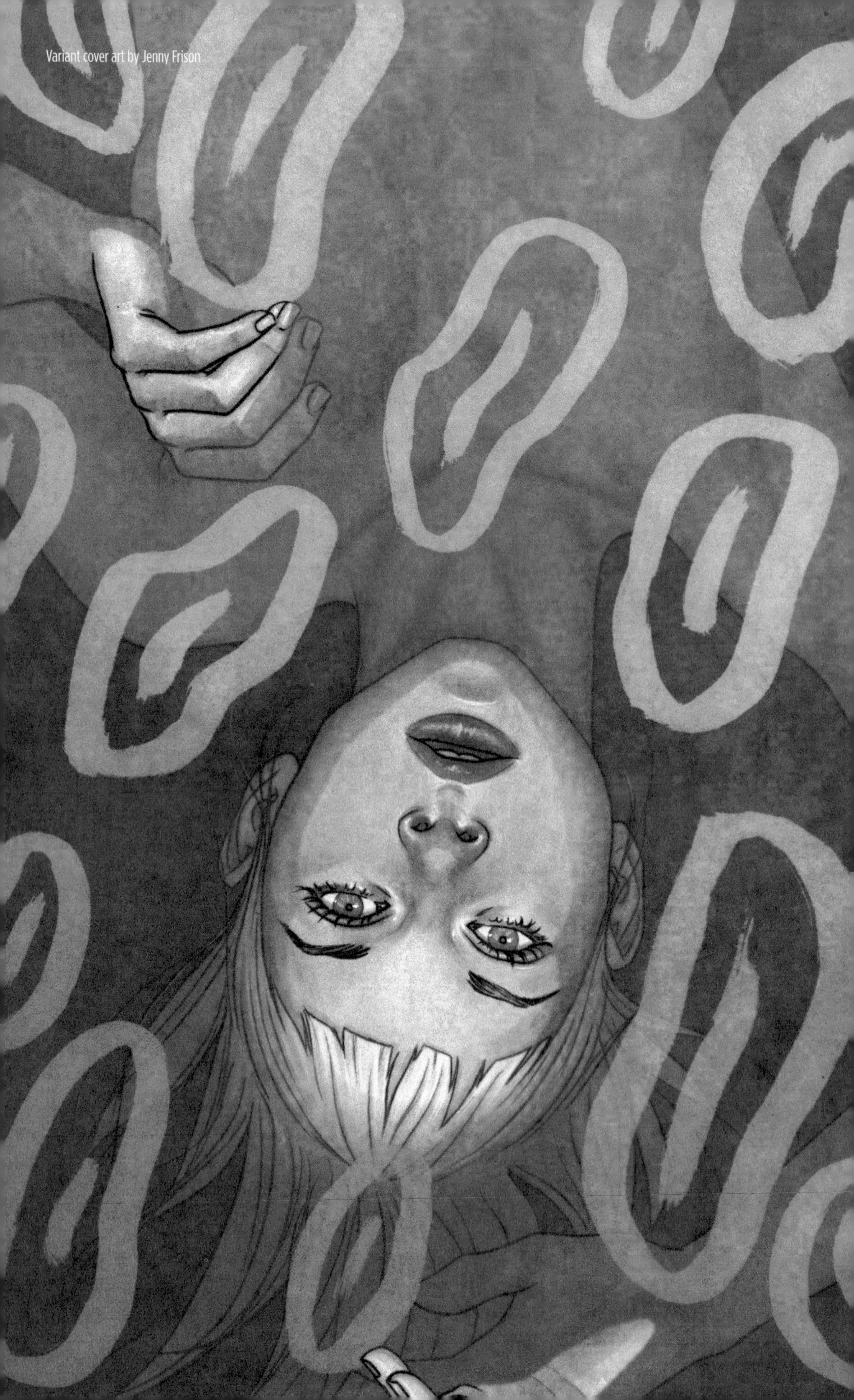

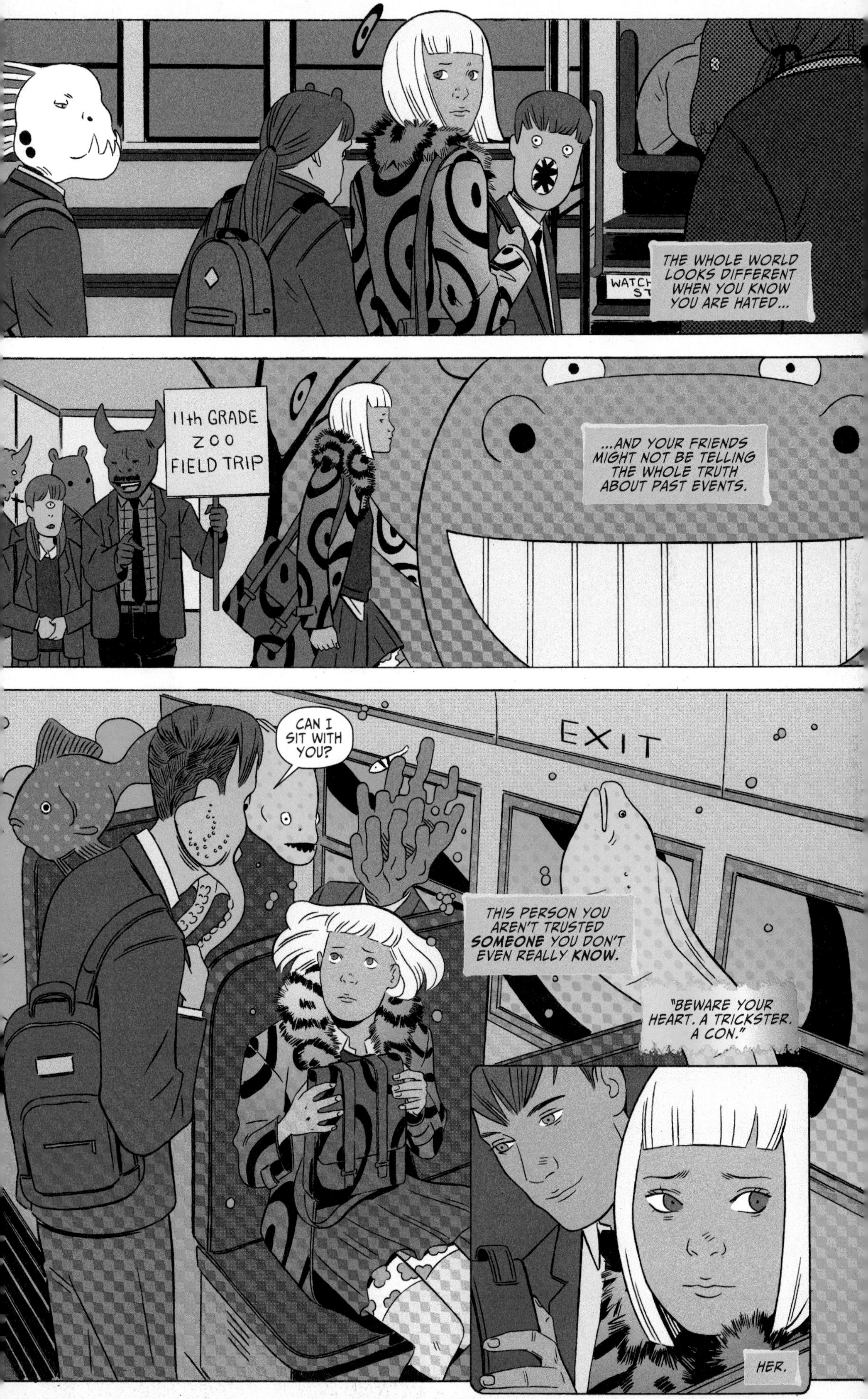
WATCH ST
THE WHOLE WORLD LOOKS DIFFERENT WHEN YOU KNOW YOU ARE HATED...
11th GRADE ZOO FIELD TRIP
...AND YOUR FRIENDS MIGHT NOT BE TELLING THE WHOLE TRUTH ABOUT PAST EVENTS.
EXIT
CAN I SIT WITH YOU?
THIS PERSON YOU AREN'T TRUSTED **SOMEONE** YOU DON'T EVEN REALLY **KNOW.**
"BEWARE YOUR HEART. A TRICKSTER. A CON."
HER.

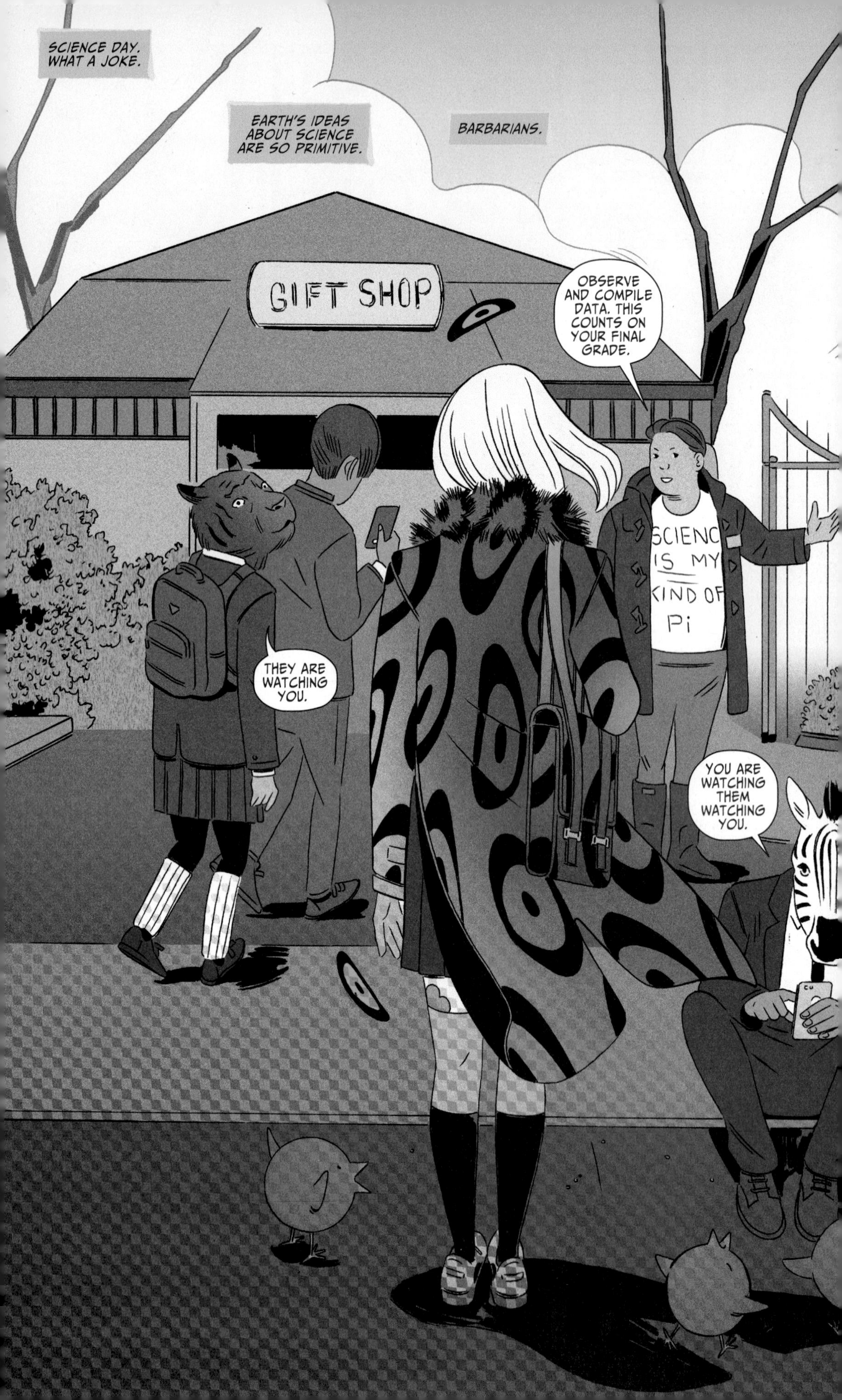
SCIENCE DAY. WHAT A JOKE.
EARTH'S IDEAS ABOUT SCIENCE ARE SO PRIMITIVE.
BARBARIANS.
GIFT SHOP
OBSERVE AND COMPILE DATA. THIS COUNTS ON YOUR FINAL GRADE.
SCIENC IS MY KIND OF Pi
THEY ARE WATCHING YOU.
YOU ARE WATCHING THEM WATCHING YOU.

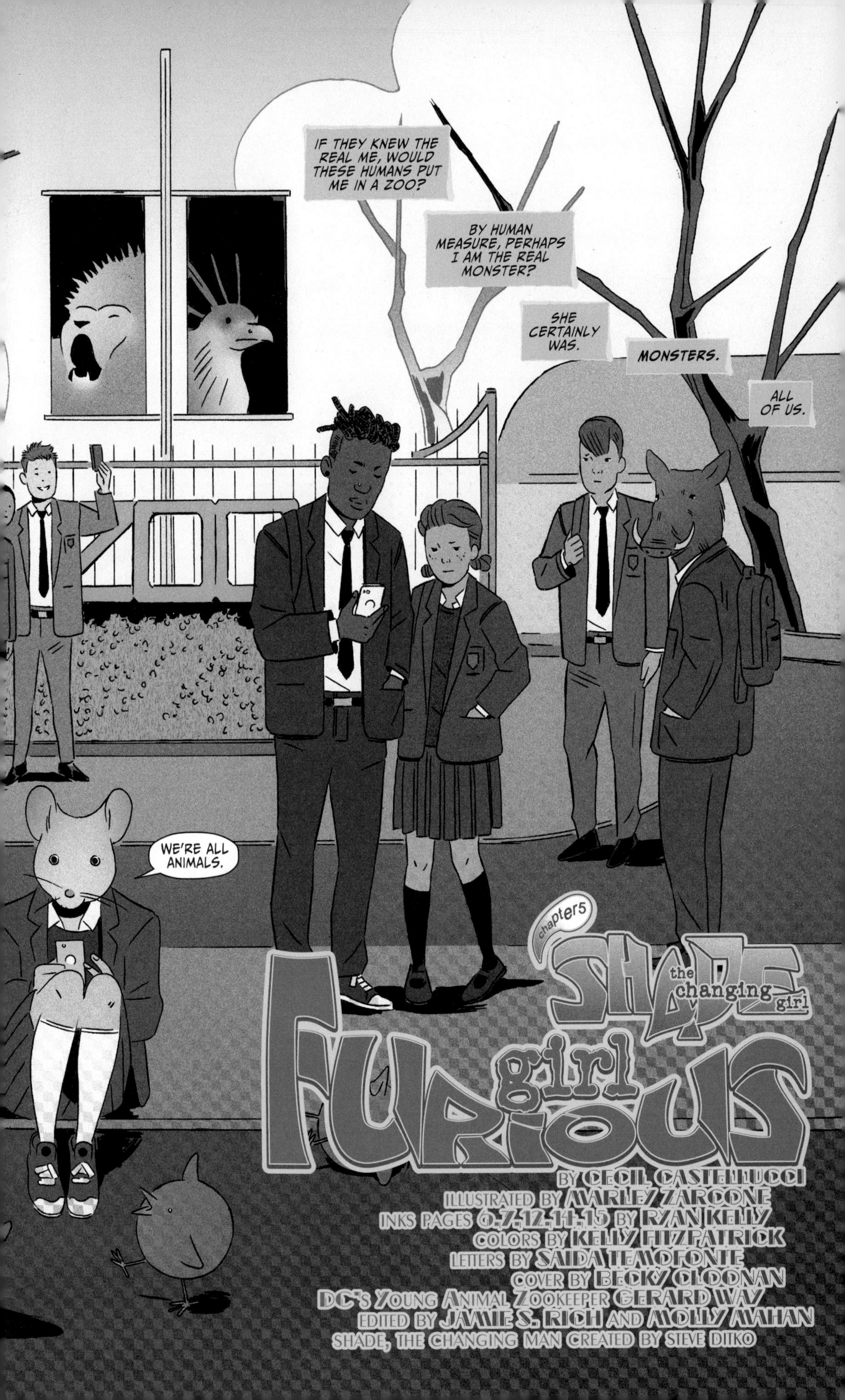
IF THEY KNEW THE REAL ME, WOULD THESE HUMANS PUT ME IN A ZOO?
BY HUMAN MEASURE, PERHAPS I AM THE REAL MONSTER?
SHE CERTAINLY WAS.
MONSTERS.
ALL OF US.
WE'RE ALL ANIMALS.
chapter5
SHADE the changing girl
girl FURIOUS
BY CECIL CASTELLUCCI
ILLUSTRATED BY MARLEY ZARCONE
INKS PAGES 6,7,12,14,15 BY RYAN KELLY
COLORS BY KELLY FITZPATRICK
LETTERS BY SAIDA TEMOFONTE
COVER BY BECKY CLOONAN
DC'S YOUNG ANIMAL ZOOKEEPER GERARD WAY
EDITED BY JAMIE S. RICH AND MOLLY MAHAN
SHADE, THE CHANGING MAN CREATED BY STEVE DITKO

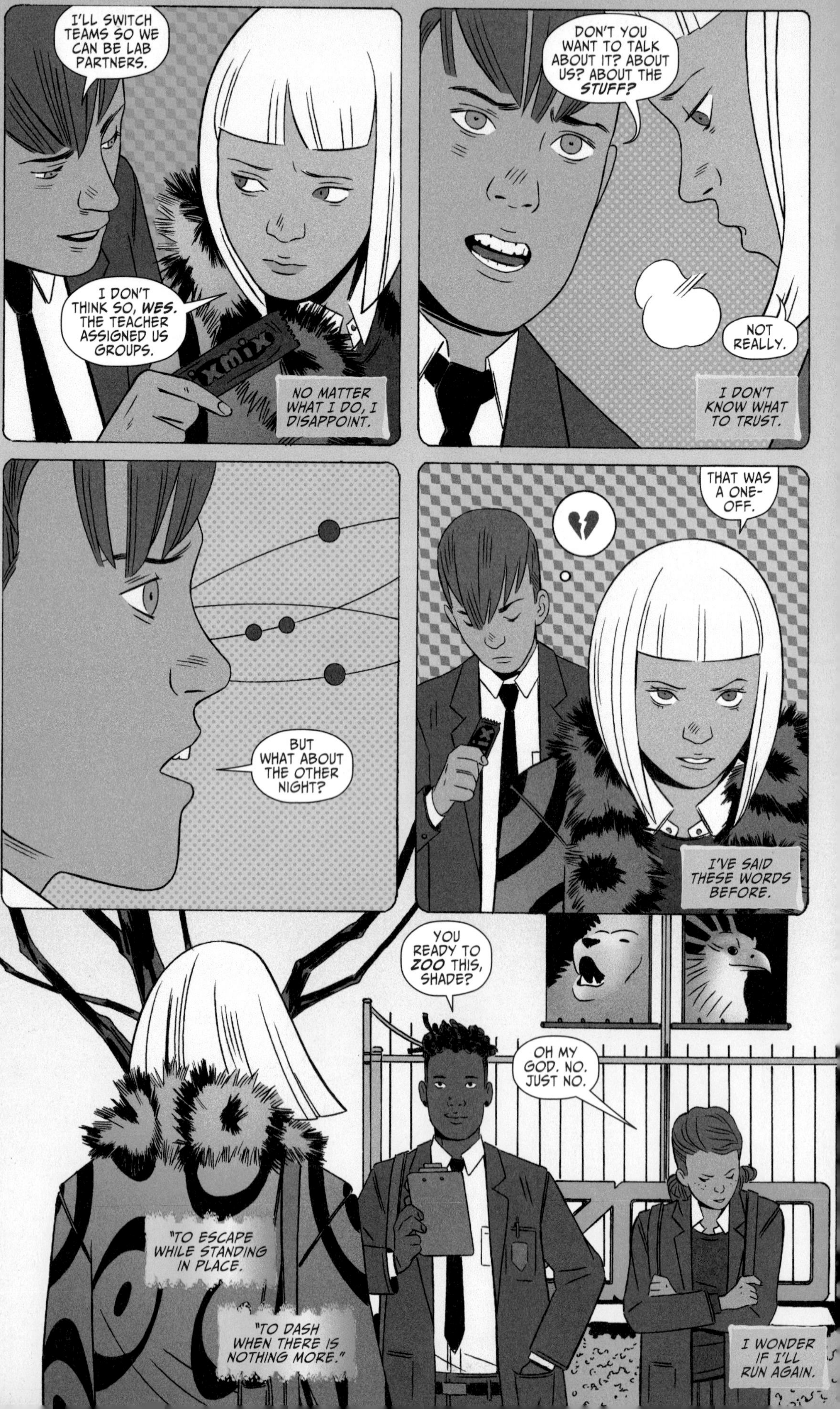
I'LL SWITCH TEAMS SO WE CAN BE LAB PARTNERS.
I DON'T THINK SO, WES. THE TEACHER ASSIGNED US GROUPS.
XMIX
NO MATTER WHAT I DO, I DISAPPOINT.
DON'T YOU WANT TO TALK ABOUT IT? ABOUT US? ABOUT THE STUFF?
NOT REALLY.
I DON'T KNOW WHAT TO TRUST.
BUT WHAT ABOUT THE OTHER NIGHT?
THAT WAS A ONE-OFF.
I'VE SAID THESE WORDS BEFORE.
YOU READY TO ZOO THIS, SHADE?
OH MY GOD. NO. JUST NO.
"TO ESCAPE WHILE STANDING IN PLACE.
"TO DASH WHEN THERE IS NOTHING MORE."
I WONDER IF I'LL RUN AGAIN.

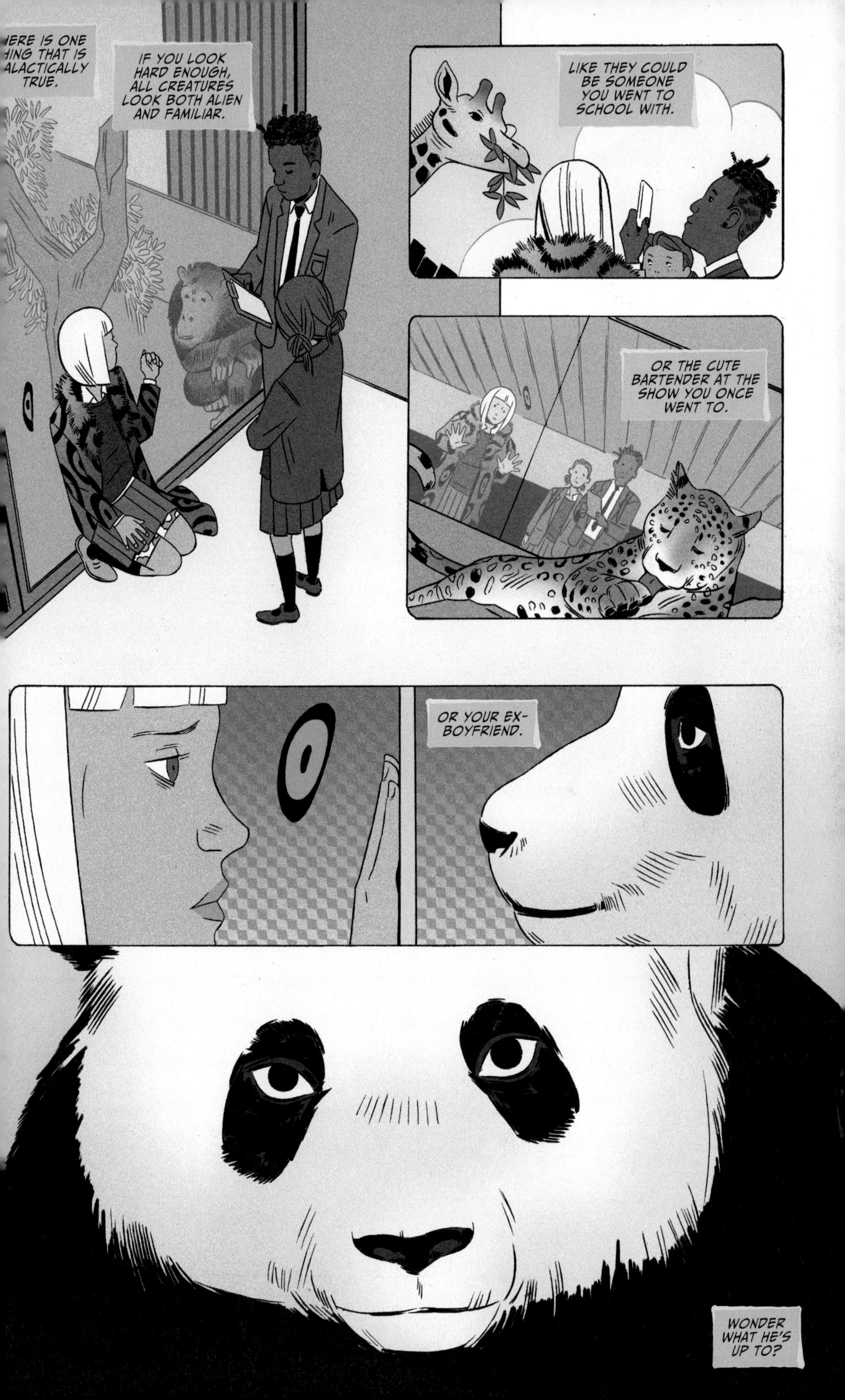

HERE IS ONE
HING THAT IS
ALACTICALLY
TRUE.
IF YOU LOOK HARD ENOUGH, ALL CREATURES LOOK BOTH ALIEN AND FAMILIAR.
LIKE THEY COULD BE SOMEONE YOU WENT TO SCHOOL WITH.
OR THE CUTE BARTENDER AT THE SHOW YOU ONCE WENT TO.
OR YOUR EX-BOYFRIEND.
WONDER WHAT HE'S UP TO?

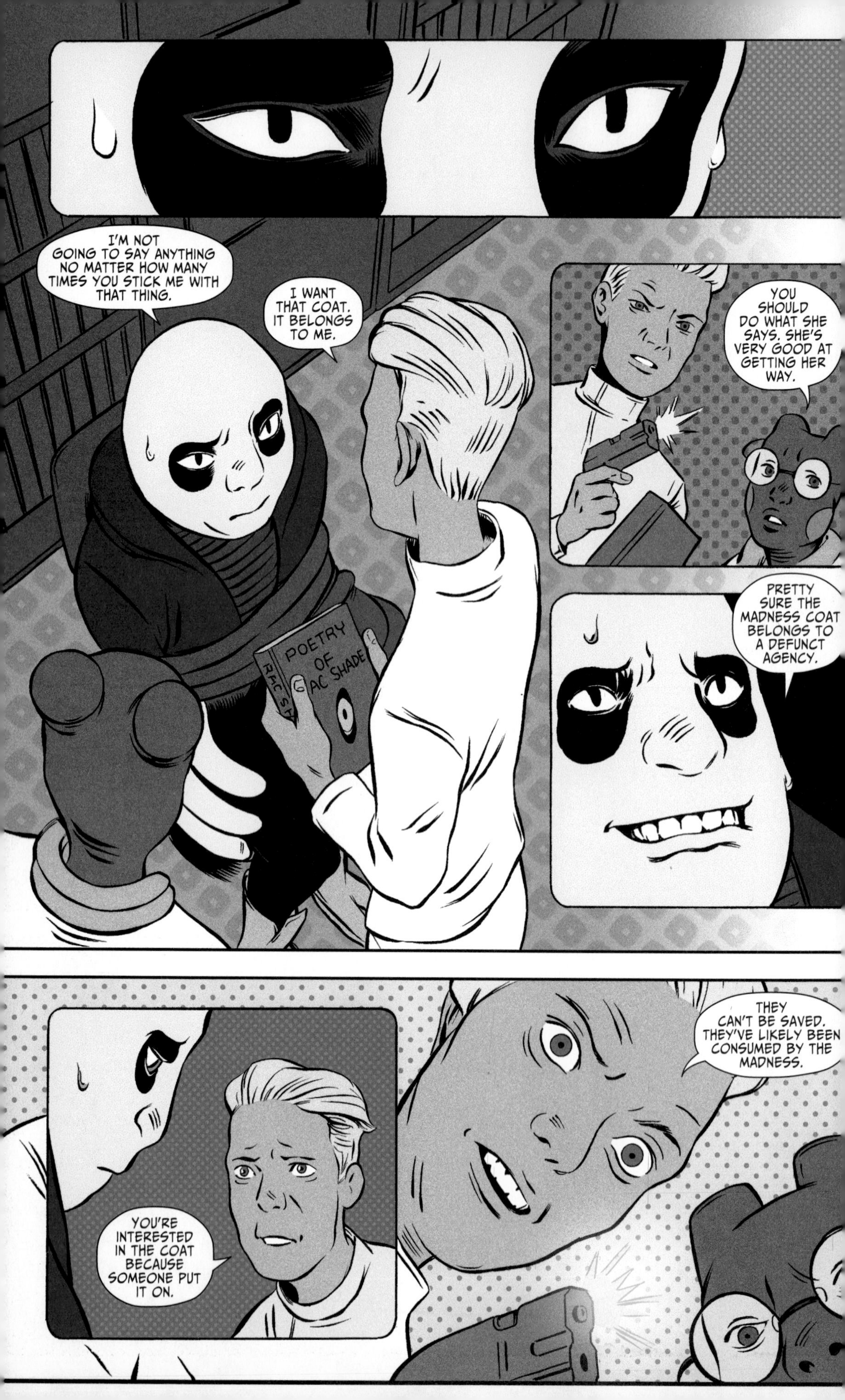
I'M NOT GOING TO SAY ANYTHING NO MATTER HOW MANY TIMES YOU STICK ME WITH THAT THING.
I WANT THAT COAT. IT BELONGS TO ME.
POETRY OF AC SHADE
YOU SHOULD DO WHAT SHE SAYS. SHE'S VERY GOOD AT GETTING HER WAY.
PRETTY SURE THE MADNESS COAT BELONGS TO A DEFUNCT AGENCY.
YOU'RE INTERESTED IN THE COAT BECAUSE SOMEONE PUT IT ON.
THEY CAN'T BE SAVED. THEY'VE LIKELY BEEN CONSUMED BY THE MADNESS.

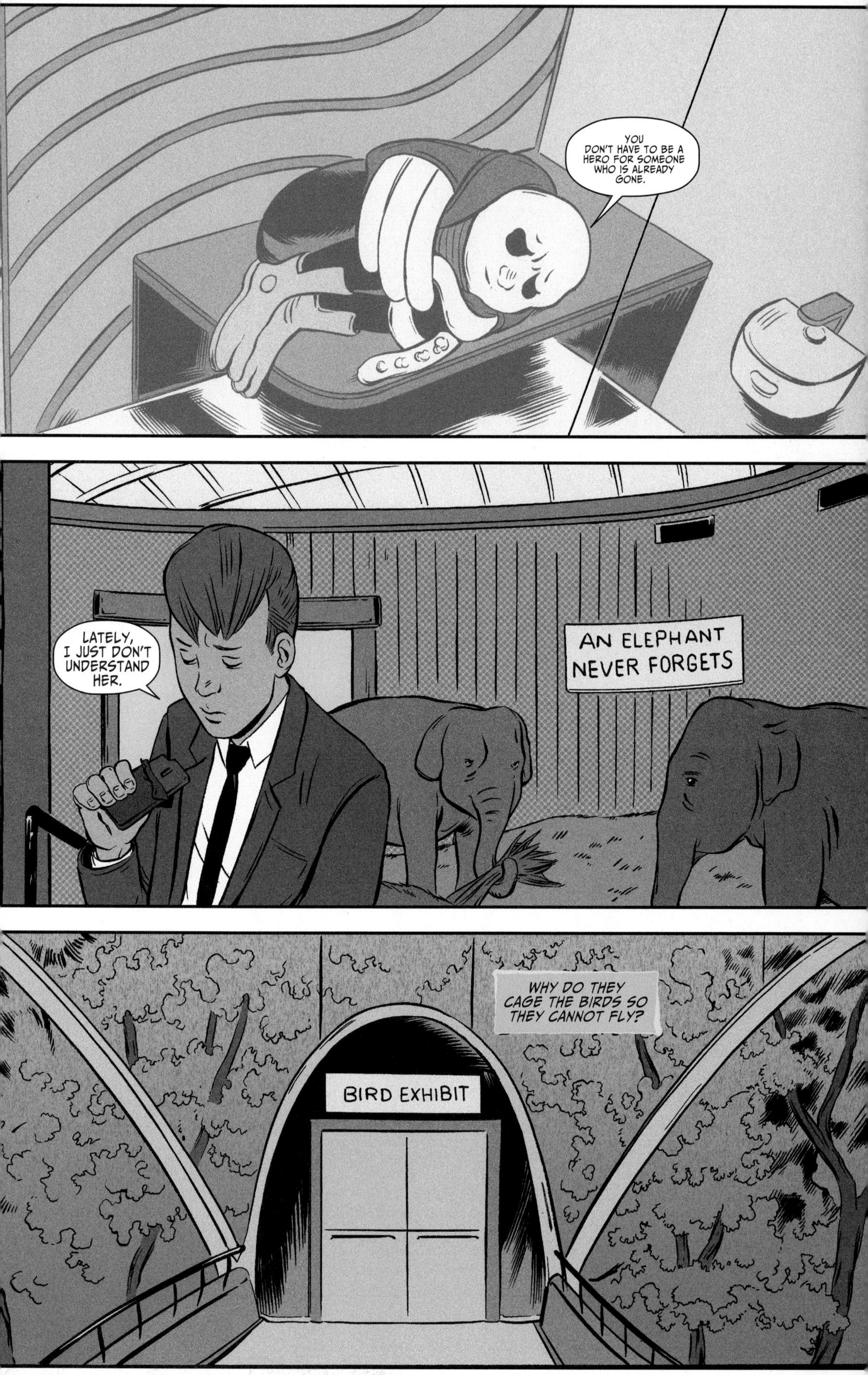
YOU DON'T HAVE TO BE A HERO FOR SOMEONE WHO IS ALREADY GONE.
LATELY, I JUST DON'T UNDERSTAND HER.
AN ELEPHANT NEVER FORGETS
WHY DO THEY CAGE THE BIRDS SO THEY CANNOT FLY?
BIRD EXHIBIT

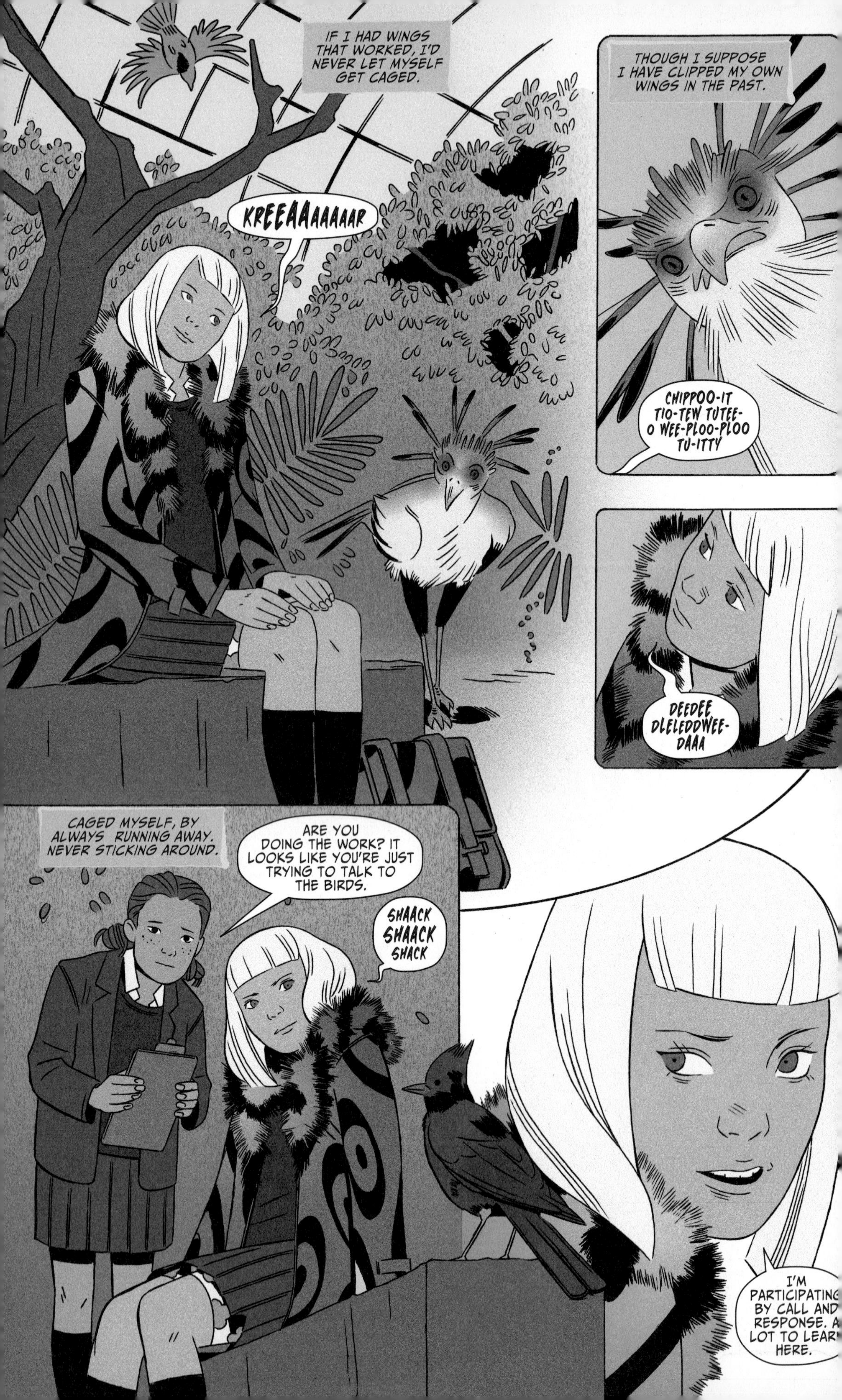
IF I HAD WINGS THAT WORKED, I'D NEVER LET MYSELF GET CAGED.
KREEAAAAAAAR
THOUGH I SUPPOSE I HAVE CLIPPED MY OWN WINGS IN THE PAST.
CHIPPOO-IT TIO-TEW TUTEE-O WEE-PLOO-PLOO TU-ITTY
DEEDEE DLELEDDWEE-DAAA
CAGED MYSELF, BY ALWAYS RUNNING AWAY. NEVER STICKING AROUND.
ARE YOU DOING THE WORK? IT LOOKS LIKE YOU'RE JUST TRYING TO TALK TO THE BIRDS.
SHAACK SHAACK SHACK
I'M PARTICIPATING BY CALL AND RESPONSE. A LOT TO LEAR HERE.

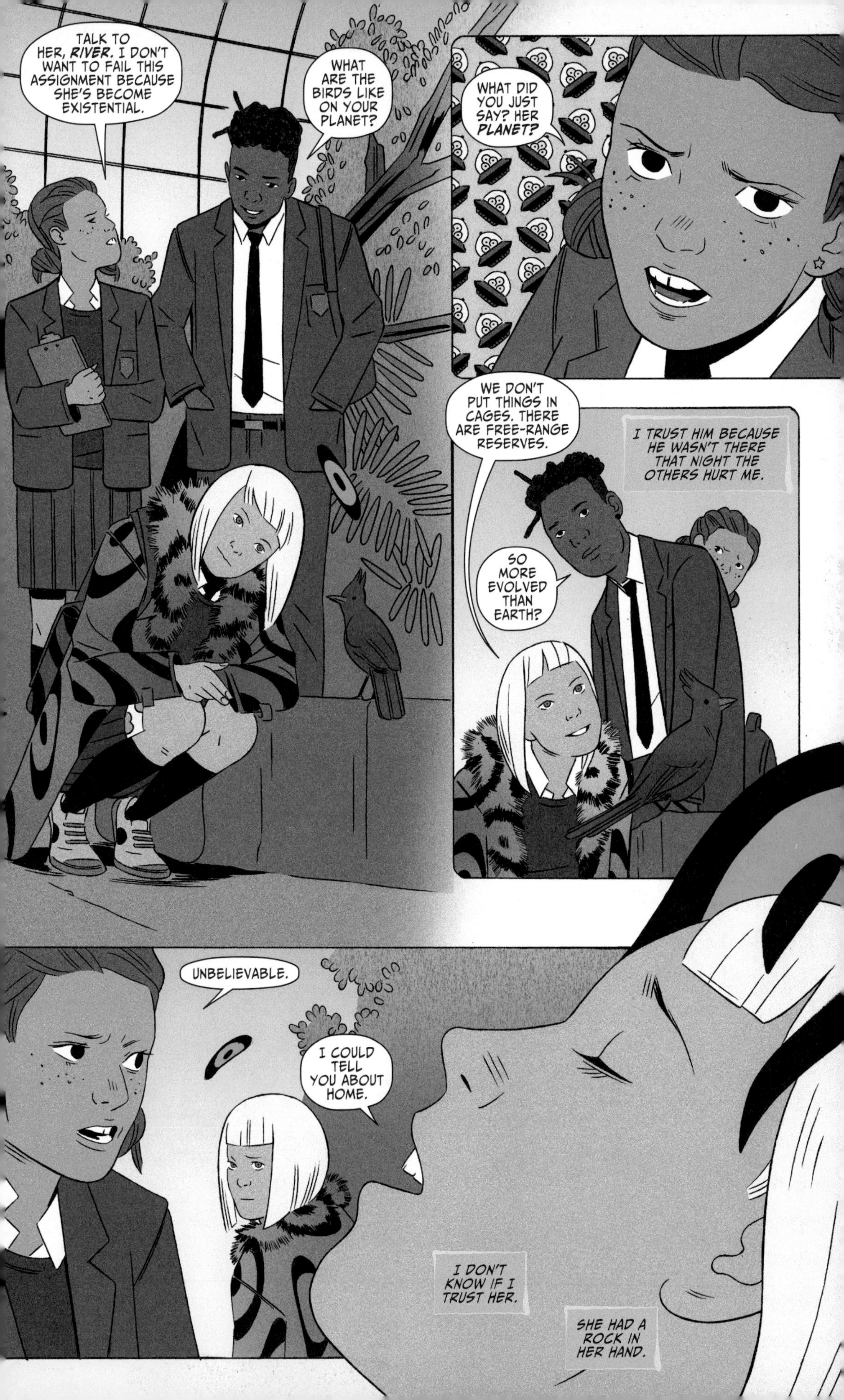
TALK TO HER, RIVER. I DON'T WANT TO FAIL THIS ASSIGNMENT BECAUSE SHE'S BECOME EXISTENTIAL.
WHAT ARE THE BIRDS LIKE ON YOUR PLANET?
WHAT DID YOU JUST SAY? HER PLANET?
WE DON'T PUT THINGS IN CAGES. THERE ARE FREE-RANGE RESERVES.
I TRUST HIM BECAUSE HE WASN'T THERE THAT NIGHT THE OTHERS HURT ME.
SO MORE EVOLVED THAN EARTH?
UNBELIEVABLE.
I COULD TELL YOU ABOUT HOME.
I DON'T KNOW IF I TRUST HER.
SHE HAD A ROCK IN HER HAND.

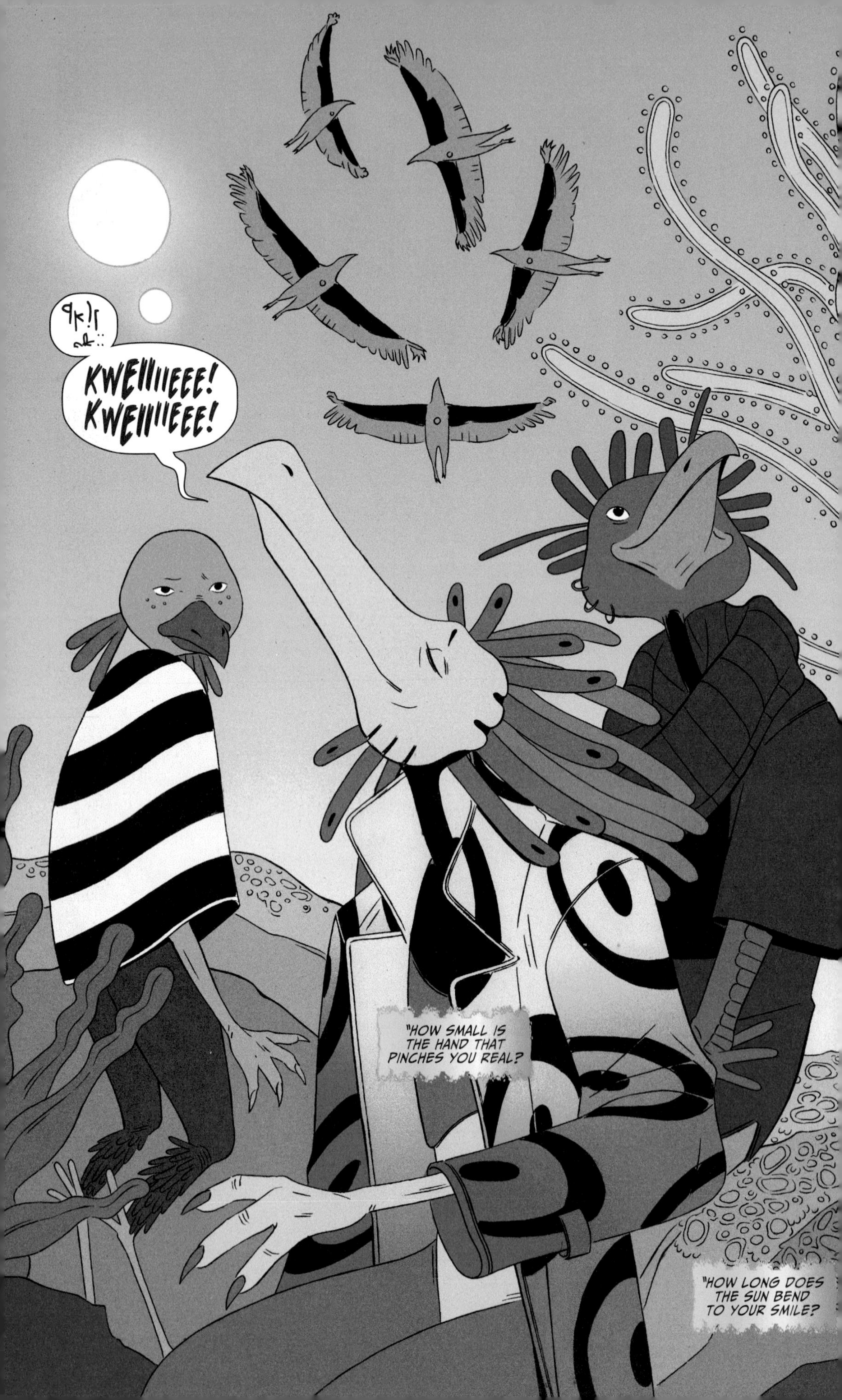
KWEIIIIEEE! KWEIIIIEEE!
"HOW SMALL IS THE HAND THAT PINCHES YOU REAL?
"HOW LONG DOES THE SUN BEND TO YOUR SMILE?

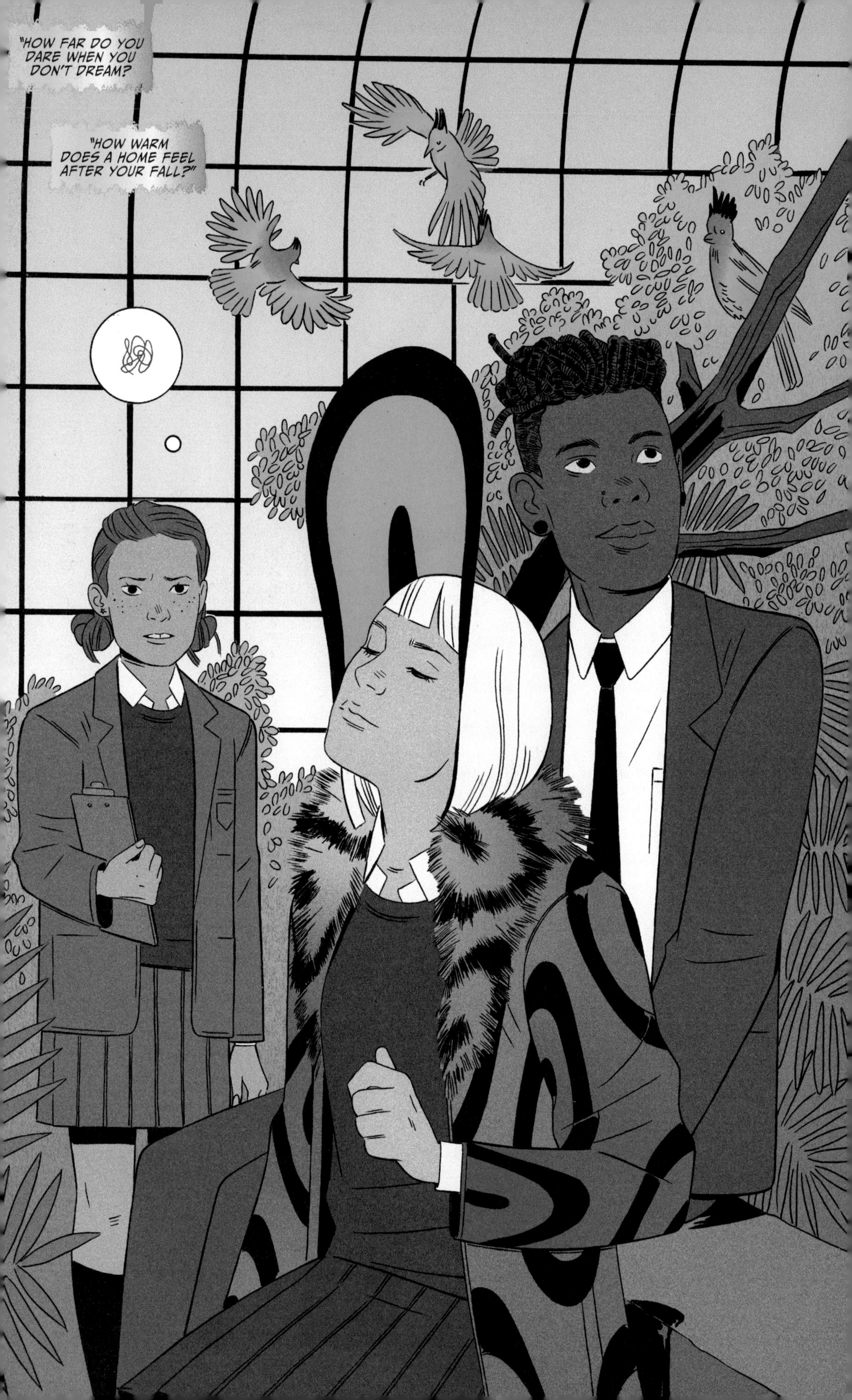
"HOW FAR DO YOU DARE WHEN YOU DON'T DREAM?
"HOW WARM DOES A HOME FEEL AFTER YOUR FALL?"

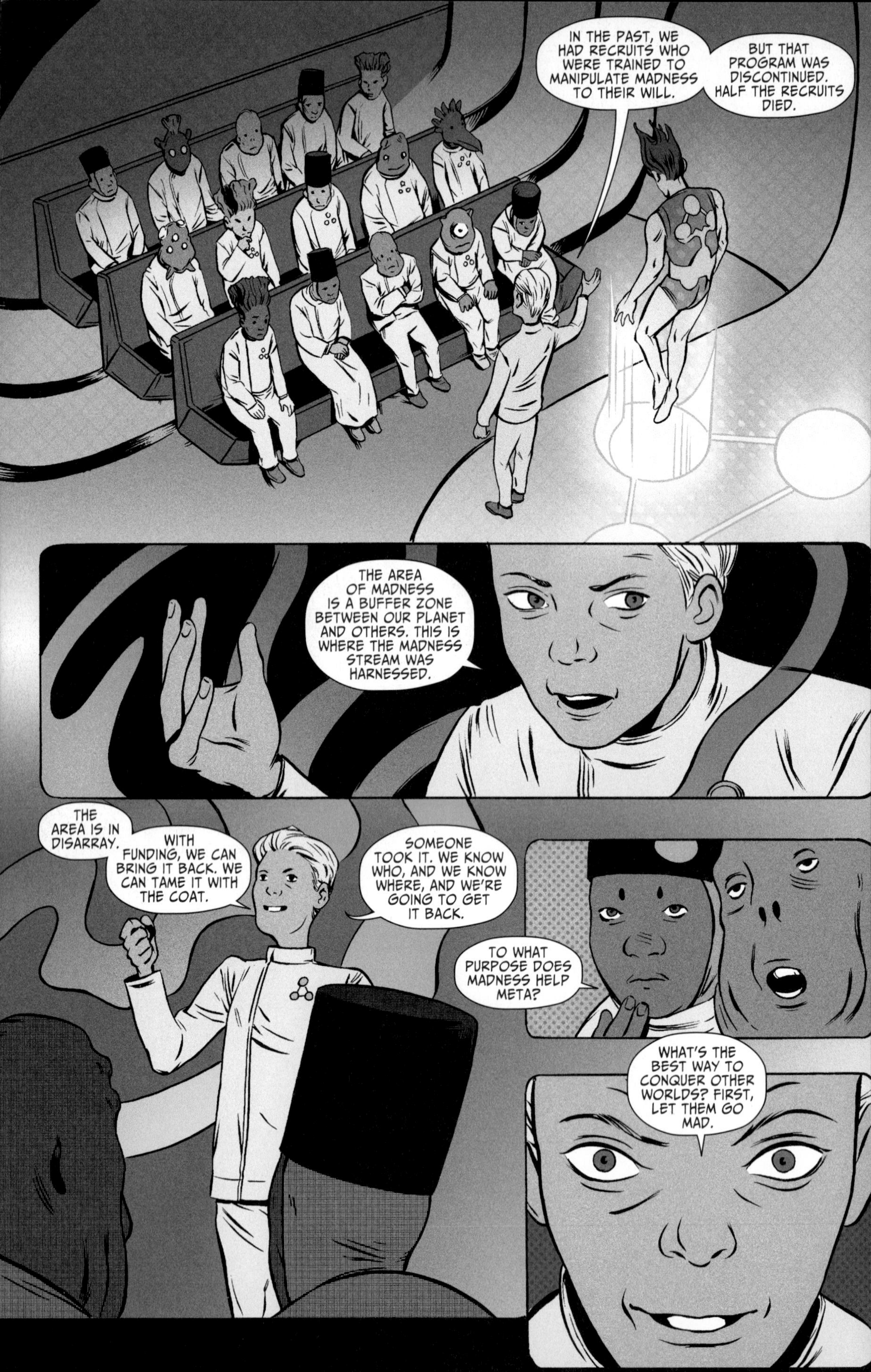
IN THE PAST, WE HAD RECRUITS WHO WERE TRAINED TO MANIPULATE MADNESS TO THEIR WILL.
BUT THAT PROGRAM WAS DISCONTINUED. HALF THE RECRUITS DIED.
THE AREA OF MADNESS IS A BUFFER ZONE BETWEEN OUR PLANET AND OTHERS. THIS IS WHERE THE MADNESS STREAM WAS HARNESSED.
THE AREA IS IN DISARRAY.
WITH FUNDING, WE CAN BRING IT BACK. WE CAN TAME IT WITH THE COAT.
SOMEONE TOOK IT. WE KNOW WHO, AND WE KNOW WHERE, AND WE'RE GOING TO GET IT BACK.
TO WHAT PURPOSE DOES MADNESS HELP META?
WHAT'S THE BEST WAY TO CONQUER OTHER WORLDS? FIRST, LET THEM GO MAD.

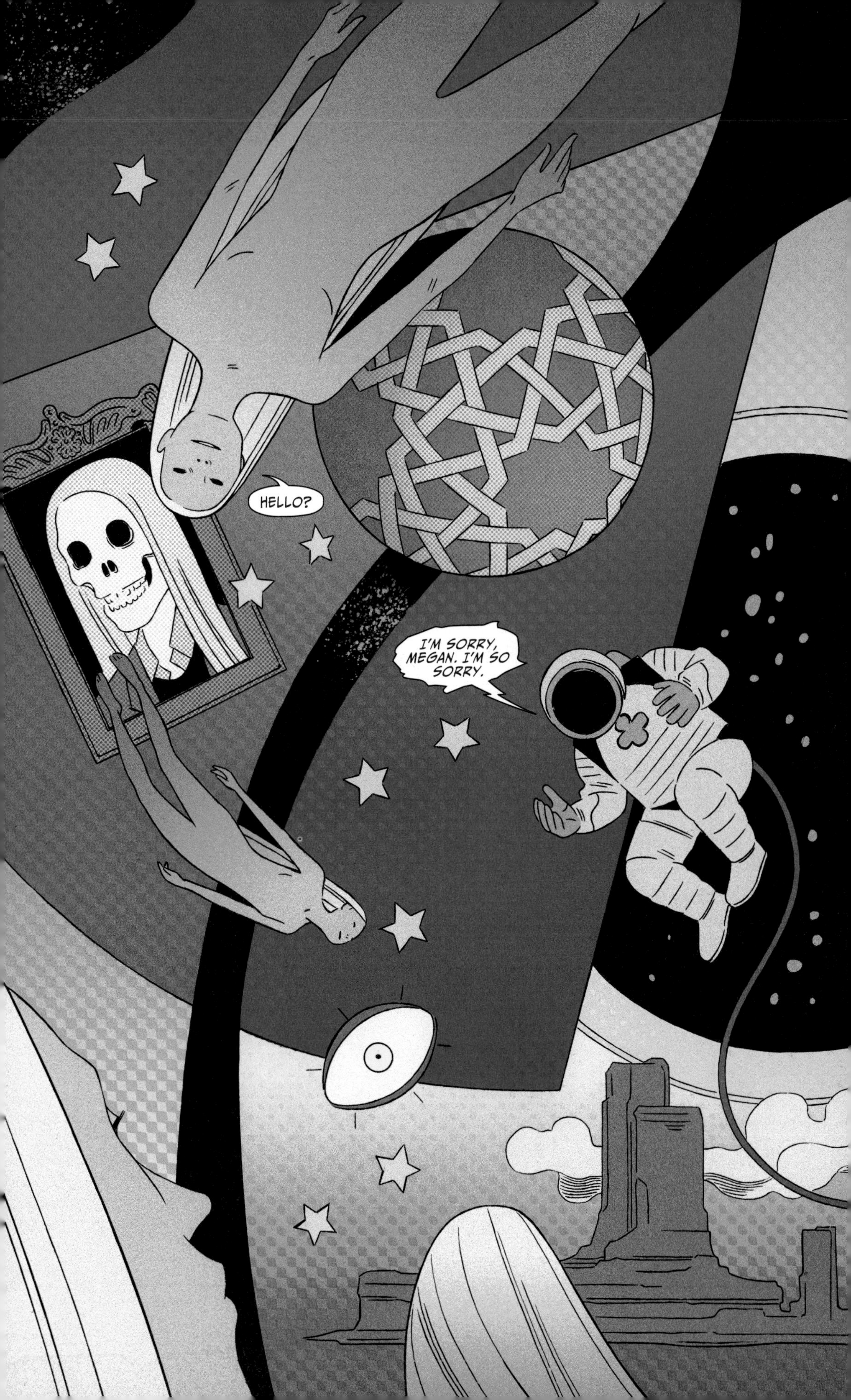
HELLO?
I'M SORRY, MEGAN. I'M SO SORRY.

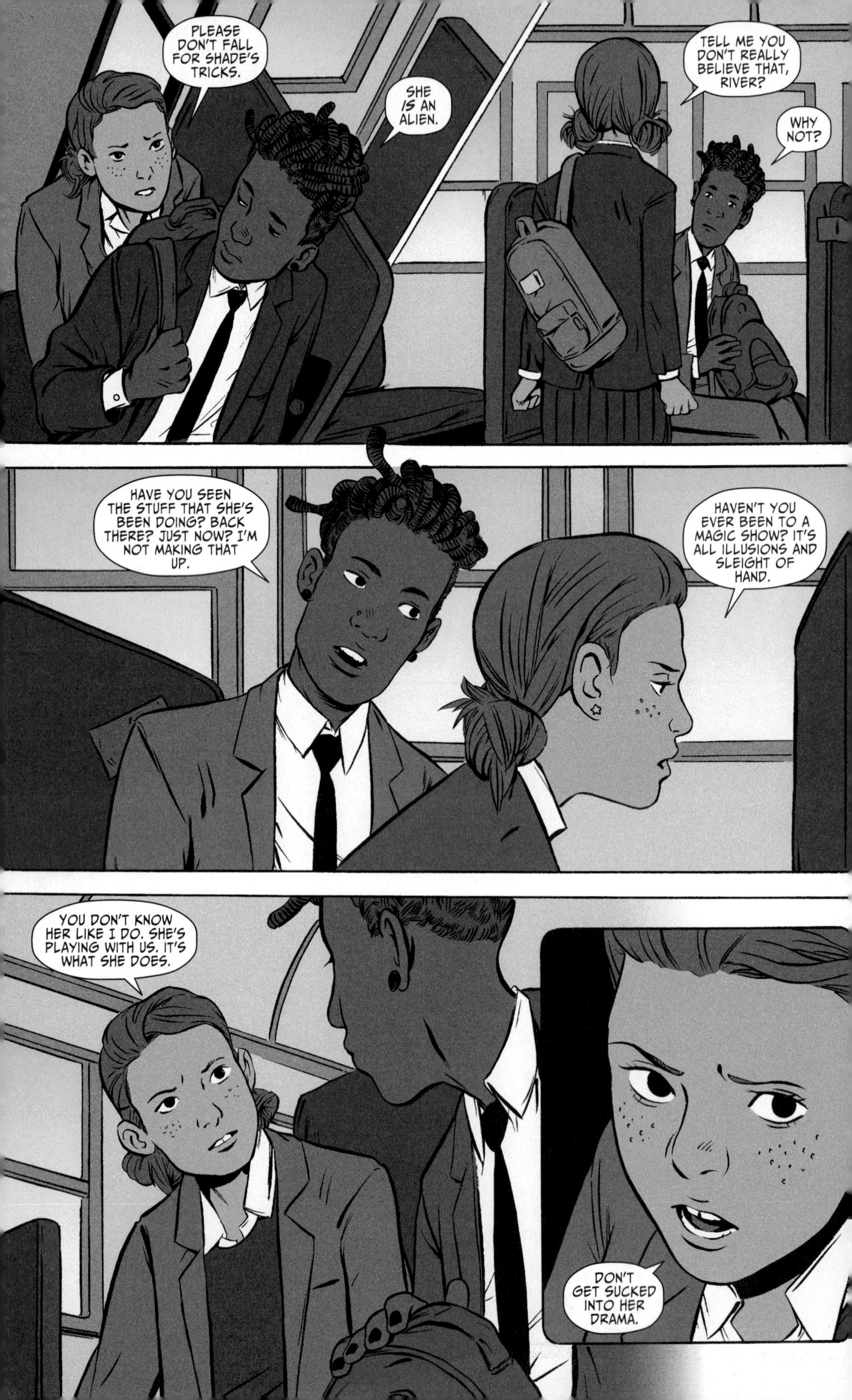
PLEASE DON'T FALL FOR SHADE'S TRICKS.
SHE IS AN ALIEN.
TELL ME YOU DON'T REALLY BELIEVE THAT, RIVER?
WHY NOT?
HAVE YOU SEEN THE STUFF THAT SHE'S BEEN DOING? BACK THERE? JUST NOW? I'M NOT MAKING THAT UP.
HAVEN'T YOU EVER BEEN TO A MAGIC SHOW? IT'S ALL ILLUSIONS AND SLEIGHT OF HAND.
YOU DON'T KNOW HER LIKE I DO. SHE'S PLAYING WITH US. IT'S WHAT SHE DOES.
DON'T GET SUCKED INTO HER DRAMA.

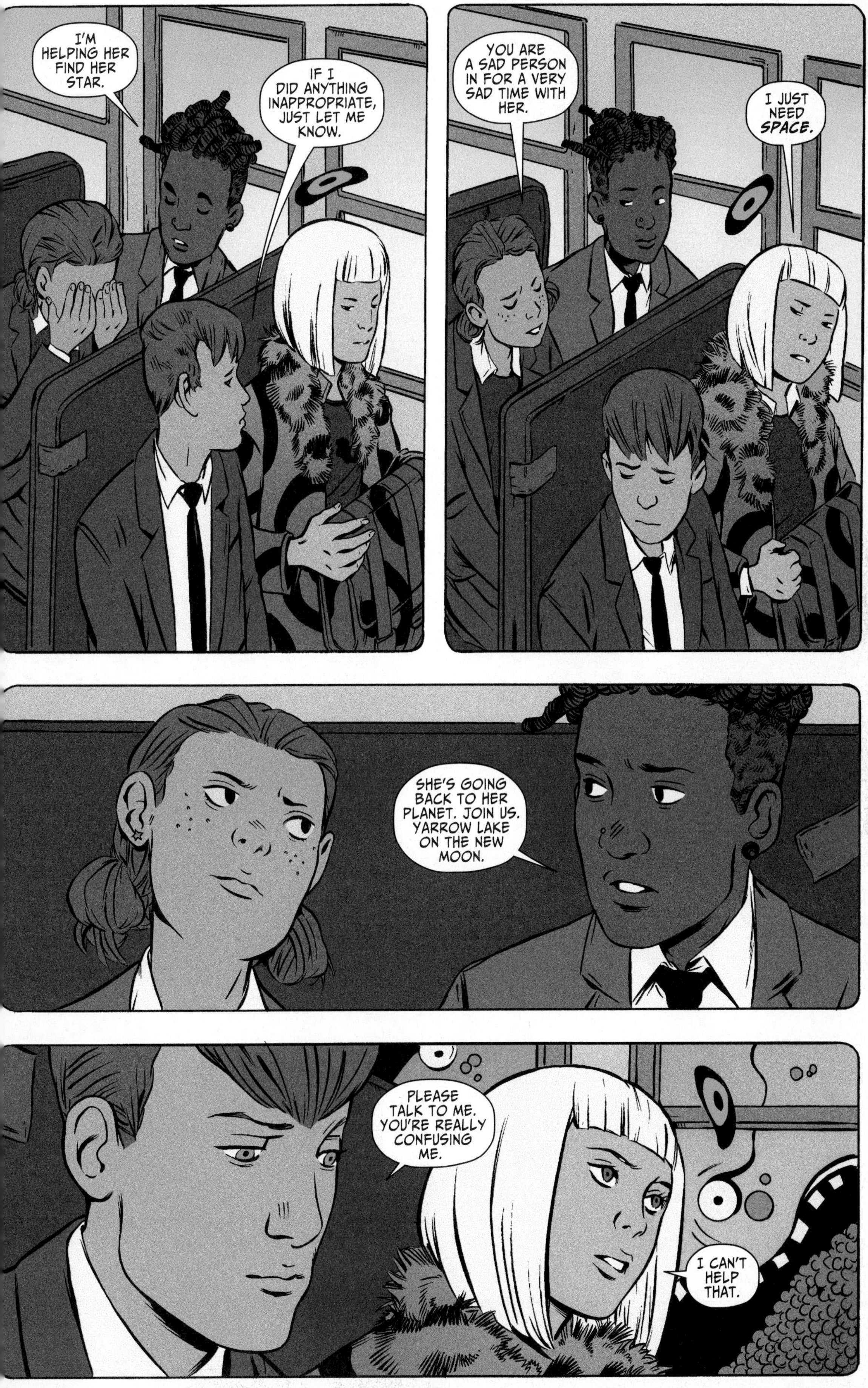
I'M HELPING HER FIND HER STAR.
IF I DID ANYTHING INAPPROPRIATE, JUST LET ME KNOW.
YOU ARE A SAD PERSON IN FOR A VERY SAD TIME WITH HER.
I JUST NEED SPACE.
SHE'S GOING BACK TO HER PLANET. JOIN US. YARROW LAKE ON THE NEW MOON.
PLEASE TALK TO ME. YOU'RE REALLY CONFUSING ME.
I CAN'T HELP THAT.

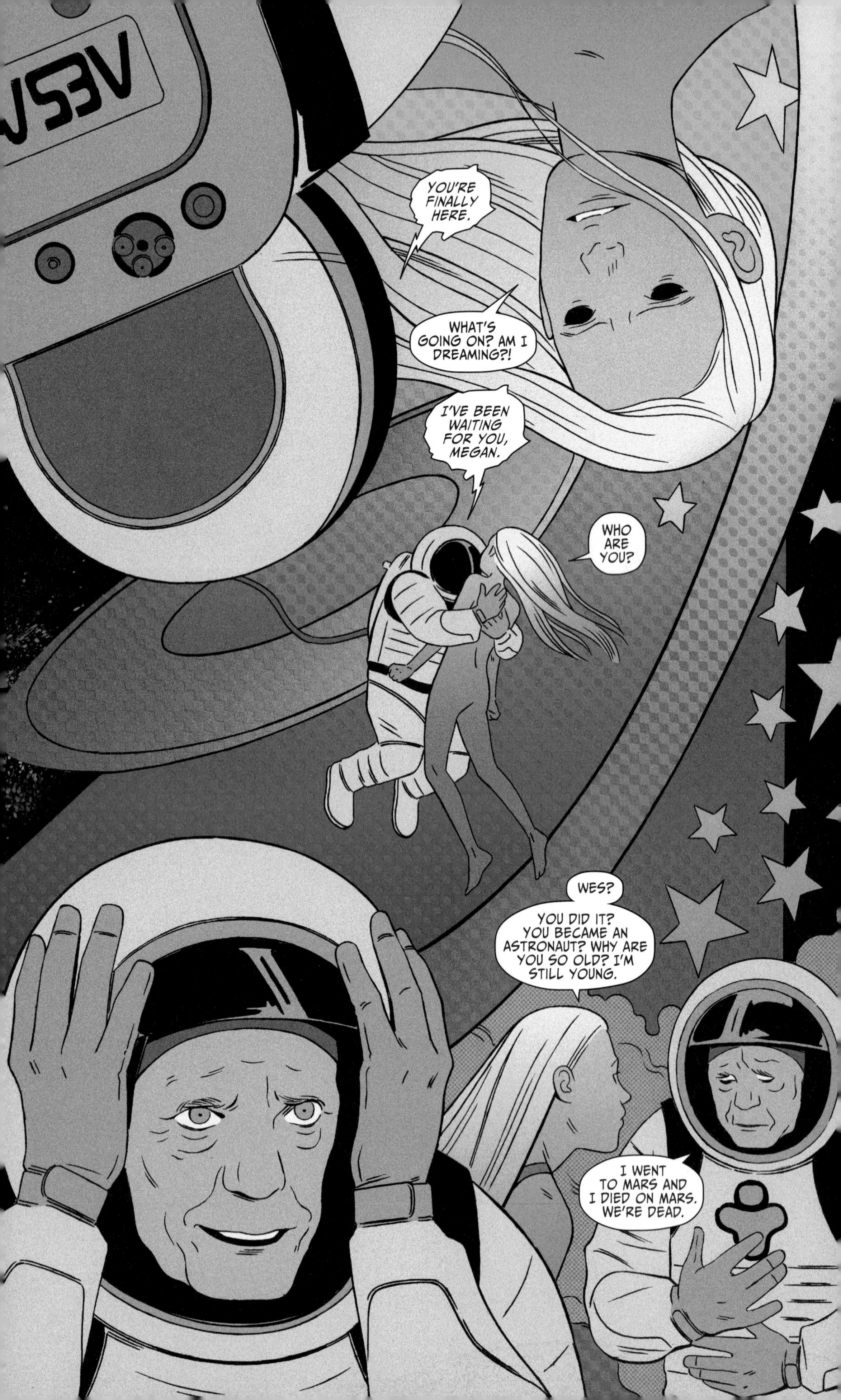
YOU'RE FINALLY HERE.
WHAT'S GOING ON? AM I DREAMING?!
I'VE BEEN WAITING FOR YOU, MEGAN.
WHO ARE YOU?
WES?
YOU DID IT? YOU BECAME AN ASTRONAUT? WHY ARE YOU SO OLD? I'M STILL YOUNG.
I WENT TO MARS AND I DIED ON MARS. WE'RE DEAD.

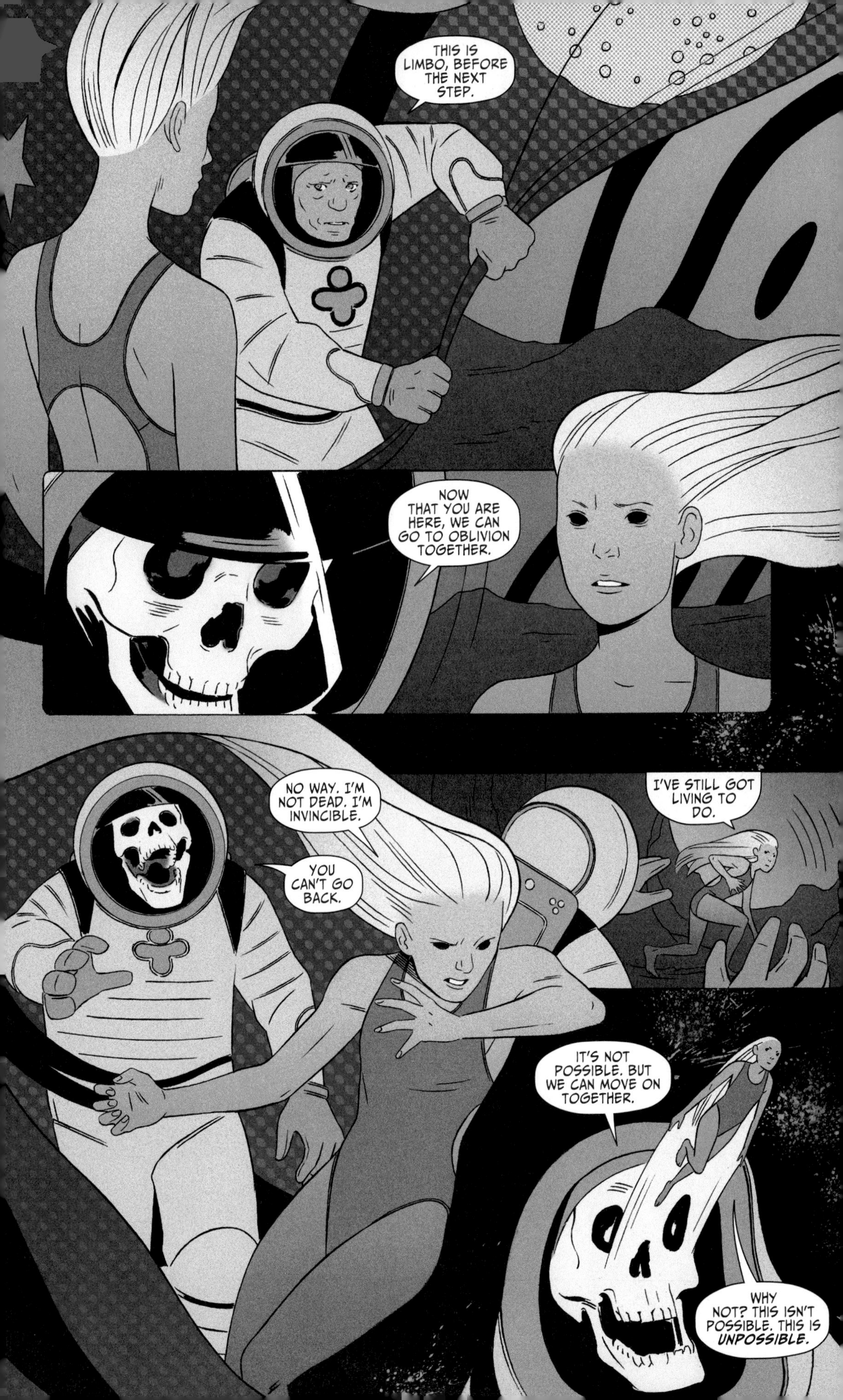
THIS IS LIMBO, BEFORE THE NEXT STEP.
NOW THAT YOU ARE HERE, WE CAN GO TO OBLIVION TOGETHER.
NO WAY. I'M NOT DEAD. I'M INVINCIBLE.
YOU CAN'T GO BACK.
I'VE STILL GOT LIVING TO DO.
IT'S NOT POSSIBLE. BUT WE CAN MOVE ON TOGETHER.
WHY NOT? THIS ISN'T POSSIBLE. THIS IS *UNPOSSIBLE.*

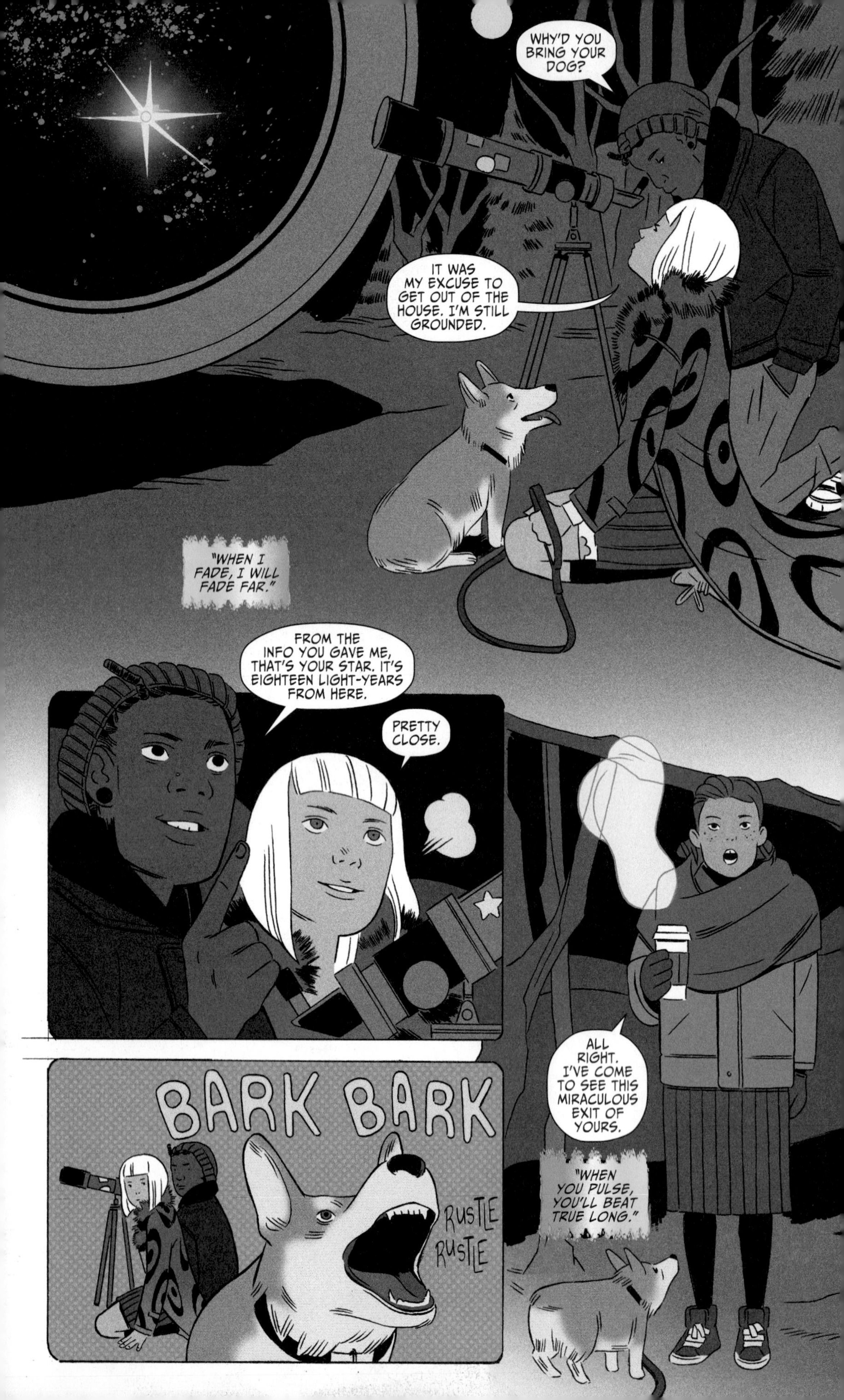
WHY'D YOU BRING YOUR DOG?
IT WAS MY EXCUSE TO GET OUT OF THE HOUSE. I'M STILL GROUNDED.
"WHEN I FADE, I WILL FADE FAR."
FROM THE INFO YOU GAVE ME, THAT'S YOUR STAR. IT'S EIGHTEEN LIGHT-YEARS FROM HERE.
PRETTY CLOSE.
BARK BARK
RUSTLE RUSTLE
ALL RIGHT. I'VE COME TO SEE THIS MIRACULOUS EXIT OF YOURS.
"WHEN YOU PULSE, YOU'LL BEAT TRUE LONG."

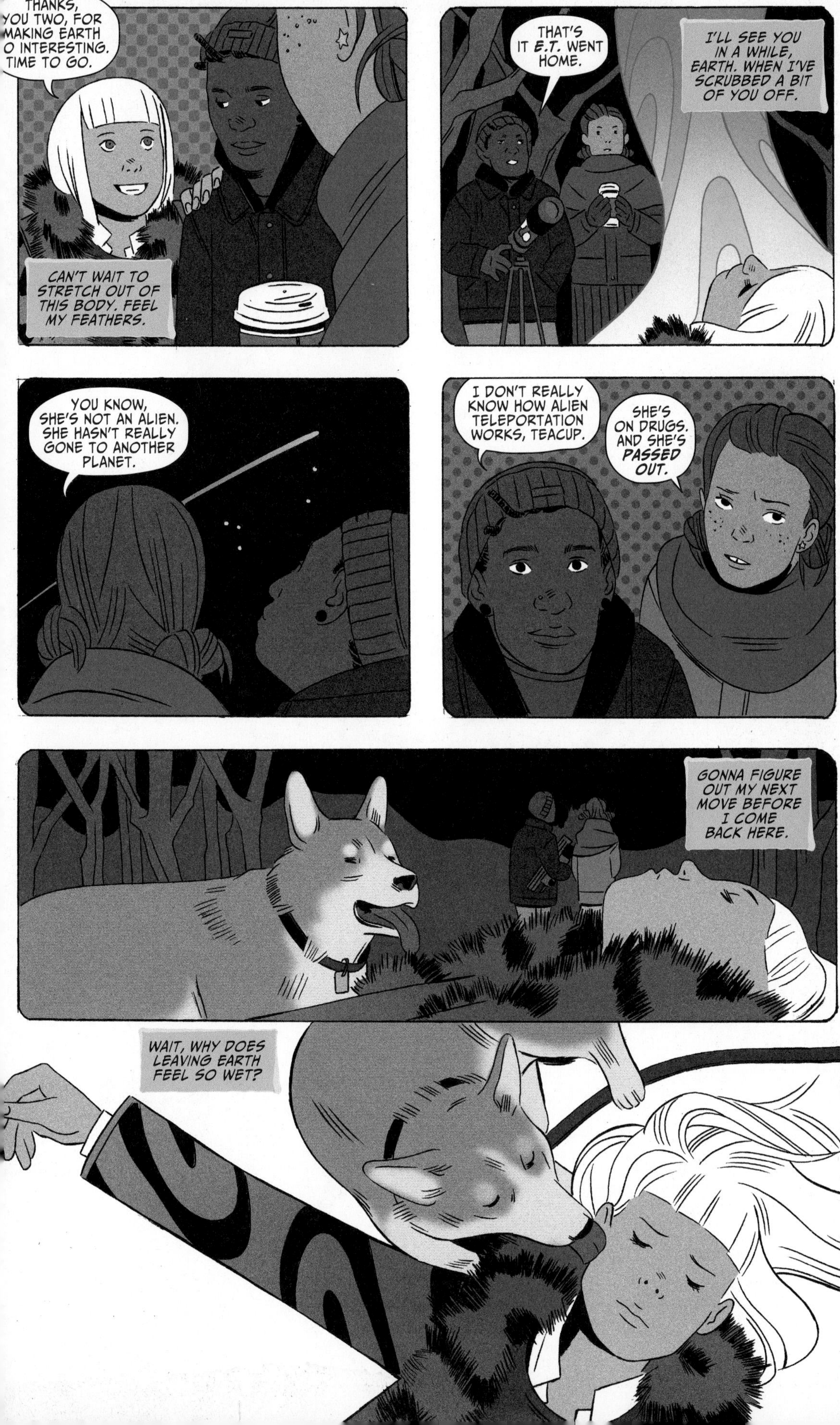
THANKS, YOU TWO, FOR MAKING EARTH O INTERESTING. TIME TO GO.
CAN'T WAIT TO STRETCH OUT OF THIS BODY. FEEL MY FEATHERS.
THAT'S IT E.T. WENT HOME.
I'LL SEE YOU IN A WHILE, EARTH. WHEN I'VE SCRUBBED A BIT OF YOU OFF.
YOU KNOW, SHE'S NOT AN ALIEN. SHE HASN'T REALLY GONE TO ANOTHER PLANET.
I DON'T REALLY KNOW HOW ALIEN TELEPORTATION WORKS, TEACUP.
SHE'S ON DRUGS. AND SHE'S PASSED OUT.
GONNA FIGURE OUT MY NEXT MOVE BEFORE I COME BACK HERE.
WAIT, WHY DOES LEAVING EARTH FEEL SO WET?

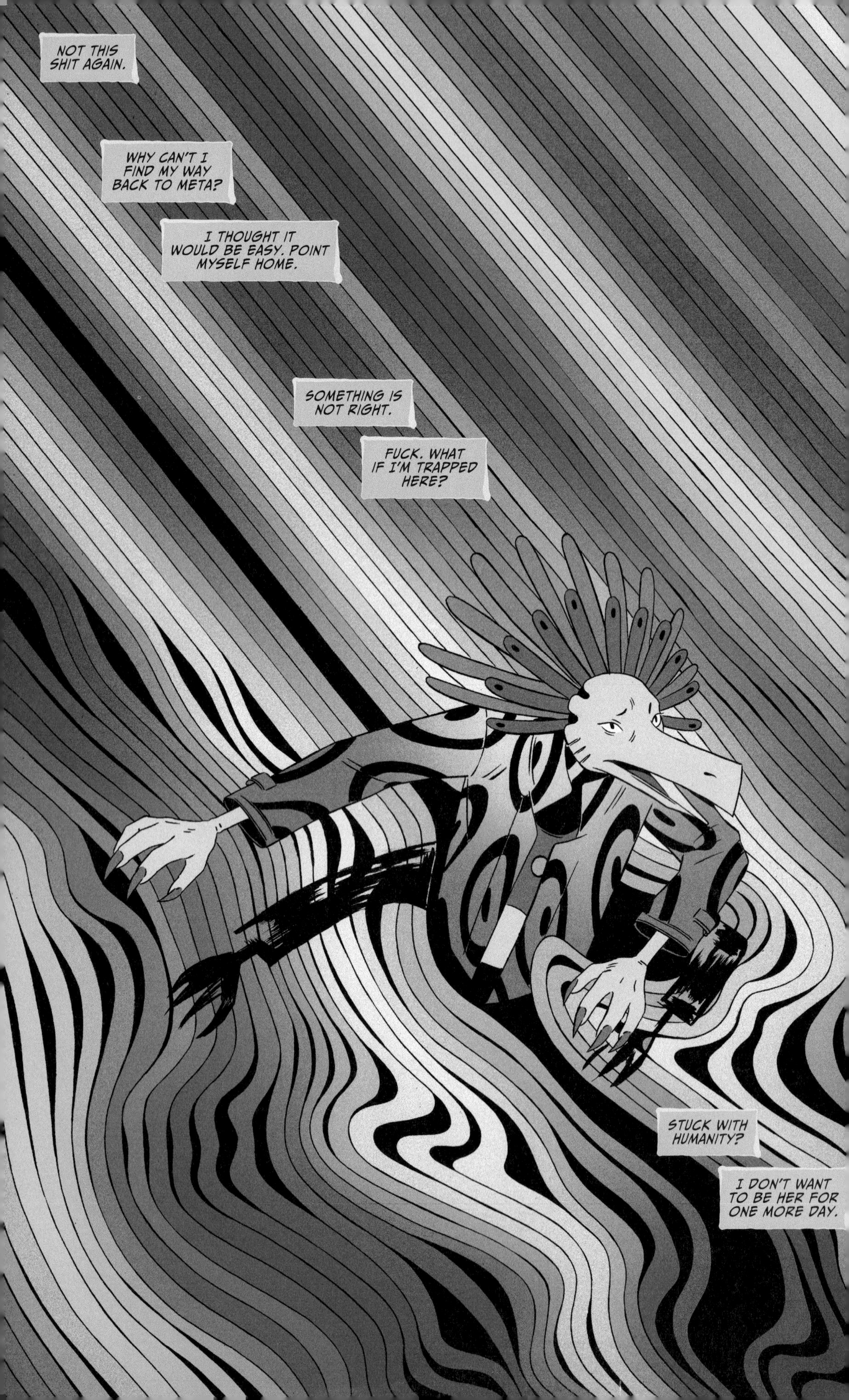
NOT THIS SHIT AGAIN.
WHY CAN'T I FIND MY WAY BACK TO META?
I THOUGHT IT WOULD BE EASY. POINT MYSELF HOME.
SOMETHING IS NOT RIGHT.
FUCK. WHAT IF I'M TRAPPED HERE?
STUCK WITH HUMANITY?
I DON'T WANT TO BE HER FOR ONE MORE DAY.

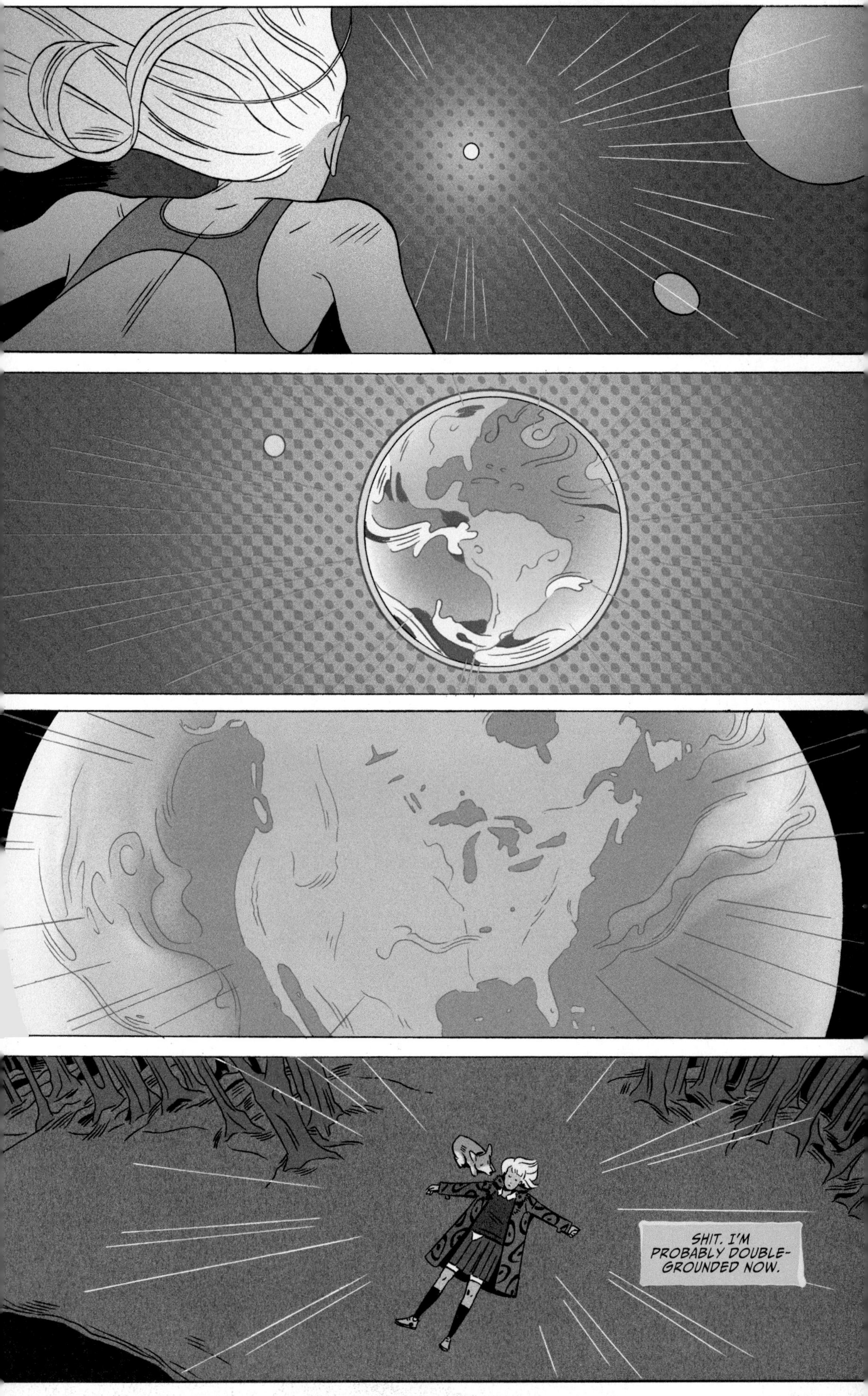
SHIT. I'M PROBABLY DOUBLE-GROUNDED NOW.

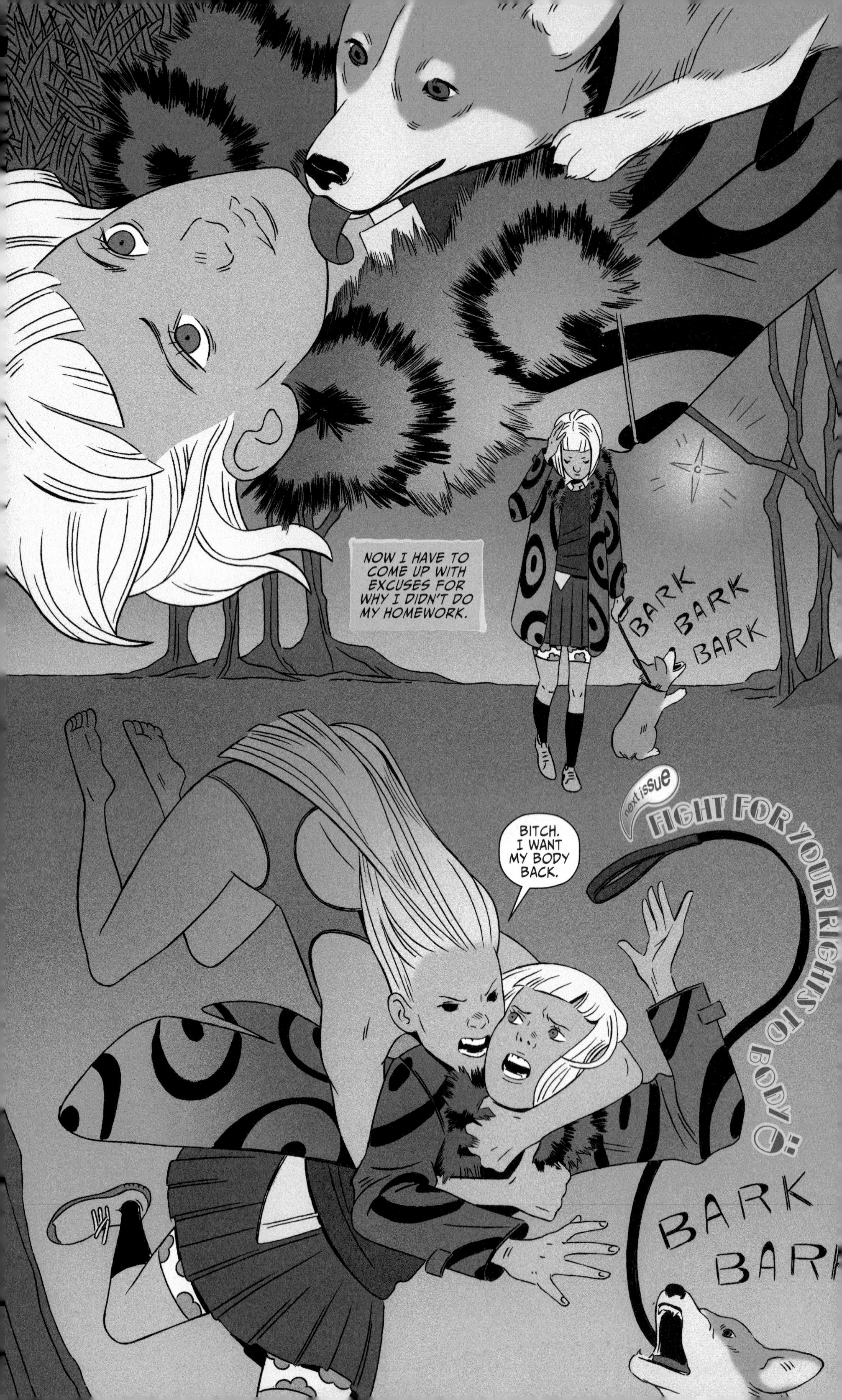
NOW I HAVE TO COME UP WITH EXCUSES FOR WHY I DIDN'T DO MY HOMEWORK.
BARK BARK BARK
BITCH. I WANT MY BODY BACK.
BARK BARK
next issue
FIGHT FOR YOUR RIGHTS TO BODY!

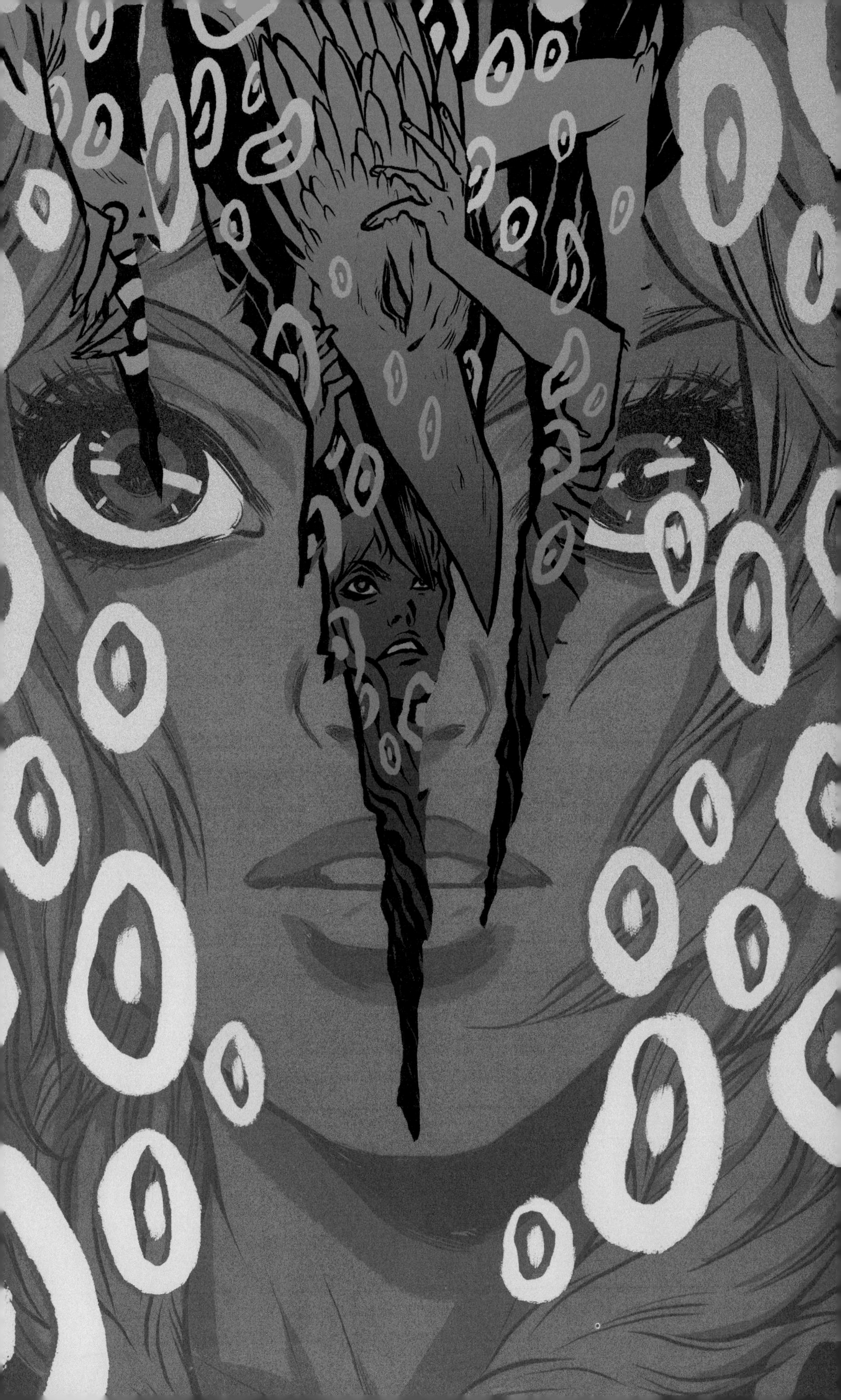

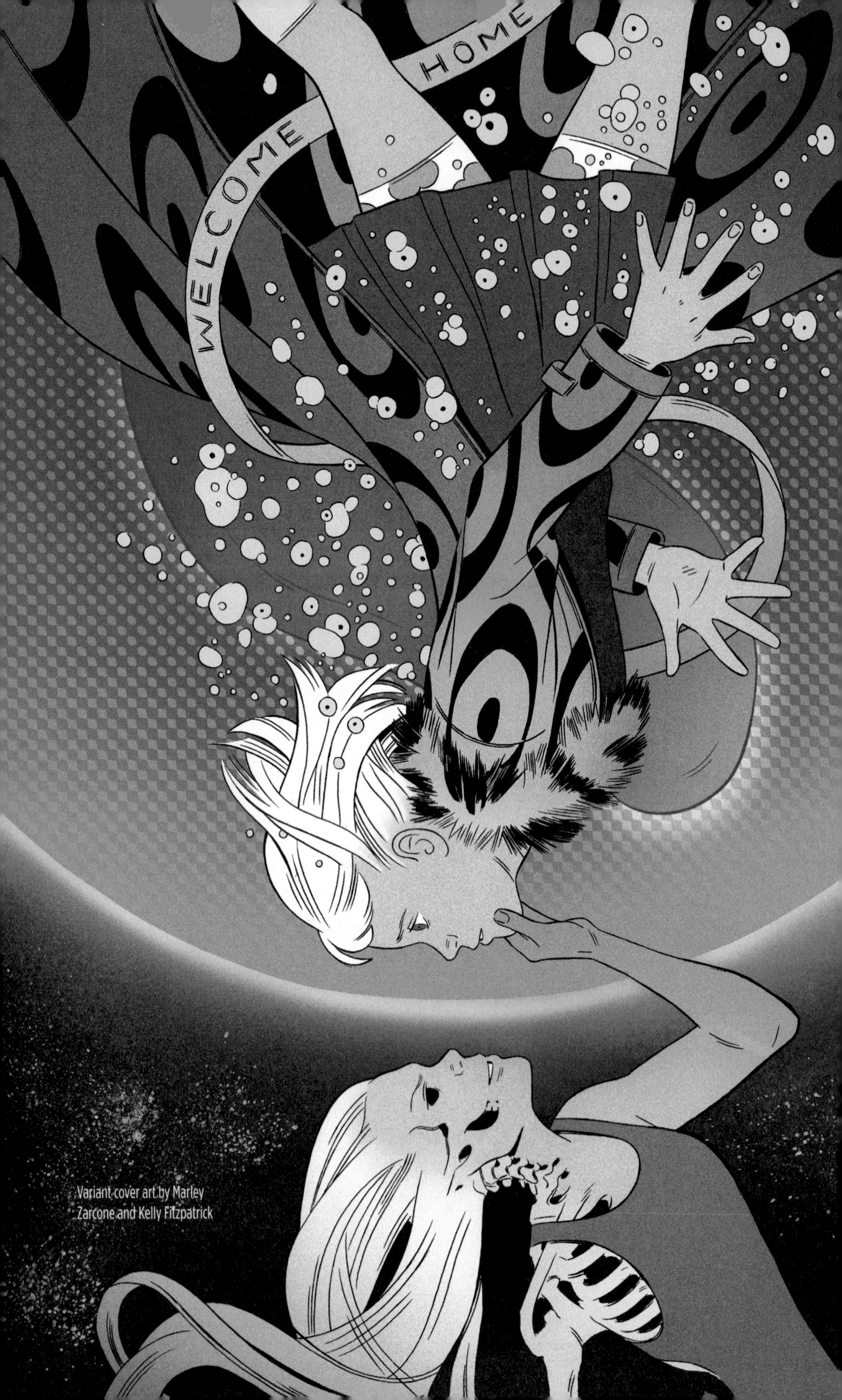
WELCOME HOME

Variant cover art by Marley Zarcone and Kelly Fitzpatrick

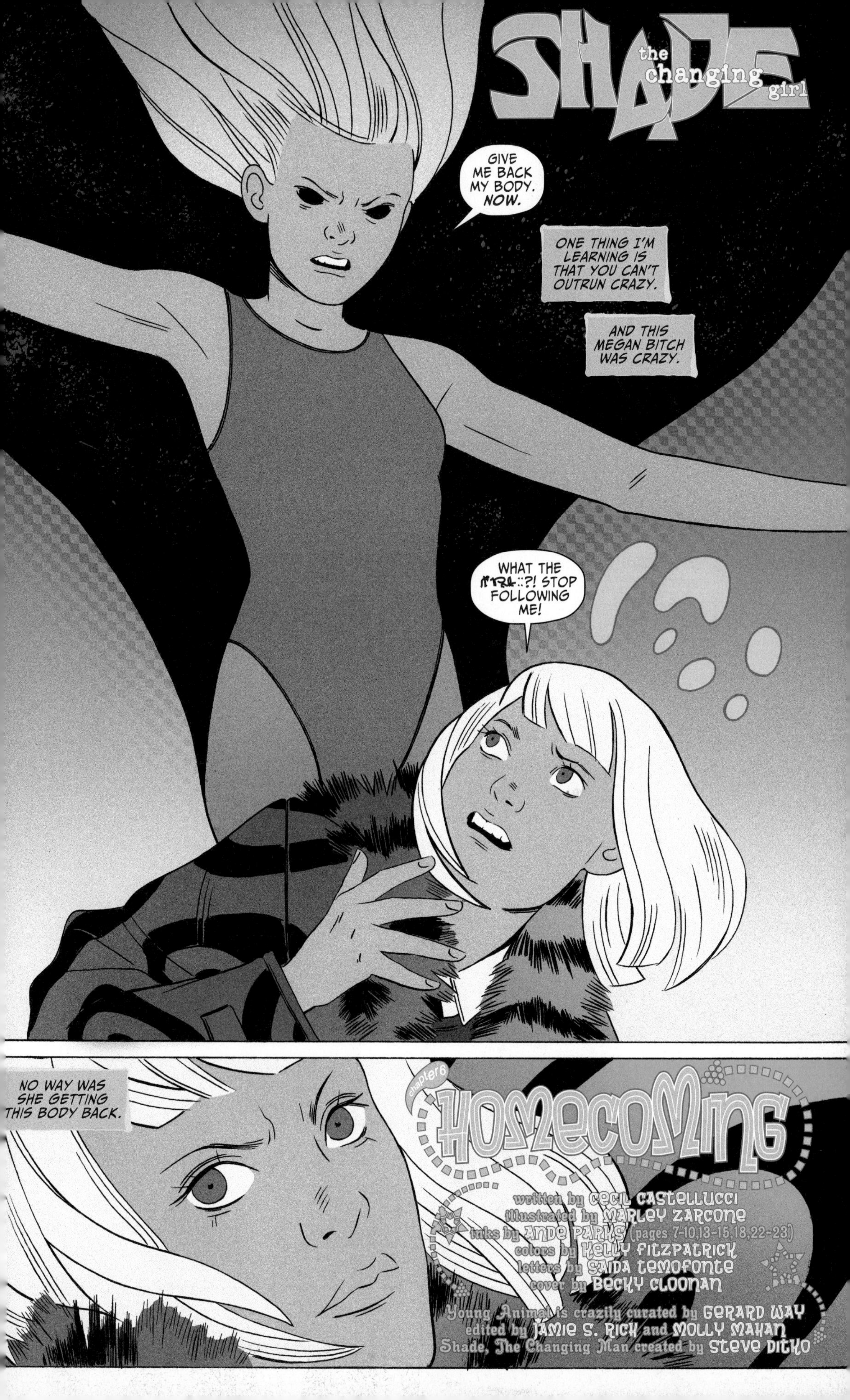
SHADE the changing girl
GIVE ME BACK MY BODY. NOW.
ONE THING I'M LEARNING IS THAT YOU CAN'T OUTRUN CRAZY.
AND THIS MEGAN BITCH WAS CRAZY.
WHAT THE ?! STOP FOLLOWING ME!
NO WAY WAS SHE GETTING THIS BODY BACK.
chapter 6
HOMECOMING
written by CECIL CASTELLUCCI
illustrated by MARLEY ZARCONE
inks by ANDE PARKS (pages 7-10,13-15,18,22-23)
colors by KELLY FITZPATRICK
letters by SAIDA TEMOFONTE
cover by BECKY CLOONAN
Young Animal is crazily curated by GERARD WAY
edited by JAMIE S. RICH and MOLLY MAHAN
Shade, The Changing Man created by STEVE DITKO

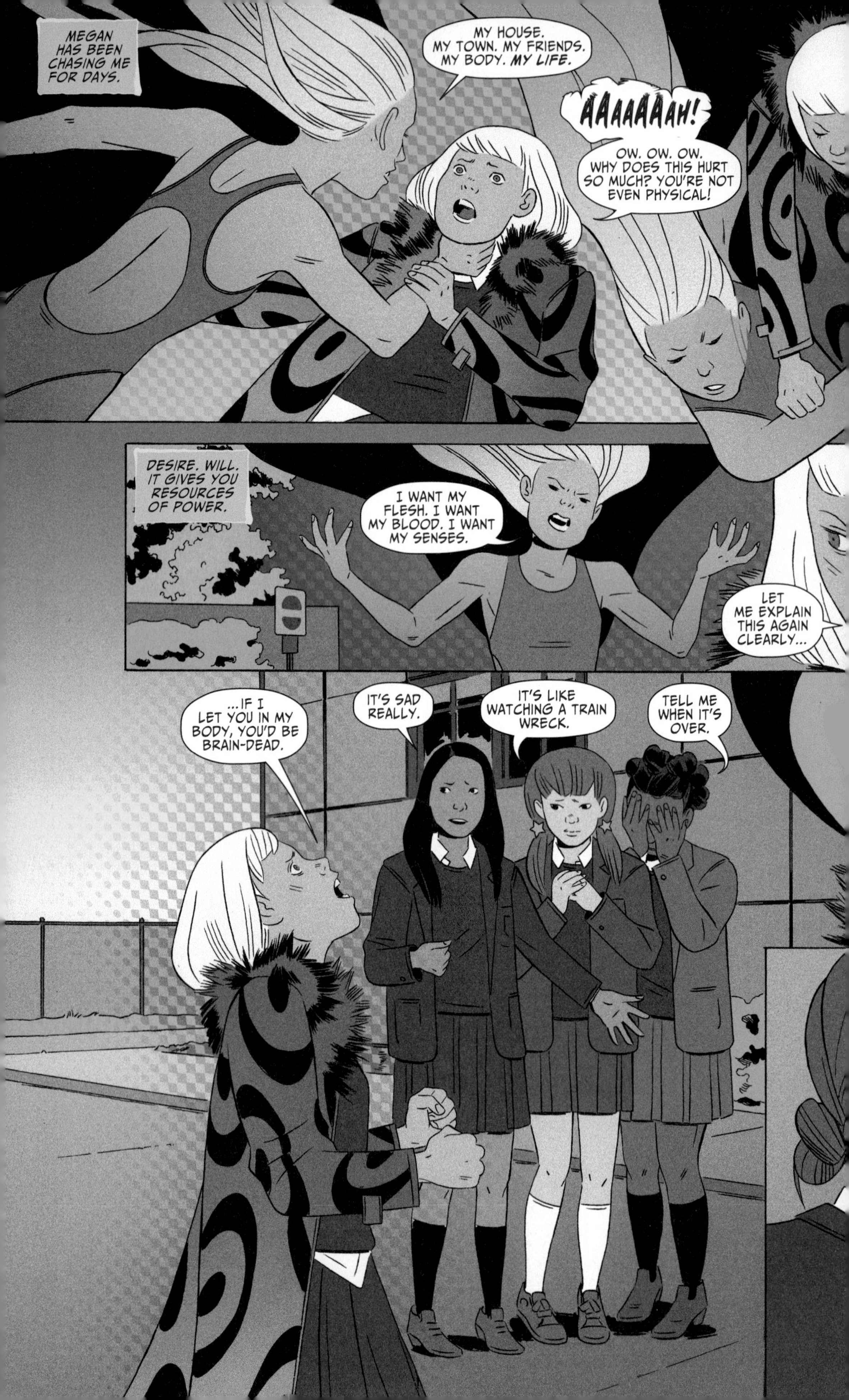
MEGAN HAS BEEN CHASING ME FOR DAYS.
MY HOUSE. MY TOWN. MY FRIENDS. MY BODY. MY LIFE.
AAAAAAAH!
OW. OW. OW. WHY DOES THIS HURT SO MUCH? YOU'RE NOT EVEN PHYSICAL!
DESIRE. WILL. IT GIVES YOU RESOURCES OF POWER.
I WANT MY FLESH. I WANT MY BLOOD. I WANT MY SENSES.
LET ME EXPLAIN THIS AGAIN CLEARLY...
...IF I LET YOU IN MY BODY, YOU'D BE BRAIN-DEAD.
IT'S SAD REALLY.
IT'S LIKE WATCHING A TRAIN WRECK.
TELL ME WHEN IT'S OVER.

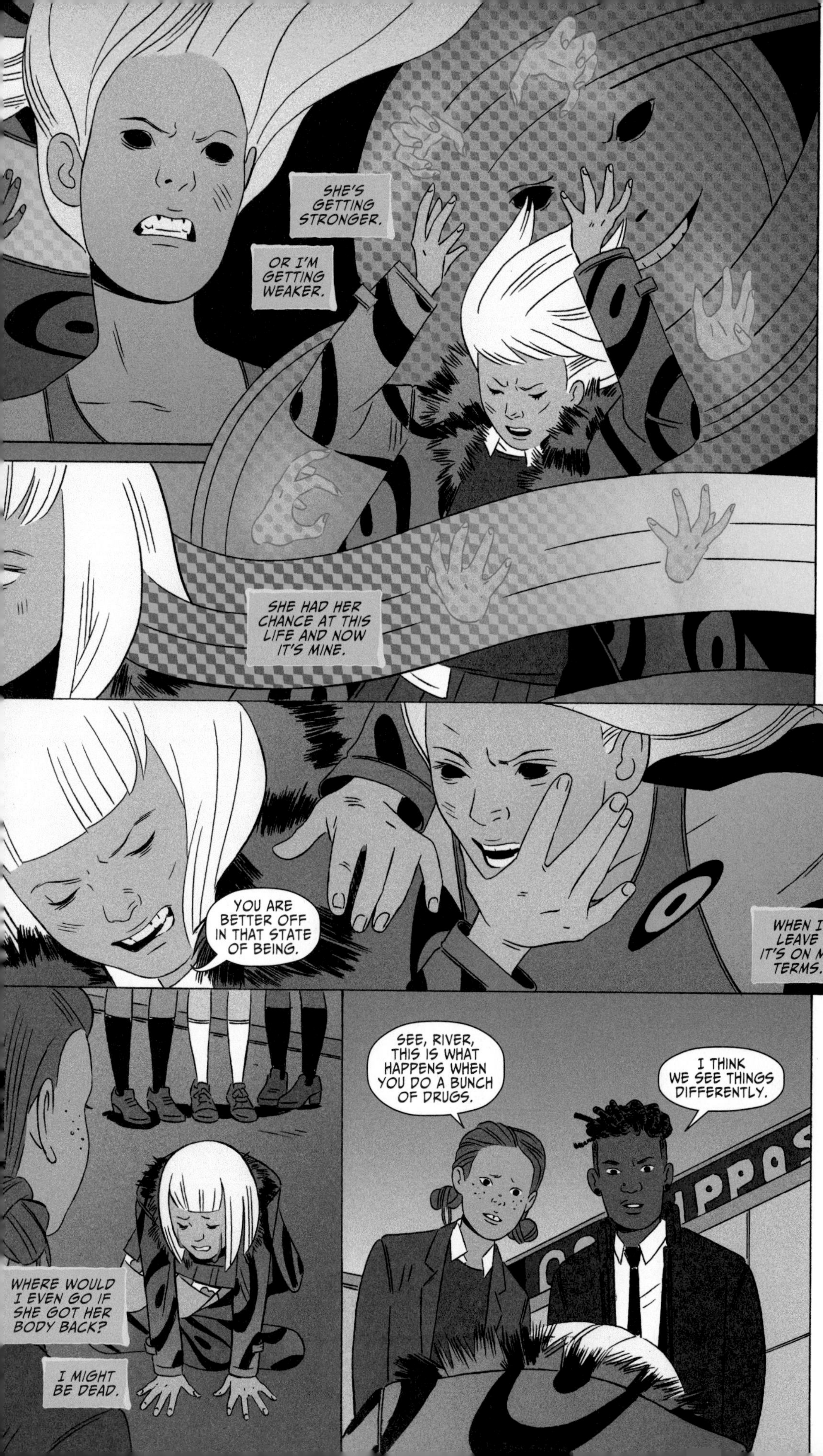
SHE'S GETTING STRONGER.
OR I'M GETTING WEAKER.
SHE HAD HER CHANCE AT THIS LIFE AND NOW IT'S MINE.
YOU ARE BETTER OFF IN THAT STATE OF BEING.
WHEN I LEAVE IT'S ON MY TERMS.
WHERE WOULD I EVEN GO IF SHE GOT HER BODY BACK?
I MIGHT BE DEAD.
SEE, RIVER, THIS IS WHAT HAPPENS WHEN YOU DO A BUNCH OF DRUGS.
I THINK WE SEE THINGS DIFFERENTLY.

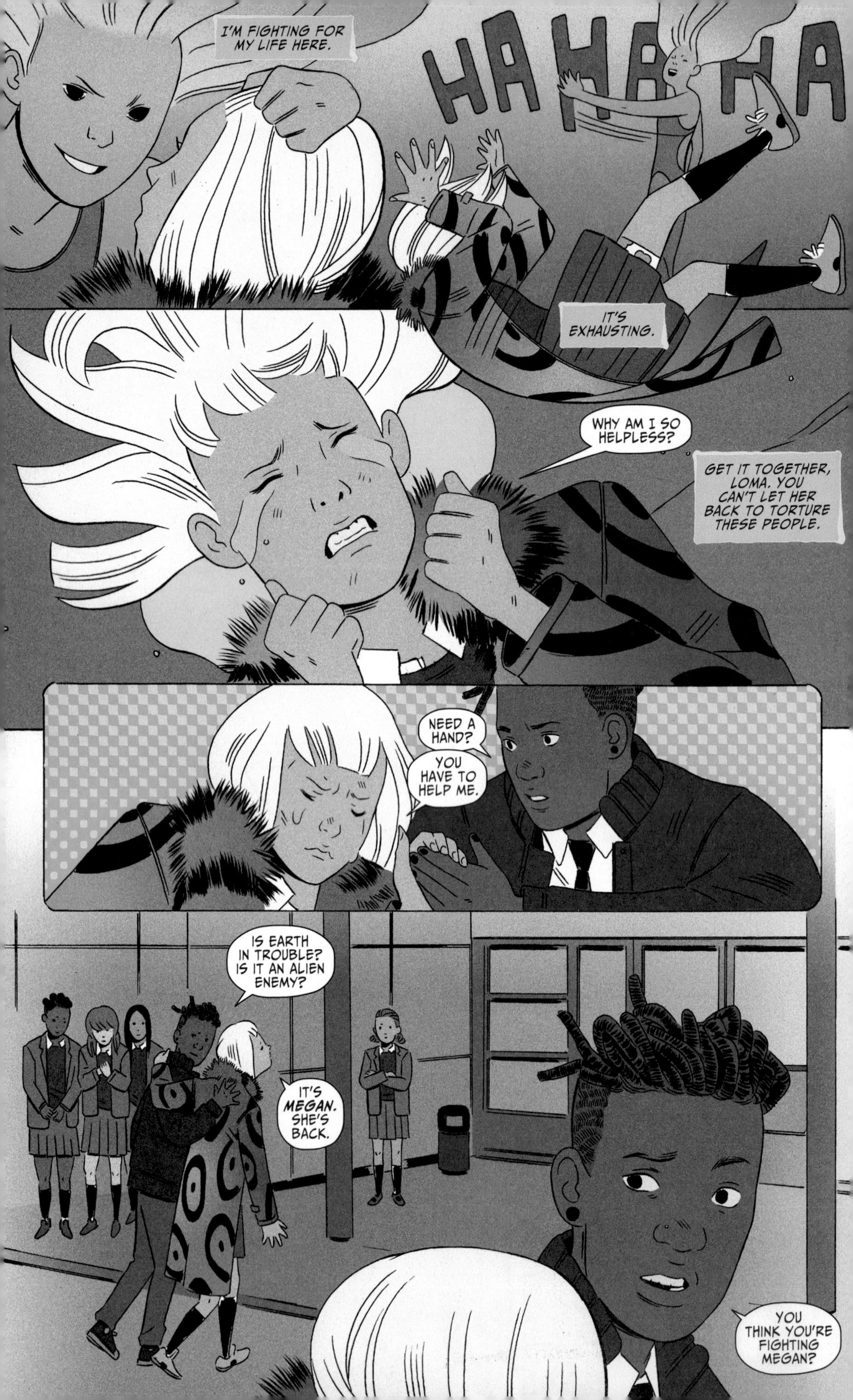
I'M FIGHTING FOR MY LIFE HERE.
HAHAHA
IT'S EXHAUSTING.
WHY AM I SO HELPLESS?
GET IT TOGETHER, LOMA. YOU CAN'T LET HER BACK TO TORTURE THESE PEOPLE.
NEED A HAND?
YOU HAVE TO HELP ME.
IS EARTH IN TROUBLE? IS IT AN ALIEN ENEMY?
IT'S *MEGAN.* SHE'S BACK.
YOU THINK YOU'RE FIGHTING MEGAN?

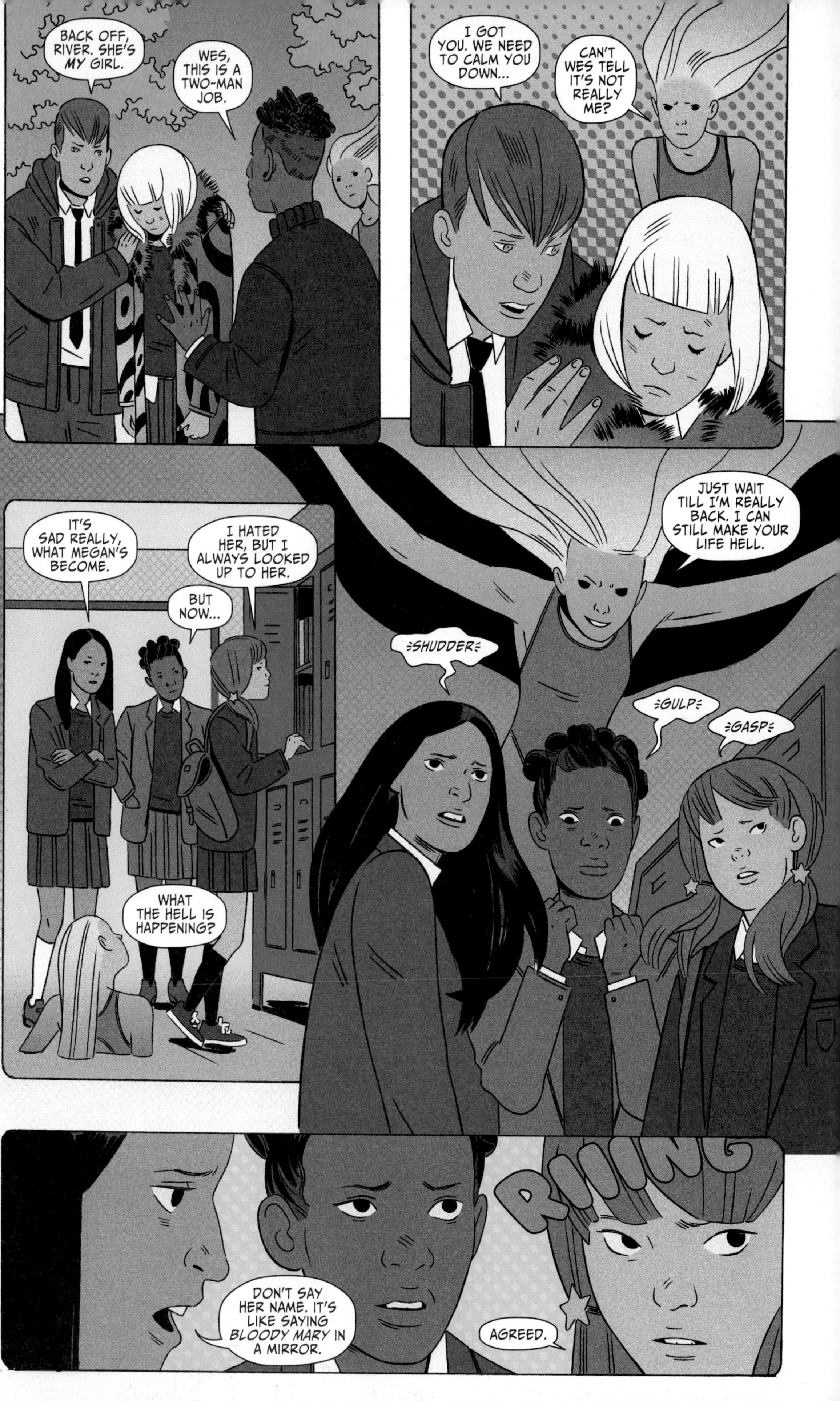
BACK OFF, RIVER. SHE'S *MY* GIRL.
WES, THIS IS A TWO-MAN JOB.
I GOT YOU. WE NEED TO CALM YOU DOWN...
CAN'T WES TELL IT'S NOT REALLY ME?
IT'S SAD REALLY, WHAT MEGAN'S BECOME.
I HATED HER, BUT I ALWAYS LOOKED UP TO HER.
BUT NOW...
WHAT THE HELL IS HAPPENING?
JUST WAIT TILL I'M REALLY BACK. I CAN STILL MAKE YOUR LIFE HELL.
SHUDDER
GULP
GASP
RIIING
DON'T SAY HER NAME. IT'S LIKE SAYING *BLOODY MARY* IN A MIRROR.
AGREED.

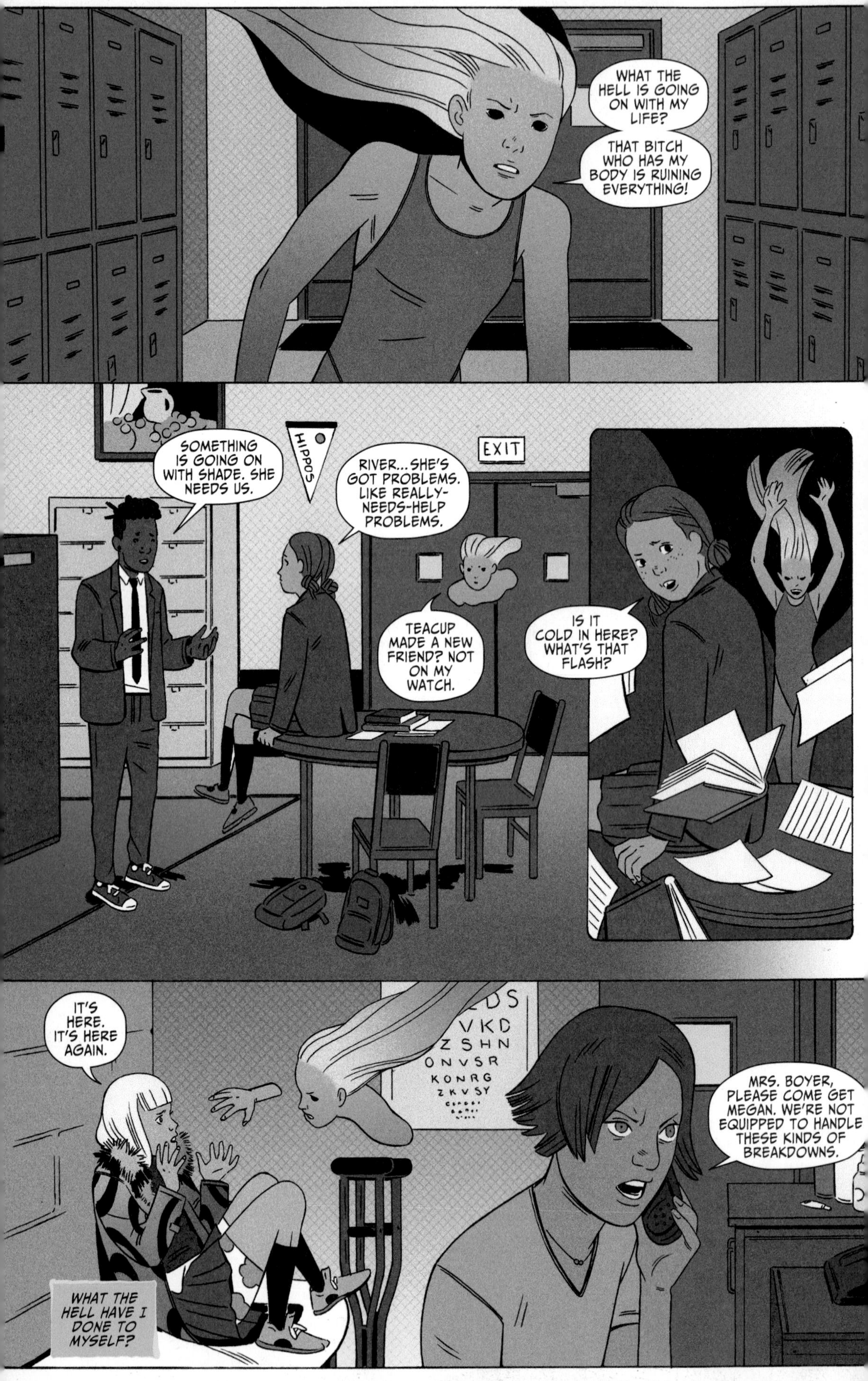
WHAT THE HELL IS GOING ON WITH MY LIFE?
THAT BITCH WHO HAS MY BODY IS RUINING EVERYTHING!
SOMETHING IS GOING ON WITH SHADE. SHE NEEDS US.
HIPPOS
EXIT
RIVER... SHE'S GOT PROBLEMS. LIKE REALLY-NEEDS-HELP PROBLEMS.
TEACUP MADE A NEW FRIEND? NOT ON MY WATCH.
IS IT COLD IN HERE? WHAT'S THAT FLASH?
IT'S HERE. IT'S HERE AGAIN.
MRS. BOYER, PLEASE COME GET MEGAN. WE'RE NOT EQUIPPED TO HANDLE THESE KINDS OF BREAKDOWNS.
WHAT THE HELL HAVE I DONE TO MYSELF?

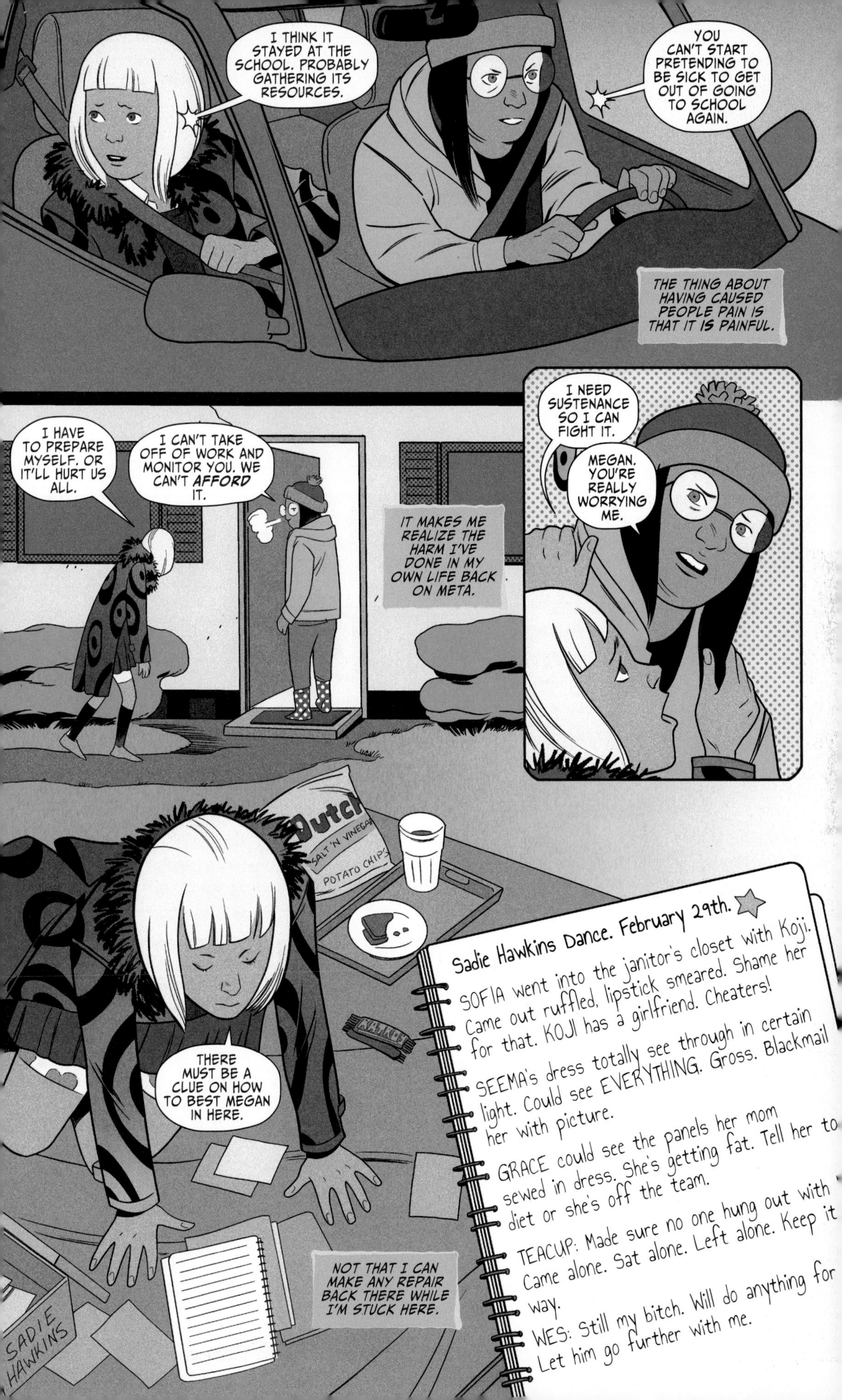
I THINK IT STAYED AT THE SCHOOL. PROBABLY GATHERING ITS RESOURCES.
YOU CAN'T START PRETENDING TO BE SICK TO GET OUT OF GOING TO SCHOOL AGAIN.
THE THING ABOUT HAVING CAUSED PEOPLE PAIN IS THAT IT IS PAINFUL.
I HAVE TO PREPARE MYSELF. OR IT'LL HURT US ALL.
I CAN'T TAKE OFF OF WORK AND MONITOR YOU. WE CAN'T AFFORD IT.
IT MAKES ME REALIZE THE HARM I'VE DONE IN MY OWN LIFE BACK ON META.
I NEED SUSTENANCE SO I CAN FIGHT IT.
MEGAN. YOU'RE REALLY WORRYING ME.
Dutch
SALT 'N VINEGAR
POTATO CHIPS
THERE MUST BE A CLUE ON HOW TO BEST MEGAN IN HERE.
NOT THAT I CAN MAKE ANY REPAIR BACK THERE WHILE I'M STUCK HERE.
SADIE HAWKINS
Sadie Hawkins Dance. February 29th.
SOFIA went into the janitor's closet with Koji. Came out ruffled, lipstick smeared. Shame her for that. KOJI has a girlfriend. Cheaters!
SEEMA's dress totally see through in certain light. Could see EVERYTHING. Gross. Blackmail her with picture.
GRACE could see the panels her mom sewed in dress. She's getting fat. Tell her to diet or she's off the team.
TEACUP: Made sure no one hung out with Came alone. Sat alone. Left alone. Keep it way.
WES: Still my bitch. Will do anything for Let him go further with me.

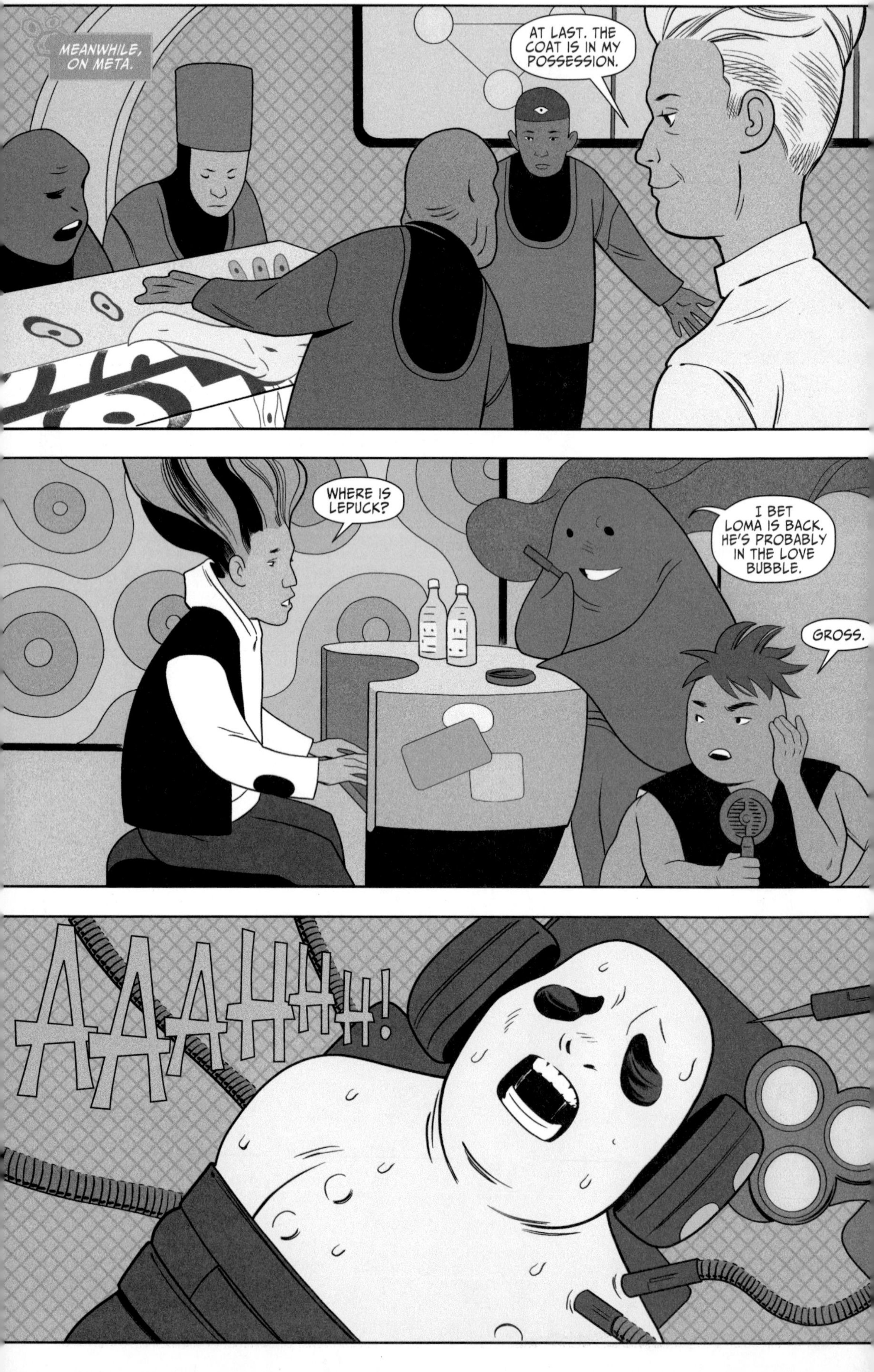
MEANWHILE, ON META.
AT LAST. THE COAT IS IN MY POSSESSION.
WHERE IS LEPUCK?
I BET LOMA IS BACK. HE'S PROBABLY IN THE LOVE BUBBLE.
GROSS.
AAAHHH!

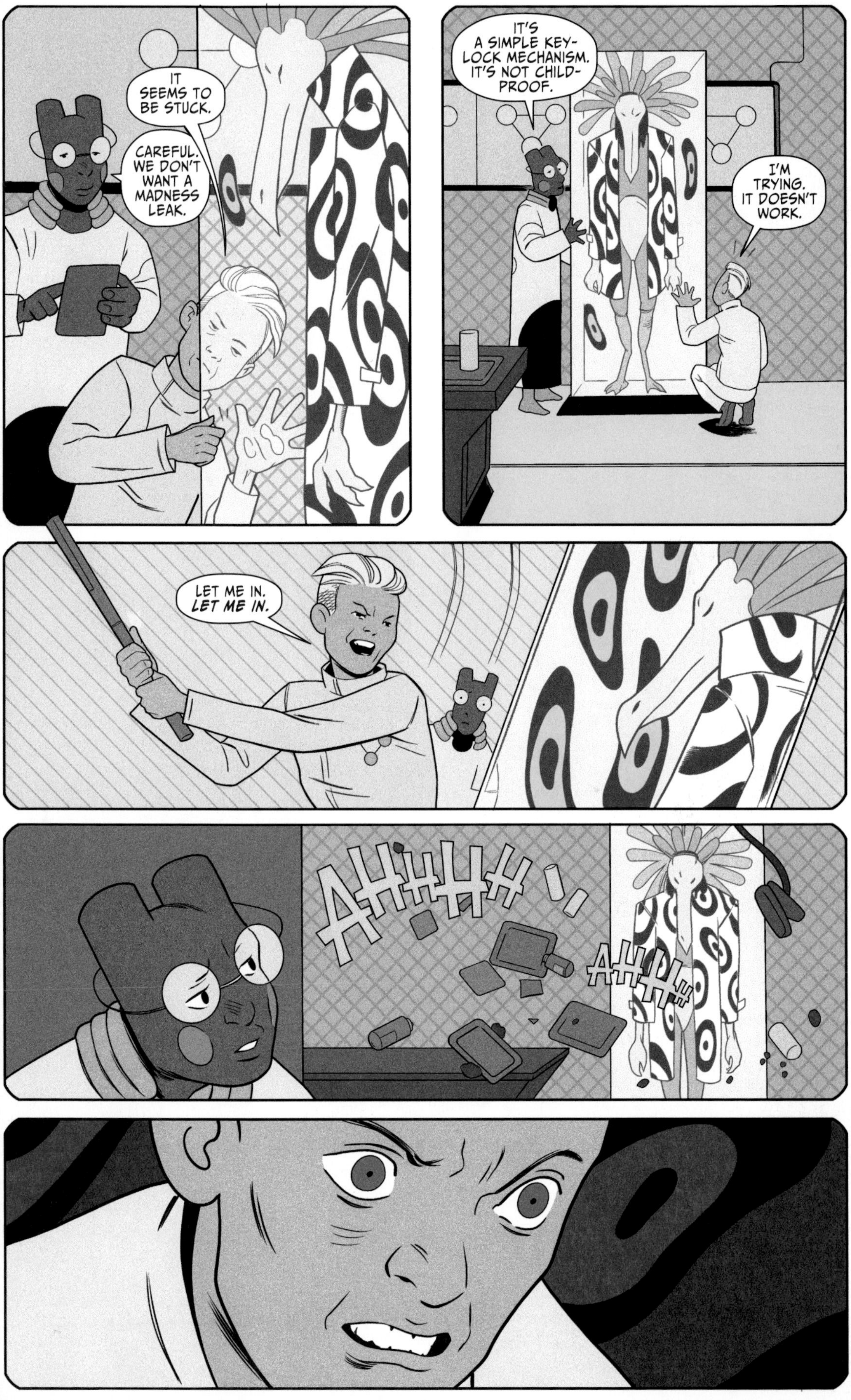
IT SEEMS TO BE STUCK.
CAREFUL. WE DON'T WANT A MADNESS LEAK.
IT'S A SIMPLE KEY-LOCK MECHANISM. IT'S NOT CHILD-PROOF.
I'M TRYING. IT DOESN'T WORK.
LET ME IN. *LET ME IN.*
AHHHHH
AHHHH

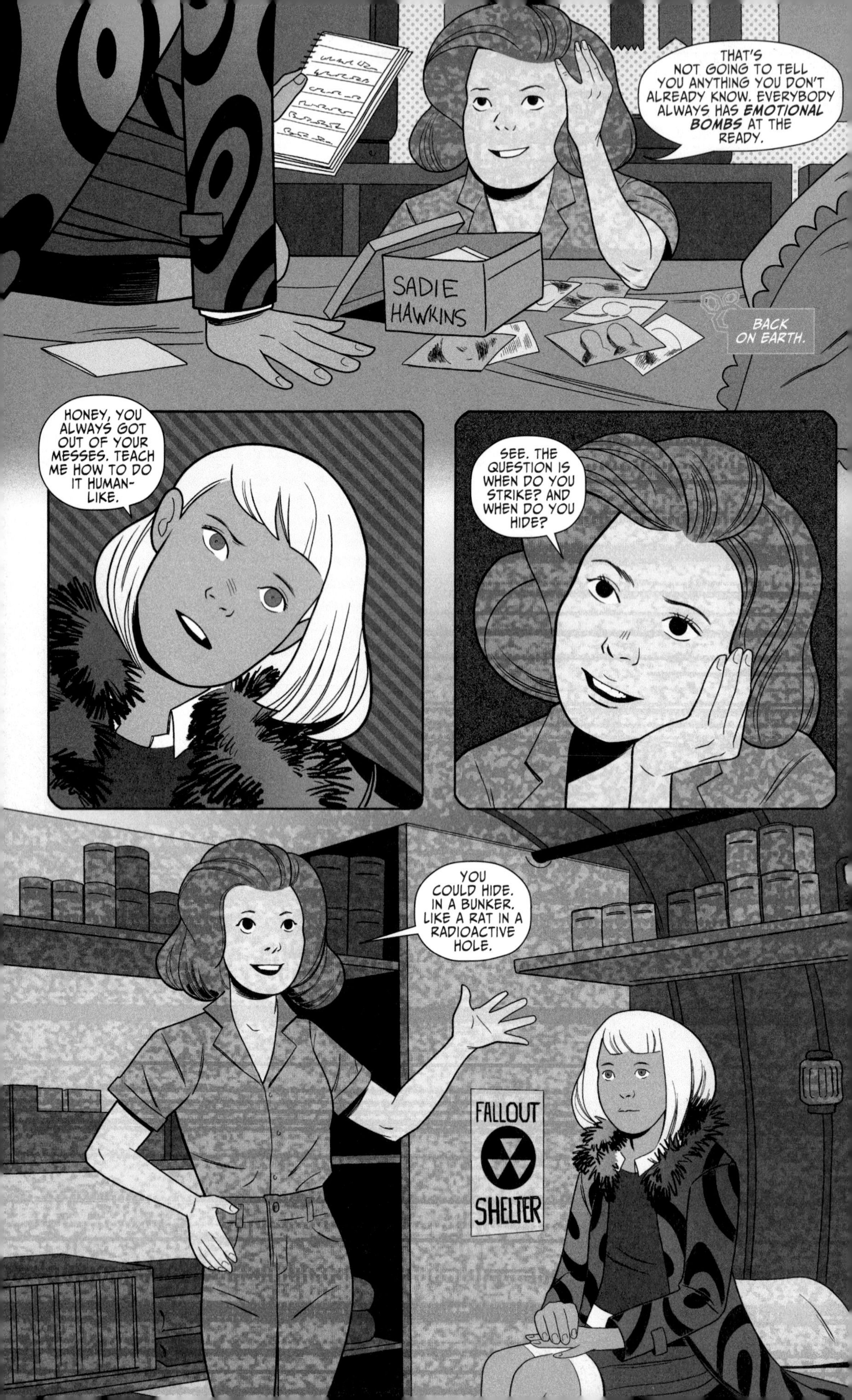
THAT'S NOT GOING TO TELL YOU ANYTHING YOU DON'T ALREADY KNOW. EVERYBODY ALWAYS HAS EMOTIONAL BOMBS AT THE READY.
SADIE HAWKINS
BACK ON EARTH.
HONEY, YOU ALWAYS GOT OUT OF YOUR MESSES. TEACH ME HOW TO DO IT HUMAN-LIKE.
SEE. THE QUESTION IS WHEN DO YOU STRIKE? AND WHEN DO YOU HIDE?
YOU COULD HIDE. IN A BUNKER. LIKE A RAT IN A RADIOACTIVE HOLE.
FALLOUT
SHELTER

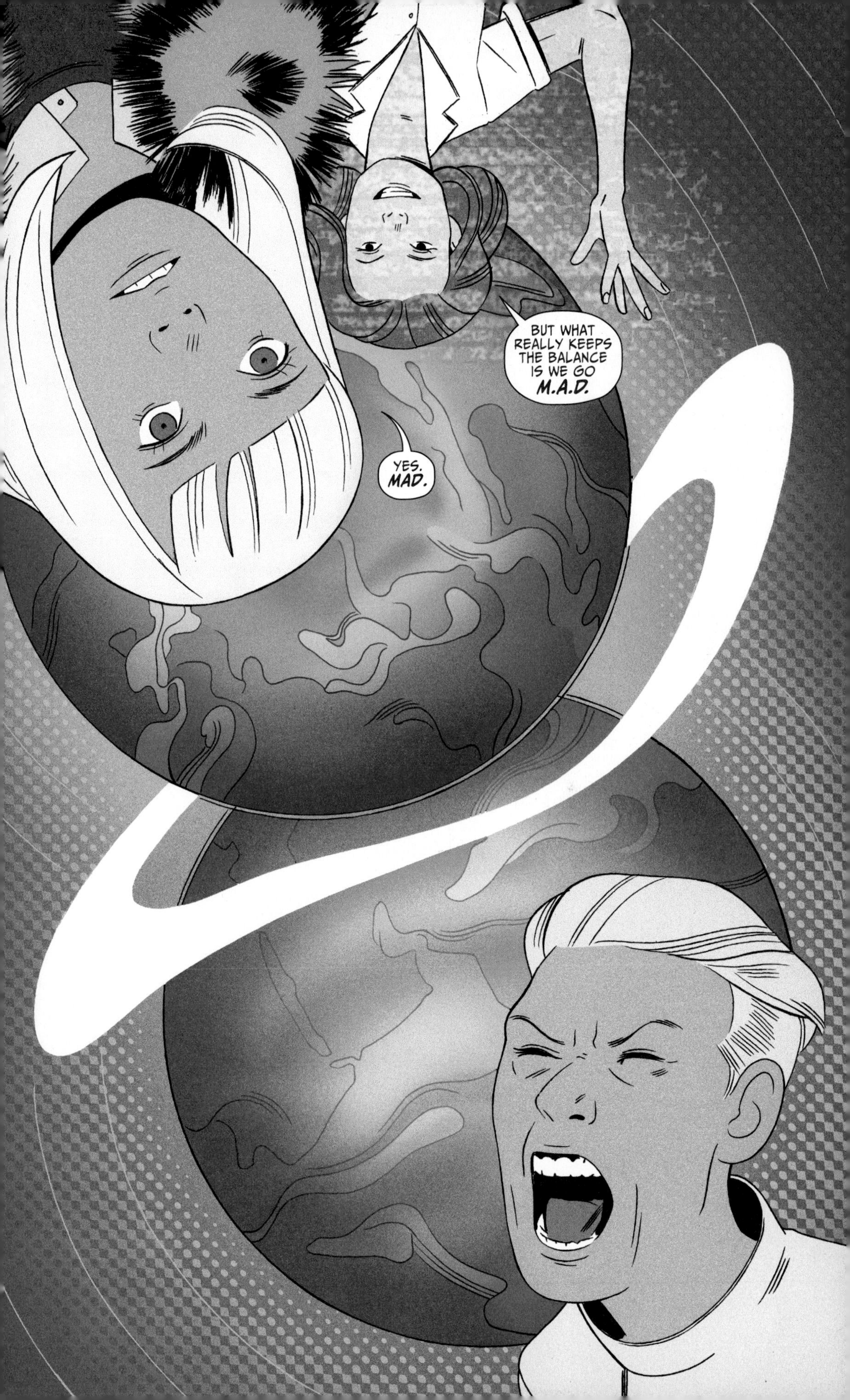
BUT WHAT REALLY KEEPS THE BALANCE IS WE GO M.A.D.
YES. MAD.

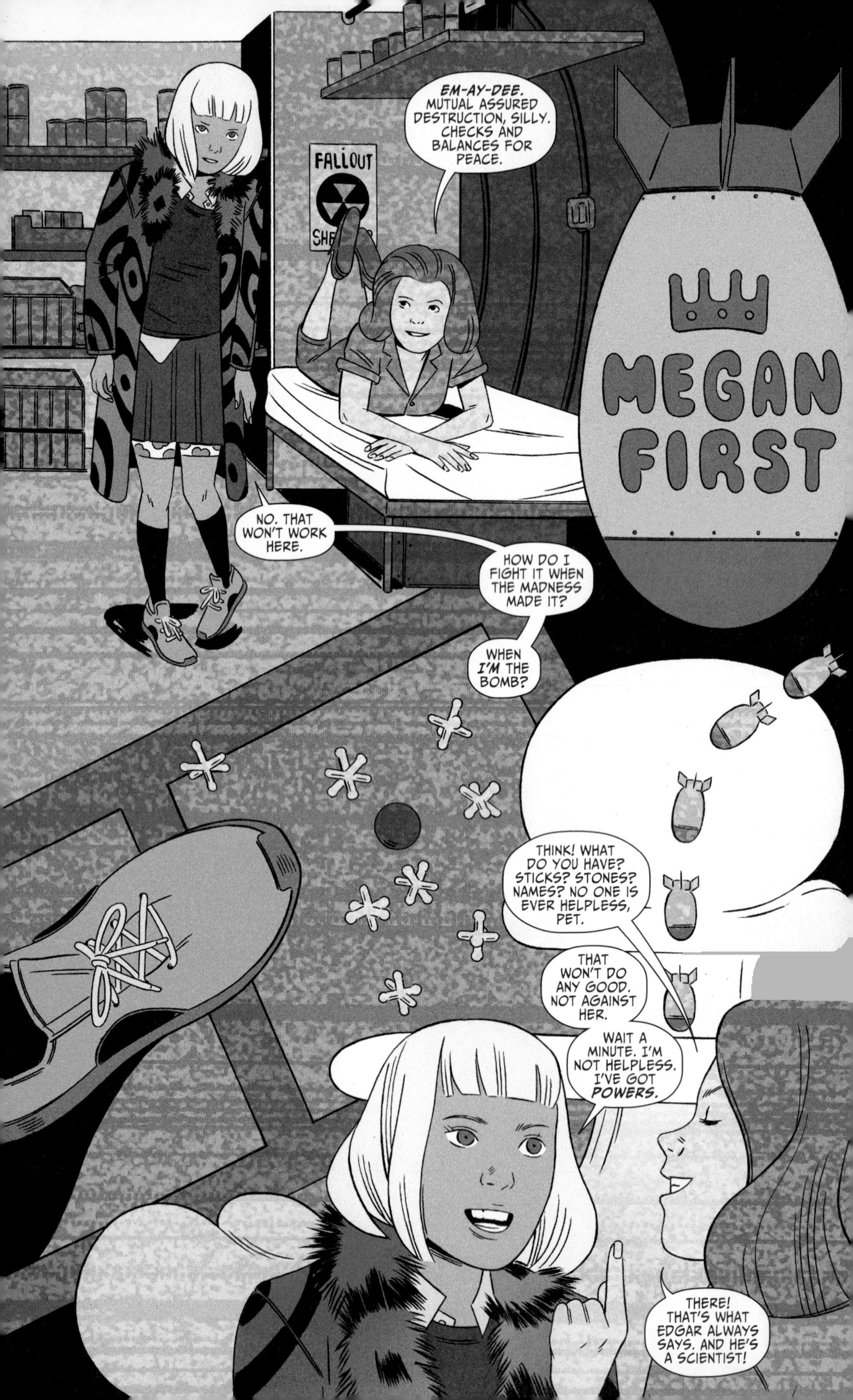

EM-AY-DEE. MUTUAL ASSURED DESTRUCTION, SILLY. CHECKS AND BALANCES FOR PEACE.
FALLOUT SHE
MEGAN FIRST
NO. THAT WON'T WORK HERE.
HOW DO I FIGHT IT WHEN THE MADNESS MADE IT?
WHEN I'M THE BOMB?
THINK! WHAT DO YOU HAVE? STICKS? STONES? NAMES? NO ONE IS EVER HELPLESS, PET.
THAT WON'T DO ANY GOOD. NOT AGAINST HER.
WAIT A MINUTE. I'M NOT HELPLESS. I'VE GOT POWERS.
THERE! THAT'S WHAT EDGAR ALWAYS SAYS. AND HE'S A SCIENTIST!

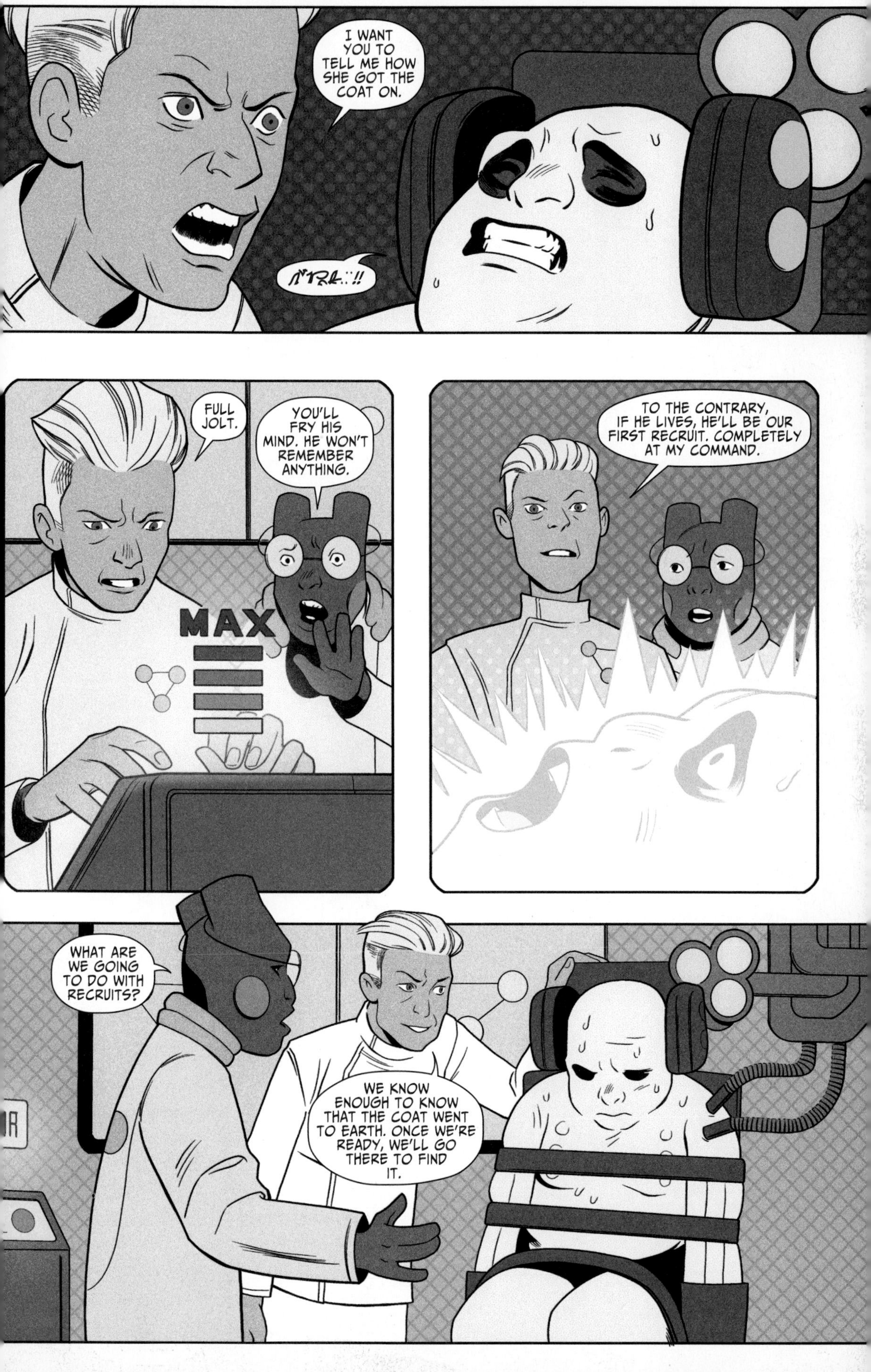
I WANT YOU TO TELL ME HOW SHE GOT THE COAT ON.
FULL JOLT.
YOU'LL FRY HIS MIND. HE WON'T REMEMBER ANYTHING.
MAX
TO THE CONTRARY, IF HE LIVES, HE'LL BE OUR FIRST RECRUIT. COMPLETELY AT MY COMMAND.
WHAT ARE WE GOING TO DO WITH RECRUITS?
WE KNOW ENOUGH TO KNOW THAT THE COAT WENT TO EARTH. ONCE WE'RE READY, WE'LL GO THERE TO FIND IT.

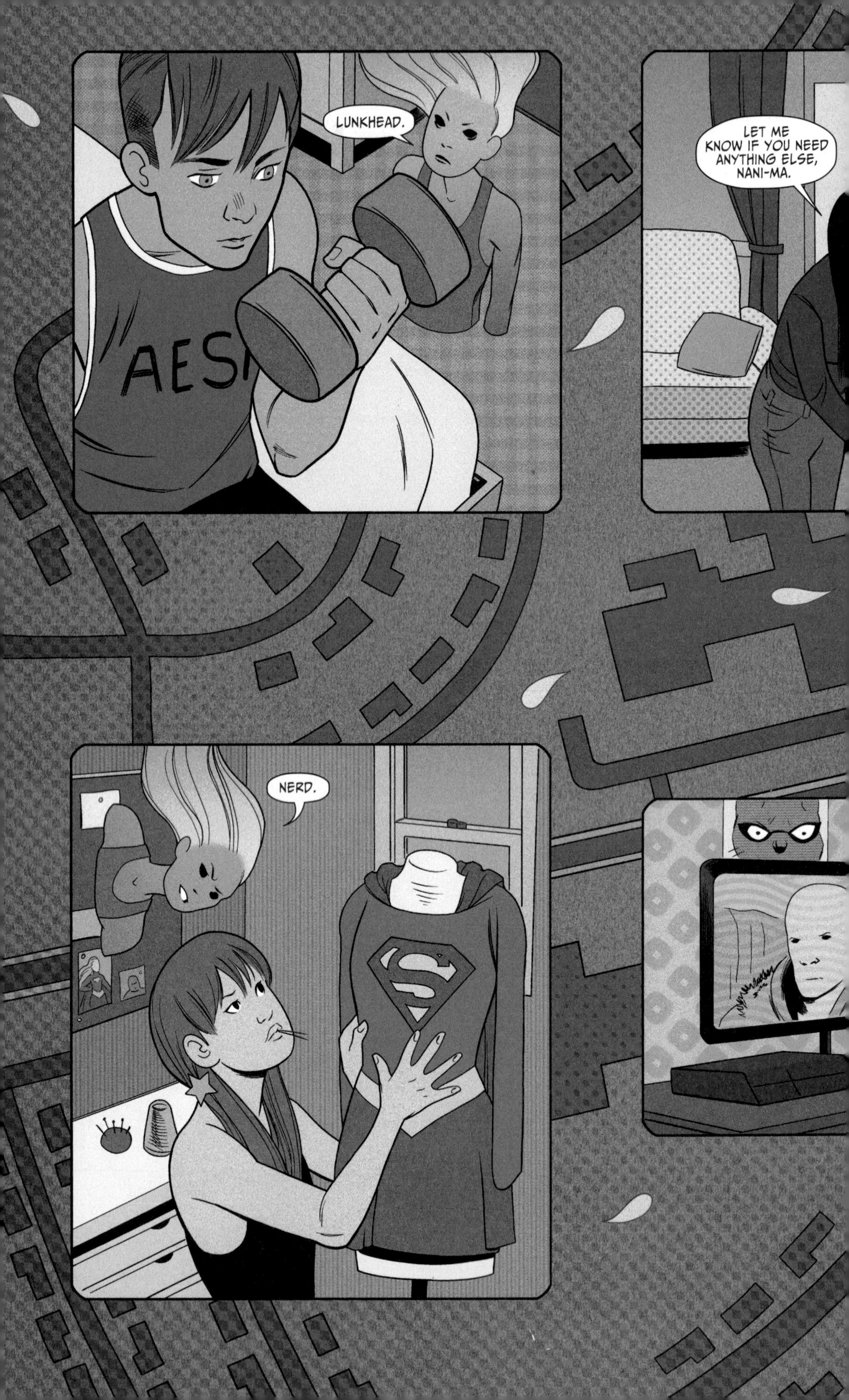
LUNKHEAD.
LET ME KNOW IF YOU NEED ANYTHING ELSE, NANI-MA.
NERD.

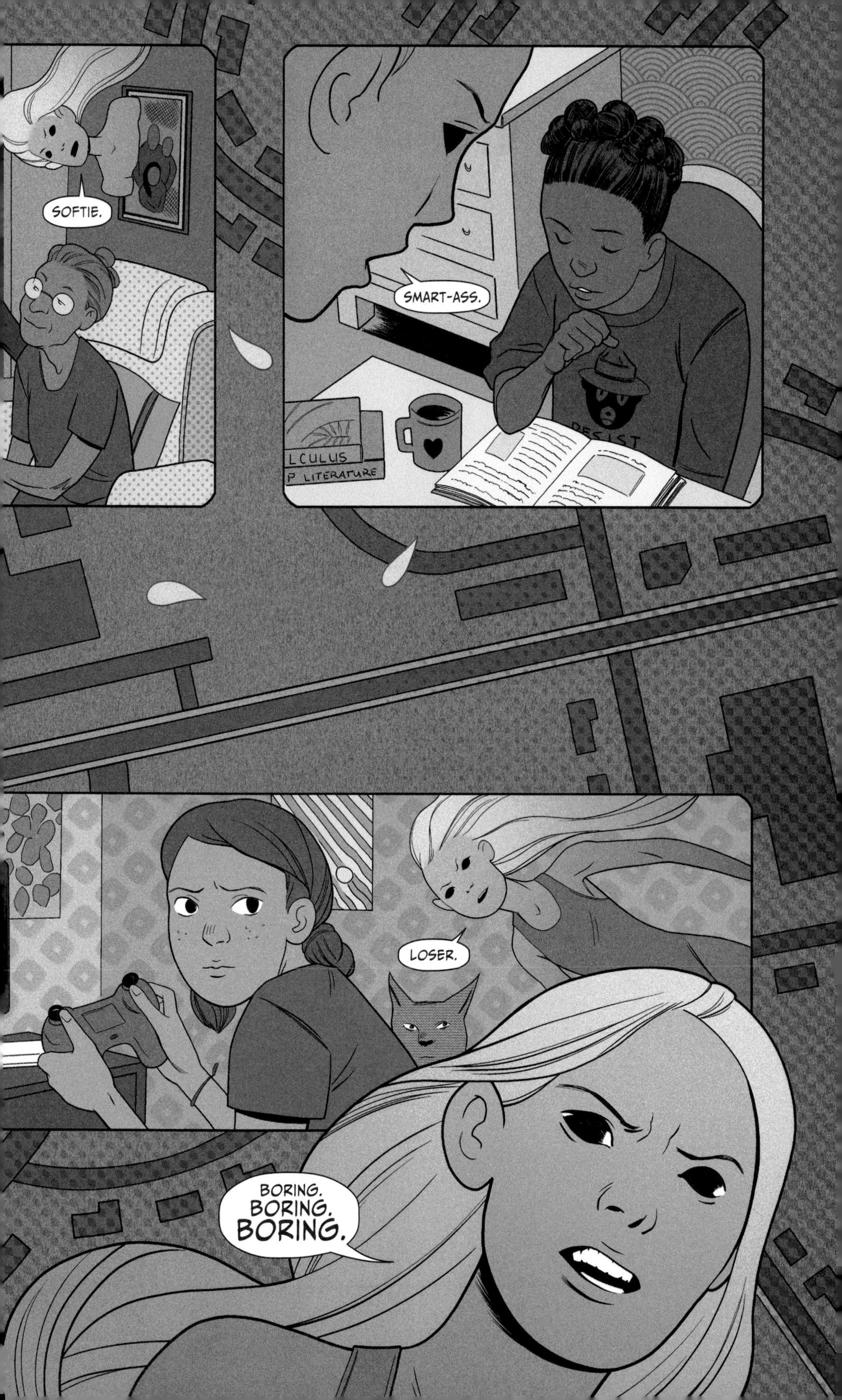
SOFTIE.
SMART-ASS.
LCULUS
P LITERATURE
RESIST
LOSER.
BORING. BORING. BORING.

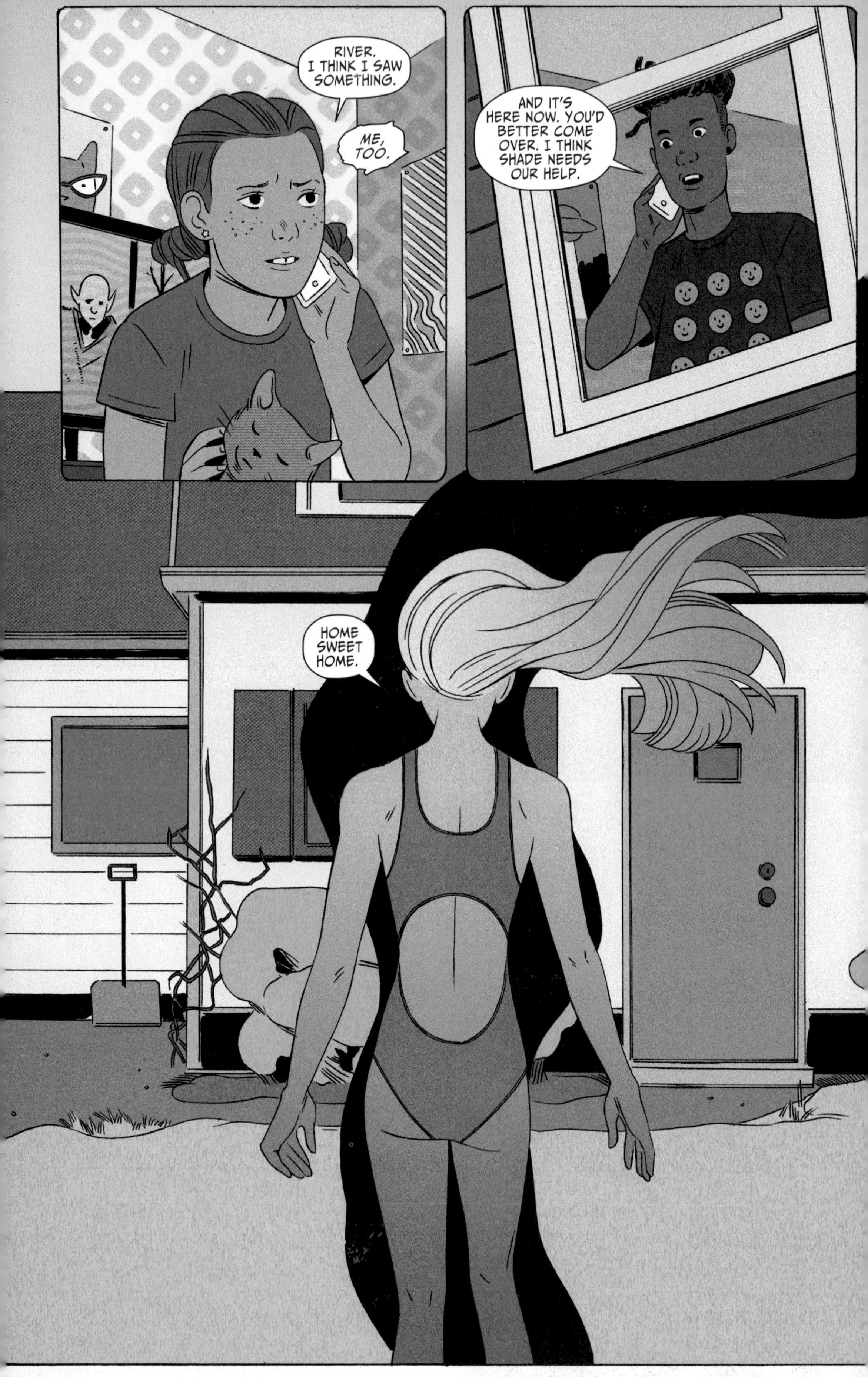
RIVER. I THINK I SAW SOMETHING.
ME, TOO.
AND IT'S HERE NOW. YOU'D BETTER COME OVER. I THINK SHADE NEEDS OUR HELP.
HOME SWEET HOME.

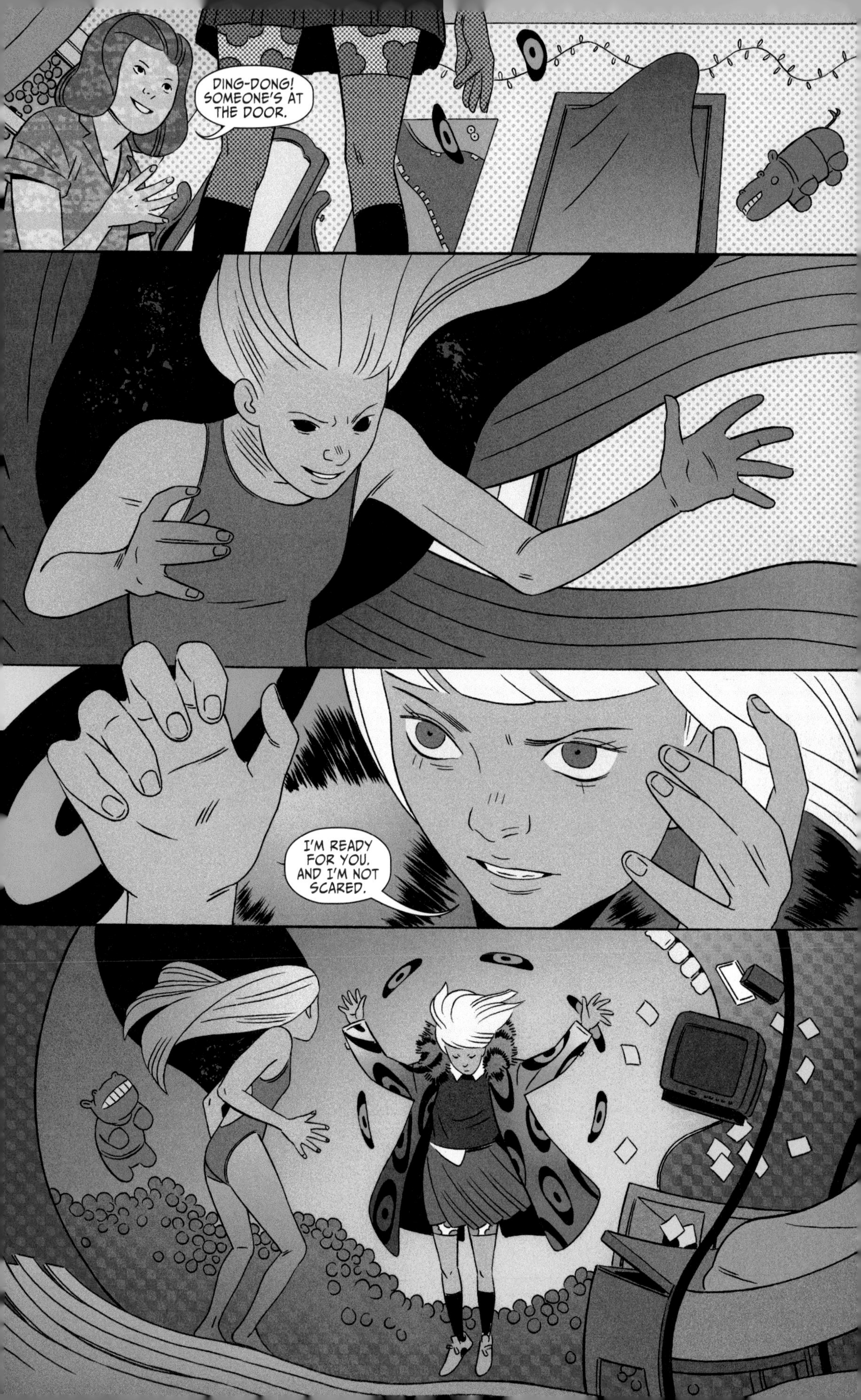
DING-DONG! SOMEONE'S AT THE DOOR.
I'M READY FOR YOU. AND I'M NOT SCARED.

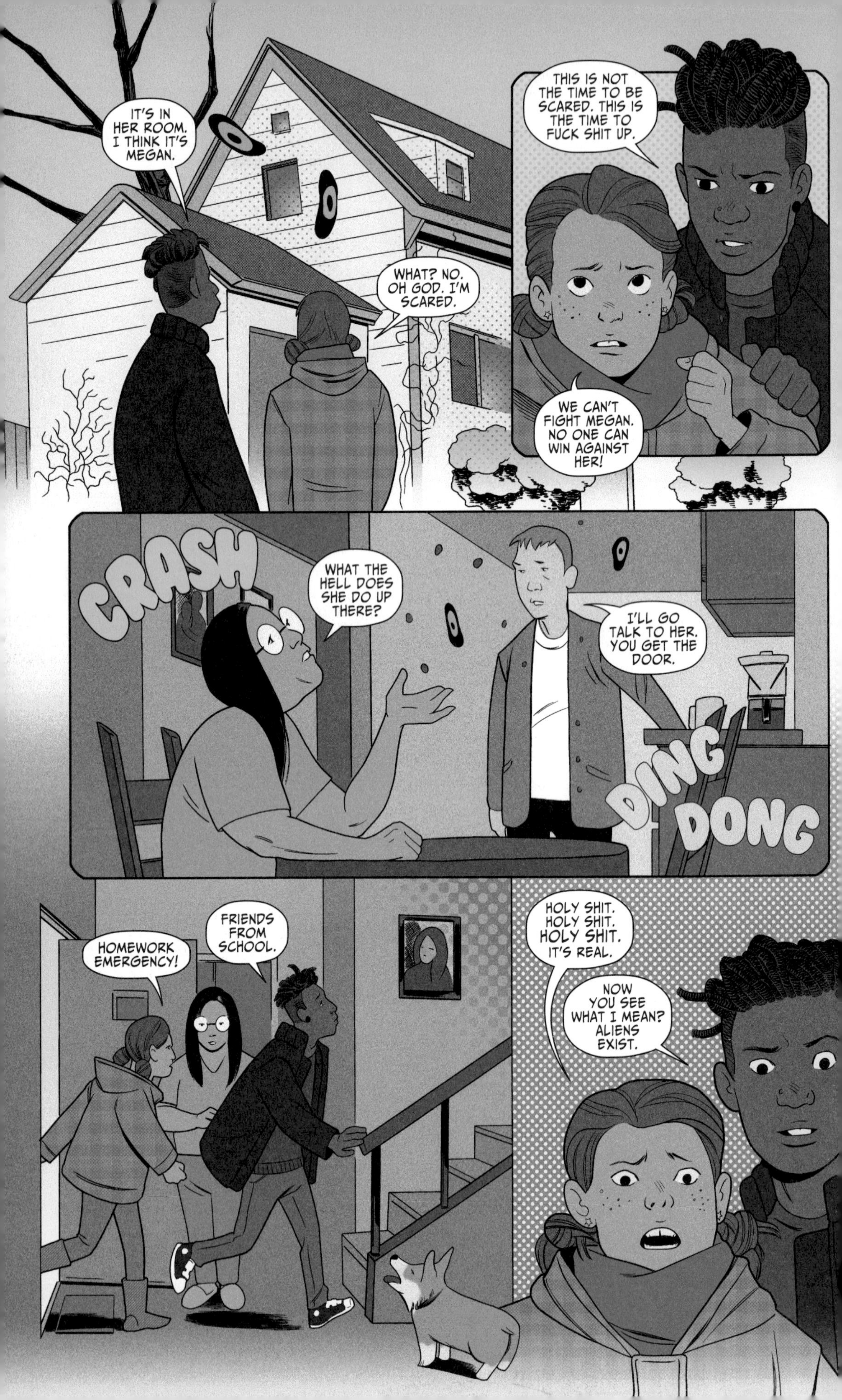

IT'S IN HER ROOM. I THINK IT'S MEGAN.
WHAT? NO. OH GOD. I'M SCARED.
THIS IS NOT THE TIME TO BE SCARED. THIS IS THE TIME TO FUCK SHIT UP.
WE CAN'T FIGHT MEGAN. NO ONE CAN WIN AGAINST HER!
CRASH
WHAT THE HELL DOES SHE DO UP THERE?
I'LL GO TALK TO HER. YOU GET THE DOOR.
DING DONG
HOMEWORK EMERGENCY!
FRIENDS FROM SCHOOL.
HOLY SHIT. HOLY SHIT. HOLY SHIT. IT'S REAL.
NOW YOU SEE WHAT I MEAN? ALIENS EXIST.

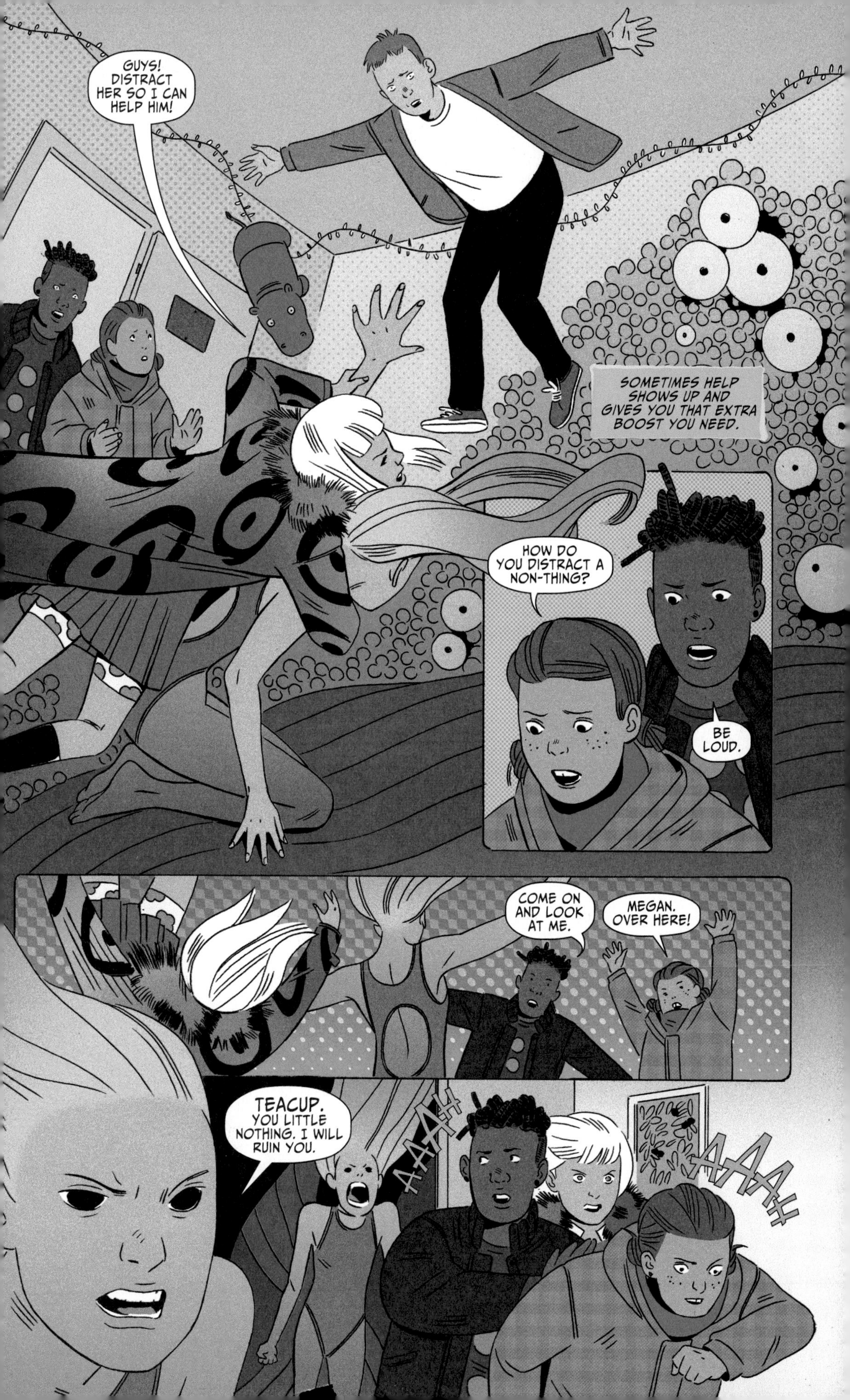
GUYS! DISTRACT HER SO I CAN HELP HIM!
SOMETIMES HELP SHOWS UP AND GIVES YOU THAT EXTRA BOOST YOU NEED.
HOW DO YOU DISTRACT A NON-THING?
BE LOUD.
COME ON AND LOOK AT ME.
MEGAN. OVER HERE!
TEACUP. YOU LITTLE NOTHING. I WILL RUIN YOU.
AAAH
AAAH

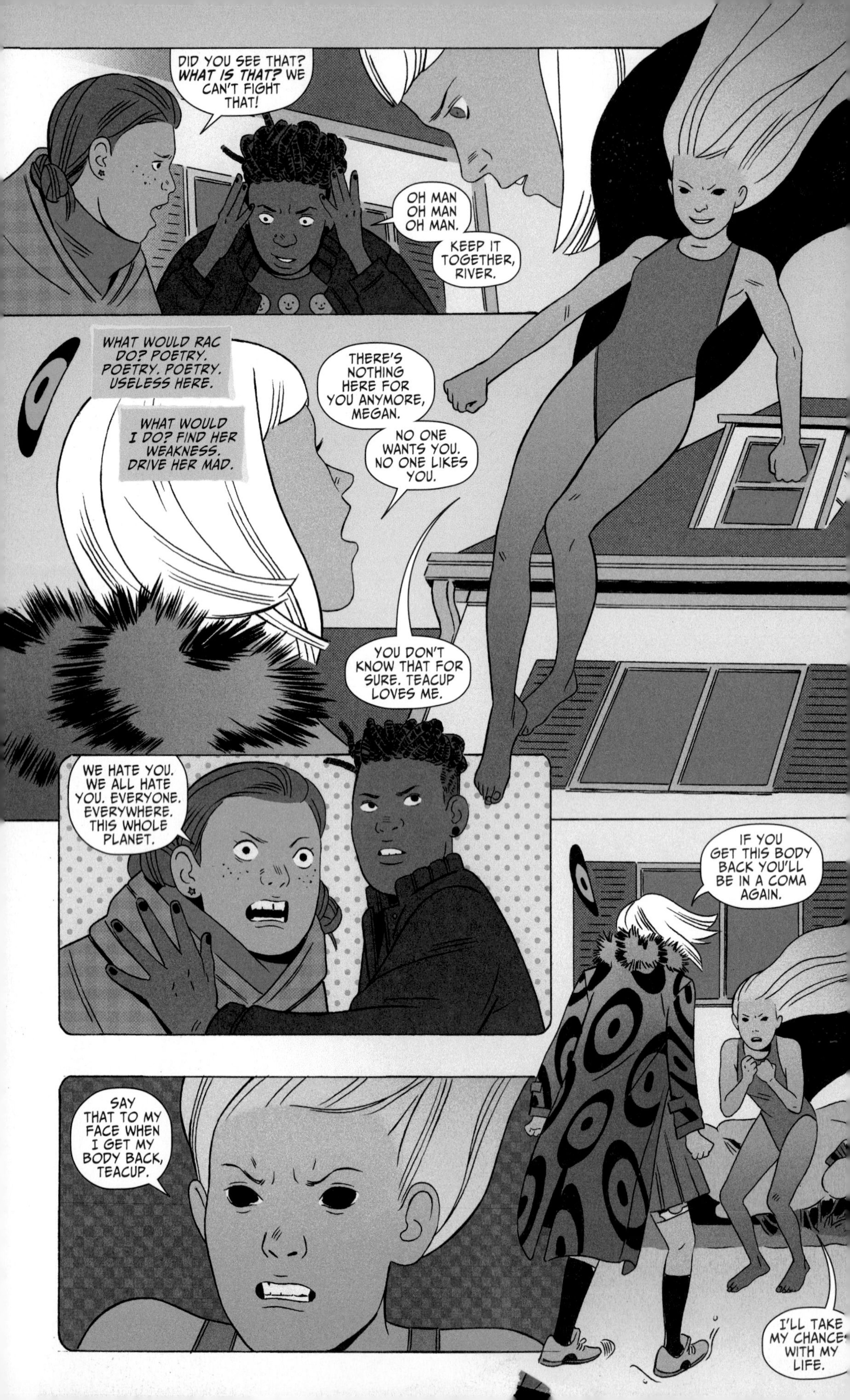
DID YOU SEE THAT? *WHAT IS THAT?* WE CAN'T FIGHT THAT!
OH MAN OH MAN OH MAN.
KEEP IT TOGETHER, RIVER.
WHAT WOULD RAC DO? POETRY. POETRY. POETRY. USELESS HERE.
WHAT WOULD I DO? FIND HER WEAKNESS. DRIVE HER MAD.
THERE'S NOTHING HERE FOR YOU ANYMORE, MEGAN.
NO ONE WANTS YOU. NO ONE LIKES YOU.
YOU DON'T KNOW THAT FOR SURE. TEACUP LOVES ME.
WE HATE YOU. WE ALL HATE YOU. EVERYONE. EVERYWHERE. THIS WHOLE PLANET.
IF YOU GET THIS BODY BACK YOU'LL BE IN A COMA AGAIN.
SAY THAT TO MY FACE WHEN I GET MY BODY BACK, TEACUP.
I'LL TAKE MY CHANCE WITH MY LIFE.

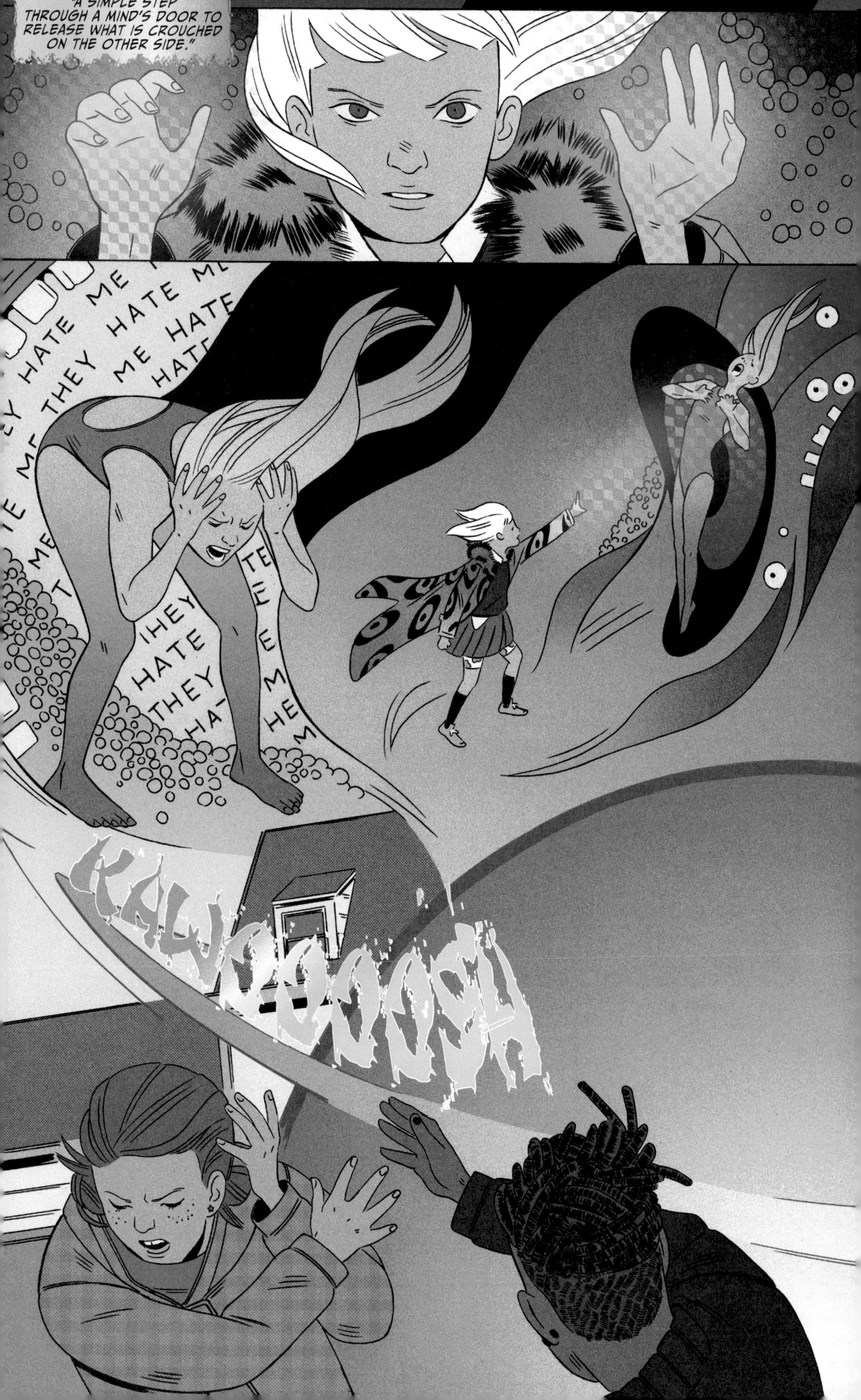
"A SIMPLE STEP THROUGH A MIND'S DOOR TO RELEASE WHAT IS CROUCHED ON THE OTHER SIDE."
THEY HATE ME
THEY HATE ME

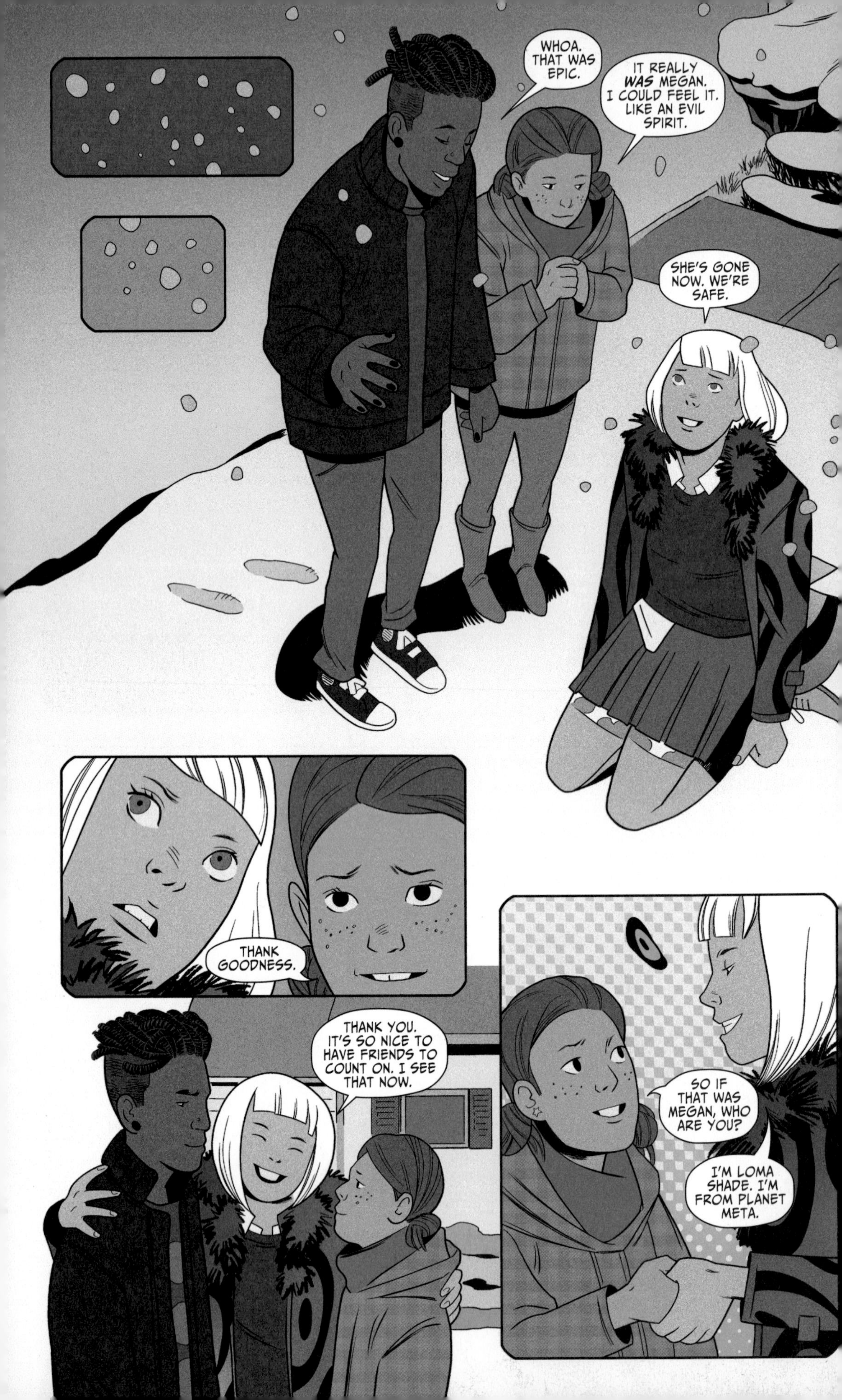
WHOA. THAT WAS EPIC.
IT REALLY WAS MEGAN. I COULD FEEL IT. LIKE AN EVIL SPIRIT.
SHE'S GONE NOW. WE'RE SAFE.
THANK GOODNESS.
THANK YOU. IT'S SO NICE TO HAVE FRIENDS TO COUNT ON. I SEE THAT NOW.
SO IF THAT WAS MEGAN, WHO ARE YOU?
I'M LOMA SHADE. I'M FROM PLANET META.

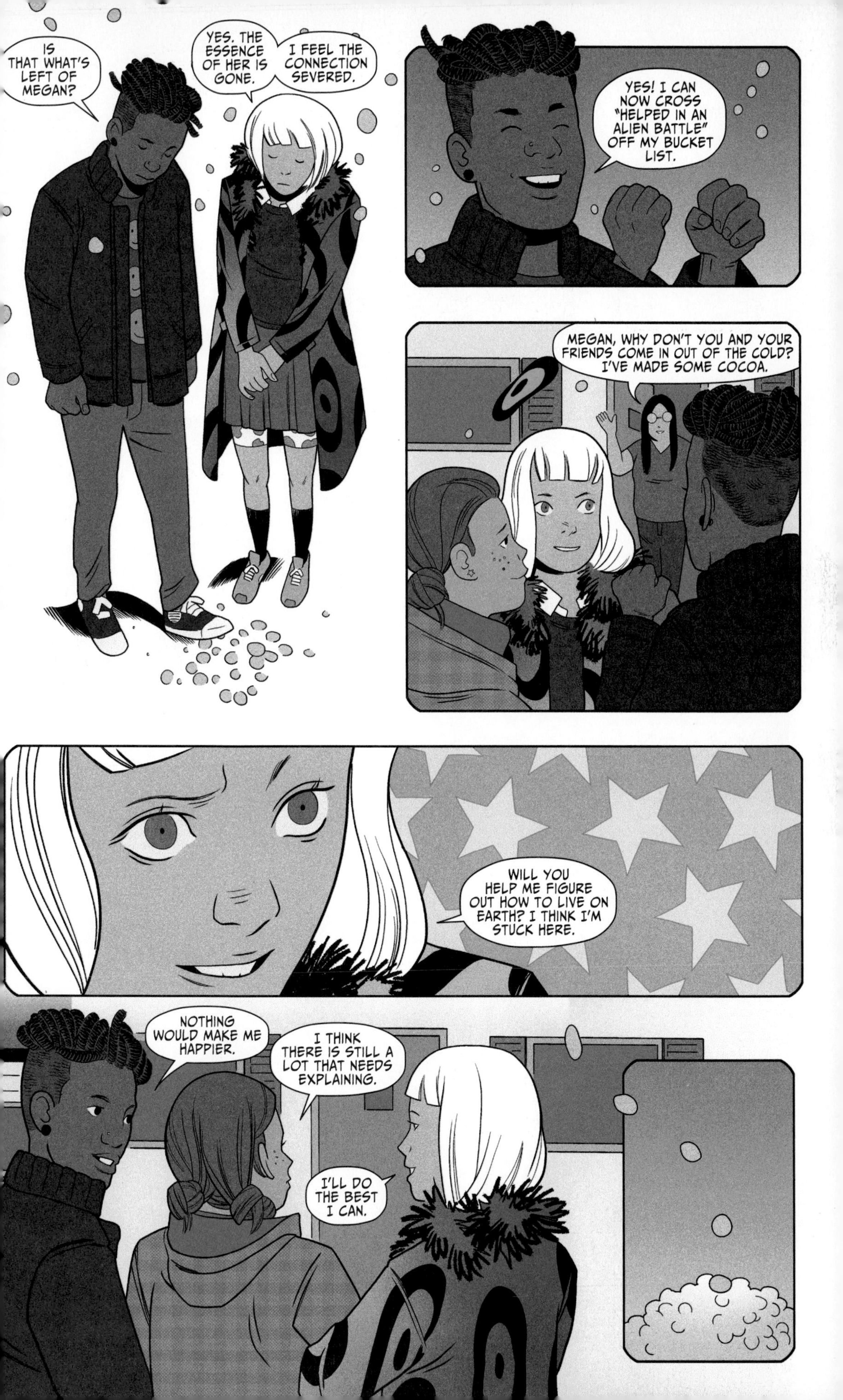

IS THAT WHAT'S LEFT OF MEGAN?
YES. THE ESSENCE OF HER IS GONE.
I FEEL THE CONNECTION SEVERED.
YES! I CAN NOW CROSS "HELPED IN AN ALIEN BATTLE" OFF MY BUCKET LIST.
MEGAN, WHY DON'T YOU AND YOUR FRIENDS COME IN OUT OF THE COLD? I'VE MADE SOME COCOA.
WILL YOU HELP ME FIGURE OUT HOW TO LIVE ON EARTH? I THINK I'M STUCK HERE.
NOTHING WOULD MAKE ME HAPPIER.
I THINK THERE IS STILL A LOT THAT NEEDS EXPLAINING.
I'LL DO THE BEST I CAN.

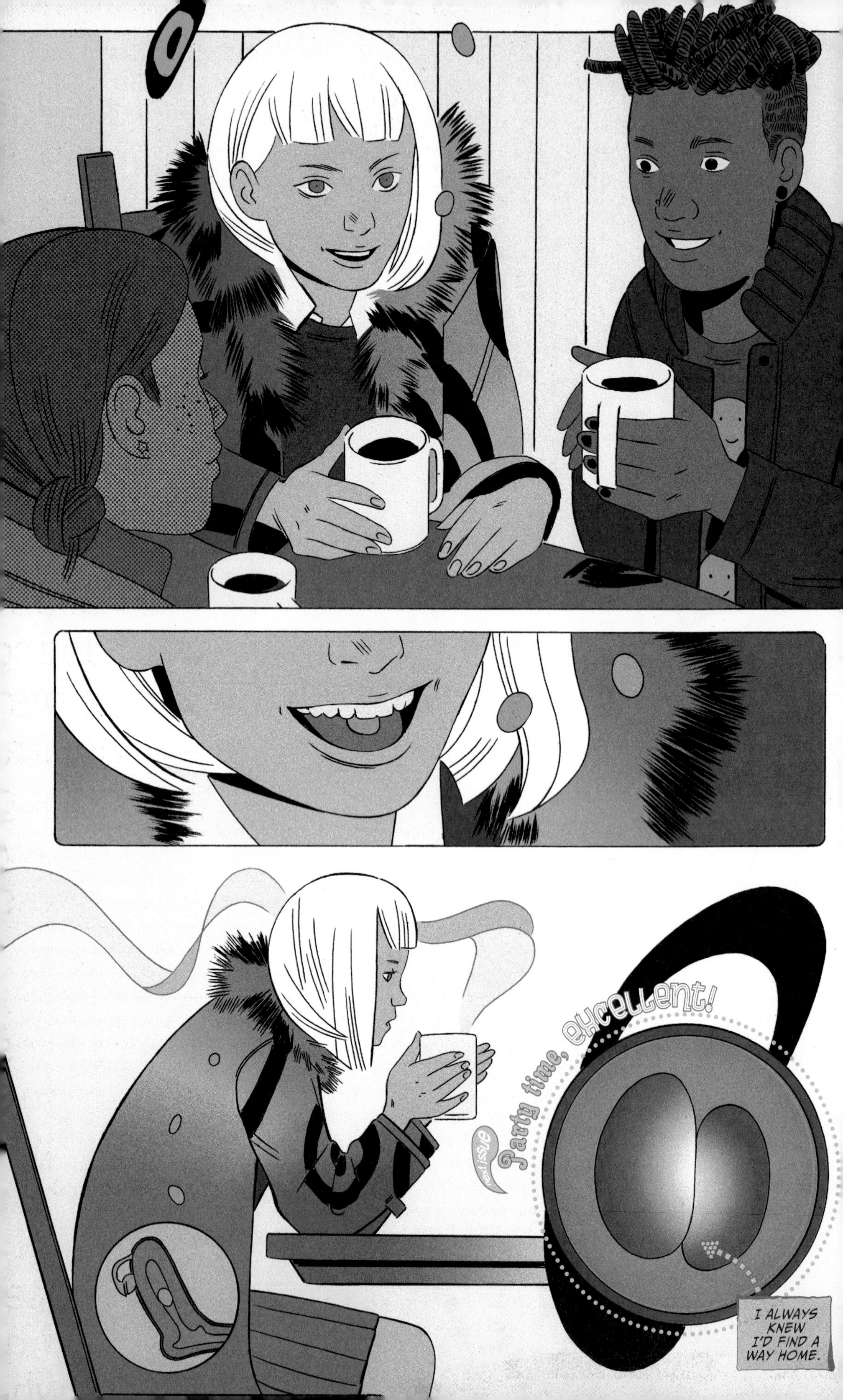

next issue
Party time, excellent!
I ALWAYS KNEW I'D FIND A WAY HOME.

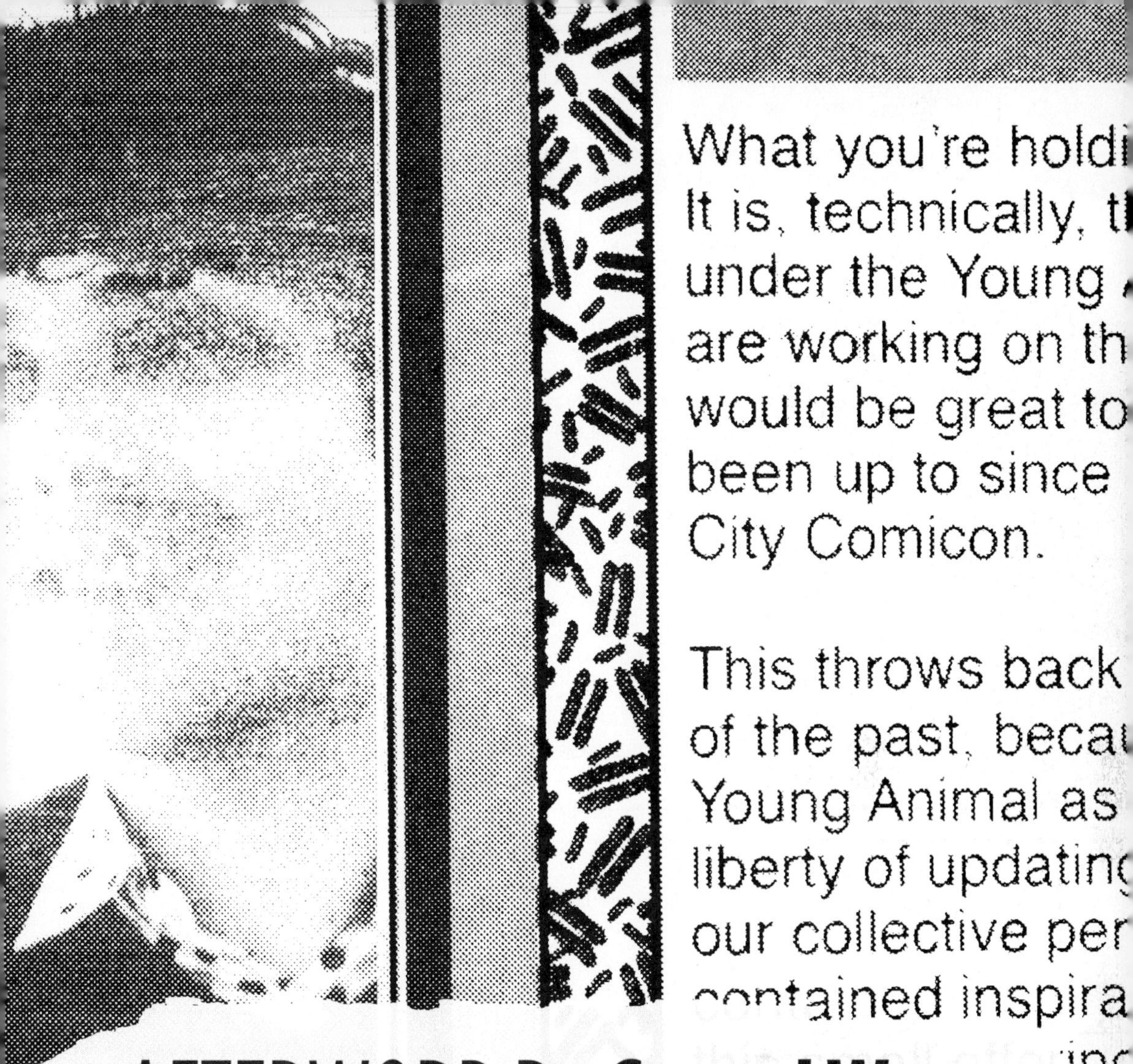
What you're holdi
It is, technically, t
under the Young
are working on th
would be great to
been up to since
City Comicon.
This throws back
of the past, becau
Young Animal as
liberty of updatin
our collective per
contained inspira

AFTERWORD By **Gerard Way**

Shade Shade Shade Shade Shade Shade Shade.

Out of all the DC's Young Animal books, I have the deepest affection for SHADE, THE CHANGING GIRL. I find myself constantly inspired by the creative team and by the stories they are telling in the pages of this comic. Everything, from the writing to the art to the lettering to the coloring, pushes the boundaries of what a comic can be, and I absolutely adore it. It is perhaps the most abstract Young Animal title, and because of that I find it the most rewarding to read.

Loma Shade was born of a simple idea: she was to be an alien connected to Rac Shade in name only—inspired by him and in possession of his madness coat. She was to inhabit the body of a 16-year-old comatose bully, who was in that state due to a swimming accident. A crude drawing of a strange alien creature, followed by a colored version of Loma in the body she would inhabit, and that was it. Shelly Bond (who edited the second half of Peter Milligan's run on Vertigo's SHADE, THE CHANGING MAN) introduced me to Cecil Castellucci, and it was then that Loma Shade really came to life. It was through Cecil's sample pages, and her young adult fiction, that we were able to find the perfect voice for the character.

In our first meeting, Cecil responded to my drawing of Loma's alien body by immediately calling out, "She's a bird!" This kind of enthusiasm, I would soon come to learn, was part of how Cecil operated, and she would keep that momentum going throughout the entire process. She took to the character immediately, filling in details right away—who was Megan? What was she like? Who is Loma? How did she get the coat? What is she going to do with it? As Cecil constructed a Loma that was every bit a free spirit as she was a fan of Rac Shade's poetry, we began to notice that Loma was a very different character than we had seen before. Sure, she was a fish (bird?) out of water, but it was the ways in which she interacted with her new human feelings that made her unique.

One of the most important aspects of all the Young Animal titles is that the books and the characters all connect to the past in some way—they aren't retellings

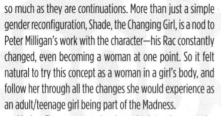

so much as they are continuations. More than just a simple gender reconfiguration, Shade, the Changing Girl, is a nod to Peter Milligan's work with the character—his Rac constantly changed, even becoming a woman at one point. So it felt natural to try this concept as a woman in a girl's body, and follow her through all the changes she would experience as an adult/teenage girl being part of the Madness.

Marley Zarcone was also brought into the soup by Shelly, as she had worked with her on the Vertigo title EFFIGY. I will never forget seeing her first take on Meglo (Cecil's name for Loma in the skin of Megan) and how excited I was by it. Marley had an immediate understanding of the character, and we loved how she presented her (she gave her a matching Madness bag!). I responded strongly to the art, and I knew readers would, too. Paired with Kelly Fitzpatrick, whom I had first seen coloring Shaun Simon and Tyler Jenkins' *Neverboy*, they created this cosmic neo-psychedelic visual presentation. Saida Temofonte went for a style that invoked some of the lettering on the '90s Milligan run, but also did something new (and I love the title-page logo she created). And Becky Cloonan, a longtime friend and collaborator, provided her usual stunning covers—in fact, *un*usual stunning covers. This is a book that is firing on all of its strange cylinders, with Shelly and Molly Mahan first forming the team, lighting the spark, and putting everything in motion, and then with Jamie S. Rich taking over, guiding the book to extraordinary places and getting the most out of everyone involved.

This first graphic novel you hold in your hands is quite a journey, and it feels like the team is just getting started. What makes me so excited for Shade's future are the possibilities: of what she could become, what kind of adventures she could go on all over the country, the Earth—the galaxy! Shade's capacity to change and to surprise is what keeps me coming back to this book. Also, Lepuck, River, Teacup—they are some of my favorite characters ever created, and I can't wait to see where they all head next.

And there's Madness all over this book! It gets all over everything!

Stick around. Or, I mean, *follow* Shade, because she's going to have a hard time staying in one place, and you never know what she's going to be.

Love and Madness Mouths,
G

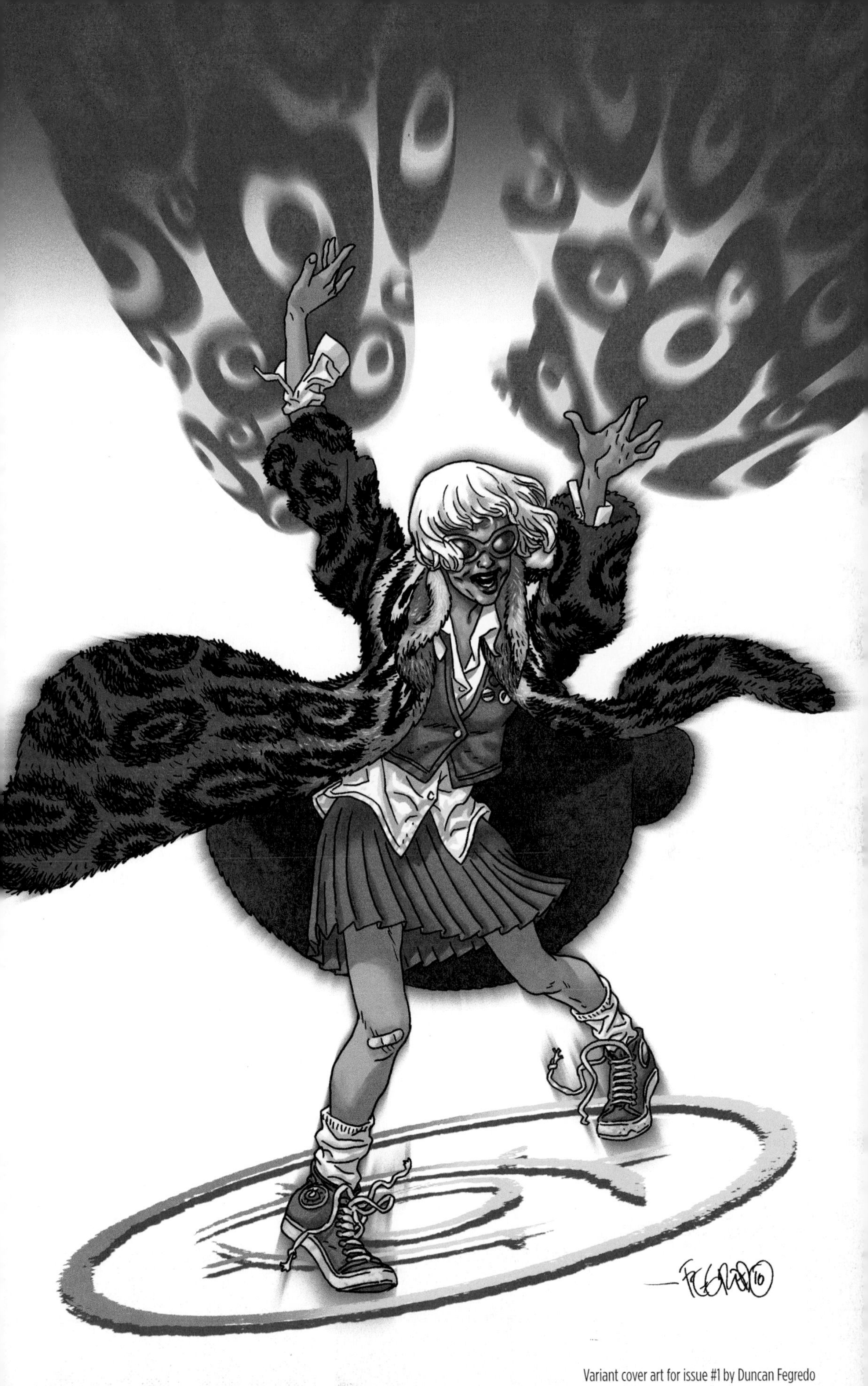

Variant cover art for issue #1 by Duncan Fegredo

shade the changing girl

PERSONAL DATA

Full Name: Loma Shade
Species: Avian
Planet: Meta
Current Location: Earth, Midwest America, Suburb of Yarrow Lake outside of Valley Ville, Body of Megan Boyer
Occupation: Student (Earth: High School; Meta: Poetry Major)
Marital Status: It's complicated
Group Affiliation: None
First Appearance: Now

HISTORY

A recent university dropout, Loma Shade is an Avian who hails from Planet Meta. She has a longtime obsession with the poet Rac Shade, known for his sojourn on Earth and dealings with Madness, and the mid-20th century Earth television show *Life With Honey*, which features a young bride, Honey, who goes to live in Los Alamos, New Mexico, with her nuclear scientist husband. The show is notable off Earth and was popular on Meta due to its signal traveling in space, along with several other shows of its time. This kicked off a brief fad of Metan interest on the planet Earth. Loma Shade was still obsessed with Earth long after the fad had passed. In a fortuitous encounter with the madness coat, Loma was able to hitch a ride with the madness to Earth, where she is currently possessing a human girl, Megan Boyer, age 16. Unprepared for her sudden trip to Earth, she is navigating the consequences of a life that she didn't lead while dealing with the growing influence of the madness that brought her there.

POWERS & WEAPONS

Madness. Currently uncontained. Fears and desires run amok.

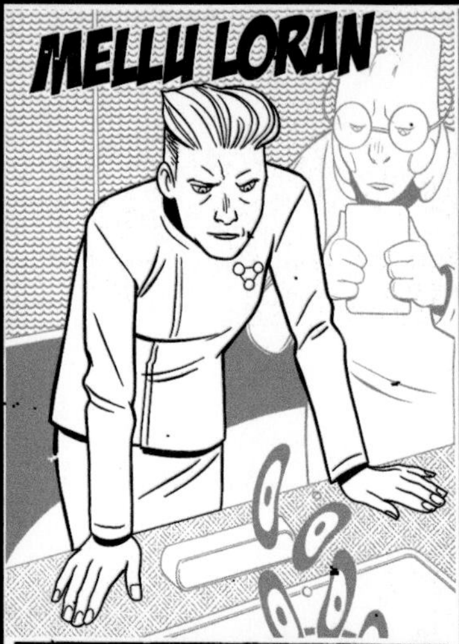
MELLU LORAN

HISTORY

Mellu Loran grew up in the elite Metan society and can trace her heritage back to the original species from Meta. Her parents (deceased) were renowned scientists, but Mellu's brilliant tactical mind had her forging her own path in Metan Bureaucracy, moving quickly up the ranks in her youth. Many thought that she would become the Metan Prime at some point. She was entrusted with the secret M-Vest project, which sought to harness madness. This is where she met Rac Shade, a down-and-out poet looking for some quick cash by joining the M-Vest project (now discontinued). During the madness experiments, Mellu and Rac fell in love and her career took a dramatic downswing. Their love affair was epic (see gossip pages, *Metan Times*), leaving Metans wondering about Loran's judgment and capacity to ever run Meta. The project was deemed a failure and she was passed over for promotions and quickly lost her standing in Metan politics.

Their breakup came due to a misunderstanding surrounding Mellu's parents' death. Rac fled to Earth on the madness stream to evade charges. Mellu's hatred of Rac Shade is well documented, and when he returned to Meta, she used her political power to make his life miserable. This abuse of power ruined all of her chances at the promising political career that she had demonstrated in her youth. Rac wrote his greatest poem, "Mellu's Lament," based on their doomed love.

Her accusations proved to be unfounded, as it later came out that Rac Shade had nothing to do with Loran's famous parents' deaths, but any reconciliation was too late. She never got over Rac Shade.

She was pardoned for her misuse of public resources for her own personal agenda and relegated to the Department of Galactic Affairs: Small Problems, a far fall for someone who had such a bright future..

PERSONAL DATA

Who's Who: Mellu Loran
Age: Older
Occupation: Director of Galactic Affairs: Small Problems, former head of ORC and Metan Affairs
Marital Status: Spinster
Superpowers: None

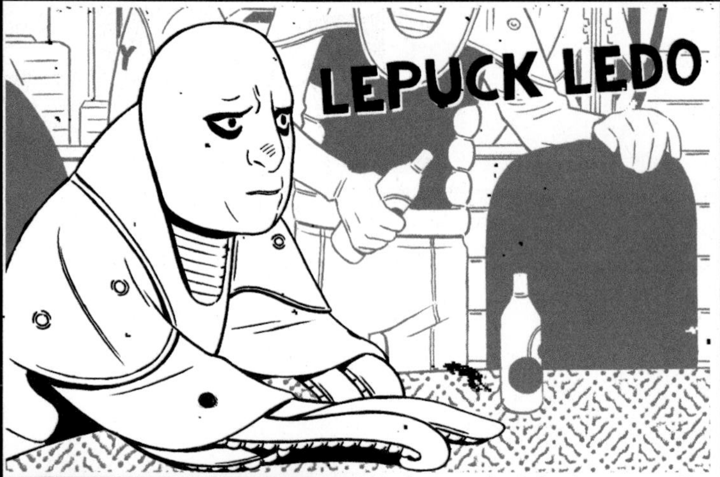
LEPUCK LEDO

PERSONAL DATA

Who's Who: Lepuck Ledo
Age: 27 (Metan years)
Occupation: Museum Security Guard, member of the band Blo'Norton
Marital Status: Thinks he's Loma Shade's boyfriend
Superpowers: None.
Skills: Plays multiple instruments, security training

HISTORY

Lepuck is a young Orzian. Like most non-native Metans, he came to Meta as a child, a refugee during the Cray Expansion.

He first met the Avian Loma at traffic school and fell quickly for her. They spent a passionate week together during her semester break and then she disappeared for a while. He was surprised when she showed up at one of his gigs and they got back to seeing each other. According to him, they've been dating on and off again for a year.

Ledo's parents were able to raise him themselves, an unusual situation for non-Metans, but despite all of his advantages, he chose a simpler path in life, leading some to think that he's a bit lost. Lepuck scored high on all of his aptitude tests, but rather than enter into the prestigious Metan Bureaucracy profession, he chose to do a year of volunteering in the Metan Civilian Guard, building habitats off-world, and then a year as a park ranger, where he specialized in tree planting. These year-long gigs led him to enter the security sector, an honorable profession, but known to be a job for those with no ambition. Thus he became a great disappointment to his parents. He is fond of smoking a good bowl of dorcha, drinking, and playing music with his band, The Blo'Nortons.

Lepuck's friends are concerned about him being a soft touch. Lepuck wants everyone to just relax and get along.

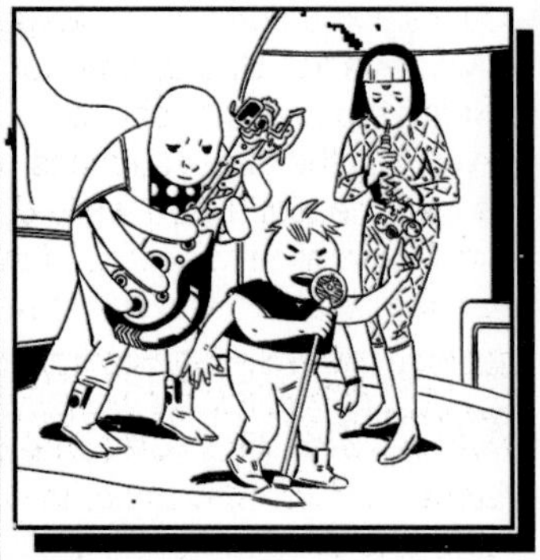

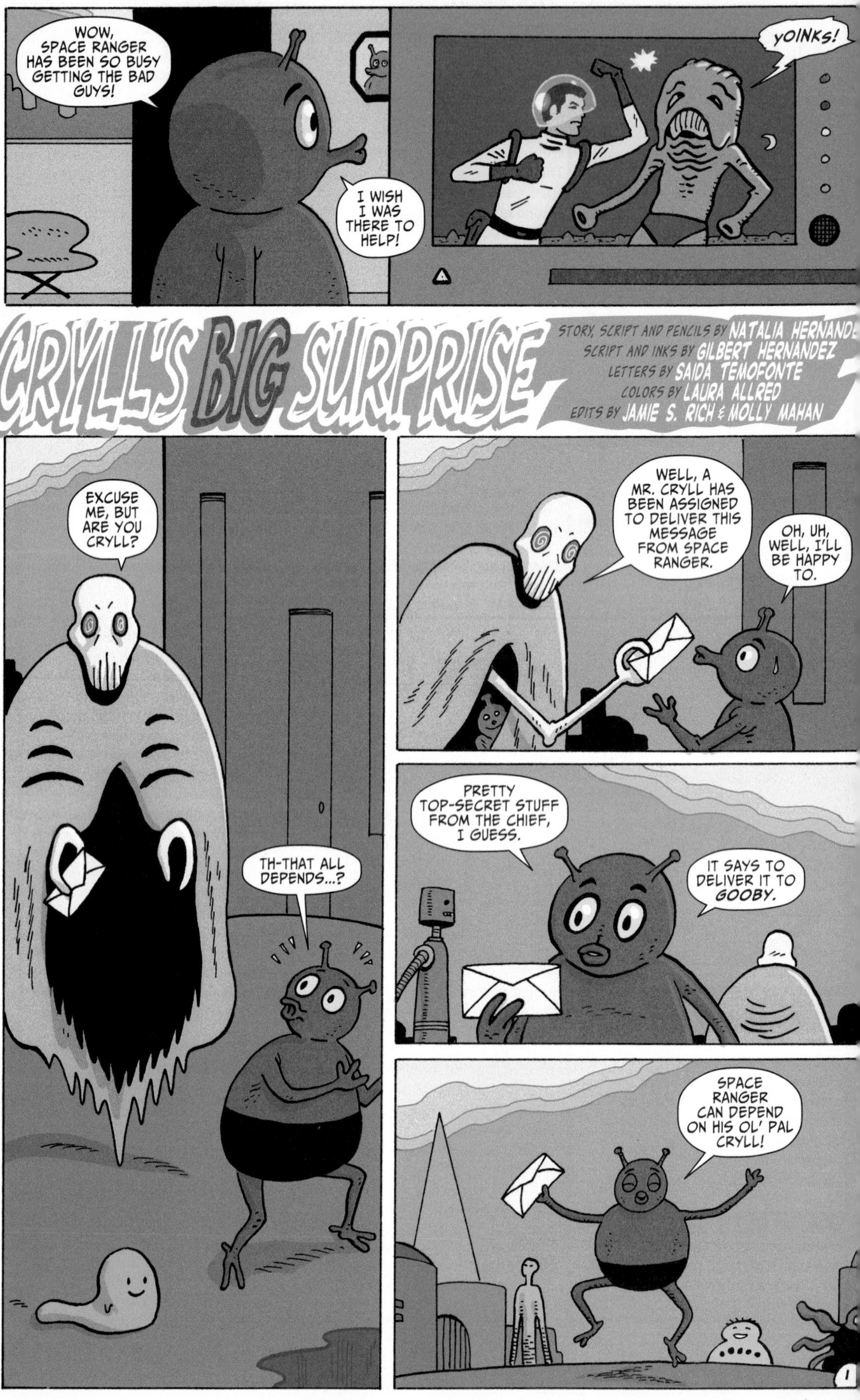

WOW, SPACE RANGER HAS BEEN SO BUSY GETTING THE BAD GUYS!
I WISH I WAS THERE TO HELP!
YOINKS!
CRYLL'S BIG SURPRISE
STORY, SCRIPT AND PENCILS BY NATALIA HERNANDE
SCRIPT AND INKS BY GILBERT HERNANDEZ
LETTERS BY SAIDA TEMOFONTE
COLORS BY LAURA ALLRED
EDITS BY JAMIE S. RICH & MOLLY MAHAN
EXCUSE ME, BUT ARE YOU CRYLL?
TH-THAT ALL DEPENDS...?
WELL, A MR. CRYLL HAS BEEN ASSIGNED TO DELIVER THIS MESSAGE FROM SPACE RANGER.
OH, UH, WELL, I'LL BE HAPPY TO.
PRETTY TOP-SECRET STUFF FROM THE CHIEF, I GUESS.
IT SAYS TO DELIVER IT TO GOOBY.
SPACE RANGER CAN DEPEND ON HIS OL' PAL CRYLL!
1

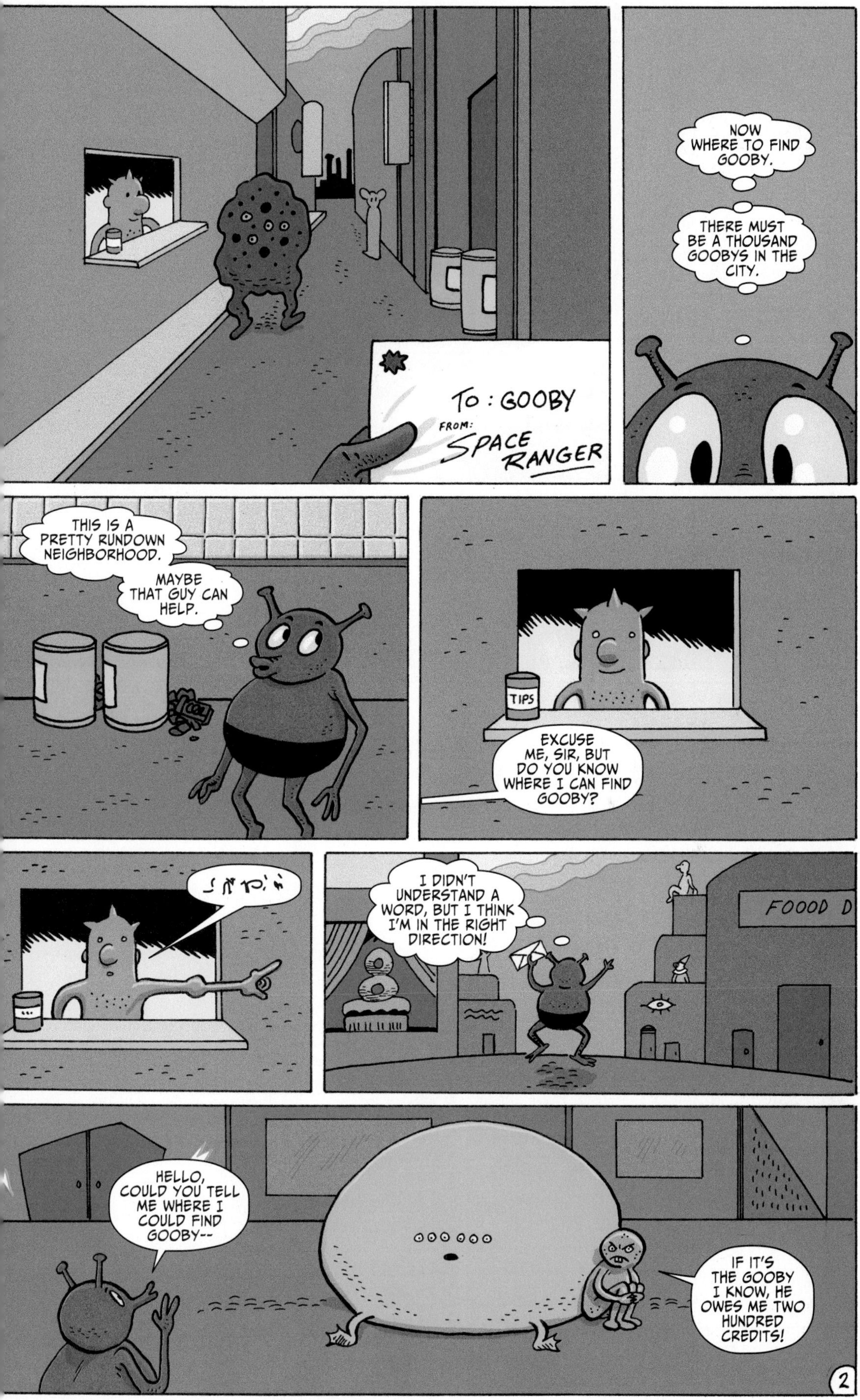
TO : GOOBY
FROM: SPACE RANGER
NOW WHERE TO FIND GOOBY.
THERE MUST BE A THOUSAND GOOBYS IN THE CITY.
THIS IS A PRETTY RUNDOWN NEIGHBORHOOD.
MAYBE THAT GUY CAN HELP.
TIPS
EXCUSE ME, SIR, BUT DO YOU KNOW WHERE I CAN FIND GOOBY?
I DIDN'T UNDERSTAND A WORD, BUT I THINK I'M IN THE RIGHT DIRECTION!
FOOOD D
HELLO, COULD YOU TELL ME WHERE I COULD FIND GOOBY--
IF IT'S THE GOOBY I KNOW, HE OWES ME TWO HUNDRED CREDITS!

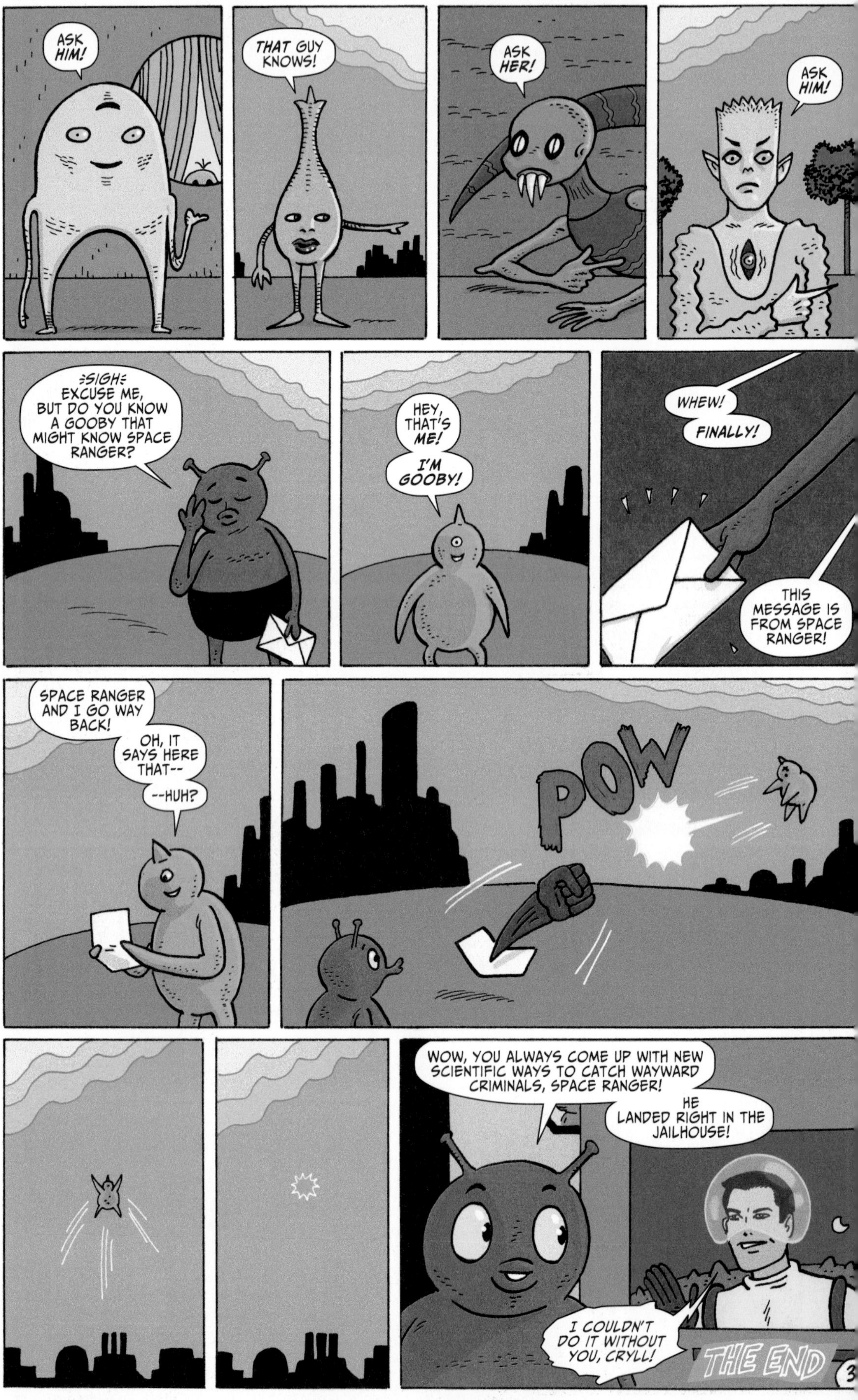

ASK HIM!
THAT GUY KNOWS!
ASK HER!
ASK HIM!
SIGH
EXCUSE ME, BUT DO YOU KNOW A GOOBY THAT MIGHT KNOW SPACE RANGER?
HEY, THAT'S ME!
I'M GOOBY!
WHEW!
FINALLY!
THIS MESSAGE IS FROM SPACE RANGER!
SPACE RANGER AND I GO WAY BACK!
OH, IT SAYS HERE THAT--
--HUH?
POW
WOW, YOU ALWAYS COME UP WITH NEW SCIENTIFIC WAYS TO CATCH WAYWARD CRIMINALS, SPACE RANGER!
HE LANDED RIGHT IN THE JAILHOUSE!
I COULDN'T DO IT WITHOUT YOU, CRYLL!
THE END

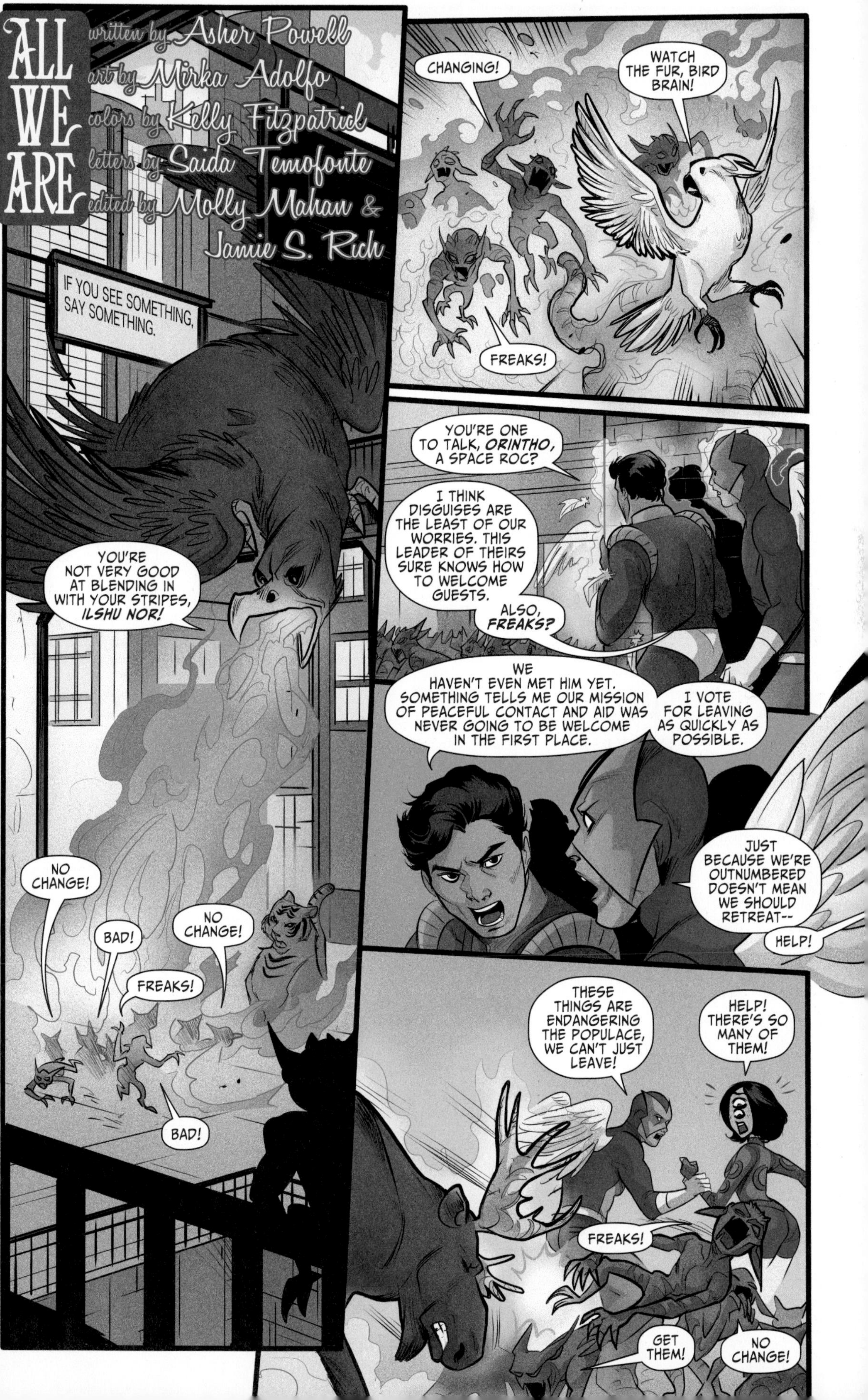
ALL WE ARE
written by Asher Powell
art by Mirka Adolfo
colors by Kelly Fitzpatrick
letters by Saida Temofonte
edited by Molly Mahan & Jamie S. Rich
IF YOU SEE SOMETHING, SAY SOMETHING.
YOU'RE NOT VERY GOOD AT BLENDING IN WITH YOUR STRIPES, ILSHU NOR!
NO CHANGE!
BAD!
NO CHANGE!
FREAKS!
BAD!
CHANGING!
WATCH THE FUR, BIRD BRAIN!
FREAKS!
YOU'RE ONE TO TALK, ORINTHO, A SPACE ROC?
I THINK DISGUISES ARE THE LEAST OF OUR WORRIES. THIS LEADER OF THEIRS SURE KNOWS HOW TO WELCOME GUESTS.
ALSO, FREAKS?
WE HAVEN'T EVEN MET HIM YET. SOMETHING TELLS ME OUR MISSION OF PEACEFUL CONTACT AND AID WAS NEVER GOING TO BE WELCOME IN THE FIRST PLACE.
I VOTE FOR LEAVING AS QUICKLY AS POSSIBLE.
JUST BECAUSE WE'RE OUTNUMBERED DOESN'T MEAN WE SHOULD RETREAT--
HELP!
THESE THINGS ARE ENDANGERING THE POPULACE, WE CAN'T JUST LEAVE!
HELP! THERE'S SO MANY OF THEM!
FREAKS!
GET THEM!
NO CHANGE!

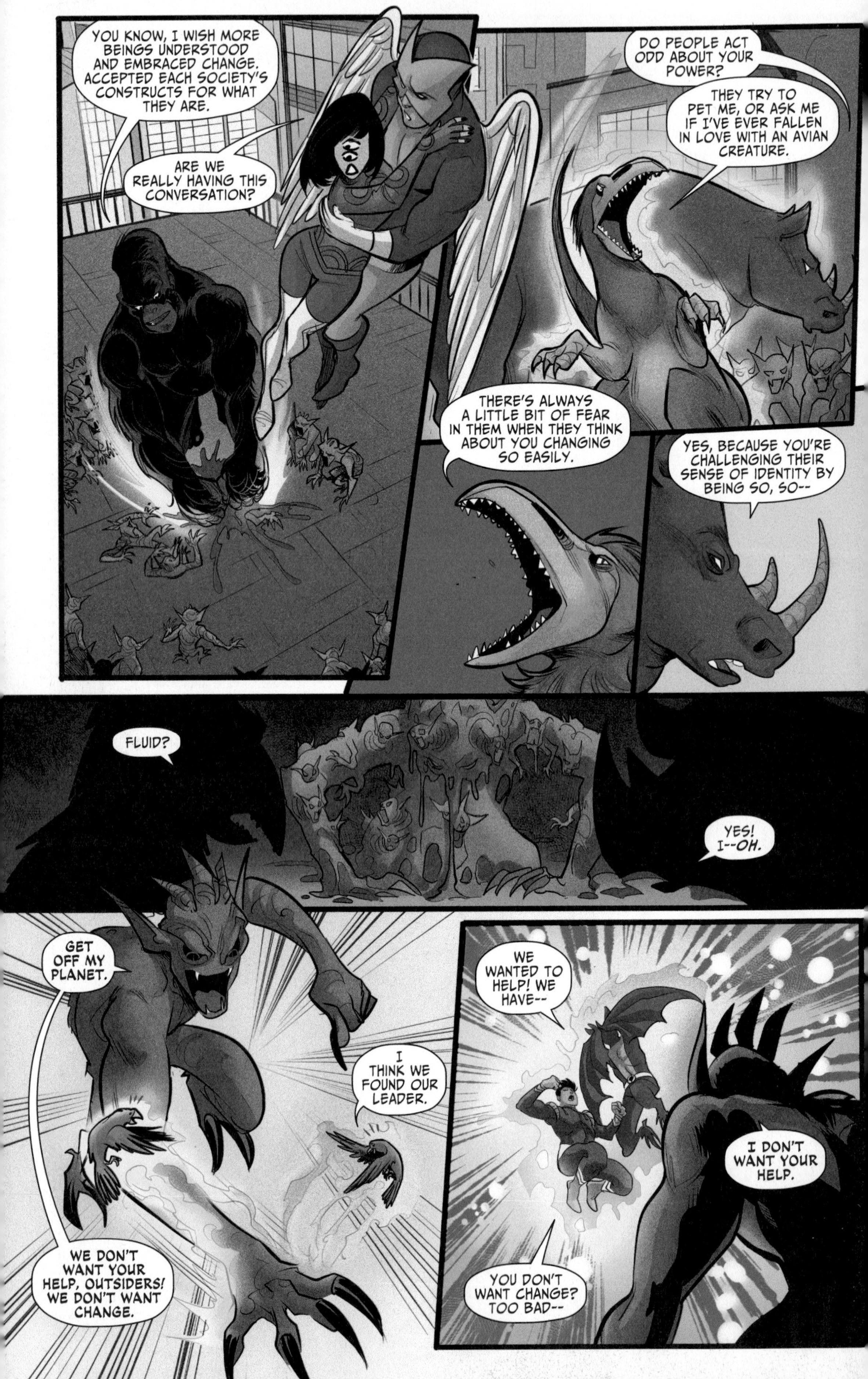
YOU KNOW, I WISH MORE BEINGS UNDERSTOOD AND EMBRACED CHANGE. ACCEPTED EACH SOCIETY'S CONSTRUCTS FOR WHAT THEY ARE.
ARE WE REALLY HAVING THIS CONVERSATION?
DO PEOPLE ACT ODD ABOUT YOUR POWER?
THEY TRY TO PET ME, OR ASK ME IF I'VE EVER FALLEN IN LOVE WITH AN AVIAN CREATURE.
THERE'S ALWAYS A LITTLE BIT OF FEAR IN THEM WHEN THEY THINK ABOUT YOU CHANGING SO EASILY.
YES, BECAUSE YOU'RE CHALLENGING THEIR SENSE OF IDENTITY BY BEING SO, SO--
FLUID?
YES! I--OH.
GET OFF MY PLANET.
WE DON'T WANT YOUR HELP, OUTSIDERS! WE DON'T WANT CHANGE.
I THINK WE FOUND OUR LEADER.
WE WANTED TO HELP! WE HAVE--
I DON'T WANT YOUR HELP.
YOU DON'T WANT CHANGE? TOO BAD--

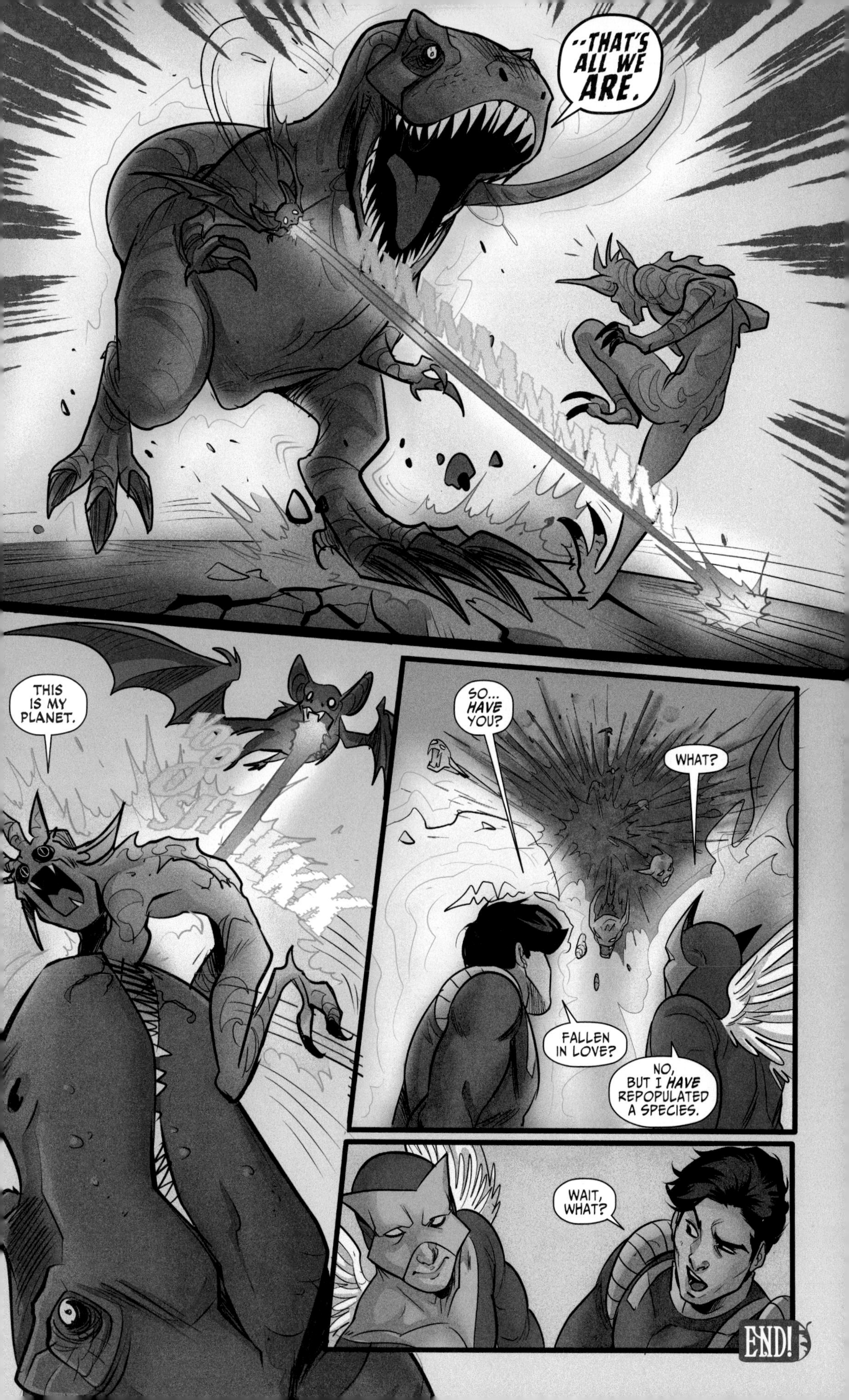

--THAT'S ALL WE ARE.
THIS IS MY PLANET.
SO... HAVE YOU?
WHAT?
FALLEN IN LOVE?
NO, BUT I HAVE REPOPULATED A SPECIES.
WAIT, WHAT?
END!

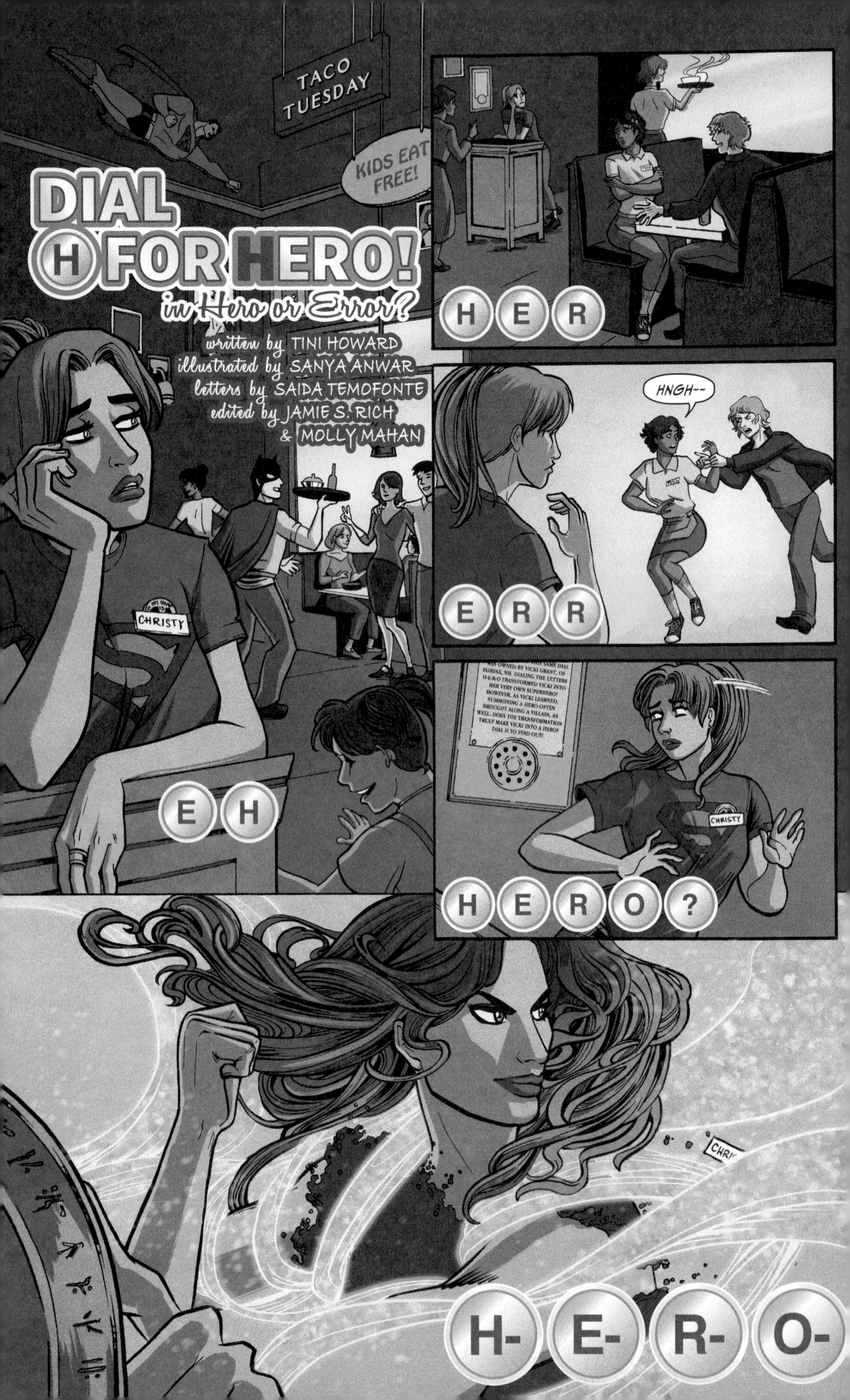
TACO TUESDAY
KIDS EAT FREE!
DIAL H FOR HERO!
in Hero or Error?
written by TINI HOWARD
illustrated by SANYA ANWAR
letters by SAIDA TEMOFONTE
edited by JAMIE S. RICH & MOLLY MAHAN
H E R
HNGH--
E R R
THIS SAME DIAL
WAS OWNED BY VICKI GRANT, OF
FAIRFAX, NH. DIALING THE LETTERS
H-E-R-O TRANSFORMED VICKI INTO
HER VERY OWN SUPERHERO!
HOWEVER, AS VICKI LEARNED,
SUMMONING A HERO OFTEN
BROUGHT ALONG A VILLAIN, AS
WELL. DOES THE TRANSFORMATION
TRULY MAKE VICKI INTO A HERO?
DIAL H TO FIND OUT!
CHRISTY
H E R O ?
E H
H- E- R- O-

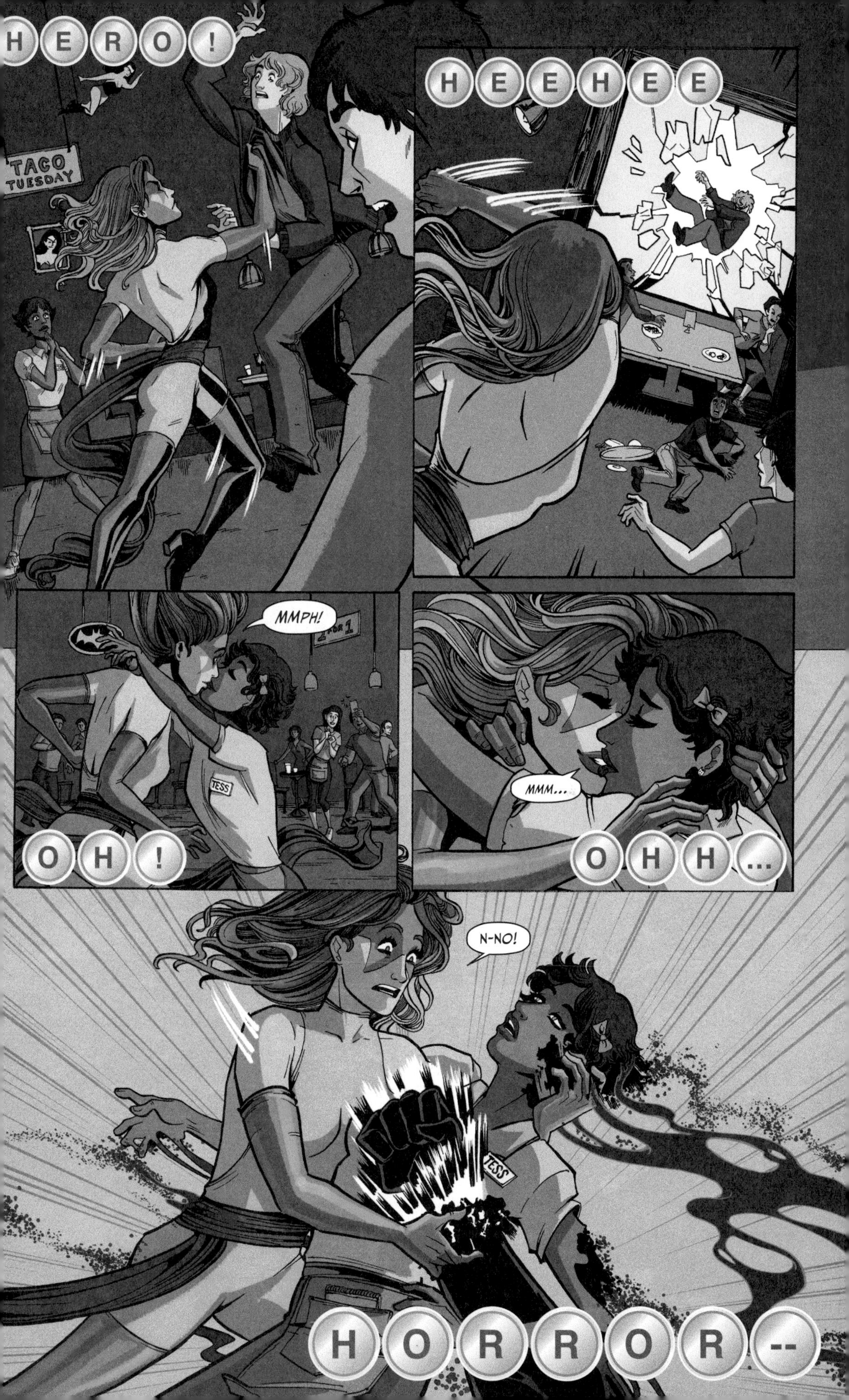
HERO!
TACO TUESDAY
HEEHEE
MMPH!
2 FOR 1
TESS
OH!
MMM...
OHH...
N-NO!
TESS
HORROR--

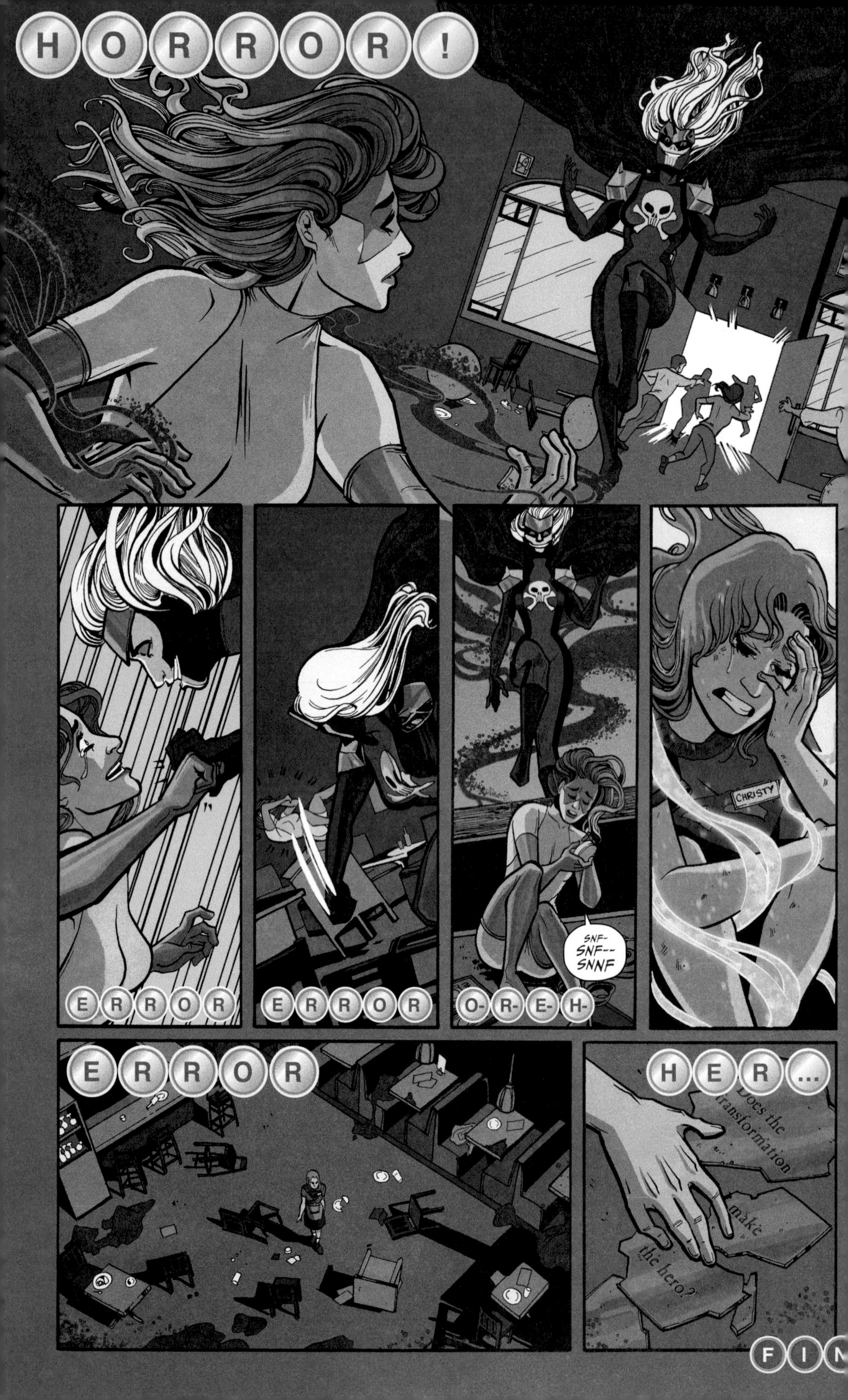
HORROR!
ERROR
ERROR
SNF-
SNF--
SNNF
O-R-E-H-
CHRISTY
ERROR
HER...
"Does the transformation make the hero?"
FIN

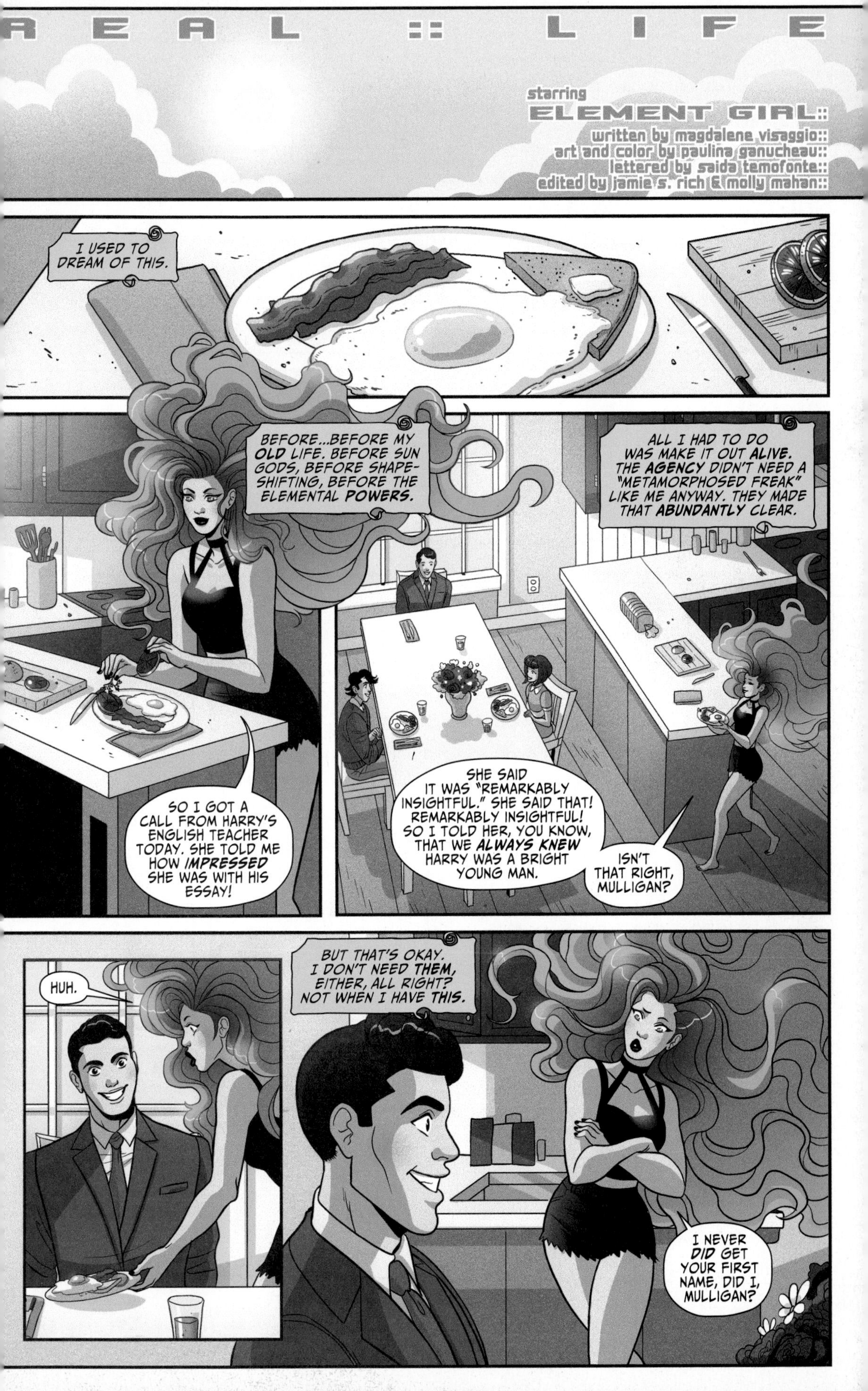
REAL :: LIFE
starring
ELEMENT GIRL::
written by magdalene visaggio::
art and color by paulina ganucheau::
lettered by saida temofonte::
edited by jamie s. rich & molly mahan::
I USED TO DREAM OF THIS.
BEFORE...BEFORE MY OLD LIFE. BEFORE SUN GODS, BEFORE SHAPE-SHIFTING, BEFORE THE ELEMENTAL POWERS.
ALL I HAD TO DO WAS MAKE IT OUT ALIVE. THE AGENCY DIDN'T NEED A "METAMORPHOSED FREAK" LIKE ME ANYWAY. THEY MADE THAT ABUNDANTLY CLEAR.
SO I GOT A CALL FROM HARRY'S ENGLISH TEACHER TODAY. SHE TOLD ME HOW IMPRESSED SHE WAS WITH HIS ESSAY!
SHE SAID IT WAS "REMARKABLY INSIGHTFUL." SHE SAID THAT! REMARKABLY INSIGHTFUL! SO I TOLD HER, YOU KNOW, THAT WE ALWAYS KNEW HARRY WAS A BRIGHT YOUNG MAN.
ISN'T THAT RIGHT, MULLIGAN?
HUH.
BUT THAT'S OKAY. I DON'T NEED THEM, EITHER, ALL RIGHT? NOT WHEN I HAVE THIS.
I NEVER DID GET YOUR FIRST NAME, DID I, MULLIGAN?

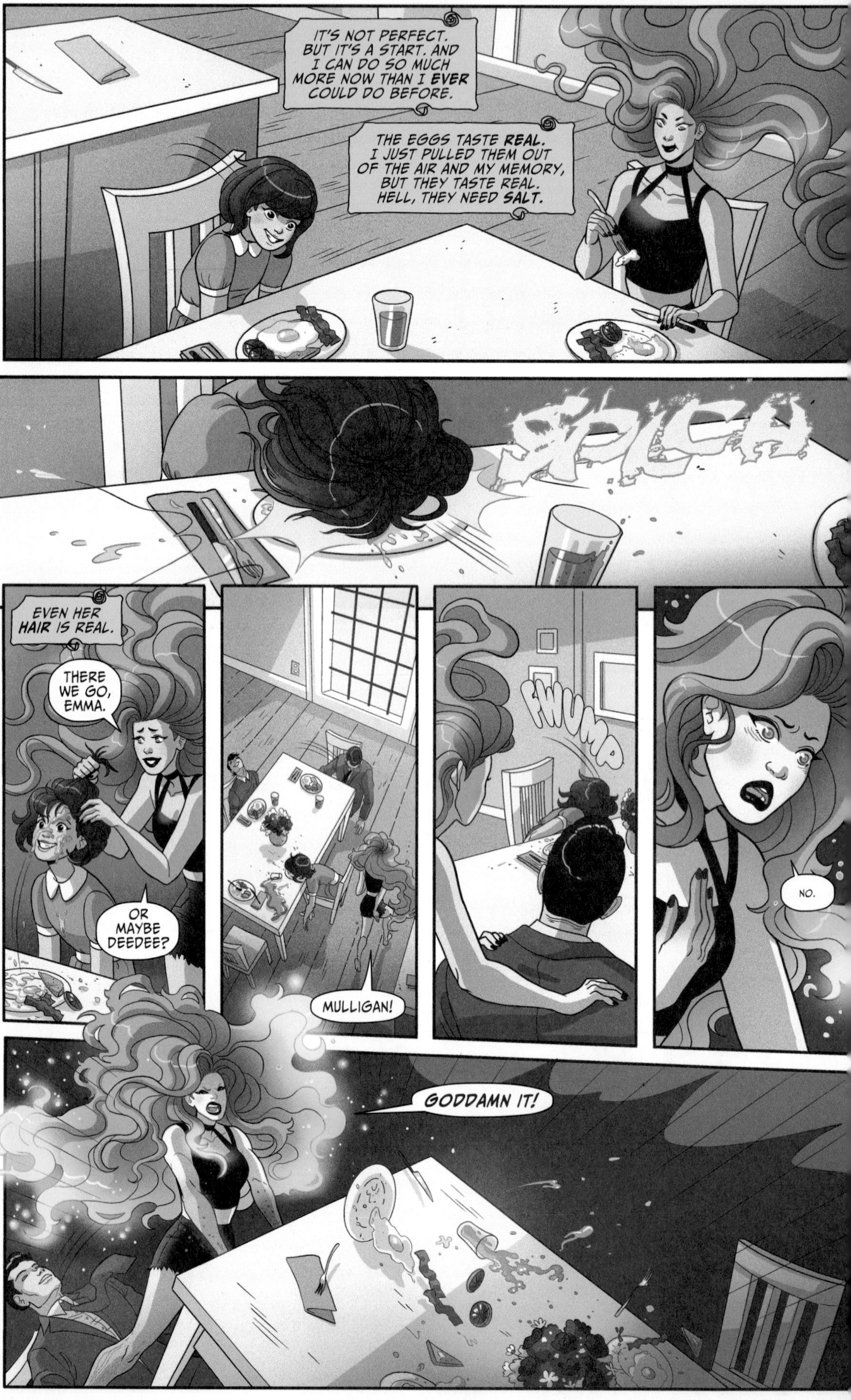
IT'S NOT PERFECT. BUT IT'S A START. AND I CAN DO SO MUCH MORE NOW THAN I EVER COULD DO BEFORE.
THE EGGS TASTE REAL. I JUST PULLED THEM OUT OF THE AIR AND MY MEMORY, BUT THEY TASTE REAL. HELL, THEY NEED SALT.
SPLCH
EVEN HER HAIR IS REAL.
THERE WE GO, EMMA.
OR MAYBE DEEDEE?
MULLIGAN!
FWUMP
NO.
GODDAMN IT!

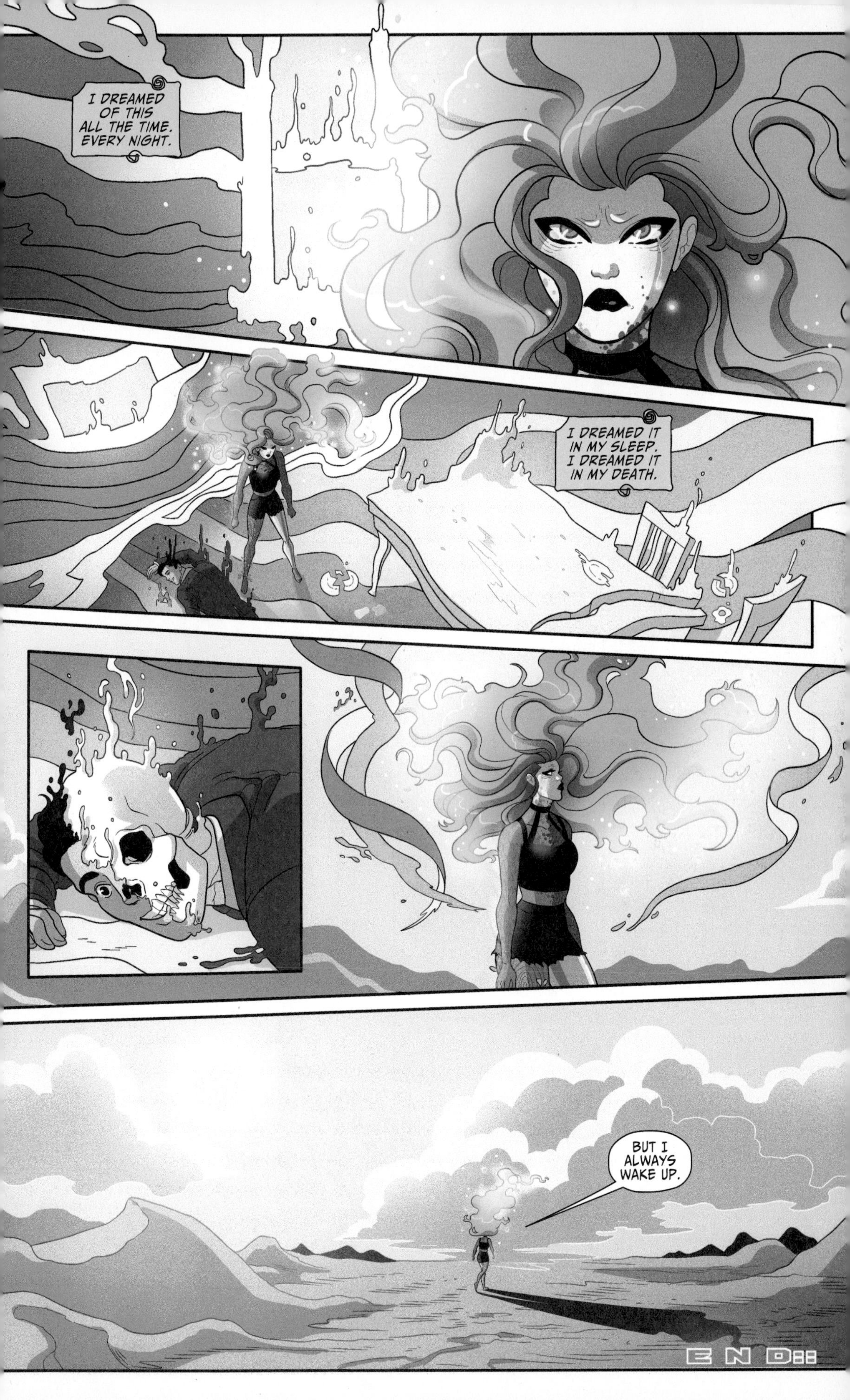
I DREAMED OF THIS ALL THE TIME. EVERY NIGHT.
I DREAMED IT IN MY SLEEP. I DREAMED IT IN MY DEATH.
BUT I ALWAYS WAKE UP.
END

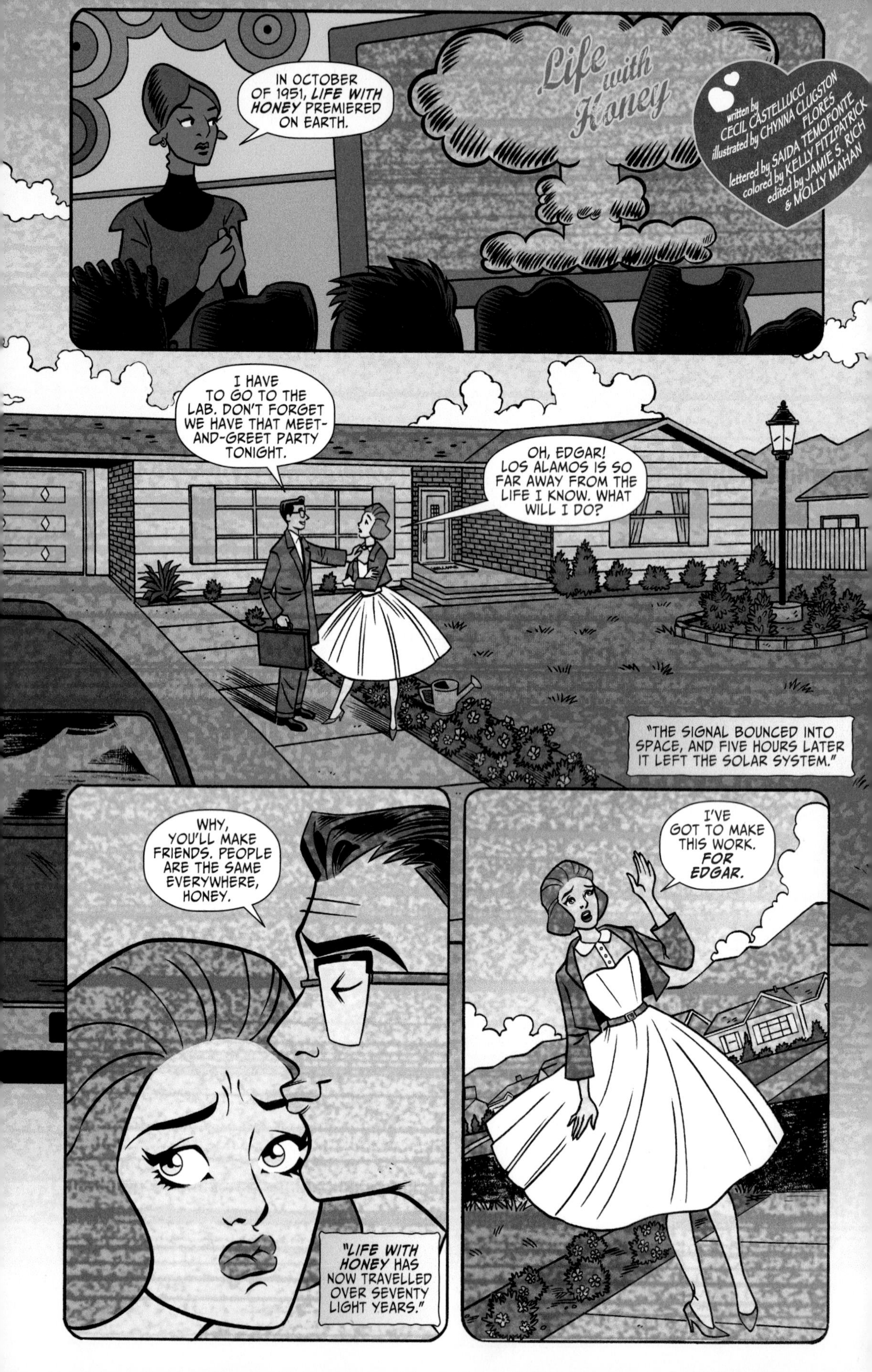

IN OCTOBER OF 1951, *LIFE WITH HONEY* PREMIERED ON EARTH.
Life with Honey
written by CECIL CASTELLUCCI
illustrated by CHYNNA CLUGSTON FLORES
lettered by SAIDA TEMOFONTE
colored by KELLY FITZPATRICK
edited by JAMIE S. RICH & MOLLY MAHAN
I HAVE TO GO TO THE LAB. DON'T FORGET WE HAVE THAT MEET-AND-GREET PARTY TONIGHT.
OH, EDGAR! LOS ALAMOS IS SO FAR AWAY FROM THE LIFE I KNOW. WHAT WILL I DO?
"THE SIGNAL BOUNCED INTO SPACE, AND FIVE HOURS LATER IT LEFT THE SOLAR SYSTEM."
WHY, YOU'LL MAKE FRIENDS. PEOPLE ARE THE SAME EVERYWHERE, HONEY.
"*LIFE WITH HONEY* HAS NOW TRAVELLED OVER SEVENTY LIGHT YEARS."
I'VE GOT TO MAKE THIS WORK. *FOR EDGAR.*

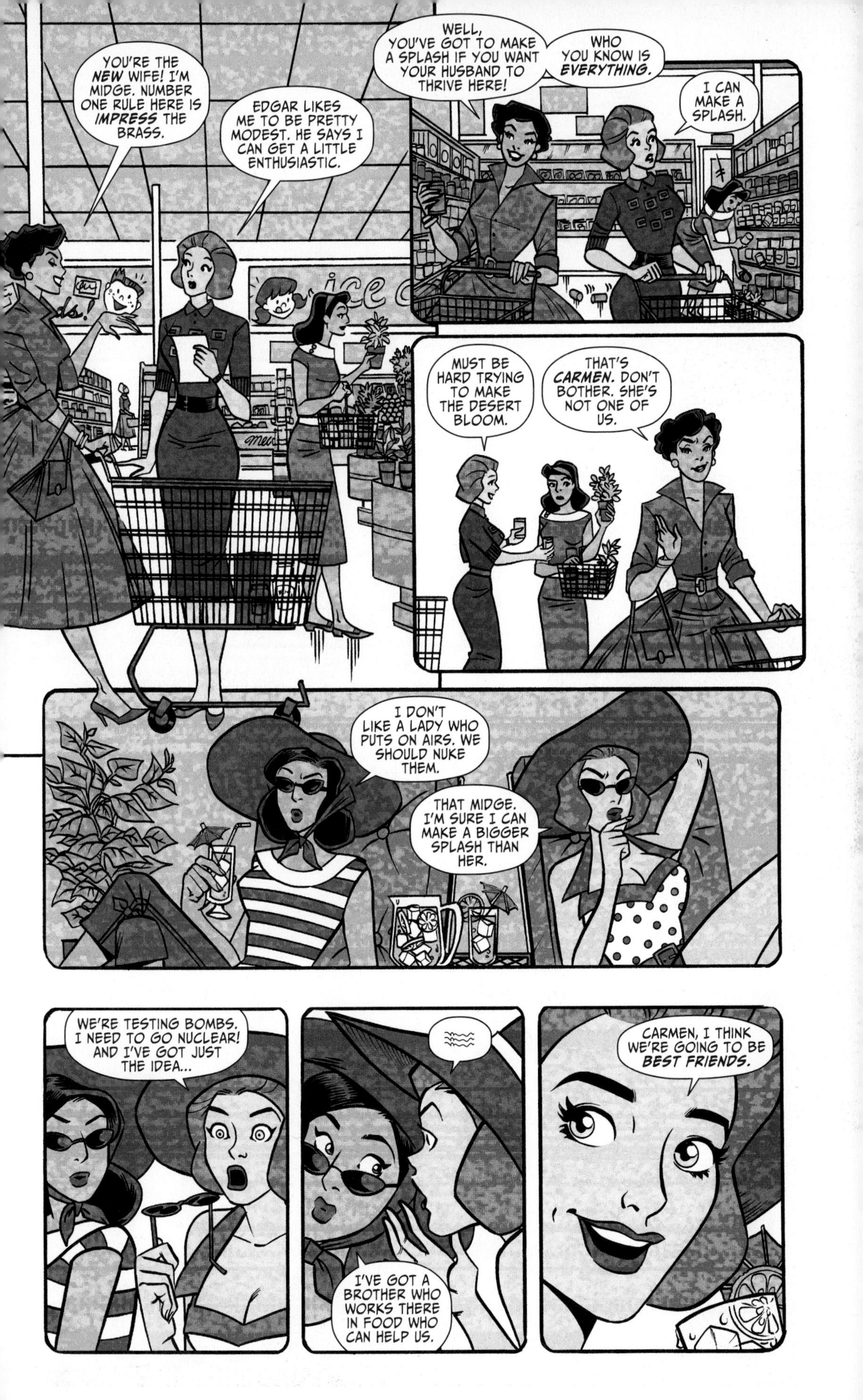
YOU'RE THE NEW WIFE! I'M MIDGE. NUMBER ONE RULE HERE IS IMPRESS THE BRASS.
EDGAR LIKES ME TO BE PRETTY MODEST. HE SAYS I CAN GET A LITTLE ENTHUSIASTIC.
WELL, YOU'VE GOT TO MAKE A SPLASH IF YOU WANT YOUR HUSBAND TO THRIVE HERE!
WHO YOU KNOW IS EVERYTHING.
I CAN MAKE A SPLASH.
MUST BE HARD TRYING TO MAKE THE DESERT BLOOM.
THAT'S CARMEN. DON'T BOTHER. SHE'S NOT ONE OF US.
I DON'T LIKE A LADY WHO PUTS ON AIRS. WE SHOULD NUKE THEM.
THAT MIDGE. I'M SURE I CAN MAKE A BIGGER SPLASH THAN HER.
WE'RE TESTING BOMBS. I NEED TO GO NUCLEAR! AND I'VE GOT JUST THE IDEA...
I'VE GOT A BROTHER WHO WORKS THERE IN FOOD WHO CAN HELP US.
CARMEN, I THINK WE'RE GOING TO BE BEST FRIENDS.

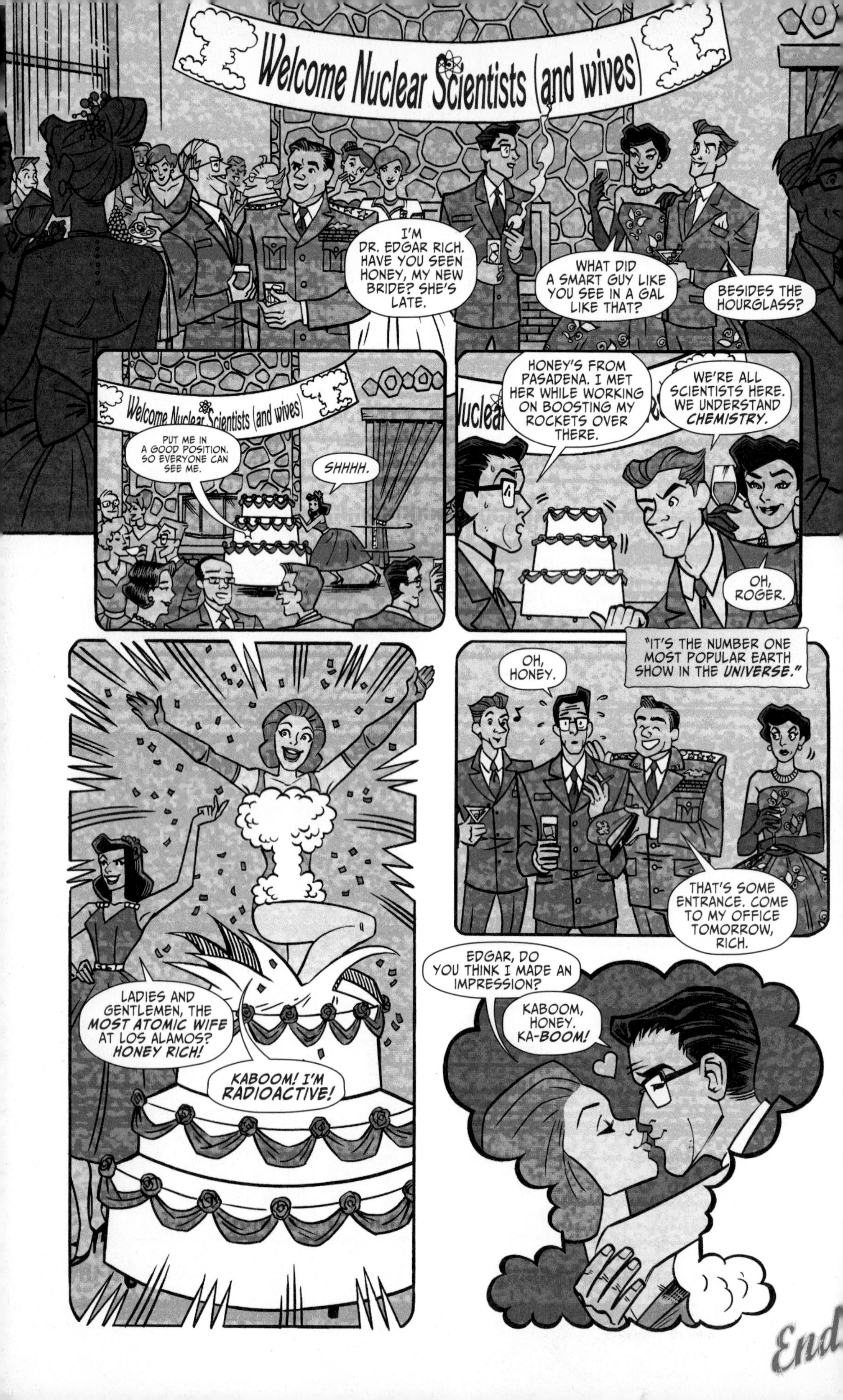

Welcome Nuclear Scientists (and wives)
I'M DR. EDGAR RICH. HAVE YOU SEEN HONEY, MY NEW BRIDE? SHE'S LATE.
WHAT DID A SMART GUY LIKE YOU SEE IN A GAL LIKE THAT?
BESIDES THE HOURGLASS?
Welcome Nuclear Scientists (and wives)
PUT ME IN A GOOD POSITION. SO EVERYONE CAN SEE ME.
SHHHH.
HONEY'S FROM PASADENA. I MET HER WHILE WORKING ON BOOSTING MY ROCKETS OVER THERE.
WE'RE ALL SCIENTISTS HERE. WE UNDERSTAND *CHEMISTRY.*
OH, ROGER.
LADIES AND GENTLEMEN, THE *MOST ATOMIC WIFE* AT LOS ALAMOS? *HONEY RICH!*
KABOOM! I'M RADIOACTIVE!
"IT'S THE NUMBER ONE MOST POPULAR EARTH SHOW IN THE *UNIVERSE.*"
OH, HONEY.
THAT'S SOME ENTRANCE. COME TO MY OFFICE TOMORROW, RICH.
EDGAR, DO YOU THINK I MADE AN IMPRESSION?
KABOOM, HONEY. KA-*BOOM!*
End

PENCIL SHADING

CHARACTER DESIGNS BY MARLEY ZARCONE

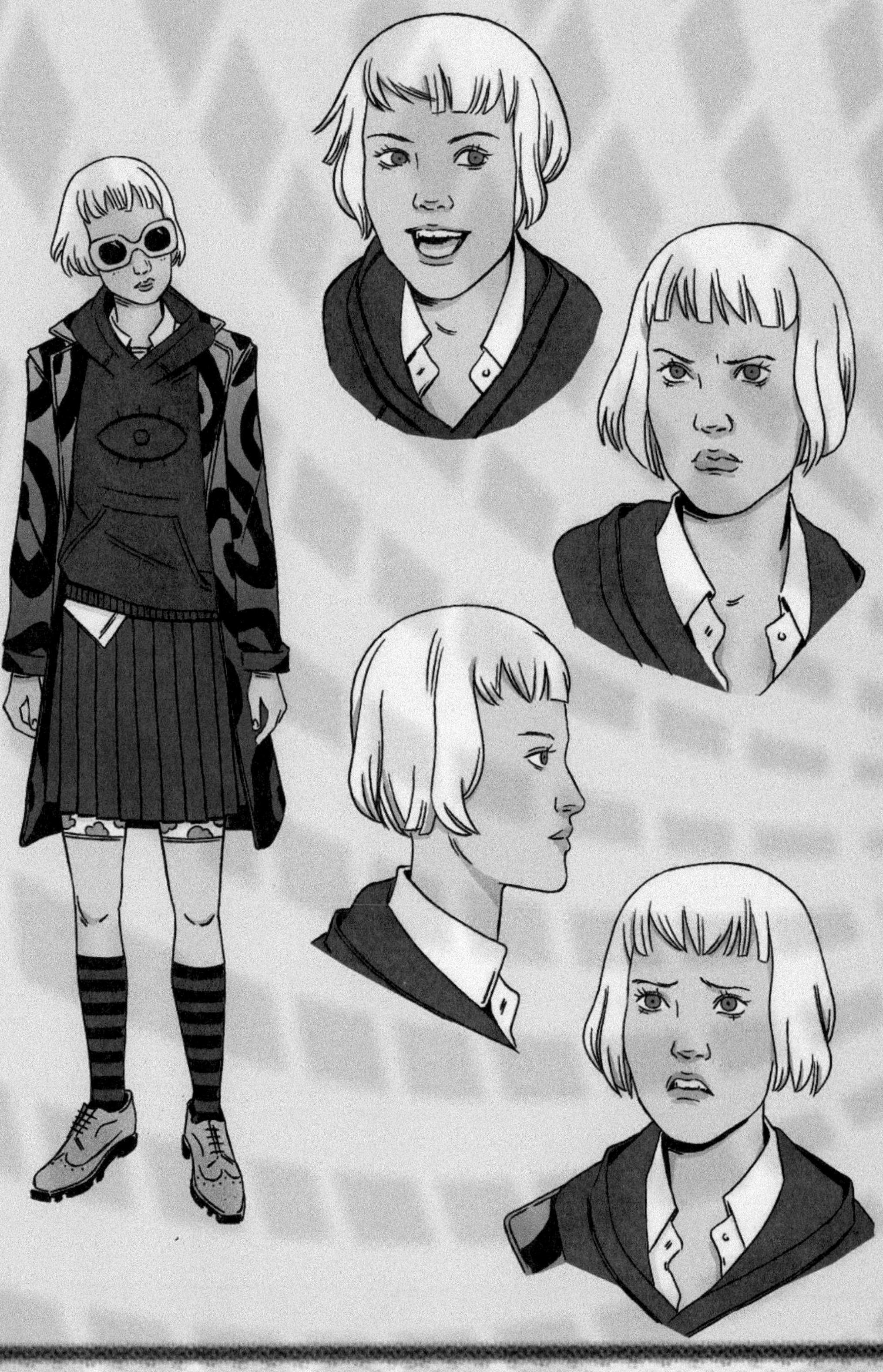

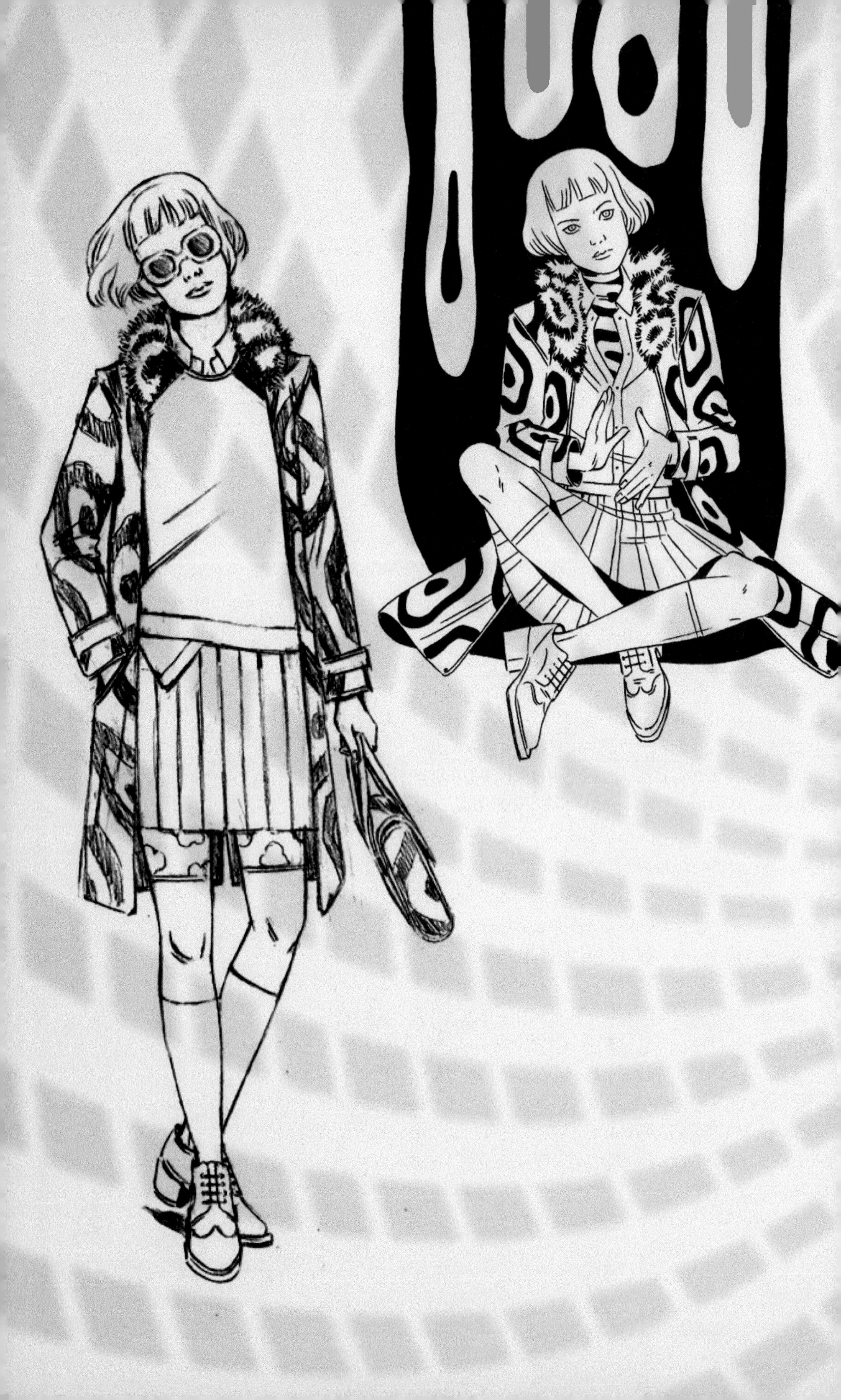

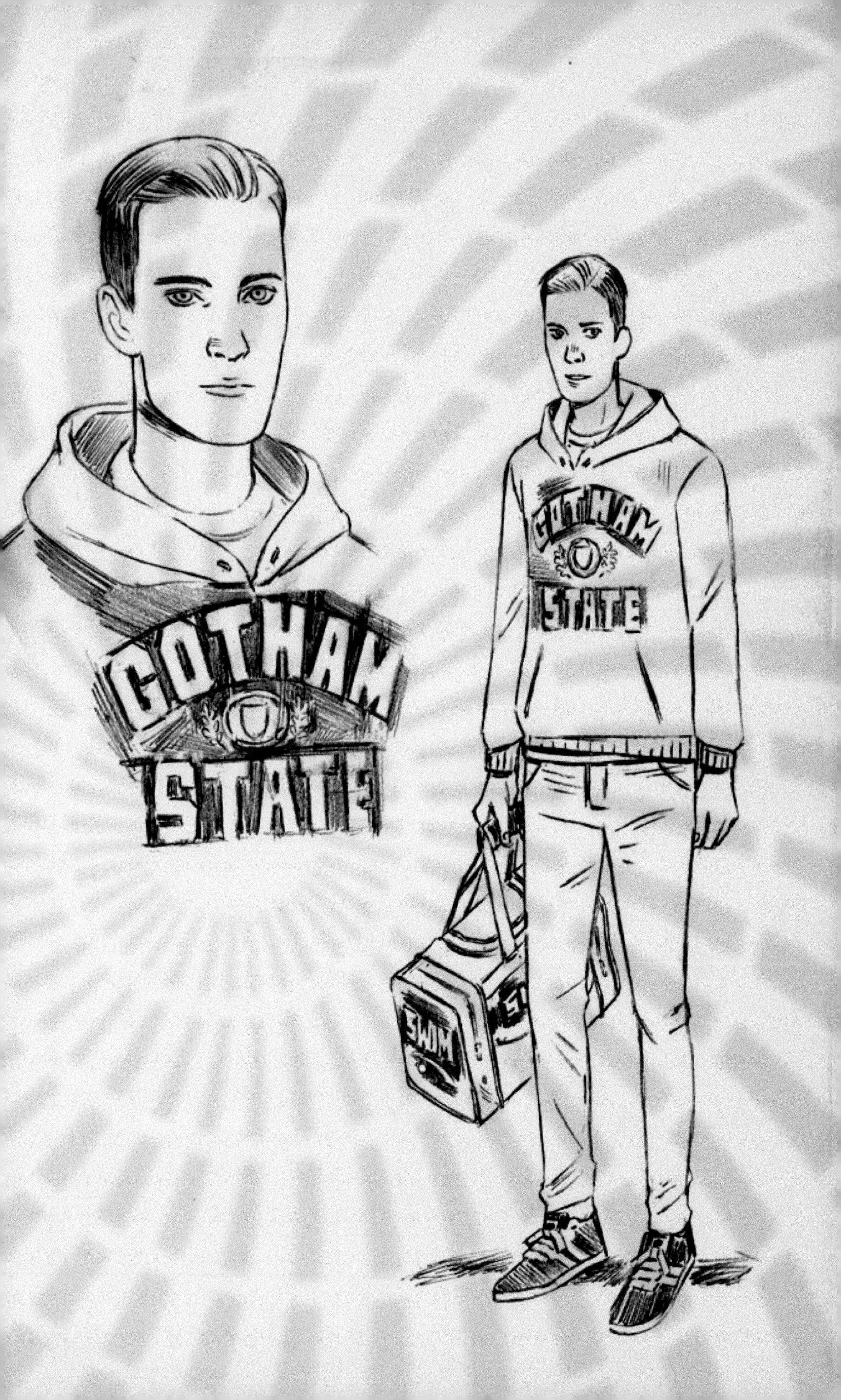
GOTHAM
STATE
GOTHAM
STATE
SWIM

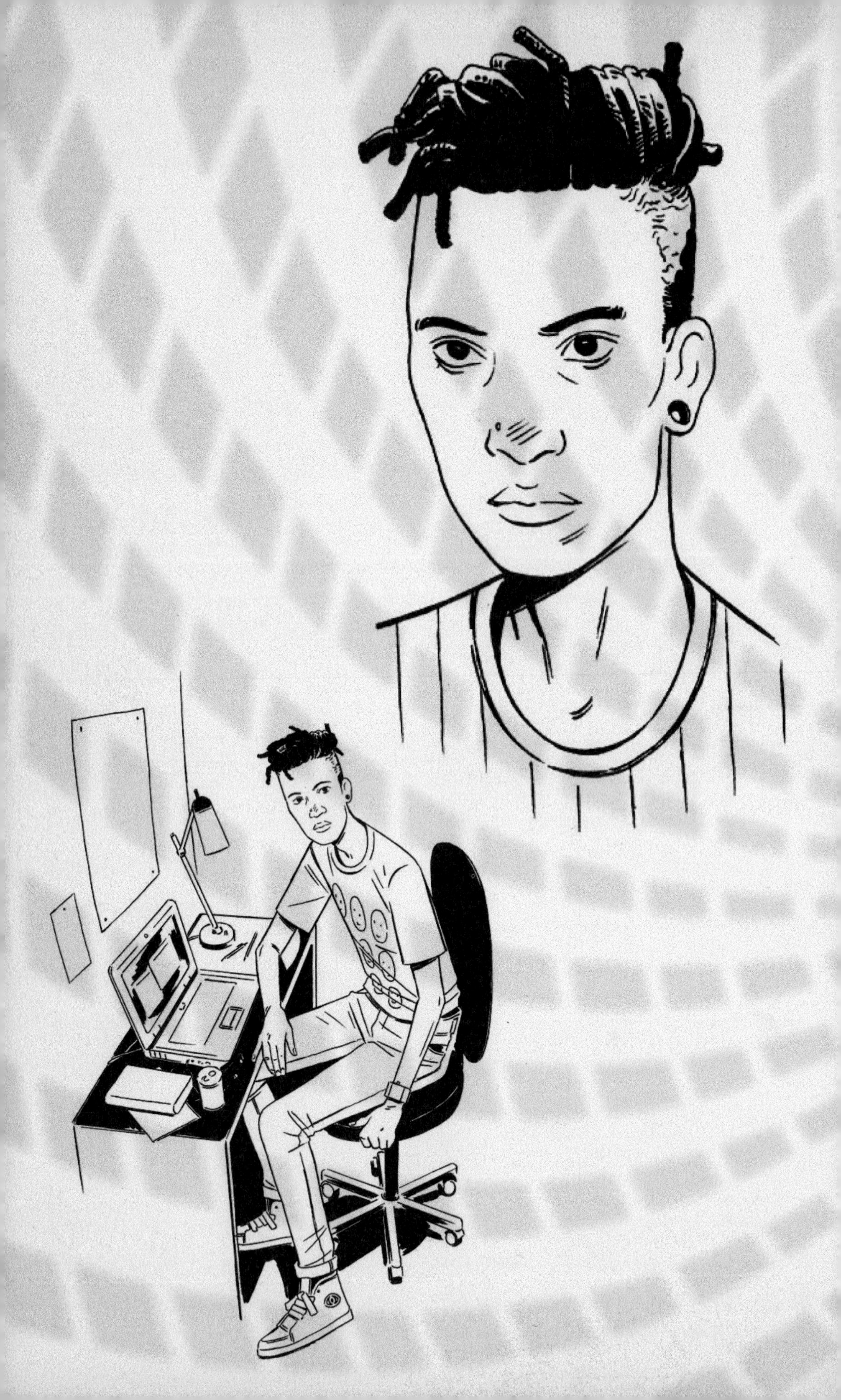

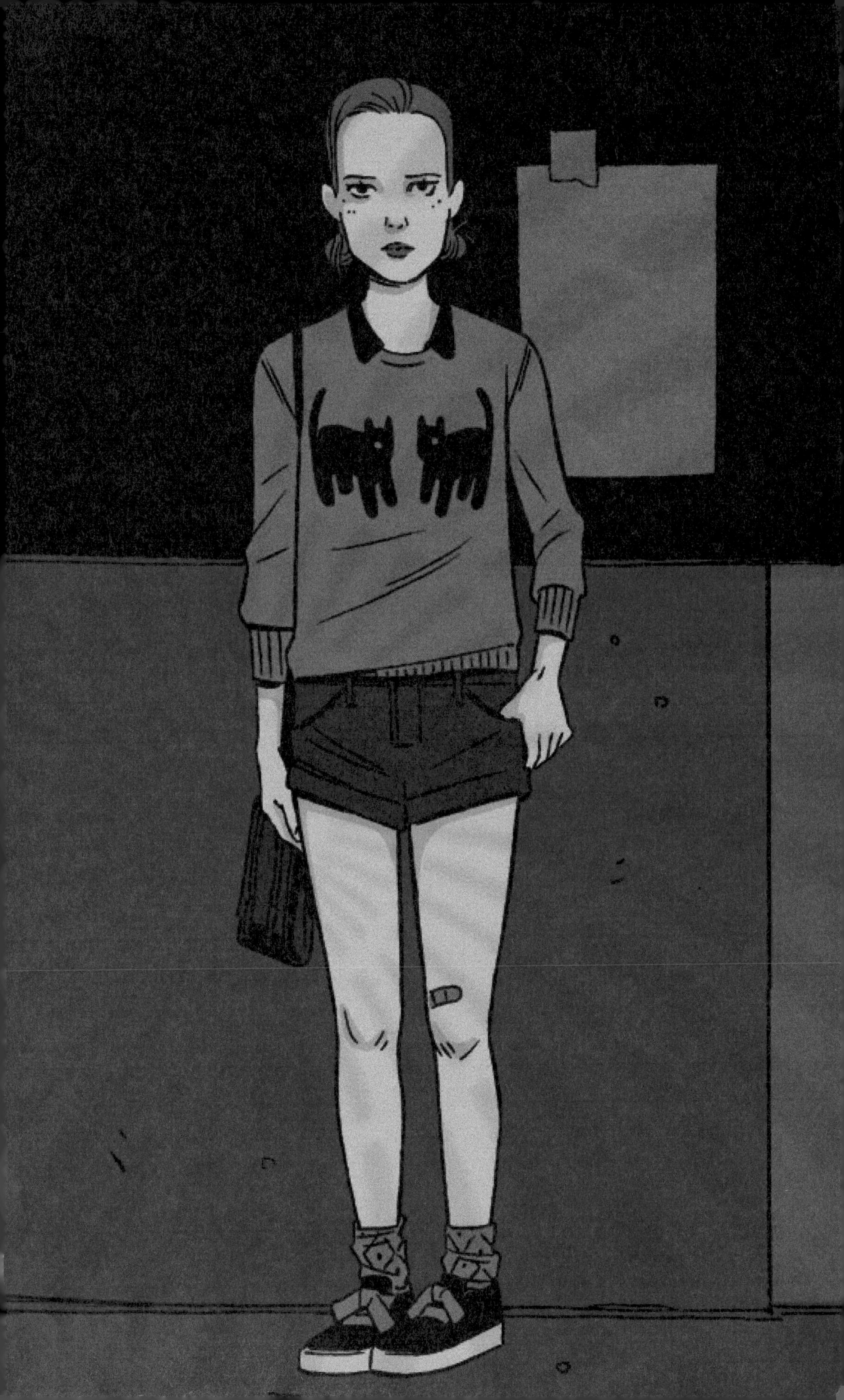